George B. Stewart

Centennial Memorial

English Presbyterian congregation in Harrisburg

George B. Stewart

Centennial Memorial
English Presbyterian congregation in Harrisburg

ISBN/EAN: 9783337235543

Printed in Europe, USA, Canada, Australia, Japan

Cover: Foto ©Lupo / pixelio.de

More available books at **www.hansebooks.com**

1794——1894.

CENTENNIAL MEMORIAL

ENGLISH

PRESBYTERIAN CONGREGATION,

HARRISBURG, PA.

GEO. B. STEWART, *Editor.*

HARRISBURG, PA.:
HARRISBURG PUBLISHING CO.
1894.

HARRISBURG DAILY TELEGRAPH
PRINT.

PREFATORY.

Pursuant to a resolution of the Centennial Committee, the following account of the Centennial services is given to the public. The work of editing, entrusted to Rev. Dr. George B. Stewart, has been done with conscientious fidelity to fact, and in a manner as gratifying to the committee as it will no doubt be to the Congregation.

M. W. McAlarney, *Chairman.*

E. J. Stackpole,

Charles H. Bergner,

Samuel C. Miller,

Henry C. Spicer.

TABLE OF CONTENTS.

INTRODUCTION.

CENTENNIAL WEEK.

INTRODUCTION.

CENTENNIAL MEMORIAL.

PRELIMINARY WORK.

A CENTURY of history must be insignificant indeed if it is not worth recording. A church whose history stretches over a century ought to have a story to tell. Especially if the century has been lived in these last days when every year is crowded with great events, and life is full of intense activity. Hence it was that on September 14th, 1891, the Session of the English Presbyterian Congregation of Harrisburg, Pennsylvania, commonly known as the Market Square Church, resolved to celebrate in a fitting manner the Centennial anniversary of the founding of their church, February 16th, 1794. As a first step in the execution of this purpose they invited Rev. Thomas H. Robinson, D. D., Reunion Professor of Sacred Rhetoric, Church Government, and Pastoral Theology in the Western Theological Seminary of Allegheny, Pennsylvania, to deliver a historical address on that occasion. This choice was eminently wise, since Dr. Robinson's long connection with this church as its fourth pastor, and his fondness for historical study, had given him much familiarity with the church and the community. Though the selection was made at an early date, it allowed none too long a time for the performance of the onerous task laid upon him.

Several months later, on May 1st, 1893, the Session resolved to call a meeting of the three official boards of the
church for the purpose of further considering the proper
celebration of the Centennial. This meeting was held in
the parlor of the church on May 15th, 1893. There were
present: George B. Stewart, Minister; Jacob A. Miller, J.
Henry Spicer, John C. Harvey, Elders; Robert H. Moffitt,
M. Wilson McAlarney, Trustees; Jacob J. Franck, David
Fleming, Luther R. Kelker, Samuel C. Miller, Melancthon
S. Shotwell, Peter K. Sprenkel, Deacons. The pastor was
made Chairman of the meeting, and Dr. Jacob A. Miller,
Clerk. After a full discussion of the subject, it was resolved
to endorse the action of the Session, and to celebrate the
Centennial anniversary of the founding of the church by
appropriate exercises during the week beginning February
11th, 1894. It was further decided that there should be a
Centennial Committee, together with various sub-committees, for the purpose of making the necessary arrangements
for this celebration, the Chairmen of the sub-committees,
together with the general Chairman, to constitute the Centennial Committee. The Pastor, Rev. George B. Stewart,
D. D., was chosen General Chairman. The meeting then
adjourned to the evening of May 29th, 1893, for the further
consideration of the arrangements.

On May 29th, 1893, the second meeting of the officers was
held pursuant to adjournment. The following were present:

George B. Stewart, Minister; Jacob A. Miller, J. Henry
Spicer, John C. Harvey, Elders; M. Wilson McAlarney,
Trustee; Charles W. Foster, Luther R. Kelker, Samuel C.
Miller, Melancthon S. Shotwell, Peter K. Sprenkel, Deacons.

The following sub-committees and their chairmen were appointed:

Invitation Committee—Charles L. Bailey, Chairman.

Programme Committee—Samuel J. M. McCarrell, Chairman.

Entertainment Committee—Gilbert M. McCauley, Chairman.

Publication Committee—M. Wilson McAlarney, Chairman.

Finance Committee—Samuel W. Fleming, Chairman.

Decoration Committee—Mrs. Isabella S. Kerr, Chairman.

Reception Committee—Mrs. Gilbert M. McCauley, Chairman.

Music Committee—George R. Fleming, Chairman.

Ushers—Peter K. Sprenkel, Chairman.

The names of the several committees indicate their respective duties. The Programme Committee was to arrange a proper programme of events for the celebration, and to have charge of its execution. The Invitation Committee to have charge of extending invitations in the name of the congregation to its friends. The Entertainment Committee to arrange for the suitable exercise of hospitality by the members of the congregation toward its guests. The Decoration Committee to have charge of the preparation and the decoration of the church. The Music Committee to direct the musical features of the celebration. The Reception Committee to have charge of a social reception. The Ushers to serve in that capacity during the week. The Publication Committee to arrange for such publications as might be found desirable in commemoration of the occasion. The Finance Committee to provide means for defraying the expenses. Of all these committees the General Chairman was a member ex-officio, and all committees were to act under the supervision of the Centennial Committee. The scheme combined the advantages of a single responsible head with the advantages of adequate specialization. The Centennial Committee, through its Chairman and several members, was in close touch both for information and for direction with all the sub-committees, while the sub-committees each had their definite and well understood duties.

The Pastor was requested to inform the congregation on the following Wednesday evening, May 31st, of the action of their officers, and invite their co-operation in making the celebration worthy of the occasion. After authorizing the Centennial Committee to fill up the sub-committees, the further arrangements were entrusted to the committees, and the joint meeting of the officers adjourned.

On the following Wednesday evening, the Pastor, as requested by the officers, addressed the congregation on the subject, and there was cordial and universal approval of the action of the officers in planning for the fitting observance of the first centennial of the church.

On September 22d, 1893, the first meeting of the Centennial Committee was held in the parlor of the church. Mr. Peter K. Sprenkel was chosen secretary of the committee. This date was the beginning of the active work of the committees. From this time until the celebration was completed they were busy planning and executing the various details incident to such an undertaking.

Too much praise cannot be bestowed upon these committees. They worked with great diligence, with unceasing fidelity, with imperturbable good nature, and with discriminating judgment. The perfection of the arrangements even to the minutest detail, the entire absence of friction, and the

complete success of the whole celebration gave abundant
evidence of their ability and faithfulness.

The work of the committees almost from the first was determined by certain leading ideas, and aimed at certain definite
results. While this was to be the Centennial of the English
Presbyterian Congregation, the mother of Presbyterianism in
Harrisburg, nevertheless, our wish was to have all the Presbyterian churches of the city enjoy with us the pleasure of
the occasion. This thought was kept prominently before the
committees, shaped many features of the programme, and
prompted the Union Communion Service. The pastors
and all the officers of the Presbyterian churches and their
families were personally invited, and a formal invitation to
all of the Events was extended through their church Sessions to the several congregations.

As the church has always given a prominent place to
music in its services, and has been favorably known for the
high character and attractiveness of its music throughout
all of its history, it seemed eminently appropriate that
special prominence should be given to music during the celebration. This led the Music Committee to plan a musical
festival of a high order, and to arrange for exceptional musical features in the other services. A large Centennial Choir
was organized, composed of our own and singers from the
Pine Street Presbyterian choir, with Mr. George R. Fleming
as director, and Mr. David E. Crozier as organist. This
choir, by its skillful rendering of beautiful music contributed
in a large degree to the delightfulness of the occasion.

The history of the church was naturally the principal
theme of the occasion. It was fitting that a whole evening

should be set apart for it. Nevertheless there was associate history which must receive attention that the celebration might be complete. Therefore, the occasion was appropriately inaugurated by an address on "The Beginnings of Presbyterianism in the Middle Colonies," by the Rev. John DeWitt, D. D., LL. D., Professor of Church History in Princeton Theological Seminary, and the eminent son of the Rev. William R. DeWitt, D. D., who for fifty years was pastor of the church. And an evening was devoted to the past history and present condition of the several Presbyterian churches whose life is directly connected with this church, and to the present condition of this church.

That the congregation might have the pleasure of renewing acquaintance with former members and friends in attendance upon the celebration, and that delightful fellowship might characterize the occasion, an evening was set apart to social festivities.

As the church has a history already written and preserved in monuments of the past, it was arranged to have an historical exhibition of church relics, pictures, books, musical instruments, diagrams of pews, and memorabilia of pastors and officers. This exhibition was displayed in the church parlor, and was an attractive feature of the celebration. It is probably not saying too much to record that the plan proved to be a most symmetrical and harmonious blending of varied and necessary features of such an occasion.

By beginning the celebration on Sunday, February 11th, and concluding it on Friday, February 16th, the two dates especially connected with the organization of the church were commemorated. For it was on Tuesday, February 11th, 1794, that the first Bench of Elders in the congregation was elected, and on Sunday, February 16th, 1794, that they were ordained to their sacred office.

Invitations were sent in the name of the congregation to members of the church not residing in the city, to former members so far as their address could be ascertained, to descendants of former Pastors and officers, to members of the Presbytery of Carlisle, the officers of the Synod of Pennsylvania and of the General Assembly, to former Pastors of the other Presbyterian churches in the city and other Presbyterian ministers having had some relation with this church, the editors of the Presbyterian religious journals, to the Pastors and officers of the city Presbyterian churches, to all the clergymen of the city, without distinction of creed or race. It was the intention of the congregation to celebrate the occasion on the broadest lines of catholicity, and their desire to have all their friends enjoy with them the pleasures of the celebration.

The Committee on Programme prepared a full descriptive programme and had it printed as an elegant souvenir.

Centennial week arrived. Everything was in readiness. The decorations of auditorium, lecture-room, and parlor, under the skillful guidance of the committee in charge were harmonious, appropriate, complete. The ushers were organized for their onerous duty of caring for the comfort of the large audiences anticipated. Nothing remained to be done. There were no last things to be thought of and no hurried final arrangements.

On the morning of Sunday, February 11th, the sun

shone forth beautifully upon the crisp and not severely cold
air. Everything to be desired in the weather was found.
The day remained perfect to its close. It was a most
auspicious beginning. Joy seemed to be in the very atmosphere, and friend remarked to friend as they met on the
way to the house of God : " We could not have had a more
beautiful day." That this weather should continue throughout the whole of the second week of this winter month was
not to be expected. It was not surprising, therefore, that
Monday brought with it a violent snowstorm. The storm
raged throughout the day and night, and with longer or
shorter intervals continued through Thursday of the week.
On Friday the heavens were bright and the sun was warm.
With the exception of Monday evening when the storm
was especially violent, the size of the audiences was not
affected by the weather. Though many would have attended the services had the weather been more propitious, yet
with the single exception mentioned, more could hardly
have been accommodated. The church was on some evenings crowded, and many were turned away.

The programme was carried out as printed with only some
slight modifications made necessary at the last moment. The
sole important change in the programme of the week was
due to the sudden illness of Hon. Samuel J. M. McCarrell,
who was to have presented at the Wednesday evening
meeting the paper setting forth the present condition of
this church. In the emergency the Pastor took his place
both in the preparation of the paper and in presenting it.

On each morning during the Centennial Week, from 11
to 12 o'clock, Mr. David E. Crozier gave an informal organ

recital. These recitals comprised selections from the best composers for the organ, chiefly those of the German and French schools. Every day except Monday, when the weather was especially inclement, the audience was large and its interest in the recitals manifested by close attention and numerous requests for favorite pieces. These recitals were a most delightful feature of the celebration.

The historical exhibition in the parlor attracted large numbers of visitors, who received valuable object lessons in church history in general, and the history of the Market Square church in particular, from the curios and relics displayed.

From Sunday morning until Friday night this centenary celebration was a season of unbroken joy. It was in all its features a brilliant success. Throughout there was a deep and true sense of gratitude to the risen and adorable Lord, the Head of the Church, for his multiplied goodness and grace toward this congregation during all its history and in the present moment. It was pre-eminently an occasion for rejoicing before the Lord. All the people praised him in his sanctuary for his mighty acts according to his excellent greatness. "This honor have all his saints."

This story of the Centennial would not be complete without mention of the most delightful closing of the work of the Centennial Committee. On Wednesday afternoon, February 28th, at 4 o'clock, the committee met at Mrs. Isabella S. Kerr's in final session. There were present Mrs. Kerr, Mrs. McCauley, Messrs. Stewart, Bailey, McAlarney, Mc-Cauley, Samuel W. Fleming, George R. Fleming and Sprenkel. Mr. McCarrell was the only member of the com-

mittee not present, being at Atlantic City for a season of rest. Reports of the work of the several sub-committees were made by their respective chairmen. These reports were all approved, the committees commended, and expenses ordered paid by the Finance Committee. This committee reported that voluntary contributions had been made by the congregation to an amount sufficient to meet all the expenses incurred. The committee then "adjourned without day."

After adjournment, together with Mrs. George B. Stewart, Miss Rachel T. Briggs, Miss Mary W. Kerr, Rev. David M. Skilling and Mr. David E. Crozier, especially invited, the committee sat down as the guests of Mrs. Kerr to an elegant supper. It was a most enjoyable hour and a delightful and fitting conclusion to the arduous but pleasant work of the committee.

The Centennial is a thing of the past, but the memory of it will linger in the mind of every one participating in it as a precious treasure never to be lost. The monument is reared. The praises of a grateful people for the goodness of God are inscribed thereon. Whatever He may have seen in it or us that was unworthy may He forgive. To glorify Him in the earth and hasten His kingdom was the purpose of it all. May He be pleased to accept the purpose as an ample mantle wherewith to cover the imperfections in its execution. "Hitherto hath the Lord helped us."

> " This shall be known when we are dead,
>   And left on long record,
> That ages yet unborn may read,
>   And trust, and praise the Lord."

ENGLISH PRESBYTERIAN CHURCH—INTERIOR.

TAKEN FEBRUARY 12TH 1894.

DECORATIONS AND HISTORICAL EXHIBIT.

The ornate auditorium of the church was greatly beautified by the tasteful and appropriate decorations made for the occasion, under the direction of the Decoration Committe. The central feature was the pulpit. From the Corinthian capitals of the columns there hung in graceful lines smilax and asparagus fern. On the two side columns were suspended blue banners, on which in gilt letters were inscribed "Jesus Christ and Him Crucified," and "Jesus Christ, the Chief Corner-stone." The arch which spans the pulpit recess was draped with blue and red bunting' which furnished a background for the bright lettering of the two mottoes, "Vox Clamantis in Deserto" and "Philadelphia Maneto," meaning respectively, "The Voice of One Crying in the Wilderness," and "Let Brotherly Love Continue." In and about the pulpit were century plants. The varied green of these harmonized with the lillies, roses and other cut flowers renewed from day to day.

In the two front angles of the room were red and blue banners bearing the historic names of John Calvin and John Knox. On the window ledges, in gilt letters on a background of blue or red, were the names of Francis Herron, Jonathan Edwards, John Witherspoon, John Rogers, John McMillan, Archibald Alexander, David Elliot, Charles Hodge, Albert Barnes, Philemon Fowler, John Elder, Charles Nisbet, William R. DeWitt. Many of these were men who have been identified with this church in some part of its history, and many were men whom the whole church delighted to honor. The red and blue, the colors of the Scotch Presbyterian church, were prominent also in the decorations of the choir gallery in the rear of the auditorium. The front of the gallery was covered with blue bunting, fluted in vertical lines and drawn together at regular intervals, and fastened with red bows midway between top and base. The effect was heightened by the delicate green of the licopodium and the sheen of the rhododendron leaves. A line of ground pine ran around the wainscoting, windows and doorways, making a pretty border of living green for the woodwork.

The whole was a poem in color. The prevailing white of the room lent itself sympathetically to the red and blue of the decorations and to the green of plant and vine.

The tasteful distribution and graceful arrangement of material gave a symmetrical completeness to the design. The historical appropriateness of mottoes and names, added intellectual finish to the æsthetic effect. Color, form, significance, all conspired to produce an effect, full of delight, and "whispered of peace, and truth, and friendliness unequalled."

As one passed from the auditorium into the lecture-room and parlor, still further evidence of the decoration committee's activity was seen. On the walls of the former room to the right of the platform were a large water-colored picture of the present church edifice and a large crayon portrait of Rev. Thomas Hastings Robinson, D. D., pastor from 1854 to 1884. To the left of the platform were large crayon

portraits of Rev. William Radcliffe DeWitt, D. D., pastor
from 1818 to 1867, and of James Wallace Weir, Superintendent of the Sunday-school from 1834 to 1878.

The parlor walls were adorned with photographs of the
first and second church edifices, the old Court house, called
"the cradle of Sunday-school enterprise in Harrisburg,"
Brant's Hall, in which the congregation worshiped while
the present edifice was being constructed, and Calvary
Chapel. There were also floor plans of the first church,
before and after it was remodeled in 1826, and the second
church. Over the mantel was a large frame containing a
photograph of the present pastor, his assistant and the five
elders of the present session. On one of the sidewalls was
another large frame containing photographs of nineteen
former elders. The committee found that there are no
likenesses in existence of the other six former elders. Near
this hung a crayon loaned by Rev. Henry C. McCook, D. D.,
of Philadelphia, showing an early sacramental occasion
in the woods; also a frame containing several handsomely
painted church seals; another frame containing pictures of
the log colleges out of which grew Princeton and Jefferson,
and a typical pioneer Scotch-Irish school-house, and two
flags of the Scotch Covenanter Church, all loaned by Doctor
McCook.

In large glass cases there were gathered and carefully preserved many early records and relics of church and Sunday-
school. There were the account books of John Kean,
Treasurer of the congregation from 1790–1792, old receipts,
lottery tickets used in the lottery, from the proceeds of which
the first church was built, the first Sunday-school minute

book, a complete set of the different hymn books used in the church lecture room and Sunday-school, several of the musical instruments used in the choir, the communion sets of Paxtang and Derry churches, communion tokens formerly in use in these congregations, a communion cup from old Hanover church, printed and manuscript sermons by former pastors. Indeed the memorabilia and curios were numbered by hundreds and cannot be mentioned, much less described. Many persons in the city and out of it kindly co-operated with the committee in making this interesting collection—so many, in fact, that it is impossible to name them in this place. The exhibit was visible history. It told the story of the church's progress from primitive days through the most active century of the world's life. It revealed that this church has kept abreast of the best thought and life. It has evidently not marched through the years with laggard steps.

ENGLISH PRESBYTERIAN CHURCH—INTERIOR.

TAKEN FEBRUARY 12TH 1894.

CENTENNIAL COMMITTEE.

Rev. George B. Stewart, D. D., *Chairman;* Samuel J. M. McCarrell, M. Wilson McAlarney, Mrs. Isabella S. Kerr, Peter K. Sprenkel, Charles L. Bailey, Gilbert M. McCauley, Samuel W. Fleming, George R. Fleming, Mrs. Gilbert M. McCauley.

SUB-COMMITTEES.

INVITATION COMMITTEE.—Charles L. Bailey, *Chairman;* David Fleming, Mrs. Julia A. Briggs, Mrs. David Fleming, Mrs. George B. Stewart, Alexander Roberts, John H. Weiss, Dr. Jacob A. Miller, Mrs. Sarah Doll, Mrs. Jacob Haldeman, Miss Sibyl M. Weir, Samuel D. Ingram, George W. Boyd, Lyman D. Gilbert.

PROGRAMME COMMITTEE.—S. J. M. McCarrell, *Chairman;* John C. Harvey, David Fleming, Spencer C. Gilbert, John G. Orr, Robert H. Moffitt.

ENTERTAINMENT COMMITTEE.—G. M. McCauley, *Chairman;* John C. Harvey.

PUBLICATION COMMITTEE.—M. Wilson McAlarney, *Chairman;* Charles H. Bergner, Edward J. Stackpole, J. Henry Spicer, Samuel C. Miller.

FINANCE COMMITTEE.—Samuel W. Fleming, *Chairman;* Robert H. Moffitt, Henry C. Orth, Spencer C. Gilbert, David Fleming, Dr. Cherrick Westbrook, Jr.

DECORATION COMMITTEE.—Mrs. Isabella S. Kerr, *Chairman;* Mrs. Gilbert M. McCauley, Mrs. Elizabeth C. Kunkel, Miss Carrie Pearson, Mrs. William O. Hickok, Jr., Mrs. George R. Fleming, Mrs. William E. Bailey, Miss Margaret B. Mowry,

Miss Caroline Reily, Miss Mary W. Kerr, Melancthon S. Shotwell, George W. Reily, Miss Anna C. Weir, Mrs. Edward Bailey, Mrs. Samuel J. M. McCarrell, Miss Rachel T. Briggs, Mrs. Frank R. Schell, Mrs. John C. Harvey, Mrs. Samuel C. Miller, Miss Sara B. Chayne, Miss Annie R. Kelker, John C. Harvey, James B. Bailey. William E. Bailey.

RECEPTION COMMITTEE.—Mrs. Gilbert M. McCauley, *Chairman* ; Mrs. Charles H. Bergner, Mrs. George C. Bent, Mrs. Anna M. Bigler, Mrs. David Fleming, Jr., Mrs. Dr. Jacob A. Miller, Mrs. Ellen W. Stees, Mrs. D. Truman Boyd, Miss Maud A. Hench, Mrs. Luther R. Kelker, Mrs. David Martin, Mrs. Howard F. Martin, Mrs. Dr. Henry L. Orth, Mrs. M. Wilson McAlarney, Miss Caroline B. Sheafer, Mrs. Elizabeth Reily, Mrs. M. Elizabeth Cathcart, Mrs. Horace A. Chayne, Mrs. Samuel W. Fleming, Mrs. Lyman D. Gilbert, Miss Ella L. Hart, Mrs. J. Henry Spicer, Miss Mary Vandling, Mrs. John H. Weiss, Mrs. Henry F. Quickel, Mrs. Spencer C. Gilbert.

MUSIC COMMITTEE.—George R. Fleming, *Chairman* ; William G. Underwood, Mrs. John C. Harvey, David E. Crozier, Miss Sara B. Chayne, Miss Margaret B. Mowry.

USHERS.—Peter K. Sprenkel, *Chairman* ; Charles W. Foster, William H. Sharp, Horace A. Chayne, Melancthon S. Shotwell, William M. Fahnestock, William M. Graydon, William H. Shaffer, Edward J. Stackpole, Edward Baily, Samuel W. Fleming, Dr. John B. McAlister, Joseph G. Ewing, B. Edward Taylor, Luther R. Kelker, Charles F. Spicer, Henry F. Quickel, Jacob J. Franck, George W. Reily, Warren H. Wasson, Dr. Cherrick Westbrook, Jr., Lucian Notestine, Edward L. Groff, William H. Middleton, Gilbert M. McCauley

CENTENNIAL CHOIR.

George R. Fleming, *Director*.
David E. Crozier, *Organist*.

SOLOISTS.—Miss Rachel T. Briggs, Miss Reba Bunton, Miss Sara B. Chayne, Miss Helen Espy, Mr. Edward Z. Gross, Mrs. Edward Z. Gross, Miss Lillian M. Kline, Mr. Wm. G. Underwood, Mr. Geo. R. Fleming.

SOPRANO.—Miss Helen Espy, Mrs. David Fleming, Jr., Miss Addie Geiger, Mrs. William M. Graydon, Miss Margaret P. Grayson, Mrs. Edward Z. Gross, Mrs. Edward J. Hardy, Miss Maud A. Hench, Miss Mary Killough, Miss Lillian M. Kline, Mrs. Gilbert M. McCauley, Miss Sara J. Miller, Miss Margaret B. Mowry, Miss Marie A. Segelbaum, Mrs. Joshua W. Sharpe, Mrs. J. Henry Spicer, Miss Elizabeth F. L. Walker.

CONTRALTO.—Miss Reba Bunton, Miss Sara B. Chayne, Miss Elizabeth Given, Miss Louisa Given, Mrs. John C. Harvey, Miss Cora L. Snyder, Miss Mabel E. Vaughn.

TENOR.—Mr. David Fleming, Mr. George R. Fleming, Mr. Edward Z. Gross, Mr. Peter K. Sprenkel, Mr. Augustus G. Shantz.

BASS.—Mr. J. Roberts Given, Mr. Henry A. Kelker, Jr., Mr. Harvey J. Miller, Mr. Samuel C. Miller, Mr. Geo. B. Roberts, Mr. John B. Roberts, Mr. George F. Sharp, Mr. William G. Underwood.

ORDER OF SERVICES.

SUNDAY MORNING,
February 11th, 1894, at 10.30 o'clock.

PUBLIC WORSHIP.—The Minister of the Church conducting the service, assisted by the Minister's Assistant and by Rev. Thomas H. Robinson, D. D., and the Rev. JOHN DEWITT, D. D., LL. D., Professor of Church History in Princeton Theological Seminary, preaching the Sermon.   Theme of the Sermon, "THE BEGINNINGS OF PRESBYTERIANISM IN THE MIDDLE COLONIES."

ORDER OF SERVICE.

ORGAN PRELUDE—Iste Confessor, ... *Guilmant*

DOXOLOGY, in Long Meter, ... [Congregation standing]

INVOCATION, closing with the Lord's Prayer [Congregation standing], ... Rev. David M. Skilling

HYMN,* . . . . No. 718, vs. 1, 2, 3

SCRIPTURE LESSON, ... Isaiah 60 : 1–9; Colossians 1 : 1–18

PRAYER, ... Rev. George B. Stewart, D. D.

ANNOUNCEMENTS.

ANTHEM—Jubilate Deo, ... *Buck*

OFFERTORY—Adagio from Sonata in C Minor, . . . *Guilmant*

HYMN,† . . . . No. 575, vs. 1, 2, 6

SERMON, ... Rev. John DeWitt, D. D., LL. D.

PRAYER, ... Rev. Thomas H. Robinson, D. D.

HYMN, ... No. 730, vs. 1, 2

BENEDICTION, ... Rev. Dr. John DeWitt

ORGAN POSTLUDE—March in D, ... *Smart*

*In place of the hymn, Miss Rachel T. Briggs sang "The Good Shepherd," by Barrie.

†Omitted.

SUNDAY EVENING,
February 11th, 1894, at 6.00 o'clock.

SEVENTY-EIGHTH ANNIVERSARY OF THE SUNDAY-SCHOOL.
Mr. SAMUEL J. M. McCARRELL, Superintendent, presiding.

ORDER OF SERVICE.

ORGAN PRELUDE—March in F, ... *Silas*
ANTHEM—I was Glad, ... Choir of Senior Department
INVOCATION,* . . . . [Congregation standing]
LORD'S PRAYER, ... [Chanted, all standing]
HYMN, ... No. 30, vs. 1, 3, Winnowed Songs
REPORT OF PRIMARY DEPARTMENT.

EXERCISES BY PRIMARY DEPARTMENT.

ANTHEM—Lord, Thy Mercy Streameth, ...
. . . . Choir of Senior Department
ADDRESS, ... † Rev. John DeWitt, D. D., LL. D.
REPORT OF INTERMEDIATE DEPARTMENT.

EXERCISES BY INTERMEDIATE DEPARTMENT.

HYMN, . . No. 48, vs. 1, 3, Winnowed Songs, [All standing]
ADDRESS, ... Rev. Thomas H. Robinson, D. D.
REPORT OF SENIOR DEPARTMENT.

SCRIPTURE LESSON, . . . [All standing and read responsively]

Supt. Ye are the light of the world. A city that is set on a hill cannot be hid.

School. Neither do men light a candle, and put it under a bushel, but on a candlestick; it giveth light unto all that are in the house.

Supt. Let your light so shine before men that they may see your good works, and glorify your Father which is in heaven.

* Offered by Rev. William P. Patterson.

† Rev. Dr. DeWitt was unable to be present. Mr. Geo. E. Sterry, of New York City, gave an address.

School. Lay not up for yourselves treasures upon earth, where moth and rust doth corrupt, and where thieves break through and steal :

Supt. But lay up for yourselves treasures in heaven where neither moth nor rust doth corrupt, and where thieves do not break through nor steal :

School. For where your treasure is, there will your heart be also.

Supt. Ask, and it shall be given you ; seek, and ye shall find ; knock, and it shall be opened unto you :

School. For every one that asketh receiveth ; and he that seeketh findeth ; and to him that knocketh it shall be opened.

ANTHEM—Thee will We Worship, Choir of Senior Department

REPORT OF CHINESE DEPARTMENT.

REPORT OF CALVARY CHAPEL SCHOOL.

SUMMARY OF REPORTS.

ANTHEM—Rest for the Weary, Choir of the Senior Department

ADDRESS, ... The Pastor

DISTRIBUTION OF PRIZES—For unbroken attendance during the year.

HYMN, . . . No. 104, v. 1, Winnowed Songs [All standing]

BENEDICTION, ... Rev. David M. Skilling

ORGAN POSTLUDE—Chorus in D Major, ... *Guilmant*

MONDAY EVENING,
February 12th, 1894, at 7.30 o'clock.

SACRAMENT OF THE LORD'S SUPPER. Rev. GEORGE S. CHAMBERS, D. D., Minister of Pine Street Presbyterian Church, presiding ; and Rev. Albert B. Williamson, Minister of Paxtang Presbyterian Church, Rev. George B. Stewart, D. D., Minister of Market Square Presbyterian Church, Rev.

David M. Skilling, Minister's Assistant of Market Square Presbyterian Church, Rev. Reuben H. Armstrong, Minister of Elder Street Presbyterian Church, Rev. George S. Duncan, Minister of Westminster Presbyterian Church, and Rev. William P. Patterson, Minister of Olivet Presbyterian Church, assisting.

The Elders * of Paxtang, Market Square, Pine Street, Elder Street, Covenant, Westminster and Olivet Churches distributing the Emblems as followeth :

The Bread : Elders Spencer C. Barber, Jacob A. Miller, Gilbert M. McCauley, John C. Harvey, H. Murray Graydon, Francis Jordan, Cassius M. Brown, William J. Adore, Turner Cooper, Sr., John Curwen, John J. Craig, William Jones, J. Wallace Elder, William S. Shaffer, Sr., and Abram L. Groff.

The Wine : Matthew B. Elder, Francis W. Rutherford, Samuel J. M. McCarrell, J. Henry Spicer, Jacob F. Seiler, Daniel W. Cox, Thomas J. Miller, Walter W. Williams, John

---

* All the elders were not present. Those not present sent reasons for non-attendance. Those present distributed the Emblems according to the following arrangement :

Left side aisle ; The Bread, Daniel W. Cox, Dr. Jacob A. Miller ; The Wine, J. Henry Spicer, Thomas J. Miller.

Left center aisle, left side ; The Bread and the Wine, Jacob F. Seiler, Gilbert M. McCauley.

Left center aisle, right side ; The Bread and the Wine, Francis Jordan, Matthew B. Elder.

Right center aisle, left side ; The Bread and the Wine, John M. Stewart, Abram L. Groff.

Right center aisle, right side ; The Bread, William S. Shaffer, J. Wallace Elder ; The Wine, William S. Shaffer, Samuel H. Garland.

Right side aisle : The Bread, William Jones, John J. Craig ; The Wine, David R. Elder, Alexander Adams.

Gallery : The Bread and The Wine, John C. Harvey.

M. Stewart, Samuel H. Garland, John E. Patterson, David R.
Elder, John E. Daniel, Jacob K. Walker and Alexander
Adams.

ORDER OF SERVICE.

ORGAN PRELUDE—Chorus from Passion Music, ... *Bach*
ANTHEM—Holy Spirit, Come, O Come,* . . . . *Martin*
INVOCATION, ... Rev. Reuben H. Armstrong
HYMN—No. 696, vs. 1, 2, 6, . . . Rev. Albert B. Williamson
SCRIPTURE LESSON. . . . . Rev. David M. Skilling
ADDRESS, ... Rev. Geo. S. Chambers, D. D.
WORDS OF INSTITUTION, . . . Rev. Geo. S. Chambers, D. D.
PRAYER, ... Rev. William P. Patterson
DISTRIBUTION OF THE BREAD, . Rev. Geo. S. Chambers, D. D.
DISTRIBUTION OF THE WINE, . . Rev. Geo. B. Stewart, D. D.
PRAYER OF THANKSGIVING, ... Rev. Geo. S. Duncan
HYMN—No. 688, vs. 1, 4, 5, . . Rev. Geo. S. Chambers, D. D.
BENEDICTION, ... Rev. Geo. S. Chambers, D. D.
ORGAN POSTLUDE—Hymn of the Apostles from the Re-
demption, ... *Gounod*

TUESDAY EVENING,
February 13th, 1894, at 7.30 o'clock.

Rev. DAVID M. SKILLING, Minister's Assistant, presiding.

MUSICAL FESTIVAL. Mr. George R. Fleming, Director.
Mr. David E. Crozier, Organist.

PROGRAMME.

ORGAN PRELUDE—Vorspiel to Parsifal, ... *Wagner*
ANTHEM—Festival Te Deum, ... *Buck*
PRAYER.†

---

*"Lead, Kindly Light," was substituted.
†Prayer by Rev. Harris R. Schenck, Chambersburg, Pa.

SCRIPTURE LESSON,* . . . . Psalm cl.

SOLO, ... † Miss Rachel T. Briggs

ORGAN INTERLUDE—Andante in F, ... *Mozart*

ANTHEM—Lo! It is I, ... *Faure-Shelly*

SOLO,‡ . . . . Miss Reba Bunton

HYMN, by the Congregation, all standing, sung as in ye

olden time, ... No. 456, vs. 1, 2, 4

DUET,§ . . . . Mr. and Mrs. Edward Z. Gross

ORGAN INTERLUDE—Pastoral from Sonata in D Minor,

. . . . *Reinberger*

ANTHEM—O! Clap Your Hands, ... *Buck*

ADDRESS—The Hymnology of the Mother Presbyterian

Church of Harrisburg, with Some Reminiscences of

Choirs and Choir Days, . . . H. Murray Graydon, Esq.

ANTHEM—Qui Tollis, ... *Farmer*

SOLO,‖ . . . . Miss Helen Espy

HYMN, Congregation standing and singing as in the

days of the fathers, ... No. 394, vs. 1, 3, 4

BENEDICTION, ... ¶ Rev. David M. Skilling

ORGAN POSTLUDE—Marche Pontifical, ... *Lemmens*

WEDNESDAY EVENING,
February 14th. 1894, at 7.30 o'clock.

Rev. WILLIAM A. WEST, Stated Clerk of the Presbytery of
Carlisle, Welsh Run, Penna., presiding.

---

*Lesson read by Rev. James Fraser, Ph. D., of Sparrow's Point. Md.

†Miss Briggs did not sing. William G. Underwood sang, "Glory to Thee, my God, this Night."

‡Miss Bunton sang, "Eye hath not Seen." from Gaul's "Holy City."

§Mr. and Mrs. Gross sang, "Forever with the Lord."

‖Miss Espy sang, "Jerusalem," by Henry M. Parker.

¶Benediction by Rev. Charles Edward Greig, Paris, France.

THE PRESBYTERIAN CHURCHES OF HARRISBURG.   Addresses by representatives appointed by the several Sessions.

ORDER OF SERVICE.

ORGAN PRELUDE—Marche Religieuse, ... *Guilmant*
ANTHEM—Hark, Hark, My Soul ! * . . . . *Buck*
SCRIPTURE LESSON,† . . . . Philippians 2 : 1–11
PRAYER.‡
HYMN, ... No. 232, vs. 1, 3, 4
ADDRESS—Paxtang Church, organized about 1726, . . .
. . . . Rev. Albert B. Williamson
ADDRESS—Market Square Church, Organized February
	16, 1794, ... ₿ Hon. Samuel J. M. McCarrell
ADDRESS—Pine Street Church, Organized May 22, 1858,
. . . . Prof. Jacob F. Seiler, Ph. D.
HYMN, ... ·. . . . No. 92, vs. 1, 3
ADDRESS—Elder Street Church, Organized October 28,
	1858, ... Mr. Cassius M. Brown
ADDRESS—Covenant Church, Organized September 9, 1866,
. . . . Mr. Samuel H. Garland
ADDRESS—Westminster Church, Organized June 19, 1873,
. . . . Rev. George S. Duncan
ADDRESS—Olivet Church, Organized October 15, 1889, .
. . . . Rev. William P. Patterson
PRAYER.
HYMN, ... No. 639, vs. 1, 3
BENEDICTION, ... Rev. William A. West
ORGAN POSTLUDE—Chorus in D Minor, ... *Guilmant*

*Martin's " Holy Spirit, Come, O Come " was substituted.
†Read by Rev. Reuben H. Armstrong, Pastor of Elder Street Presbyterian Church, City.
‡ Prayer offered by Rev. Benjamin F. Beck, City Missionary.
₿ Mr. McCarrell detained by illness.   The Pastor took his place.

THURSDAY EVENING.
February 15th, 1894, at 7.30 o'clock.

Rev. GEORGE B. STEWART, D. D., Minister, presiding.

HISTORICAL EVENING.—The Rev. THOMAS H. ROBINSON, D. D., Reunion Professor of Sacred Rhetoric, Church Government and Pastoral Theology in Western Theological Seminary, Allegheny, Penn'a, delivering the address.

ORDER OF SERVICE.

ORGAN PRELUDE—Benedictus, ... *Mackenzie*

ANTHEM—Hallelujah Chorus, ... *Handel*

THE APOSTLES' CREED, . . [In unison, congregation standing]

INVOCATION,* . . . . [Congregation standing]

HYMN, ... No. 2, vs. 1, 4, 5

SCRIPTURE LESSON.†

HYMN—No. 435, vs. 1, 2, 3, 5, . . . [Congregation standing]

HISTORICAL ADDRESS—A Century Plant, . . .

By Rev. Thomas H. Robinson, D. D.

HYMN—No. 953, ... [Congregation standing]

LORD'S PRAYER, ... [In unison, congregation standing]

BENEDICTION, ... By Rev. Thomas H. Robinson, D. D.

ORGAN POSTLUDE—Chorus in E Flat, ... *Guilmant*

FRIDAY EVENING,
February 16th, 1894, at 7.30 o'clock.

A RECEPTION BY THE CONGREGATION TO THEIR GUESTS. Entrance by side door. Hon. JOHN B. McPHERSON, Lebanon, Pa., presiding. During the evening there will be an informal

---

* By Rev. I. Potter Hayes, Wrightsville, Pa.
† Psalm 89 : 1-11 by Rev. John L. McKeehan, Steelton, Pa.

musical programme,* and brief impromptu addresses by some of the guests. †

---

* The musical programme consisted of " The Angel Came," F. H. Cowen, by Miss Reba Bunton ; "They Shall Hunger no More," from Gaul's "The Holy City," Miss Reba Bunton and Mr. Geo. R. Fleming ; "Come Unto Me," Coenen, Mr. Geo. R. Fleming. These were sung in the auditorium. In the lecture-room were given two numbers by Messrs. Henry A. Kelker, Jr., J. F. Hutchinson, H. L. Vance, Charles F. Etter, Frank S. Morrow, members of the Harrisburg Banjo Club ; a piano duet, overture to "Rienzi," Wagner, by Mrs. Frank R. Schell and Mrs. David Fleming, Jr.: "The Miller of the Dee," "Ben Bolt," "Annie Laurie," "Blue Bells of Scotland," by "The Mendelssohn Quartette," composed of Mr. Geo. R. Fleming, Mr. Edward Z. Gross, Mr. William G. Underwood, Mr. Lucius S. Bigelow.

† Addresses were made by Rev. Wm. C. Cattell, D. D., Philadelphia ; Major General Geo. R. Snowden, Philadelphia ; Col. J. Ross Thompson, Erie, Pa.; Rev. Henry E. Niles, D. D., York, Pa.; Mr. Franklin W. Rutherford, Paxtang.

PROGRAMME OF ORGAN RECITALS.

MONDAY, *February 12th.*

Adagio from 6th Organ Symphony, ...	*Wider*
Fantasia in A Minor, ...	*Lemmens*
Andante from Fifth Symphony, . . .	*Beethoven*
Cantilene Pastorale, ...	*Guilmant*
Gothic March, ...	*Salome*
Induant Justiciam, ...	*Guilmant*

TUESDAY, *February 13th.*

Sonata in E Minor, ...	*Merkel*
Pictures from the Orient, Nos. II., III., VI., . . .	*Schumann*
Andante from Symphony in C, ...	*Schubert*
Song to the Evening Star from Tannhauser, ...	*Wagner*
Funeral March and Song of the Seraphs, ...	*Guilmant*

WEDNESDAY, *February 14th.*

Concerto for Organ, No. III., ...	*Handel*
Adagio from Opus, 97, ...	*Beethoven*
Sonata in E flat, ...	*Buck*
Two Hymn Tunes of the Olden Time, ...	*Anon*
Old Hebrew Prayer, ...	*Anon*
Judex, from Mors et Vita, ...	*Gounod*
Torchlight March, ...	*Guilmant*

THURSDAY, *February 15th.*

Concerto, No. I., ...	*Handel*
Sonata, No. IV., ...	*Mendelssohn*
Andante in A Minor, ...	*Merkel*
Rhapsody in D, ...	*Saint-Saens*

Tremmerei, ... *Schumann*
Prayer from Lohengrin, ... *Wagner*
Funeral March and Song of the Seraphs (by request), ...
. . . . *Guilmant*

FRIDAY, *February 16th.*

Allegretto from Symphony No. 7, ... *Beethoven*
Sonata in D Minor, ... *Guilmant*
Adagio, ... *Liszt*
Andante Religioso, ... *Liszt*
Pilgrim's Chorus from Tannhauser, ... *Wagner*
Ave Maria, ... *Arcadelt-Liszt*
Funeral March and Song of the Seraphs (by request), . . .
. . . . *Guilmant*

CENTENNIAL WEEK.

SUNDAY MORNING,

February the 11th, 1894, at 10.30 o'clock.

Cowper, speaking of the "soft music of the village bells," says:

> "With easy force it opens all the cells,
> Where Memory slept."

This was the experience of many as the sweet, deep tones of the Market Square Church bell announced that the hour had arrived for commencing the Centennial commemoration of the founding of this church, and called the people to the house of prayer.

The cells where Memory slept were unlocked, and the sleeping occupant was called to his task. It was an easy and pleasant task. Three generations of worshipers have passed along these streets to the house of God. The forms of many are recalled with loving veneration, the names of others are rehearsed with a deep appreciation of the sterling worth and valiant service of those who bore them, while in the shadows of Memory's cell, half-revealed, half-hidden are many, many more who are only known now by what they have done. Memory is busy. Joyful, tender, solemn feelings are evoked as we enter the sanctuary and recall past experiences and departed friends. The day with its crisp air and "blue vault without a cloud"; the occasion provoking historical reminiscence; the sanctuary beautifully decorated, and now filled with an audience crowding into every vacant space; the pulpit tastefully ornamented with century plants and cut flowers, and occupied by a beloved former Minister, the honored son of another former Minister, the present Minister and his Assistant; all conspire to make the opening service of Centennial Week impressive.

The hour appointed having arrived, the service was begun with the organ prelude, Guilmant's " Iste Confessor," a set of elaborate variations on the old Latin hymn of that name. At the conclusion of the prelude the congregation arose and united in singing the Doxology in long meter:

> Praise God from whom all blessings flow ;
> Praise him all creatures here below ;
> Praise him above, ye heavenly host ;
> Praise Father, Son and Holy Ghost.

While the congregation remained standing, Rev. David M. Skilling, Minister's Assistant, offered the Invocation, the congregation uniting in the Lord's Prayer at its close. Miss Rachel T. Briggs sang with great acceptance Barrie's "The Good Shepherd." The Minister read for the Scripture lesson from the Old Testament, Isaiah lx. 1-9, and from the New Testament, Colossians i. 1-18, and offered prayer.

He then gave an account of the preparations for the Centennial observances, and called particular attention to some of the special features of the week upon which the church was entering. He closed his statement in the following words:

" Those who founded this church and those who have succeeded them in its membership wrought faithfully, fearing God and serving man in all earnestness and sincerity. It is meet that we celebrate their deeds and treasure the memory of their virtue. The Great Head of the Church, our God and Saviour, has been pleased for a hundred years to show favor unto this portion of his glorious church. It is fitting that we bear testimony to his abounding goodness and superabounding grace toward our beloved Zion. This is our double purpose in these Centennial services: to recount the deeds of our fathers, and to exalt the name of our God.

It is our prayer that these days may be the dawn of a new era of activity, purity, and consecration on the part of us who have fallen heir to such a goodly heritage; and of continued and increasing favor from the God of our fathers, our God, and the God of our children to all generations."

Dudley Buck's bright, vigorous "Jubilate Deo" was rendered with spirit by the large Centennial Choir. While an offering for the Synodical Sustentation Fund was being gathered, Guilmant's Adagio from Sonata in C Minor, a slow, graceful movement, was rendered on the grand organ. The Minister introduced the speaker of the occasion in the following words:

"The Rev. Dr. DeWitt, who will now address us on 'The Beginnings of Presbyterianism in the Middle Colonies,' needs no introduction to this congregation. Born and reared in this city and church, he is personally known to many of you. Consecrated to the Gospel ministry, he has become the worthy and honored son of his revered father. First as a pastor, in Irvington on the Hudson, Boston and Philadelphia, then as a professor in Lane Theological Seminary, McCormick Theological Seminary, and now in

Princeton Theological Seminary, the Church has honored herself in recognizing his ability and in honoring him. We are proud to claim him as one of us, and most happy to have him now stand in the pulpit his father so long occupied, and inaugurate these Centennial services."

BEGINNINGS OF PRESBYTERIANISM IN THE MIDDLE COLONIES.

By Rev. JOHN DeWITT, D. D., LL. D.

I need not assure you of the great pleasure with which I
received your invitation to take part in the services by
which you had decided to celebrate the hundred years of
our church's life. I say our church; because, after all, this
church must always be mine in a sense in which no other
church can be. I was born one of its members; and when
my membership in the Church of God was recognized in the
sacrament of baptism, it was among the children of this
church that my name was enrolled. It was in the cata-
chetical class and in the Sunday-schools of this church that
I was instructed in the principles of our religion; and when
I was led to confirm by my own act the vows of baptism, it
was here that I united with some of you in partaking for
the first time of the Lord's Supper. From this church I
went to the Theological Seminary; and I must always
remember, with great distinctness, that it was in the lecture-
room of this church, while my father and Dr. Robinson
were sitting in the pulpit, that I preached my first sermon
to a company of friends, of whom some are before me at
this time.

And Harrisburg can never be anything to me but home;
my own city, the city of my people. A month or two ago I
had occasion to spend two days here, and brought with me

one of my nephews. Both of us were deeply interested in visiting the resting places of five generations of our ancestors; and it was with no ordinary feelings that, in reading the epitaphs of those from whom we were descended, we found among them the names* of the first white settler of the place, of the founder of the city, of the first Senator from the Commonwealth, of the first president of the town's eldest bank, and of one who for a half century was pastor of the city's eldest Christian congregation.

One who was born and reared in this place must always think of the beauty of its situation with enthusiasm. It is my good fortune always to have lived in the presence of some strikingly beautiful natural object. My first parish was on the banks of the Hudson, just at the southern edge of the broad Tappan-zee. Northward my vision was bounded by the bold outlines of the lower Highlands, while looking down the river, I could

> See sunrise rest or sunset fade
> Along the frowning palisade.

From the banks of the Hudson I went to Boston and the banks of the Charles where it broadens into the Back-bay. Around me were the hills and uplands made memorable by a great history, and made to sing with beauty by the energy and intelligence of a great people; while a short walk brought me to the noble harbor and bay, "where," as Emerson has said,

> Twice a day the loving sea
> Takes Boston in his arms.

---

* John Harris, the first; John Harris, the second; William Maclay William Wallace; William Radcliffe DeWitt.

From Boston I went to Philadelphia; to the loveliness of Fairmount and the Wissahickon, and the broad and shining glory of the stately Delaware. From Philadelphia I was called to Lane Theological Seminary, and lived on Walnut Hills. The banks of the Ohio are beautiful from Pittsburg to the Mississippi; but at no point are the hills clothed with a more glorious green or with statelier trees, than at Cincinnati. From the valley of the Ohio I moved to the great City of the Lake; and I am sure that all of you who last summer saw the living waters of Lake Michigan must have been profoundly impressed with the magnificence of that great inland sea. And now at Princeton—whether looking eastward over the great plain lands toward the ocean, or westward to the first foothills of the mountains, or about me on the stately trees which have helped to give fame to our University town—I rejoice that my lot has again been cast in a place "suffused and saturated with the element of beauty."

But the beauty of Harrisburg has a charm for me which that of no other place possesses. And sometimes, when I begin to fear that the charm resides, not in the scene but in my relation to it, I dissipate the fear by reading what another Harrisburger, the late Dr. Benjamin Wallace, has written of it; and I will please myself by reading it to you. "If there be a more beautiful spot on earth," writes Dr Wallace in his paper on the Insurrection of the Paxton Boys, "if there be a more beautiful spot on earth than that where the men of Paxton settled, we have never seen it. From its source in Otsego Lake, along by its lovely windings where the Chemung intersects the North Branch, by the Valley of the Wyoming which lives forever in the imagination of Campbell, but which is fairer even than the semi-tropical fancy of which he was enamored; on by the bold scenery of the meeting of its waters at Northumberland, to its broad glory and its magnificent union with the Chesapeake, every mile of the Susquehanna is beautiful. Other rivers have their points of loveliness or of grandeur; the Susquehanna has every form of beauty and sublimity that belongs to rivers. Everywhere its course is deflected. It begins a wooded lake; it winds a limpid brook by meadows and over silver pebbles; it makes its way through mountains; it loiters restingly by their base; it sweeps in broad courses by the valleys. Its vast width in its mad Spring freshets, when, swollen by the melted snows, it rushes from the hills with irrestible force, leaves with its fall island after island in its mid channel of the richest green and the most surpassing beauty; while those passages through the mountains afford points of scenery, which it is no exaggeration to call sublime. The Susquehanna makes the grandest of these passages just below the mouth of the Juniata. Its course there is several miles long, before it entirely disengages itself from the rapids called Hunter's Falls, which are the remains of the rocky barrier that once resisted its way. Entirely at liberty, it pours its stream, a mile wide, along a channel some fifty feet beneath its eastern bank. About seven miles below the mountains, at a point where they look blue in the distance, flows in a little stream, which the Indians called called Pextang, Paixtang, or Paxton. This mountain range is the northern boundary of the great valley, which, under-laid with blue limestone, covered originally with the richest and noblest forest growth, and including within it the garden of the Atlantic slope extends from Newburg on the Hudson, by Easton on the Delaware, by Reading on the Schuylkill, by Harrisburg on the Susquehanna, by Carlisle and Chambersburg, and Hagerstown and Winchester, until it loses itself in the North Carolina hills. The point of greatest beauty in all that valley is the spot where it is cloven by the Susquehanna." * So a son of Harrisburg and of this church wrote more than a third of a century ago, of the beauty of the place of which every foot of ground was precious dust to him. And so doubtless all her scattered sons and daughters feel, as they think of the mountains, and the valley, and the trees, and the gorgeous sunsets, and the shining river, that glorified their childhood.

I dare not trust myself to speak of the tender personal associations and the sacred memories which make a return to Harrisburg almost a holy pilgrimage. For, though I am tempted to be very free and personal to-day, I must pause before I stir up the deepest fountains of feeling in you and in myself. But I cannot forbear to say, that every Harris-burger, who is also a son of this church, must feel himself made better by returning to the place in which that man of God and friend of man, James Wallace Weir, so long did justice and loved mercy and walked humbly with his God.

Among the many traits of Harrisburg that endear it to a native, who has been called to live away from it, is its charming social life. This social life derives no small part of its charm from the fact that Harrisburg, with its surrounding country, was settled not by one class of people,

---

*Presbyterian Quarterly Review, April, 1860.

but by two classes. We are beginning to-day the celebration
of the establishment a century ago of a church called the
English Presbyterian Congregation. But we must not forget
that, during the most of its life there has existed by its
side in Christian amity a German Presbyterian Congregation. While here the spiritual descendants of John Knox
have been fed on the catechism of Westminster, there the
spiritual descendants of Ulrich Zwingli have been fed on
the catechism of Heidelberg. The union of these two
peoples has made a broader and kindlier, a far more
genial social life than either would have made. Since the
Scotch or Scotch-Irish has always been the dominant element in this congregation, and since in the course of this
address I shall have a good deal to say about it, it will not
be out of place now to remind ourselves how much we all
owe to the other, the distinctively Teutonic element, with its
less polemic and more genial, though perhaps more lax
modes of religious thinking; with its home-loving, earth-
hungering sentiment; with its *gemuthlichkeit*, which, though
the word is perhaps untranslatable into English, our
German brethren have imparted to the social life of this
whole district. This union is seen in the union of family
names. It is not long since you were accustomed to meet
on the streets of your city one of the eldest members
of the Harrisburg bar, whose geniality and courtesy were
always a benediction; who, in his Christian name, preserved the memory of his Scotch, and in his surname preserved the memory of his Netherland ancestors; I refer to the
late Mr. Hamilton Alricks. But the union of the Scotch
Hamilton and the Teutonic Alricks, is only an instance of

what is typical and common in Harrisburg families and Harrisburg names. So are united the German Wiestling and the Scotch Weir; so Egle and Beatty; so Kerr and Orth; so Orth and Reily; so Kunkel and Rutherford; so Buehler and McCormick; so Ross and Haldeman; so Haldeman and Cameron; so Gross and Criswell; so Spangler and Hamilton; so Bucher and Ayres; so Fahnestock and McKinley; and so, to refer to the pulpit of this church, the Scotch Robinson and the German Buehler. When I think of the great social and religious value, to Harrisburg of this union of the Scotch and Teutonic elements of its early population, I encourage the hope that it will be continued in the future. And the social news of the city that comes to me from time to time leads me to the conclusion that the hope is quite certain of fulfillment.

I have thus told you many reasons—and I could tell you as many more—why my affection for Harrisburg has not abated with absence and the lapse of time, and why it is a pleasure to return to the city, especially to take some part in such a celebration as you begin to-day: the celebration of the establishment a hundred years ago of this venerated church; the church of my family, the church my father and of my forefathers, the church that sprang from Paxtang, the church of my elder ancestry. And since we are looking backward to-day, it has occurred to me that it would be well if we were to begin at a point even earlier than a century ago, and call up before our minds a picture of the beginnings of Presbyterianism in this part of the United States. Of course, I must be very brief and fragmentary in my treatment of a large historical subject; but brief and incomplete as I shall be, what I shall say may prove a not inappropriate introduction to the celebration of the week which this day begins.

The name of the church gives us a convenient order for the treatment of the subject I have to present: the English Presbyterian Congregation of Harrisburg. It is a Presbyterian congregation; a congregation of that peculiar type of Presbyterianism known as English speaking, and the place in which it has stood for a hundred years brings before us the fact that it belongs to the second generation of those English speaking Presbyterian churches that were planted in the Middle Colonies.

When, on All Saints' day, in fifteen hundred and seventeen, Martin Luther nailed on the door of his church in Wittenberg the *theses* on grace and indulgences which he was prepared to defend against the world, a step was taken which divided Western Christianity against itself. In the enthusiasm of the new movement, it seemed as if the churches of the Reformation must be as closely united, externally, as the Latin church of the Middle Ages had been. But events soon showed that the organizing, or Roman spirit, which had determined the external life of European Christianity since the pontificate of Gregory the Great, had given place to the Protestant, the critical and divisive spirit, which has marked the career of the modern church. This is not the time to discuss the question whether Christianity has gained most or lost most by the domination, during the last three centuries and a half, of the spirit of protest, of criticism and of dissent; whether or not the attainment of clearer views of truth, and of the internal unity, of which we Protestants make so much, is an adequate compensation for the loss of that one fold with one shepherd, to which the Protestant world is so often invited to return. I believe that the compensation is more than adequate. But, to-day, I note simply the great historical fact that, with the first blow of Luther's hammer began the history of national churches and of modern denominational Christianity. This tendency to divide, supported by the relations of the Protestant churches to the civil governments, revealed itself first in the memorable controversy between Luther and Zwingli, touching the presence of the body of Christ in the Sacrament of the Supper. That controversy resulted in setting over against each other the Lutheran and the Reformed, as the two great families of National Protestant Churches. The resources of diplomacy and of theological analysis were exhausted in the fruitless endeavor to unite them. Since the Conference of Marburg, each of the two great types of Protestantism has developed along lines distinct from those of the other's history.

In dividing Protestant Europe between them, Lutheranism, broadly speaking, took Northern Germany and the Scandanavian countries. Its territories were contiguous, and it possessed, during the fight of Protestantism for life and for recognition on the map and in the politics of Europe, all the advantage that belongs to a compacted empire and to racial unity. The Reformed type of Protestantism, the more radical and thorough-going type, pushed itself into those countries which lay nearest to Rome, or which had felt most keenly the evils of the Papacy. Reformed Protestantism was the more widely spread, and the less racially united. It appeared in South Germany, in German Switzerland and French Switzerland, in France, in Spain, in Italy and in Scotland. But for the fact that, for reasons personal to himself, the monarch of England took the lead in, and so largely limited the progress of the Reformation in England, it would have taken possession of South as it did of North Britain, and the modern religious history of the island would have been the history of a single national church.

The Reformed Churches were not so closely related to the State as were the Lutheran; and for this reason, as for others which I need not stop to mention, they required for their healthful development a form of government, both strong enough for the church's struggle with an adverse environment and representative enough of the faithful who composed it. For such a government, our spiritual fathers repaired to the Scriptures which they had accepted as their rule of faith ; and they were convinced that they found its elements in the organization of the churches founded by the Apostles. But there was needed a genius, who could seize these elements and, employing them to form an actual church, could show to the Reformed Churches of Europe a living example of the revived Apostolic church organization. Such a genius appeared in John Calvin, first among the exegetes, first among the theologians and one of the first statesmen of his age. It is among the wonders of the world that he organized, seemingly without difficulty or hesitation, both the theology and the polity which have distinguished the great family of Reformed Churches. The church of Christ in Geneva became the model of the Pres-

byterian Churches of the world. The characteristic traits of
this church order are familiar to us all; its exaltation of the
truth and of the preacher, its provision for the representation of the people, its insistence on the church's autonomy,
on the efficiency of its discipline, and on the subjection of
a part to the whole. But we are not all so familiar with
the fact that those who have given to the subject severe
study, as historians and publicists, find it hard to resist
the conclusion, to which our own historian Mr. Bancroft
gives expression, when he assigns to Calvin's theology and
polity a high if not the highest place among the causes of
our system of general education and of our enjoyment of
civil liberty and self-government.

The Reformed theology and the Presbyterian order
were eagerly accepted by the people of Scotland. They
were made the national religion and church order against
the enmity of the crown, and they were maintained
against a succession of hostile monarchs. Of these no
one was more persistently hostile than James the Sixth,
afterward James the First of England. He tried the
strength and temper of the Scottish character, and found
that he could not bend it to his will. When, therefore, the
Ulster plantations needed settlers, he invited the Scotch to
furnish them; and the Scotch, accepting his invitation and
becoming the Scotch-Irish, began at once to justify the boast
of their King, that here at least was a people, unlike the
English of the Pale, too vigorous to be absorbed or modified
by the Irish Celts. There in Ireland our Scotch forefathers
lived for a hundred years before the great emigrations to
America began. The training of their Irish life was severe

indeed. It robbed the Scotchmen of some of their most
engaging traits; notably that gift for poetry which makes
the Scotch ballad the most pathetic of popular songs. This
gift seems to have died out during their stay in Ireland.
But if the exile robbed the Scotch of this great gift, "their
training in Ireland," as Mr. Bancroft has said, "kept the
spirit of liberty and the readiness to resist unjust government as fresh in their hearts as though they had just been
listening to the preachings of Knox or musing over the
political creed of the Westminster Assembly"*

It is a sad story, that of the persecutions and oppressions
which at last drove them from their new home in Ulster,
and across the sea. We can understand the persecutions
in the days of the Stuarts, of Charles the First and Charles
the Second and James the Second. But the oppressions of
the reigns of Anne and the earlier Georges, after all that
Ulster had done to make their reigns a possibility; after
Derry and Enniskillen and the Battle of the Boyne; these
are hard to understand. Certainly, if ever a people purchased by patriotic self-sacrifice the right, I will not say to
religious toleration, but to absolute religious liberty, our
Presbyterian fathers of Ulster purchased it during the cam-
paign of William of Orange against the followers and allies
of the rejected James. Yet it was precisely in these latter
reigns that the oppressions became intolerable and the great
migrations to America took place. I shall not tell at length
the outrageous story, but my subject requires me at least to
say something. How can I speak adequately of the begin-

---

* Hist. of the U. S., Vol. iii., p. 29.

nings of Presbyterianism in the Middle Colonies. unless I tell in brief what were the facts that compelled the Briggses and Brysons of Silver's Spring, that compelled the Flemings and Simontons and McCormicks and Wallaces of Hanover, the Rutherfords and Elders and Gilmors and Cowdens of Paxtang, the Kerrs and Wilsons and Boyds and McNairs of Derry, to leave their Irish homes and clear the forests at distant out-posts of civilization in the province of Pennsylvania?

William the Third highly valued his Scotch-Irish subjects, and during his reign they enjoyed a liberty of religion to which they had not been accustomed. The act of toleration was faithfully executed and the policy of toleration was not changed. But after the accession of Anne, the execution of the act became tardy and unequal, and measures were taken by the High Church party for its amendment. Such an amendment was secured in the sacramental "Test act," by which conscientious Presbyterians were effectively driven or excluded from all public positions of honor or trust. And there were other methods of persecution. "No sooner," writes Dr. Blackwood, "had Anne ascended the throne than the same intolerant High Church party that had formerly oppressed them began to renew their assaults. At one time the annoyances of the Presbyterians of Ulster arose from embarrassments about marriages. At another time they were assailed because their ministers obeyed their Presbyteries by preaching in vacant churches; while the most absurd charges of disloyalty were urged against them in pamphlets and often made the subject of legal investiga-

tion by magistrates." *   At last in 1714, an act was passed
to prevent the growth of schism, in which under penalty of
three months imprisonment and disqualification as a teacher,
every teacher of children was forbidden " to be willingly
present at any conventicle of dissenters for religious worship." The fifth year of the reign of the First George is
marked by the passage of an act which gave back legal
toleration to the Presbyterians in Ireland. But the relief
came too late; and the effect was only to substitute the
oppression of the wealthy land owner for the oppression
of the Church, the Parliament and the Crown.

To escape this prosecution the Ulster Presbyterians sailed
in large numbers for America.   " In Ireland," says Mr. Bancroft, " the disfranchised Scotch Presbyterians who still drew
their ideas of Christian government from the Westminister
Confession began to believe that they were under no obligation to render obedience to Britain, and had all Ireland
resembled them, it could not have been held in subjection.
But what could be done by unorganized men constituting
only about a tenth of the population, in the land in which
they were but sojourners? They were willing to quit a soil
which was endeared to them by no traditions; and the
American colonies opened their arms to receive them. They
began to change their abode as soon as they felt oppression,
and every successive period of discontent swelled the tide of
emigrants." † We are told by another authority, that "year
after year, from the second quarter of the eighteenth cen-

---

*Introduction to Webster's History of the Presbyterian Church of
United States.

†History of the United States. Vol. III, pp. 28, 29.

tury, it is estimated that 12,000 people annually sailed for America from the north of Ireland. Such was the drain indeed that it was computed that in 1773, and the five preceding years, the north of Ireland lost by emigration to America, one-fourth of the trading cash and a like proportion of the manufacturing people." *

Thus in the eighteenth century there flowed wave after wave of Presbyterian immigrants into America. They poured themselves over the whole Atlantic country south of New England and New York. There were two or three small colonies in New England; but New Jersey, and Pennsylvania, and Maryland, and Virginia, and the Carolinas received by far the largest share. They brought with them vivid and bitter recollections of the injustice of their treatment at the hands of Great Britain; and therefore when the War of Independence was begun, they were unanimously for the cause of the Colonies and against the mother country. We should never forget, or forget to acknowledge the great debt we all owe to the New England Colonies for the part they bore in the Revolutionary war. But New England would have been powerless without the Scotch Irish people, scattered, as the latter were, throughout the middle and the southern colonies, and as ready as the New Englanders to take up arms for independence; as ready indeed for war as their fathers had been to fight in order to ensure the safety of the Protestant William's throne.

When the Scotch-Irish began their settlements in the middle colonies, and particularly in the Commonwealth of Penn-

*History of the Irish Presbyterian Church, by Rev. Thomas Hamilton, p. 133.

sylvania, they stood in a relation to the civil government entirely different from that of the Episcopalians in Virginia, the Dutch-Reformed and afterwards the Episcopalians in New York, or the Congregationalists in New England. The latter were legally related to the State, their church order was in some sense the established religion; "the standing order," as it was called in New England, "the religion of His Majesty's faithful subjects," as it was called in Virginia. Our fore-fathers' Presbyterian churches were voluntary societies in the eye of the law; and whenever a Royal Governor chose to do so, he was able to make the lives of the members of the Presbyterian churches, and of their ministers in particular, exceedingly uncomfortable. In New York, the Royal Governor did all in his power to extirpate Presbyterianism. Francis Makemie and John Hampton, two of our earliest ministers, were imprisoned by Lord Cornbury; and this for the avowed purpose of putting down the pestilent heresy of Presbyterian dissent; and Makemie had already been made to suffer for the same reason in both Maryland and Virginia.

Happily our ancestors in Pennsylvania, whatever else were their trials, escaped this particular mode of suffering. This church has among its most valued members those in whose veins runs the blood of ancestors who belonged to the Society of Friends. The rest of us may well remind ourselves at this time of the indebtedness of our Presbyterian fathers to that great souled and high minded follower of the Inward Light, William Penn; who, in 1682, came to his province of Pennsylvania to begin what he called "his Holy Experiment"; which "Holy Experiment" was a frame of government, a constitution, of which these were the two distinguishing traits: first, that the people should govern, and second, that there should be liberty of conscience. Honor, everlasting honor, is due by the people of this church to the Commonwealth's great proprietor. This freedom of conscience, indeed, was one of the chief causes of the popularity of the province of Pennsylvania as a new home for the Scotch-Irish immigrants. They settled in the colony in great numbers. James Logan, William Penn's Secretary of his Province, said in reference to the movement as early as 1725: "It looks as if Ireland were to send all her inhabitants hither; if they will continue to come they will make themselves proprietors of the province." Professor Macloskie of Princeton points out that largely as the result of this movement the population of the province rose from 20,000 in 1701, to 250,000 in 1749.

At once upon their settlement the immigrants began to organize congregations for the worship of God. The evidence is clear that the initiative was taken by the people themselves. They had fought too long and too hard to maintain in the land of their sojourn the ordinances of religion, not to make immediate provision for them in the new land of liberty. And so while they were felling the trees and turning the soil, they made every sacrifice that they and their children might enjoy the stated services of the house of God. What I wish to emphasize is the fact that they were never an irreligious people requiring evangelization. They were from the first a religious people, knowing the value of the Church of God. The organization of these early churches was not due to the ministers who ministered in them, so much as to the laymen to whom they ministered. This was true of almost every congregation from Philadelphia northward to the Irish Settlement at Easton, and from Philadelphia westward through the settlements of Chester and Lancaster (then including Dauphin), and Cumberland counties.

It is true that their first ministers came from the mother country. But they did not come to evangelize an unevangelized people. They came to small communities, which were Christian from the beginning; communities whose members knew the word of God and believed it, and had studied the great system of truth embodied in the Westminster symbols, and were moulded by it. In this respect, the Scotch-Irish settlements were precisely like the early settlements on Massachusetts Bay and in the Hartford and New Haven colonies. I dwell on this fact for the reason that in the histories of Presbyterianism in America thus far written, too much relatively has been assigned to the ministry and too little to the strong, God-fearing men and women of the laity. The life of these churches at the beginning was in this respect precisely like their subsequent careers. What would the later history of this church have been but for the profound religious life, and the continuous religious activity of the laity—the godly women and God-fearing men; but for the church in the household, the training of the children by parents, and the family Bible, and the family prayers? So it was at the organization of our congregations in all the province.

Closely connected with the churches they founded were the parochial schools. I am sure that I need take no time to show you that the Calvinistic theology must lead, as in fact

it always has led, to the establishment of a system of general education. A people, fed on the religious truths of
that highly organized and profound system, will always see
to it, as a matter of the first importance, that their children
are disciplined and cultured far more carfully than themselves. We all know how true this is to-day. It was just
as true at the beginning. Our forefathers planted the church
and the school side by side. " With them," as has well been
said, "religion and education were inseparable; no religion
without the training of the intelligence; no education divorced
from piety. The school was always planted near the church,
the schoolmaster was often the pastor, often a candidate for
the ministry, often one of the pillars of the church."* So Mr.
Chambers, writing of the Scotch-Irish settlers in the Cumberland Valley, says: "Simultaneously with the organization of
congregations was the establishment of school houses in every
neighborhood. In these schools were taught the rudiments
of education, of which a part was generally obtained at home.
The Bible was the standard daily reader, and the Shorter
Catechism was to be recited and heard by all in the school
as a standard exercise on every Saturday morning."

But they were not content with this general system of
education. They had scarcely been settled in their new
homes when they began to feel that the ministry, and the
members of the other learned professions, must be provided
out of their own families. The Scotch Irish immigration
and settlement took place about one hundred years later
than the settlement of Massachusetts. The Scotch Irish
were without the advantage of a charter of their own,

---

* Prof. G. Macloskie : The Scotch-Irish and Education.

such as was possessed by the inhabitants of Massachusetts. But they began at once individually and through their church courts, to make provision for the higher education. So William Tennent established the Log College on the Neshaminy, that was merged in Princeton College in 1746. So, as early as 1739, John Thompson proposed to the Presbytery of Donegal—the Presbytery to which Paxtang and Derry and Hanover churches belonged—the erection of a school to be placed under the care of the Synod, and the Synod in the same year approved the plan ; and thus arose the school at New London in this State. So arose the Academy in Philadelphia, with Francis Allison as Principal, out of which issued the great University of Pennsylvania. So was founded the celebrated school of Samuel Finley at Nottingham, and the school of Samuel Blair at Fagg's Manor. It was precisely these schools and others like them that made the middle colonies independent at the war of Independence, and enabled them to come to the formation of the Federal and State constitutions, with culture and discipline adequate to the great work.*

As to the home life of these early Presbyterians, it must be remembered that they came to subdue to the use of man a section of the country which, if rich and fruitful, was difficult to conquer. Moreover they had to forge and frame their instruments of conquest. The modern era of labor-saving machinery was not to be ushered in for a century. When Thomas McCormick, in 1745, took up one hundred acres of land in Hanover township of this county, he did not have the advantage in reaping his crops, of the great "harvester," which his great grandson Cyrus Hall McCormick invented almost ninety years later. Our forefathers rose early and toiled hard. Theirs was not the generation that formed towns and cities. It was not the first, but the second John Harris, who founded Harrisburg. The first generation was a generation of farmers. They settled "near the springs and the brooks and in the valleys." They lived in log cabins, of two rooms. They found comfort on hard settees and benches. They had few dishes, and few spoons, even of pewter; and they had to be content often with cups and pitchers of gourds. Slowly the conditions changed; and all the more slowly because Great Britain's colonial policy was as harsh and tyrannical as possible. For instead of fostering, Great Britain did all that could be done to prevent the growth of manufactures in her possessions. But hard as the life was the Scotch Irish farmers were sustained by the great truths of their holy religion, and by that strong racial character that has made the Scotch the most persistent of European peoples. In that early period when they were called to conquer nature, during which, as a great American divine has pointed out, there was in the conditions of their lives great danger of a lapse into barbarism, they were held to a high ideal of life by their theology and their church life. They were lifted out of their hardships by their study of the Bible and their common and their private prayers to God.

The Scotch-Irish Presbyterian settlers of this part of the country have more than once been attacked by writers of our own State for their treatment of the red Indians, and the "Uprising of the Paxtang Boys," and the summary ven-

geance taken by them at Conestoga and at Lancaster upon
those whom the provincial government would not punish,
has been made the text of many a discourse against the
cruelty of our ancestors. That wrongs have been perpe-
trated against individuals among the Red men by individuals in every frontier settlement of the country there is no
good reason to doubt. To say that among the Scotch-Irish
Presbyterian settlers were " men of blood," is only to say
that they were like any other community. But that as communities they wronged the Indians there is no shadow of
evidence. We may lay it down as a truth based upon a
law of God, that no people could ever have had a title to
this fruitful valley as a hunting ground. At the beginning,
God gave man the Garden and placed him there "to dress
it and to keep it." And we may be sure that it is God's will
that Esau, the mere hunter, shall always go down before
the laborious Jacob, the worker in the fields, the plain man
dwelling in tents. The laborious Scotch-Irishman found
no difficulty in dwelling side by side with the laborious
German man. Together and in peace in this very county
they have turned the sod of the valley and the uplands,
and sowed and reaped the harvests.

But the hunter, the Red Indian, who would not labor
and who contemplated with envy the growing wealth of the
white man, mourned the loss of the land as mere "hunting
grounds;" and along the frontiers of the country killed or
carried off to bondage more bitter than death hundreds of
families. It is no wonder, as the historian Parkman says,
that the frontier people of Pennsylvania "were goaded to
desperation by long-continued suffering." Day after day

they lived in danger from the treachery and the cruelty of
the savages whom no kindness could make trustworthy
friends, and whom no efforts succeeded in civilizing. We,
who remember the civil war, know how easily, at so late a
date as eighteen hundred and sixty-one, the most violent
of passions were enkindled. What wonder that they were
aroused in the days of our forefathers, when it was the
custom because it was an absolute necessity of John Elder's
congregation, the minister included, to worship God in
Paxtang church under arms.* And when Lazarus Stewart
was told that the Indian settlement at Conestoga, professedly
friendly to the whites, was treacherously harboring and
entertaining an Indian known to have murdered a white
man's family, what wonder that at the time when the conspiracy of Pontiac was threatening every English settlement
on the frontier, a company was raised to inflict the punishment, which a neglectful government refused to inflict?
Whatever may be said of this particular incident, this I
think is true; that no English speaking population in the
country has ever dealt more fairly as between the Indian and
themselves than the Scotch-Irish citizens of Pennsylvania;
and no people certainly were subject to greater provocations.

The mother churches of this part of the country were
planted between the close of the first quarter and the close
of the first half of the century. Paxtang, the mother of this
church, being founded about 1732. It ought to be said that
the period was not one in which the religious life was warm
and glowing. In this respect, it was a period of deca-
dence. There was a good deal of mere formality; and

---

*Parkman's Conspiracy of Pontiac, Vol. II., p. 119, et seq.

there was a strong disposition to distrust religious experiences. This disposition was nowhere stronger than in this part of the country. But the early Presbyterian churches of the Middle Colonies had scarcely been planted when, in both England and America, there occurred the Great Evangelical Revival. *In Great Britain it infused new life into the churches of England and Scotland and Ireland. In America its influence was felt from Massachusetts to Georgia. It was marked by the earnest preaching of great preachers. The sermons of Edwards in New England of the Tennents in the Middle Colonies, and of Davies in Virginia remain to us and serve to show the type of preaching common at the time. Some of its methods were blameworthy, and some of its evils were serious; but the incidental evils were spots upon the sun. It radiated everywhere the warmth and the light the churches needed for a more vigorous life. The Scotch–Irish churches of this section fought against its methods. The Rev. John Elder, strong, honest, believing in the Bible and in the theology of his church, had no confidence in it. But, its influence was felt in all the congregations, and in most of the houses of the Valley. Even before the War of the Revolution it had wrought a great change in the life of the churches and of the people. And when the hardships of that terrible struggle had brought the people nearer to God, the more genial religious life which had been wrought by the Spirit of God during the great evangelical movement' was characteristic of the homes and the churches of our

---

*Here, as in one or two other places, I quote from my address before the Presbyterian Historical Society on the First General Assembly.

fathers. Meanwhile, the country about Harrisburg had been more thickly settled, and the son of the first settler had founded the town. Thus, in the more genial atmosphere of the great revival, this church was founded one hundred years ago.

I do not know how better to conclude this brief account of the conditions that immediately ante-dated the birth of this church, than to urge upon you the duty of keeping green the memory of your godly ancestry, that you may intelligently thank God for the blessings he has given to you, in preparing the way for this church by their faithful and laborious and religious lives. The sons and daughters of this congregation owe a large debt not only to their parents and grandparents who for three generations have been members of this church, but also, and this a debt quite as large, to those more remote ancestors, who while they spun the wool and linen and plowed the soil, read the Bible, and taught the catechism, and honored the Sabbath, and built Hanover and Derry and Paxtang churches, and established schools, and laid the foundations of a great Christian State. If Paul could glory in his people to whom belonged the covenants and the giving of the law and the promises, you may thank God for those from whom you are descended. But while we thank God for them, let us remember, that in leaving to us a great inheritance they have left to us great duties, also. The family religion which was theirs it is ours to maintain; the truth which made them strong it is for us to guard; the public schools of which they were the founders here, it is our sacred mission to defend against all open and concealed enemies; the Bible which made them strong and courageous and hopeful in life and in death, it is our duty to make our rule of faith and life; and to the God to whose service they gave themselves—the God of our fathers—it is our privilege at this time to dedicate anew all our powers and possessions in an everlasting covenant.

At the close of Dr. DeWitt's address, the Rev. Thomas H. Robinson, D. D., for thirty years pastor of this church, offered prayer. The minister announced hymn No. 730 which the congregation, having risen, sang with spirit.

> See the ransom'd millions stand,
> Palms of conquest in their hand;
> This before the throne their strain,
> "Hell is vanquish'd; death is slain;
> Blessing, honor, glory, might,
> Are the conqueror's native right;
> Thrones and powers before him fall,
> Lamb of God and Lord of all!"
>
> Hasten, Lord, the promised hour;
> Come in glory and in power:
> Still thy foes are unsubdued;
> Nature sighs to be renew'd:
> Time has nearly reach'd its sum:
> All things with the bride say "Come!"
> Jesus! whom all worlds adore,
> Come, and reign for evermore!

After the Benediction had been pronounced by the Rev. Dr. John DeWitt, Smart's March in D was rendered as an organ postlude, and the audience dispersed with the conviction that Centennial Week had been successfully inaugurated, and would be a most notable week in the history of the church.

SUNDAY EVENING,

February the 11th, 1894, at 6 o'clock.

SEVENTY-EIGHTH ANNIVERSARY OF THE SUNDAY-SCHOOL.

Mr. Samuel J. M. McCarrell, Superintendent, presiding.

A large audience, filling every available space in pew, aisle, vestibule and gallery, gathered to celebrate the Seventy-eighth anniversary of the Sunday-school. Many persons were unable to enter the church. The Primary department occupied the front seats of the middle block of pews, the Intermediate department were in the block of pews to the right of the Superintendent, while the Senior department were in the block to the left of the Superintendent, and in the middle block, back of the Primary department. Those not connected with the Sunday-school found seats or standing room as best they could. The decorations of the church were the same as those of the morning.

The services were opened promptly at 6 o'clock with the organ prelude, Silas's "March in F.," followed by an anthem, "I was glad when they said unto me, let us go into the house of the Lord," sung by the choir of the Senior department. This choir was composed of about fifteen of the best voices in the Senior department, under the direction of Mrs. John C. Harvey. Mrs. Harvey was most devoted and painstaking in training them for the accurate rendering of the solo and chorus parts in the anthems of the evening.

The SUPERINTENDENT. The Rev. William P. Patterson, Pastor of the Olivet Presbyterian church, will offer the invocation, and at its close will lead the congregation in repeating the Lord's prayer.

The congregation then united in singing the first and third stanzas of No. 30 in Winnowed Songs, the hymn book in use in the Senior department:

> True hearted, whole hearted, faithful and loyal,
> King of our lives : by thy grace we will be ;
> Under the standard exalted and royal,
> Strong in thy strength we will battle for thee.

> *Chorus.*
> Peal out the watch word ! silence it never !
> Song of our spirits rejoicing and free :
> Peal out the watch word ! loyal forever,
> King of our lives, by thy grace we will be.

> True hearted, whole hearted, Saviour all-glorious !
> Take thy great power, and reign there alone,
> Over our wills and affections victorious,
> Freely surrendered and wholly thine own—*Cho.*

Mr. Samuel C. Miller, Secretary of the Senior department, read the report of the Primary department. This report showed that there were enrolled during the year 1893 five officers and three hundred and nine scholars, a total of three hundred and fourteen. That the offerings during the same period amounted to $95.36, which sum was appropriated to the support of the school, and to missionary and benevolent causes.

Seven scholars have been present every Sabbath : May Landis, Katie Wolford, Sarah McCord, Mabel Swanberry,

Thomas McCord, Malcolm Dwyer, Freddie Ehrisman. One scholar has been present every Sabbath but one, Kenneth Dwyer. Four scholars have been present every Sabbath but two: Ellen Boyd, Minnie Wolford, Eva Smith, Helen Weidman.

The SUPERINTENDENT. We will now be glad to listen to the exercises of the Primary department.

The children of this department, with Mr. George R. Fleming leading, sang:

"ANOTHER YEAR."

Another year we've trod the way
    That leads to joy and heaven,
Then join with us and sing to-day
    Of blessings freely given.

Chorus.

Singing, singing,
    As the years go rolling by,
Working, striving,
    For a home on high.

Each trusting heart with pleasure rife
    Each eye with hope is gleaming,
While sweetly o'er the path of life
    The Saviour's smile is beaming.—*Cho.*

'Mid pastures green at last we'll rest
    Beside the flowing river,
And with the happy spirits blest
    We'll dwell in peace forever.—*Cho.*

Mrs. Gilbert M. McCauley, the Superintendent of the department, then led the children in repeating the 100th Psalm, after which they sang:

Little Workers.

Early in the morning
　When the glorious sun,
All the earth adorning,
　Has its work begun.
We will rise with gladness
　And a song of joy,
For each happy moment
　Brings us sweet employ.

Chorus.

Working for the Master,
　In his garden fair,
For he loves to see us,
　Working there.

Deeds of love and honor
　Will the Father bless,
Deeds of joy and patience,
　And of truthfulness !
All will grow together
　Till the reaper come,
Then he'll pluck them gladly
　For his harvest home.—*Cho.*

Bright as heav'nly sunshine
　Is the Father's smile :
When the shades of even
　Bid us rest awhile.
Let us listen softly,
　We may hear him say :
"Well done, little workers,
　Faithful all the day."—*Cho.*

The part the little folks take in the anniversary is always listened to with interest and delight.

The choir of the Senior department followed with the anthem, "Lord, Thy Mercy Streameth."

The SUPERINTENDENT. Dr. DeWitt, who is noted upon our programme for an address at this point in our exercises, is unable to be with us, because of the desire of Dr. Chambers, of the Pine Street Church, that he should occupy his pulpit this evening. He has, however, furnished a substitute in the person of Mr. George E. Sterry, for the past twenty-five years superintendent of Hope Chapel Sunday-school, a mission of the Fourth Avenue Presbyterian church, New York city, in which he is an elder. Mr. Sterry has had knowledge of this school in the past. Some years ago he came here upon a visit, and after repeating his visit, I cannot tell how many times, succeeded in capturing and carrying away with him a young lady who was then a scholar in this school. I am sure that he ought to have a very high regard for the school, because this young lady, to whom I have just referred, has made him a most excellent wife. On this occasion we have captured Mr. Sterry, and I know that you will be greatly gratified to hear from him at this time.

Mr. Sterry spoke substantially as follows, his address being listened to with rapt attention by old and young:

MR. GEORGE E. STERRY'S ADDRESS.

I am going to use small words so that the small folks can understand me, as I am most anxious that they should. Your superintendent has said that I have been for twenty-five years superintendent of the Hope Chapel Mission school in New York. About twenty-five years ago a little company of us went over to the east side in New York city and

established a Sunday-school which we have carried on ever
since. It has been the means of much blessing to many
people. I could tell you many stories which would show
you how much good has been done. More than three hundred young people have united with the church as a result
of this mission work. One boy entered our Sunday-school
ten years ago. He was at that time fifteen years old. He
was not very bright, but he had one good point, he was
willing to come to Sunday-school. There is always hope
for a boy who will attend Sunday-school. Now he is superintendent of a Sunday-school over in Brooklyn and is an
elder in the church.

A few Sundays ago he asked the children what was the
forbidden fruit—you know we had a lesson recently about
the forbidden fruit—and they all said it was the peach.
Probably that was because I was over there a little while
before and told them a story of a forbidden peach. If you
will listen I will tell it to you. On one occasion a mother
put a beautiful peach on an upper shelf in the cupboard,
and as she was leaving the house to go on an errand,
she told John and Mary, her children, that they must not
touch that peach. After she was gone, John said to Mary,
“I would like to see that peach.” Mary replied, “Mother
said you must not touch it.” John said, “I will not touch
it, I just want to look at it.” So he drew a chair to the
side of the cupboard and stood upon it, but he could
not see or reach the peach. After a little while he tried
again, putting a book upon the chair, but without success.
Then another book and another trial, but still he could not
reach the peach. Then a third book and a third trial.

This time he was able to reach the peach. As he held it, it looked so good he thought he would taste it. Just as he bit into it his mother opened the door, and he was caught in the very act. And what was more, the peach, instead of being a nice, ripe peach, was a wax peach, in which his teeth stuck so that he could neither open nor shut his mouth. He stood there guilty before his mother. What a foolish thing for a boy to disobey his parents.

Twenty years ago one of our girls brought fifteen new scholars into the Sunday-school in a very short time. She afterwards gave her heart to Christ, united with the church, and is now the wife of a Christian gentleman who is a lawyer and an elder in the church. He also was a scholar in the school at one time. You thus see, my dear children, that the Sunday-school is a great blessing to those who attend, and I hope that this school will be the means of leading many of you to give your hearts to Jesus Christ.

I will close what I have to say with the story of an English Lord who offered to the people round about his country residence to pay all their debts. He published it everywhere in the neighborhood that between 10 and 12 o'clock on a certain day he would pay the debts of any one who came to him and asked him to do so. When the time came many curious people gathered about his office wondering what it all meant, but no one ventured to go in and ask him to pay their debts. At last an old man and his wife came up, and as they were going in some one said "You don't think he will pay your debts, do you?" And he said, "Yes, certainly I do, for he said he would." They went in and gave him a list of all that they owed, and he drew his check upon the bank for the whole amount. They were the only ones whose debts were paid because they were the only ones who had faith to take their lord at his word. How foolish it was for those who stood about the office not to believe their lord and ask him to do what he promised to do! Our Lord Jesus has promised to pay all our debts, if we will but ask him. Let us all ask him to pay the debt of sin which we owe, and so save us from eternal death.

Mr. Miller read the report of the Intermediate department. This department had on its roll during the year 1893 seven officers, twenty-eight teachers, and two hundred and sixty-eight scholars, a total enrollment of three hundred and three.

The contributions of the department during the year amounted to $1,065.98, which were given to various missionary and benevolent causes.

The Superintendent, Mrs. David Fleming and one teacher, Miss Sarah C. Cowden, were present every Sabbath during the year. Eighteen scholars were present every Sabbath: Gertie G. Carnes, Rhoda M. Bell, Jenny Brookens, Minnie E. Snoddy, Carrie Speise, Bessie Stephens, Laura McCord, Alice E. Gingher, Blaine Fry, David Wingeard, Willie Reindel, John E. Swanberry, Milton W. Swanberry, M. Frank Bishop, Joseph Hogentogler, Charley Taylor, Frank Dwyer, John Dwyer.

Eleven scholars were absent one Sunday: Clarence P. McCoy, Harry Bradigan, Boyd E. Morrow, Frank Kittner, Robert Ehrisman, Cora W. Anderson, Annie Malseed, Viola Bell, A. Mabel Bishop, Mabel V. Chester, Cora E. Shertzer.

Seven scholars were absent two Sabbaths: Annie Spicer, Mary Arnold, Irene S. Loudenslager, Bertha M. Meredith, Mary E. Wager, Edward G. Hershman, Ronald Harvie.

The SUPERINTENDENT. We will now be interested in attending to some exercises by the Intermediate department.

The Intermediate department, with Mr. Fleming leading, sang:

COME SING WITH GLAD VOICES.

Come children, and sing with glad voices,
    The praises of Jesus our king!
The world in his coming rejoices,
    And we will adore him and sing!

Chorus.

    We'll sing of the Saviour who loves us,
        And carol with gladness our lay,
    We'll sing of the little child Jesus,
        And praise him, and praise him to-day.

O dearly we love the sweet story
    Which comes thro' the centuries long,
Of the shepherds beholding his glory,
    And hearing the wonderful song!—*Cho.*

The wise men who follow'd the leading
    Of Bethlehem's beautiful star,
Were guided to Him they were seeking
    O'er mountain and river afar!—*Cho.*

O could we but kneel at that manger,
    And lay our best offerings there,
How gladly we'd hail the sweet Stranger,
    With hearts full of worship and pray'r.—*Cho.*

Mrs. David Fleming, Superintendent of the Intermediate department, led her school in the following responsive service:

God the Ruler.

Supt.—Who rules all worlds?

School.—God rules all worlds.

Supt.—Whom does God rule in heaven?

School.—God rules all spirits in heaven.

Supt.—Whom does God rule on earth?

School.—God rules all people.

Supt.—What does God give us to obey?

School.—God gives us good laws to obey.

Supt.—What is God's law about love and worship?

School.—We must love and worship the one God.

Supt.—What is God's law about idols?

School.—We must not worship idols.

Supt.—What is God's law about the Sabbath?

School.—We must remember the Sabbath day to keep it holy.

Supt.—What is God's law about our father and mother?

School.—We must honor our father and mother.

Supt.—What is God's law about stealing?

School.—We must not steal.

Supt.—What is God's law about lying?

School.—We must not lie.

Supt.—What is God's great law?

School.—We must love God and one another: God is the ruler.

Obedience.

Supt.—Why should we obey God?

School.—We should obey God, because He is our creator; He is wise; His laws are holy, just and good, and He loves us.

Supt.—What does God want us to be?

School.—God wants us to be good and happy like himself.

Supt.—Is it a little sin to disobey God?

School.—If we disobey God, we sin greatly.

Supt.—Where cannot we go if we continue to disobey God?

School.—We cannot enter heaven.

Supt.—Whom can we see when we talk with them?

School.—Our parents and friends.

Supt.—Whom can we not see when we talk with Him?

School.—We cannot see God, but we can talk to Him; He sees us, and knows all we think and hears all we say; when we talk to God we pray.

Supt.—What must we ask God to do for us?

School.—We must ask Him to forgive us our sins, to help us to be good, to give us the things we need.

Supt.—For whom must we pray?

School.—We must pray for our parents and friends; for our teachers and schoolmates, and for the poor, sick, ignorant and wicked?

Supt.—When must we pray?

School.—We must pray every day—at home and away from home, and in the house of God.

Supt.—What can you say about God?

School.—God hears and answers prayer.

Worship.

Supt.—Where are the angels? And what do they do?

School.—The angels are in heaven; they bow before God and worship Him.

Supt.—What is a church?

School.—A church is God's house; people go into it, sit still and think about God: they should worship Him as the angels do in heaven, should listen and learn from God's servant as he preaches God's truth. God is a spirit, and we must worship Him in spirit.

Jesus Christ the Lamb of God.

Supt.—When was the temple of God in Jerusalem built?

School.—Long before Jesus came from heaven to earth.

Supt.—What was a table in the temple called?

School.—The altar.

Supt.—What was the altar for?

School.—To offer sacrifices upon. A man brought a lamb to the priest; he laid the lamb by the altar, as God had told him to do.

Supt.—About whom did the lamb help the man to understand?

School.—Helped him to understand about the Christ.

Supt.—When the man brought the lamb from his home, what did he remember about the Christ?

School.—He remembered that the Christ would come from heaven to earth.

Supt.—What should we do if we would live forever in heaven?

School.—We must repent of sin, love, obey and serve God.

Supt.—Because Jesus Christ died for us, what is He called?

School.—The Lamb of God.

Glory to God on high,
Let praises fill the sky!
Praise ye his name.
Angels His name adore,
Who all our sorrows bore,
And saints cry evermore.
" Worthy the Lamb?"

At the close of the responsive service this department sang:

Lift up Thy Voice.

Lift up Thy voice with strength, O Zion that bringeth good tidings,
Lift up, lift up thy voice with strength, for God, the Lord is here,
The fullness of the earth and the people are the Lord's,
And ev'rywhere o'er sea and land, His goodness doth appear.

Refrain.

Lift up, lift up thy voice, and cry aloud, O Zion!
Arise and shine, let all rejoice for God the Lord is here.

Lift up, be not afraid, behold your God, O Judah,
The Lord shall come, His arm shall rule with power from above,
He calls the stars by name by the greatness of His might,
He giveth power to the faint; behold his name is Love!—*Ref.*

O wait upon the Lord, and ye shall not be weary;
The youths shall faint, the young men fall who know not God, the Lord,
All nations are as nothing before the Lord of Hosts,
But we are all His people, He sustains us by His word.—*Ref.*

All of the exercises of the Intermediate department made a marked impression upon the audience and the school was justly praised.

Mr. McCarrell announced verses one and three of hymn No. 48, in Winnowed Songs, and the audience, having risen, joined heartily in the singing.

Joy bells ringing, children singing,
Fill the air with music sweet ;
Joyful measure, guileless pleasure,
Make the chain of song complete.

Chorus.

Joy bells ! joy bells ! never, never cease your singing ;
Children ! children ! never, never cease your singing ;
List, list the song that swells.   Joy bells ! Joy bells !

Earth seems brighter, hearts grow lighter,
As the tuneful melody
Charms our sadness into gladness,
Pealing, pealing, joyfully.—*Cho.*

The SUPERINTENDENT. It is a rare pleasure to have with us him who for thirty years was the Pastor of this church, and who by his active interest in everything relating to the welfare of the school, contributed largely to making the school what it is to-day.   I am sure he is glad to be with us, and I know you will be more than glad to hear him. Dr. Robinson has been with us on so many anniversaries that a formal introduction is unnecessary.   He will now address us.

REV. DR. THOMAS H. ROBINSON'S ADDRESS.

This is the seventy-eighth anniversary of the Sunday-school.   When people are seventy-eight years of age they look old.   This school does not look older than when I came to it forty years ago, probably not any older than when it was born in a little frame house down on Market street, seventy-eight years ago.   What will it be when it is one hundred years old, as this church is to-day ?   If it keeps on growing as it has grown during the last few years, then this room will not be large enough to hold it all. Not every one that looks old, however, is old. Old people can keep young just as schools keep young, even though they cannot keep young in appearance. We have here to-night a lady * who was a member of this school in very early days. She was not one of the first scholars, but she joined the school when it was not more than four or five years old. She remembers very well how the school looked and what it was then. It was a very small affair to what it is now. Though she is now more than eighty years old, yet she is as young in heart as any one.

How shall we keep young? That is a very important question. The school keeps young by bringing new scholars into it, " new blood," as they say in other organizations. We keep young by keeping the heart young, and the heart is kept young by bringing new affections and sympathy and interests into it. The heart is kept young by love. It may be that the day will come when I will need a cane to walk with, but I do not mean that the day shall come when my heart grows old. I hope we will all keep young in the same way by loving God and loving good. We can keep ourselves young and bright though we may live to be very old.

Mr. Miller read the report of the Senior department. The number enrolled in this department during the year 1893 was thirteen officers, sixty teachers and five hundred and ninety-nine scholars, a total enrollment of six hundred and

---

*Mrs. Harriet J. Agnew, daughter of Dr. Samuel Agnew, an elder in this church from 1820 to 1835, and the widow of the late Rev. John R. Agnew, of Greencastle, Pa.

seventy-two. The contributions for the year were $1,077.64, which sum was used for the support of the school and for benevolent and missionary purposes.

Three teachers were present every Sunday in the year, Mr. George W. Boyd, Mr. Peter K. Sprenkel and Mr. Sharon Stephens.

Twenty-five scholars were present every Sunday: Bertha Unger, Carrie McCord, Annie C. Wager, Carrie P. Michael, Bella Jones, Carrie Tippett, Bessie Ehrisman, Bertha Tippett, Maud Tippett, Harry Zeiter, George Deisroth, Charles W. Hartwick, Daniel Crutchley, Edward Hogentogler, William H. Shindler, William Taylor, Luther R. Kennedy, George Ehrisman, Harry Hilton, Frederick H. Stephens, Mrs. Samuel Fortney, William Steinmeier, C. Ross Colestock, Albert Metzgar, Mrs. Samuel Briggans.

Seven scholars were present every Sunday but one: Bessie L. Eckenroth, Lydia Minning, Ira Bishop, Charles Fry, John Kelker, Harvey M. Taylor, William McCord. Four scholars were present every Sunday but two: Richard M. Morrow, William Hoke, Lewis H. Carpenter, John Arnold.

Mr. McCarrell, while all were standing, read responsively with the school, the scripture lesson printed on the programme as followeth:

SCRIPTURE LESSON.

Supt.—Ye are the light of the world. A city that is set on a hill cannot be hid.

School.—Neither do men light a candle, and put it under a bushel, but on a candlestick; it giveth light unto all that are in the house.

Supt.—Let your light so shine before men that they may see your good works, and glorify your Father which is in heaven.

School.—Lay not up for yourselves treasures upon earth, where moth and rust doth corrupt, and where thieves break through and steal :

Supt.—But lay up for yourselves treasures in heaven, where neither moth nor rust doth corrupt, and where thieves do not break through nor steal :

School.—For where your treasure is, there will your heart be also.

Supt.—Ask, and it shall be given you ; seek, and ye shall find ; knock, and it shall be opened unto you:

School.—For every one that asketh receiveth ; and he that seeketh findeth ; and to him that knocketh it shall be opened.

The choir of the senior department sang the anthem, "Thee Will We Worship." Mr. Miller read the reports of the Chinese department and of Calvary Chapel school, and the summary of all the reports. These were as follow : In the Chinese department were enrolled during 1893, one officer, eleven teachers, and thirteen scholars ; total, twenty-five. The contributions amounted to $36.93, given to benevolent causes. The enrollment of Calvary Chapel school during 1893 was six officers, nineteen teachers, and four hundred and twenty-six scholars, a total enrollment of four hundred and fifty-one. The contributions amounted to $255.34, given to church and benevolent causes.

The summary of the reports showed that during the year here were enrolled in the church school, deducting duplicates on account of transfers from one department to another, and in Calvary Chapel school, thirty-one officers, one hundred and seventeen teachers, and one thousand five hundred and twenty-two scholars; a total of one thousand six hundred and seventy; and that the contributions amounted to $2,531.25.

After the senior choir sang " Rest for the Weary," Mr. McCarrell said: " No session of the Sunday-school is entirely complete without the presence of the pastor, and no Sunday-school anniversary programme would be properly made up which did not provide for an address by the pastor, and I know that you will now be very glad to hear from Dr. Stewart.

The Pastor's Address.

I am reminded to-night that though I have been pastor of this church something over nine years, yet this is the tenth anniversary of the Sunday-school which has occurred during my pastorate. This is the one hundredth anniversary of the church. There is not very much difference, for you know one hundred is only " nothing " more than ten. The fact that I have been present at ten such gatherings as this gives me my text to-night. Take the word TEN and make an acrostic of it, and you have the three heads of the sermon.

I. Time Flies.

How it does fly! Here is Mrs. Agnew with an experience stretching back to the fourth or fifth year of this Sunday-school, and yet how rapidly the years have gone for her! This Sunday-school is seventy-eight years old, the church is one hundred years old, and yet how short these periods seem as we look back over them. The official life of our present Superintendent, Mr. McCarrell, and of his revered predecessor, Mr. Weir, cover sixty years of the life of this school, Mr. Weir being Superintendent for forty-four years, and Mr. McCarrell for sixteen. May you, Mr. Superintendent, live to round out your forty-four years of service in this office which you so adorn, and in which you are such a great blessing to the school. It will not be long until you, children, are men and women, until you, young men and maidens, are old men and women. Time is going very fast. It does not wait for anybody. If you get behind in your work, if you neglect your opportunities, if you idle away your days, you cannot hope to make up the loss. Lost time is never found. Time past never returns. Be up and at your work to-day and now, for time is going rapidly.

II. *Eternity is the Measure of our Life.*

This school is seventy-eight years old, and no matter how long it may last it will be so many years old, and it must come to an end some day. This school cannot live forever. But we will live forever. We never die. These spirits and bodies of ours will be separated some day by what we call death, but it is not death in the sense that we come to an end. We live on forever. Time is the measure of the life of organizations here in the earth, but eternity is the measure of our life. We who are living to-day will always live. The most blessed and solemn fact is that we can never get away from ourselves, we can never get away from God. He and we must live on together throughout all the ages that are yet to come. How important it is that we have our hearts right with him, that we should be at peace with him, since we are to live together forever. What misery it means for us if we do not love the things he loves, and do not do the things he wants us to do. We sometimes hear people say, " I mean to be different some day, I do not mean to live this way always." Yet we must live always, and if we are going to be different we ought to begin at once. For what we are now and what we do now are going to tell much on what we are to be in the hereafter.

III. *Now is the Accepted Time.*

This word *now* is the word that is underscored and emphasized throughout the whole Bible. All duty is written in the present tense. It is very pleasant to think of the past. It is inspiring to dream of the future. The past is gone and we can never change it. The future is not here and we cannot yet have its blessings. But the present is here and it is here with all its possibilities, with all its treasures, with all its work, and with all its duty. If we are to get what it has we must get it now, because the present is rapidly becoming the past, and as soon as it is gone it is gone forever. You have a work to do, do it. You have lessons to learn, learn them. You have duties to perform, attend to them. You must not wait, you cannot delay. Now is the time. Now is the accepted time. Take hold of the present moment. Do the work that is just before you. Heed the old Scotch proverb, " Do the next thing." Do not waste your time in thinking of past deeds, or dreaming of coming honors. The past is beyond your control, and the future is yet to come into your hands. Seize the present moment, do your duty now, and you will find your life being filled with good things, and your life work being fully accomplished.

Now, you have my sermon. I do not think it will be hard for you to remember the text and the divisions. T E N : T—time flies. E—eternity is the measure of our life. N—now is the accepted time.

The Superintendent. The distribution of prizes for unbroken attendance during the last year should be made at this point. The hour, however, is growing late, and the crowded condition of the room makes it almost impossible for the librarians to reach the scholars who are entitled to the prizes. The books will therefore be handed to the scholars entitled to them upon their coming to the platform after the benediction shall have been pronounced. In connection with this distribution, I desire to call attention to the fact that these books are the gift of a former Superintendent of the school, whose love for his scholars prompted him to provide in his will a fund, from the income of which this annual distribution of gifts might be made. We are grateful for his kindness and liberality, and the school should never fail to remember him, of whom Dr. DeWitt this morning so appropriately and eloquently spoke when he characterized him as that man of God and friend of man, James Wallace Weir. These books, as they go into the hands of the scholars who have earned them, bear the imprint of the James Weir Fund, and I trust that those who are to receive them may be imbued with the spirit of the generous donor. We will now sing the first verse of hymn No. 104.

We are marching on with shield and banner bright,
We will work for God and battle for the right.
We will praise His name, rejoicing in His might,
And we will work till Jesus calls.
In the Sunday-school our army we prepare,
As we rally round our blessed standard there,
And the Saviour's cross we early learn to bear,
While we work till Jesus calls.

Chorus.

Then awake, then awake, happy song, happy song,
Shout for joy, shout for joy, as we gladly march along.

The Rev. Mr. Skilling pronounced the Benediction and while Mr. Crozier played as an organ postlude Guilmant's Chorus in D Major, the prize books were distributed to those who had maintained an unbroken attendance at Sunday-school during the year.

MONDAY EVENING,

February the 12th, 1894, at 7.30 o'clock.

UNION COMMUNION SERVICE.

On account of the violent snow-storm which prevailed at the time of the union communion service on Monday evening, and which had prevailed throughout the day, the audience was not as large as it otherwise would have been. Nevertheless the house was well filled. The Pastors and Elders of the several Presbyterian churches gathered in the lecture-room prior to the service. Several of the Elders were detained from the service by reason of illness of themselves or of members of their family. Before entering the church, Rev. William P. Patterson led in a fervent prayer for God's blessing upon the service of the evening. In view of the absence of some of the Elders, the previous arrangement for the distribution of the emblems was modified, and it was arranged that Daniel W. Cox, Dr. Jacob A. Miller, Jacob F. Seiler, Gilbert M. McCauley, Francis Jordan, Matthew B. Elder, John M. Stewart, Abram L. Groff, William S. Shaffer, Sr., William Jones, J. Wallace Elder, John J. Craig and John C. Harvey should distribute the bread; and that J. Henry Spicer, Thomas J. Miller, Jacob F. Seiler, Gilbert M. McCauley, Francis Jordan, Matthew B. Elder, John M. Stewart, Abram L. Groff, William S. Shaffer, Sr., Samuel H. Garland, David R. Elder, Alexander Adams and John C. Harvey should distribute the wine.

After the Ministers and Elders had taken their places at the Communion Table, Mr. Crozier played as an organ prelude the final chorus from the passion music according to St. Matthew, composed by Bach. The choir sang with feeling and finish Dudley Buck's setting of John Henry Newman's "Lead, Kindly Light." The invocation by Rev. Reuben H. Armstrong, Pastor of the Elder Street Church, followed. The Rev. Albert B. Williamson, Pastor of the Paxtang Church, announced hymn No. 696, verses 1, 2, 6.

> Not worthy, Lord! to gather up the crumbs
> With trembling hand that from.thy table fall,
> A weary, heavy-laden sinner comes
> To plead thy promise and obey thy call.
>
> I am not worthy to be thought thy child,
> Nor sit the last and lowest at thy board:
> Too long a wanderer and too oft beguiled,
> I only ask one reconciling word.
>
> My praise can only breathe itself in prayer,
> My prayer can only lose itself in thee:
> Dwell thou forever in my heart, and there,
> Lord! let me sup with thee; sup thou with me.

Rev. David M. Skilling, Pastor's Assistant in Market Square Church, read as the Scripture lesson the first chapter of Ephesians.

The Rev. George S. Chambers, D. D., Pastor of the Pine Street Church, delivered the Communion address.

COMMUNION ADDRESS.

By Rev. GEORGE S. CHAMBERS, D. D.

In a very special sense, the communion service which
has brought us to the house of God this evening is a
memorial service. It is a feast of memory; the memory
of Christ, and the memory of service for Christ by generations of His faithful disciples.

Primarily and pre-eminently do the great facts of our
Lord's love and death for us come before our minds.
Neither the tender memories of departed friends with
whom we have taken sweet counsel, nor the history of
the generations of Christians who preceded them, and who
laid the foundations of this Christian church, and of
whose piety and zeal, this week is a commemoration,
should obscure the Divine Person; or diminish the emphasis of the Divine Word which is the warrant of this service
—" Do this in remembrance of me." Let us give Christ
this pre-eminence to-night. And we can think of Him as
the joy of all the communion services of this church and
the others that have sprung from it, during all these years.
Not a year has passed in the century which this week
closes, without these assemblies of Christians around the
table of the Lord. Company after company, representing
all phases of Christian character and experience have thus
met to magnify his atoning love. Of them we may say,
varying the words of Paul concerning the witnesses of

Christ's resurrection—"Some of them remain unto this present, but the greater part are fallen asleep."

There is an appropriateness in making a communion service a part of this Centennial celebration. It will check any tendency to man-worship, into which we may unconsciously glide as we discuss the fortitude, and perseverance, and intelligence, and devotion of the men and women whose work at such a time comes into review. Moreover, a communion service at this time is suggestive to us of the true principle of a church's continuity. There would have been, there could have been, no Centennial celebration this week, had there been no communion celebrations during these hundred years. The history of a church is practically the history of its communion seasons. These are the signs of its growth. Upon these depends to a very considerable degree the development of individual piety. These sustain a very intimate relation to family religion. If we can conceive of a church without the observance of the Lord's Supper, it is not one with the history of a century. It is, on the contrary, an ephemeral organization, inviting and hastening its own decay by neglect of, or disobedience to, the Lord's dying command.

The Sacrament of the Lord's Supper is a very essential part of the history which we are recalling and celebrating. It has constantly reminded believers of the love which founded the church, it has been a badge of their separation from the world, it has been a testimony to the world of their loving loyalty to Christ, it has been the means by which a confession of Him has been made on the part of those who, through sanctified family training and faithful preaching, have been brought into His fold, it has kept alive the faith of the church when worldliness has come in like a flood, it has been the jubilant expression of thanksgiving when the reviving power of God's Spirit has swept over the church. With its simple symbolical presentation of the great fact of atonement, with its prophecy of a returning Lord towards the fulfillment of which every celebration of it has been a step, the Lord's Supper has been an answer to the question, What is the secret of a church's life? The church lives because Christ died for it, and rose again. Where a church lovingly holds to these facts, and repeatedly confesses them in the service which He appointed, we may expect to see it blessed with a continuity of life and a constant enlargement of life. We can give a prospective, as well as a retrospective character to this service. We can confidently predict another century of history to this church, and all churches that exalt and confess Jesus Christ as Prince and Saviour.

Thus making Him pre-eminent, we may allow ourselves to indulge in the memories of the holy men and women who have gone before us. With some of you these memories are specially vivid and tender. To all of us, of course, the knowledge of the most of these saints of God is a historical knowledge. We read of the Christians of a hundred years ago and their immediate successors, and we admire their faith, and hopefulness, and courage. But there is a knowledge which is personal and experimental, of other godly ones who have been closely identified with these churches. They have been the fathers and the mothers of some of you. They have been the ministers

and the Sunday-school teachers of some of you. They
have been the intimate friends of some of you, dearer
to you even than your very life. We cannot help thinking of them at such a time as this. If we believe (and
why should we not believe) that all the saints who
have entered glory, during these hundred years, from this
church, and the churches that have sprung from it, are
interested in the work, and the worship of the church on
earth, then with what an interest must this service be invested. They are looking upon us to-night. They are
nearer to us than we think. The limitations of our mortal
vision prevent us from seeing "this cloud of witnesses."
"From behind the thin veil which severs us from them,
they are looking down upon us." Let us take to ourselves
the comfort of that description of the church as "the family
in heaven and on earth." Let us think of that part of the
household which has entered into rest, as both watching us
and waiting for us.

> "O blest communion, fellowship Divine !
> We feebly struggle, they in glory shine :
> Yet all are one in Thee, for all are Thine.
>   Alleluia."

Coming back to the thought with which I began, let us
exalt the Son of God, our Saviour, in this service. He made
atonement for our sins. Because He lives, we live also.
Through Him they who have gone before us, and we who
follow after, are one. They obeyed His dying command, as
we are obeying it now. Through His relation to them and
to us we are their contemporaries, for He is not the God of

the dead, but of the living. This communion table is a place for memory to do a blessed work in recalling the achievements and the fellowship of the past. It is a place for gratitude that the Lord has given us some work to do as the successors of such consecrated men and women. It is a place for hope as we contemplate the greater field of service given to these churches, and the greater responsibilities which rest upon them. It is a place for fellowship as we express our interest in one another, and assert our church brotherhood. But it is all these in a peculiar sense as we think of Him who loved us, and gave himself for us. Our fellowship is with Him. Our hope is in Him. Our gratitude is to Him. Our memory is of Him,as the words, never old, always beautiful, fall with a new tenderness on our hearts, " This do in remembrance of me."

At the conclusion of Dr. Chamber's address he pronounced the words of institution of the Supper, and Rev. William P. Patterson, Pastor of Olivet Church, led in prayer. The bread was then given by Dr. Chambers to the elders appointed for receiving it, and they distributed it to the people. In like manner also the wine was given by the Rev. George B. Stewart, D. D., Pastor of the church, to the elders appointed for receiving it, and they distributed it to the people.

After the people had all communed, the Rev. George S. Duncan, Pastor of the Westminster Church, led in the concluding prayer of thanksgiving.

Dr. Chambers announced hymn No. 688, verses 1, 4, 5.

Sweet the moments, rich in blessing,
  Which before the cross I spend,
Life and health and peace possessing
  From the sinner's dying Friend.

Here it is I find my heaven,
  While upon the Lamb I gaze;
Love I much? I've much forgiven;
  I'm a miracle of grace.

Love and grief my heart dividing,
  With my tears his feet I bathe;
Constant still in faith abiding,
  Life deriving from his death.

At the conclusion of the hymn, which the congregation sang while standing, Dr. Chambers pronounced the Benediction. The organ postlude, The Hymn of the Apostles from "The Redemption," by Gounod, concluded the service. This service, with all of the Ministers, most of the Elders, and many of the People of the seven Presbyterian churches laid beautiful and solemn emphasis upon the unity of our church and the goodly fellowship of the saints.

TUESDAY EVENING,

February the 13th, 1894, at 7.30 o'clock.

MUSICAL FESTIVAL.

The harmonies that filled the souls of Israel's prophets, priests and people with divine transports are the same which wake "the echoes of Paradise in the soul" of God's people to-day. Never so much as now has the church made use of music. Never so much as now have men thought of music as a note in "the universal concert of God's love." Thoughts such as these were in the minds of some, at least, of the great throng that crowded every available space in the auditorium, vestibule, gallery and rear hall and stood in the snow on the street to hear the musical festival on Tuesday night.

Promptly at the hour, Mr. David E. Crozier, the accomplished organist of the church, began the service with Wagner's "Vorspiel to Parsifal." As the last strains of this jubilant overture died away they mingled with the first notes of Dudley Buck's "Festival Te Deum." The large choir of the church, augmented by several voices from the Pine Street Presbyterian Church choir, sang this and the other anthems of the evening with precision, sympathy and spirit. The Rev. David M. Skilling, who presided throughout the evening, introduced the Rev. Harris R. Schenck, Pastor of the Falling Spring Presbyterian Church, of Chambersburg, who led the audience in prayer. The Rev. James Fraser, Ph. D., Pastor of the Presbyterian Church at Sparrow's Point, Md., was then introduced and read the 150th Psalm as the Scripture lesson. Mr. William G. Underwood took Miss Rachel T. Briggs's place in the programme and sang with fine expression "Glory to Thee My God This Night." Mozart's "Andante in F" followed as an organ interlude by Mr. Crozier. The choir then sang "Lo! It is I," as adapted by Shelly to a chorus by Faure. Miss Reba Bunton delighted the audience with her rich contralto voice in "Eye Hath Not Seen," a solo from Gaul's "The Holy City."

Mr. Skilling then announced hymn No. 456, vs. 1, 2, 4. The congregation rising united in singing this hymn of Charles Wesley, so dear to the fathers.

> A charge to keep I have,
>   A God to glorify,
> A never-dying soul to save,
>   And fit it for the sky.
>
> To serve the present age,
>   My calling to fulfill,
> Oh, may it all my powers engage,
>   To do my Master's will.
>
> Help me to watch and pray,
>   And on thyself rely,
> Assured, if I my trust betray,
>   I shall forever die.

Mr. and Mrs. Edward Z. Gross followed with a duet, "Forever With the Lord," in which their voices blended perfectly, Reinberger's "Pastorale from Sonata in D Flat," as an organ solo, and Dudley Buck's "Oh, Clap Your Hands," as an anthem by the choir, followed.

The President of the Evening. No anniversary, and certainly not the centennial, of this church could be complete without a festival such as this one to which you have accepted an invitation this evening.

From the very beginning of this church music has had an important place in its worship. During the hundred years that are past this church has witnessed and participated in the various stages through which church music has developed.

From the period ante-dating the introduction of music books into the pews, when the hymns were "lined out," onward through the era of orchestral music, when the flutes and violins and violoncellos sounded the notes for the singers, to the introduction of the melodion and with it the "Carmina sacra;" and then to the present era of congregational singing, led by a choir so efficiently directed, accompanied by the music so skillfully brought forth on the large organ, and augmented by the anthems which we enjoy to-night, this church has sung its praise to the King of Glory.

And, therefore, it has a history of music to tell.

It is fitting that that history should be told at this time; and it is especially appropriate that it be told by the speaker whom it is my pleasure to introduce this evening. The committee could have selected no one better suited to the task. A son of the church; his father and brother for many years elders in this church; himself dedicated to God in infant baptism at its altar; in early youth received into its communion upon the public profession of his faith in Christ; a member of its choir from 1842 to 1858; and subsequently for a number of years the director of music in the Pine Street Church, he comes to us, I know, with a fund of information which shall be not only interesting but instructive. I take pleasure in presenting our brother churchman, our fellow-citizen, our friend, Mr. H. Murray Graydon; his subject is, "The Hymnology of the Mother Presbyterian Church of Harrisburg, with Some Reminiscences of Choirs and Choir Days."

THE HYMNOLOGY OF THE MOTHER PRESBYTERIAN CHURCH OF HARRISBURG, WITH SOME REMINISCENCES OF CHOIRS AND CHOIR DAYS.

By H. MURRAY GRAYDON, ESQ.

I have been asked to prepare a paper upon the hymnology of the Presbyterian Church in Harrisburg during the last hundred years. This will necessarily involve sketches and reminiscences, so far as they can be obtained, of the singers and choirs who flourished during that period, and led the congregation in their Sabbath service of song. Of course information in regard to the early part of the century must be meager in the extreme, as the memory of no living person reaches quite that far back. My own recollections of the music and musical personages connected with the church extends no farther than a year or two before the pulling down of the old and the erection of the new edifice on the corner of Second street and Cherry alley. But some few records remain, and I am indebted to Mr. A. Boyd Hamilton and to a paper prepared by the late Alexander Sloan, a short time before his death, for some facts relating to the subject under consideration, which take us back to the early part of the present century.

It is said that John Wyeth, the father of the late Francis Wyeth, was the leader of the choir before the erection of the first church building. About the year 1809, Thomas Smith became the leader, and his choir occupied the space in front of the pulpit, there being as yet no gallery constructed. This defect was remedied about the year 1820, and the singers then took possession of that part of the gallery which was allotted to the choir. James Wright seems to have succeeded Mr. Smith, then James Whitehill, and he was followed by the late John A. Weir. Of the singers of that early day, who led the praises of the sanctuary, no record remains. It is probable that Mr. Weir continued to lead the choir down to the building of the new church, when he was succeeded by Mr. R. J. Fleming. A short time before the year 1840 I can recall a few names of those who occupied the choir gallery, I presume, under the leadership of Mr. Weir. These are Mrs. J. A. Briggs, then Miss Todd, and Mrs. John J. Pearson, then Miss Mary Briggs, both of whom were, I think, soprano singers, and Alexander Sloan and Andrew Graydon, who dealt out the bass.

In the paper prepared by Mr. Sloan it is stated that the first regular choir was organized about the year 1818, and that he became a member of it about that time. This may be the fact, and the earlier singers may have been only the skirmish line, or advance guard. Congregational singing must have been at a low ebb, as it has sometimes been at a much later day, for Mr. Hamilton is responsible for the statement that the Rev. Mr. Buchanan, one of the earliest pastors, once said from the pulpit that if the congregation would not sing he would not preach.

Mr. Sloan says, in the paper referred to, that in the year 1821 or 1822 the first musical instrument was introduced in the shape of a bassoon played by a Mr. Holt, a school teacher of Harrisburg. Before that time the leader probably used a pitch pipe to get the proper key, as I have a distinct recollection of seeing an old wooden instrument of that kind in my childhood, not then in use, but kept as a relic. It was regulated by moving a slide up and down until the proper pitch was obtained.

In the month of February, 1842, the congregation occupied the new church edifice, and the choir became a more pretentious body. Mr. R. J. Fleming was then the leader, and assistance was given by an orchestra composed of Col. John Roberts, with his violin; Alexander Roberts, and afterwards George B. Ayres, on the flute; and Dr. James Fleming, with a violoncello. The flute, if I remember aright, took the soprano, whilst Col. Roberts aided the alto singers, and Dr. Fleming played the bass. Mr. Fleming, the leader, whilst not gifted with a voice of much power, was thoroughly skilled in the science of music, and took great pains to make his choir proficient in both musical science and art. It was during his leadership that an Englishman, who happened along about that time, was permitted to introduce a trombone into the choir gallery, and this materially aided the bass singers. In order to conceal the instrument from the congregation below, some of whom might have been scandalized by its introduction, a screen was erected, attached to the upper pew, behind which the player sat and performed his part of the musical exercises.

After the retirement of Mr. Fleming, Mr. Silas Ward became the leader of the choir, and remained in that position for a number of years. It was during his occupancy

of the post that the first reed organ, in the shape of a small
instrument, then called a melodeon, was used to assist the
choir. After that the flute and stringed instruments gradually gave up the service, the violoncello lingering the long-
est. No pipe organ was ever used in any of the Presbyterian churches of Harrisburg until after the separation in
1858, when first the Pine Street Church, and afterwards
this church, introduced the instruments which are now in
use. The original organ first placed in the gallery of Pine
Street Church is now transferred to the Sabbath-School
room, whilst a new one takes its place in the audience
chamber. This church still retains the one first introduced,
the gift of the late James W. Weir, of happy memory. A
larger reed organ succeeded the melodeon in the church on
Second street, and this instrument was rescued at the time
of the fire, and is probably still used in some part of this
building.

After the congregation moved into the new church, in
the year 1842, the old choir dropped out, and a younger set
of singers occupied their places. Among these were Miss
Sarah Carson, now Mrs. Wyeth; Miss Isabella Tod, now
Mrs. Kerr; Miss Lucia Simmons, afterwards Mrs. Wilson,
now deceased; Miss Susan Ayres, afterwards Mrs. Jones, also
deceased; Miss Margaret Carson, Miss Elizabeth Boyd, Miss
Kate Emerson, the Misses Nancy and Lill Shunk, daughters of Governor Shunk; Miss Mary E. Graydon, now Mrs.
Sharpe, of Indianapolis; Miss Susan Mowry, now Mrs.
Fleming, and Miss Eliza Roberts, now Mrs. Given. The
last four of these sang alto, whilst the others were soprano
singers. Among the bass were Alexander Sloan, who kept

his old place for a time; David Fleming, Joel Hinckley, Patterson Johnson, Lucius V. Parsons, and after an absence of some years, Alexander Roberts. The tenor singer was Dr. C. N. Hickok. A still younger set were gradually introduced into the choir at a later day, and they continued there until the destruction of the church edifice in the year 1858. Some of them are to-day matrons in both of the large Presbyterian churches, and as it is impossible to give the names of all, I refrain from mentioning any.

But as this paper is supposed to be a dissertation upon the hymnology of the Church, I must not omit to notice the hymn and music books in use in the church during the period of which I am writing. Mr. Hamilton, in an article recently published, speaks of a hymn book called the "New Haven Collection," which he says was the first book used by the congregation. It contained only seventy hymns. The first hymn book which I remember was the authorized version of psalms and hymns, the former being kept separate from the latter, and placed first in the book. The combined hymn and tune book, now so common, was unheard of in the church at that day, the music book, which was used only by the choir, being an entirely separate work. It contained the tunes ordinarily sung to the psalms and hymns, and in the end of the book was generally a collection of anthems and set pieces, to be used by the choir as voluntaries. The first two music books which were in use after the new church was occupied, were the "Boston Academy" and the "Carmina Sacra." At a later day the "Psaltery" and the "Mendelssohn" were introduced, and a short time before the destruction of the church, a new book, called " The Harp of David."

A lady friend residing in the West, who was a member of the choir for a year or two, sending me some reminiscences of choir days, speaks of some of the favorite tunes then in use. She mentions " Rothwell," " Cephas," " Harwell," " Oliphant," " Lischer," " Ariel," " Oberlin," " Ezra," " Ceylon," the last three being copied into our manuscript books, not being found in any of our own collections. And then the anthems, with which the morning service was generally opened, " Jerusalem my Happy Home," " Plunged in a Gulf of Dark Despair," " Wake the Song of Jubilee," " The Lord is my Shepherd," " Come unto me all ye that Labor," &c., " I will wash my Hands in Innocency," and many others. As pertinent to my mention of the anthem last named, let me here introduce a brief extract from a letter received recently from George B. Ayres, of Philadelphia, whose old flute, played by him in the choir over forty years ago, is now on exhibition in the adjoining church parlor. He says: " You may notice in ' The Psaltery ' the anthem, ' I will wash my Hands in Innocency,' has two passages (in small notes) *for the instruments alone.* Well, I remember what a MAGNIFICENT thing our people used to think *that* was—when the instruments played those passages ! I suppose *you* recognize the bass part."

We seldom hear anthems like those I have referred to nowadays. The modern voluntaries are generally more highly artistic, and relegate those of a simpler character to the rear. And yet I may be permitted to say that, in my judgment, the average congregation, even in these days, would appreciate more highly and enjoy more thoroughly some of these old anthems, than many of those which are "executed" in their hearing in perhaps the majority of our Presbyterian churches.

I know of no hymn book in use in the lecture-room, at the Wednesday evening service, until after Dr. Robinson was called to the pastorate, unless it was the one used in the church on the Sabbath. Possibly the hymns were "lined out," as was the custom in early days. Dr. DeWitt, who had a fine voice, generally started the tunes on Wednesday evening, and the range on these occasions was not a very extensive one. I remember that on one occasion a strange clergyman, who was conducting the service, gave out the hymn commencing "Now I resolve with all my heart;" and sang it to the tune "Rockingham." Dr. DeWitt was greatly pleased with the music, which was then new to us, and from that time on we had it on nearly every Wednesday evening. So surfeited did I become with the tune that to this day I dislike to hear it sung.

After Dr. Robinson became co-pastor a small book was introduced into the lecture room, called "Parish Hymns," which was used thereafter and contained many very good selections. One beautiful hymn became a favorite, and was

---

* The records of the Session contains the following item under date of March 10, 1853, more than a year prior to Dr. Robinson's coming : "Whereas many members of the church having expressed a wish that a suitable hymn book should be used in the meetings for lecture and prayer, and the Session having examined several compilations extant, it was resolved unanimously to recommend the 'Parish Hymns' for the uses proposed."—EDITOR.

often sung at a Saturday evening prayermeeting.   Its opening verse was:

> When the worn spirit wants repose,
>   And sighs her God to seek,
> How sweet to hail the evening's close
>   That ends the weary week."

The same hymn has since been arranged to appropriate
music in one of the music books, as a hymn anthem,
though I have not heard it sung for many years.

These reminiscences must close with the year 1858. From
that time two organized Presbyterian churches existed, and
with the musical arrangements of the mother church since
that day, the writer is not familiar.   The constituent
elements of the choir in Pine Street Church have varied
greatly in the passing years, as have doubtless those in
this church.   In both churches the combined hymn and
tune books are now in use, and there is less excuse than
ever for a neglect of congregational singing. Choirs, too,
have become more ambitious, and claim a much larger
share of the musical part of the service than did their
predecessors.   Within proper bounds, this is not perhaps to
be deprecated, especially if the music is entirely appropriate.   Possibly too little account was made in days past
of the praise element, but we may be in danger of running
too far to the opposite extreme.   I confess to a feeling of
misgiving when I see whole programmes published on a
Saturday evening in the newspapers, including even the
names of the composers of the pieces to be performed by the
choir, inviting the congregation seemingly to a concert of
sacred music, rather than to a meeting with the Master for

worship, and the hearing of his message from the pulpit. Let me be understood here, as objecting to the *advertising* and not to the praise service itself.

But this is treading upon what some may consider debatable ground. I give only my own opinion. It is my province in this paper to *narrate*, rather than to moralize, and I therefore leave the subject, commending it to the calm reflection of all Presbyterian hearers.

The concluding anthem by the choir was Farmer's " Qui Tollis," this was followed by a soprano solo, " Jerusalem," sung by Miss Helen Espy with sweetness and expression. Rev. Dr. Thomas H. Robinson read hymn number 394, verses one, two and four, which the congregation having risen sang "as in the days of the fathers," to the solemn majestic tune of " Windham."

> A broken heart, my God ! my King !
> Is all the sacrifice I bring :
> The God of grace will ne'er despise
> A broken heart for sacrifice.
>
> My soul lies humbled in the dust,
> And owns thy dreadful sentence just ;
> Look down, O Lord ! with pitying eye,
> And save the soul condemned to die.
>
> Oh. may thy love inspire my tongue ;
> Salvation shall be all my song,
> And all my powers shall join to bless,
> The Lord, my strength and righteousness.

The President of the Evening introduced Rev. Charles Edward Greig, Superintendent of the McCall mission work in Paris, France, who pronounced the Benediction. After the Benediction the audience tarried to hear the last of the inspiring music of the night, Lemmens' "Marche Pontificale."

The brevity of this sketch of the most complete and enjoyable musical festival given in many years in Harrisburg is justified only because there follows another sketch prepared at the request of the editor by the Rev. Thomas B. Angell, Rector of St. Stephen's Protestant Episcopal Church, who was an interested auditor, and who is most competent to write in a critical way of the evening.

THE MUSICAL FESTIVAL.

By Rev. THOMAS B. ANGELL, B. D.

In the address with which the Rev. Mr. Skilling introduced the speaker of the evening, he made a happy reference to the past that the church had a history of music
co-eval with itself. And it was therefore not only fitting
but suggestive that one evening of the Centennial week
should be devoted to a musical festival—suggestive in that
it indicated the increasing importance attached to praise as
an integral part of worship. The writer may perhaps be
allowed to congratulate the Presbyterian Church on its
increasing perception of the truth that there can be few
ways in which the higher aspirations of the spiritual nature
can be better expressed than through the instrumentality
of music; more especially as the power of such expression
in its higher forms has been given to man only of all
created beings.

It may safely be asserted that the time referred to
by Mr. Graydon, when a psalm tune, lined out by the
precentor and followed, more or less, by the congregation,
was all that was considered permissible, and when that
noblest of instruments, the organ, was looked upon as
savoring of Romish tendencies, has forever passed. And
no stronger evidence to that effect could have been brought
forward than the elaborate and satisfactory musical pro-

gramme rendered on this occasion, under the able director-
ship of Mr. George R. Fleming, assisted by the masterly
ability of Mr. David E. Crozier at the organ.

Were this notice intended for temporary purposes
only, it would be amply sufficient to print the programme
and the names of those who assisted in its rendition;
no other comment as to the adequacy of the production
to the occasion would be necessary. But as it is understood that this volume is intended to be a reminder
to future generations of this week of rejoicing a more
extended notice seems to be called for. The writer regrets
that his knowledge is not sufficient to adequately notice the
organ work rendered by Mr. Crozier. We can only say that
the selections were as happy as their rendering was satisfy-
ing to musical taste, and it is safe to add that the varied
resources of the organ were never more fully displayed.
The vocal work was in the hands of a large choir, in which
Mrs. E. Z. Gross, Miss Helen Espy, Miss Reba Bunton, Mr.
George R. Fleming, Mr. E. Z. Gross, and Mr. W. G. Underwood
ably sustained the solo parts. The opening number, Dudley
Buck's well-known Festival " Te Deum," probably the most
satisfactory piece of sacred music written by this com-
poser, was admirably rendered. Clearness of enunciation,
accuracy of attack, and pleasing blending of parts testified
to careful work and to Mr. Fleming's able leadership.
Were any criticism to be made, it might perhaps be
said that the time taken was somewhat too slow. In
the absence of Miss Briggs, Mr. W. G. Underwood sang
admirably, " Glory to thee my God this Night," a selection
well calculated to display the power of the lower range of

his voice. This was followed by an organ solo, Mozart's well known Andante in F, most satisfactorily rendered by Mr. Crozier. The anthem, "Lo! it is I," by Faure–Shelly, displayed the good training of the choir in being able to lend interest to a somewhat uninviting piece of writing. Miss Bunton then sang the contralto solo from Gaul's Cantata, The Holy City, "Eye hath not seen," &c., one of the most beautiful bits of devotional musical writing which these later years have produced. While not tuneful—as alas! some people after a long training in the meretricious music of Gospel hymns, and so forth, reckon tune—its majestic melody adequately mirrored the magnificent words to which it was wedded and no higher praise can be given than that. Miss Bunton's rendering was worthy of the music, which gave large opportunity for the display of a contralto voice, most unusual in its range and power, and specially fitted for the impressiveness of oratorio music. It was said in a metropolitan paper a few days ago that while nature afforded ample supply of soprano and bass voices, and was not niggardly in tenors, it was rarely indeed that she provided contraltos. Our city is to be congratulated on having one of the rare voices within its limits, and the choir of Market Square Church on being able to number it among its musical resources. The duet, "Forever with the Lord," was sung by Mr. and Mrs. Gross with that mutual sympathy and tender feeling which gives such a charm to their work in duet singing. The choir fully sustained their previous efforts in their rendering of the anthems, "O, Clap Your Hands," by Buck, and "Qui Tollis," by Farmer. Both of these selections were of that florid style, always popular, but with which the writer has to confess a certain want of sympathy. They are apparently composed with the main idea of showing off the agility of the human voice, the sentiment of the words being a minor consideration. The execution of them by the choir was, however, exceedingly good, though the substitution of English words in the latter anthem for the Latin, for which the music was written, detracted somewhat from the effect. A special mention is due to the solo " Jerusalem" sung by Miss Helen Espy. Suited as it was in every way to the capabilities of her voice, Miss Espy rendered it with admirable purity and force of tone, together with a warmth and justness of expression that made it exceptionally pleasing to the hearers. To Mr. George R. Fleming great credit is due for his admirable conducting, as well as for the aid which his strong, yet pleasing tenor, afforded to the choir in the concerted work. To the writer not the least satisfactory part of the programme was the closing congregational hymn. A Presbyterian lady informed him that it was among her earliest recollections as having always been sung on the occasions of the administration of the communion. The air was evidently based on one of the Gregorian tones, and it is worthy of remark that the old favorites, "Olmutz" and "Hamburg," composed by Lowell Mason, were both adaptations from Gregorian music, the former being an arrangement of the eighth tone. It is pleasant to feel that in music, as in creed, the Christian church of to-day is linked with the long distant past.

Mr. Graydon's paper of reminiscences detailing the various stages of progress and change through which the music of the congregation has passed in the last century was both interesting and appropriate.

In every way this evening of melody was a worthy and fitting contribution to the varied features of this centennial celebration. That it was appreciated was testified by the presence of a congregation that taxed the utmost resources of the church.

SOME ADDITIONAL REMINISCENCES.

By the EDITOR.

Mr. H. Murray Graydon's excellent paper upon the hymnology of the mother Presbyterian church of Harrisburg revived memories in the minds of many in the congregation These reminiscences have been gathered by the Editor into the following article :

There is a significant coincidence in the organization of the first choir in the same year that Dr. DeWitt began his ministry. It was probably one of the first fruits of his ministry.

From that time to the present there is no intimation in the testimony of persons or of records that the music of the sanctuary has been neglected. On the contrary, pastor and people have made every effort to make the music an edifying part of the worship on the Lord's day and at week day services. A former member recalls that somewhere in the twenties Mr. Joel Harmon, an itinerant music teacher formed a class for "the study of music and improvement in the art of singing" which met weekly. Many of our singers were in the class, and its meetings were frequently held in our church. Each member brought a tallow candle to supply light. Mr. Harmon would make his lighted candle serve as a baton as well. The coat and hand bespattered with melted tallow gave evidence to his energetic efforts in bringing his pupils to time and expression.

Another former member was reminded by Mr. Graydon's reference to Dr. DeWitt's custom of "raising the tune" at the week-day service, of an occasional slip. He would hum over to himself the first two lines of the tune, and then start the hymn, unconsciously joining the first line of the hymn to the third line of the tune, much to the merriment of herself and her young companions.

To the early singers mentioned by Mr. Graydon, there ought to be added the names of Misses Rose and May Wright, neices of Major Forster, afterwards Mrs. Samuel and Henry Cross, Miss Ellen Graydon, afterwards Mrs. Whitehill, Miss Theodosia Graydon, afterward Mrs. Joel Hinckley, Miss Margaret C. Berryhill, afterwards Mrs. Geo. P. Wiestling, Miss Martha S. Ingram (Mrs. William Dick Boas,) Miss Isabel Sloan, Miss Margaret Hays, Mrs. John A. Weir, *nee* Miss Catharine E. Wiestling, Messrs. Andrew Graydon, Samuel Cross and Geo. P. Wiestling. Many of these had voices worthy of more than passing notice, especially Geo. P. Wiestling and his sister, Mrs. John A. Weir, whose voices combined unusual sweetness and strength. A former member writes: "The memory of Mrs. Weir's voice, its wonderful sweetness, strength, range, rare pathos, and power to sway the feelings of her hearers, still lingers in the minds of her cotemporaries. Often has my father, returning home from trips to different parts of the State, told us about some one asking if that voice were still in our choir."

In addition to those mentioned by Mr. Graydon as singing at a later period were Miss Elizabeth Boyd, Miss Frazer, Miss Josephine Smith, Mr. Lucius V. Parsons, Mr. David

Fleming and Dr. James Fleming. Special mention is due the Fleming brothers. Mr. R. Jackson Fleming was for a period of fourteen years leader of the choir, and for many years his two brothers, David and James, were acceptable members of it. It is notable that in later days the three sons of Mr. David Fleming, and one daughter, Charles M., David, Jr., George R. and Sara, now Mrs. Joshua W. Sharpe, have been prominently identified with the music of the church.

The thirties and forties were delightful choir days. The rehearsals were held on Friday evenings, and the whole evening was given up to it. Such prominence did choir practice have in the social life of the then village that parties were never given on choir night, friends were invited to the practice, and it was regarded as one of the delightful events of the week. About this period it was the custom for our choir and that of the Reformed Salem Church, then under the leadership of Mr. Geo. P. Wiestling, to visit each other in a body once a month for social and musical enjoyment.

From time to time new voices appeared among those with which the congregation had become familiar. Among those who sang about the middle of the century referred to by Mr. Graydon, ought to be included Miss Mary J. Partch and Mr. Saxton, both of whom had voices of remarkable sweetness and power of expression; Miss Kate Doll, afterwards Mrs. Dr. Harris; Miss Esther Doll. afterward Mrs. Bradshaw, "whose voice will never be forgotten by the congregation of that day;" Miss Jeanette Street, afterwards Mrs. James Fleming, and Mr. Peter K. Boyd. In these days the choir was large and popular. Mr. George B. Ayres and others testify that "it was the best choir in town, as a whole," and that its reputation extended throughout the State.

Mr. Graydon's reminiscences ended with the year 1858. During these last thirty-five years the choir has maintained the high standard of early days. The disturbed conditions of life of the sixties, the presence of soldiers, the military hospitals, the tide of war rolling to our very doors, interfered seriously with the church life of that period. It was almost impossible to have choir practice. One of the choir of those days says, "Frequently did we have to hurry so rapidly from hospital to church that we hardly had breath enough to sing the first hymn." From 1850 for a quarter of a century Mr. Silas Ward was closely identified with the choir. His ability as a conductor, his fine tenor voice and his great enthusiasm as a musician were of invaluable service to the music of the church.

It is impossible to give a complete list of all who have been in the choir since the erection of the present church building. During this period there appear in this company the names of Miss Sibyl Fahnestock, now Mrs. Thomas H. Hubbard; Miss Ellen J. Weir, Miss Rachel T. Briggs, Miss Maggie Barnitz, Miss Annie Roberts, now Mrs. Purvis; Miss Kate Roberts, now Mrs. Lowell; Miss Ellen Roberts, afterwards Mrs. Kelker; Miss Elizabeth McCormick, now Mrs. Phillips; Miss Belle Briggs, afterward Mrs. Blaikie; Miss Carrie Hickok, now Mrs. Schell; Miss Sibyl M. Weir, Miss Nellie Fleming, now Mrs. Bruner; Miss Alice Westbrook, now Mrs. Fager; Miss Mary Detweiler, now Mrs. Quickel; Miss Sara Fleming, now Mrs. Sharpe; Miss Carrie Porter,

now Mrs. Shotwell; Miss Annie M. Robinson, Louis Fahne-
stock, Wallace W. Fahnestock, James W. Weir, Jr., Dr.
Cherrick Westbrook, Jr., Henry F. Quickel, Charles M.
Fleming, Melancthon S. Shotwell, George W. Boyd,
William R. Fleming, Luther R. Kelker, William A. Robin-
son, John W. Reily, John Porter.

Mr. Charles M. Fleming, whose sweet, rich tenor won for
him a wide reputation during his college days as a member
of the Princeton University quartette, became the leader of
the choir upon his return from college in 1875, and remained
in that capacity until his death in 1883. The choir was
without an authorized leader for some time, though his
brother, George R. Fleming, by common consent, was recognized as the leader. On March 21st, 1887, he was elected by
the Session to that position and still fills it with great
acceptance.

It is worthy of note that some families have been identified with the music of the church through a long period of
years. Mention has already been made of the two generations of Fleming brothers. Besides these are the three Doll
sisters, Miss Kate Doll (Mrs. Harris), Miss Esther Doll (Mrs.
Bradshaw), Miss Sarah Doll (Mrs. McCauley), the latter
being a member of the present choir. There have been
three generations of the Roberts family, Col. James Roberts
and his children, Mrs. Kelker, Mrs. Purvis, Mrs. Lowell,
Mrs. Given and Alexander, and the children of the two
latter, Alexander, Jr., George, John B. and James Roberts,
and Misses Elizabeth and Louisa Given. Two generations
of the Weirs have been in the choir, Mr. and Mrs. John A.
Weir, Miss Ellen J., James W., Jr., and Miss Sibyl M. Weir

and of the Briggs family, Mrs. Julia A. Briggs, Miss Belle (Mrs. Blaikie) and Miss Rachel Briggs, and of Dr. James Fleming's, Dr. and Mrs. James Fleming, Miss Nellie (Mrs. Bruner) and William R. Fleming.

The present choir is published in the Appendix to this volume among the present organizations of the church. It is only needful to call attention to the rare musical festival of Centennial Week to emphasize the high class work done by this volunteer choir. This choir, by its occasional praise services on Sunday evenings, has done much to magnify the place music has in the service of the sanctuary. These services were first introduced into the city by this church several years ago, and our example has been generally followed by the other churches.

MUSICAL INSTRUMENTS.—As full and accurate an account of the various musical instruments in use prior to the first reed instrument, as it is possible at this date, is given in Mr. Graydon's paper. He very correctly says that Mr. Silas Ward introduced the first reed organ about 1850. It was a small affair, being what is called a melodeon. This was shortly followed by a large reed organ of unusual size and superior quality. It must have been a remarkably well made instrument as it has been in use for at least forty years and is still doing duty in the lecture-room. It was rescued from the fire in 1858, and continued to serve in the public worship of the Lord's day until 1872. During nearly all these years, from 1850 to 1872, Mrs. Isabella S. Kerr, was organist. Miss Sibyl Fahnestock (Mrs. Hubbard) and Miss Mary Nutting (Mrs. Wallace W. Fahnestock) also served acceptably in this capacity.

This organ gave place in the latter year to the large Hook & Hastings pipe organ given by Mr. James W. Weir in memory of his beloved wife. This organ is still in use, and for sweetness, richness and power is not surpassed by any in this portion of the State. This organ has twenty-six stops, eleven hundred and eighty-three pipes, five mechanical registers, and four pedal movements. The case is black walnut, the pipes are silvered, with gold mouths, and its general design is made to correspond with that of the pulpit which it fronts. The silver plate on the front of the organ bears the following inscription: " Presented by Mr. James W. Weir, a memorial of his wife, Mrs. Hanna A. Weir, who died February 12th, 1872."

On September 25th, 1872, the new organ was dedicated with an elaborate recital. Mr. John Zundel, organist in Rev. Henry Ward Beecher's church, Brooklyn, together with Mr. Thomas Winn, who had just been elected organist, gave the large audience gathered for the occasion an exhibition of the many excellencies of the new instrument. The church choir sang several anthems and led the congregation in "Coronation," "Avison," "Mendon" and "Old Hundred." The soloists of the evening were Miss Rachel T. Briggs and Miss Maggie Barnitz. Mr. Silas Ward was the leader.

It is interesting to note that while the church had, up to this time, been decorated with flowers at weddings and on other week day occasions, it was not until the first Sunday the new organ was used that flowers were placed about the pulpit on the Lord's Day. The custom then inaugurated has been happily continued until the present.

From 1872 to 1879 Mr. Winn, Mr. Charles H. Small, Miss Ellen A. Walker, served as organists. On January 1st, 1879, Mr. Henry F. Quickel was selected as organist and continued to serve in that capacity until April, 1886. For several months Miss Sara B. Chayne, and Mrs. David Fleming, Jr., took charge of the instrument. Mr. David Edgar Crozier, the present accomplished organist, began his duties on the last Sunday in November, 1886.

The reed organ in use in the Senior department was a gift, at the dedication of the present Sunday-school in 1883, from the Superintendent, Mr. Samuel J. M. McCarrell, a memorial of his son, Wallace A. McCarrell, who departed this life, December 16th, 1880.

The reed organ in the Intermediate room was the gift of Mrs. David Fleming, in 1891. The piano in the Primary room was secured by the officers of that department and the Young People's Society of Christian Endeavor, in March, 1890. The reed organ used in the parlor was presented by Mr. James W. Weir many years ago.

Special reference must be made to the valuable services of Mrs. Isabella S. Kerr. For nearly fifty years Mrs. Kerr has been identified with the music of the church. Her fine musical ability, her abiding interest and untiring devotion to everything pertaining to our musical affairs, her aptitude to fill any place and meet any emergency made her indispensable. Not only did she serve in the public worship of the sanctuary, as has already been mentioned, but for many years she played the organ and led the singing in the lecture room, and had charge of the music in the Senior department of the Sunday-school. When the present

Pastor arrived in Harrisburg, she introduced herself as "Chairman of the Committee on Music, Flowers and Dirt." Her unremitting attention to the cleanliness of the sanctuary, her love for flowers and diligent care to have them each week for many years about the pulpit, her personal connection with the music as singer, organist and director, justify this rather unique and suggestive title.

Music and Hymn Books.—Mr. Graydon has given all the facts obtainable touching the music books used by the choir prior to the introduction of the modern combined hymn and tune books.

On October 22d, 1834, the Session resolved to recommend to the "congregation to adopt in their public worship the Psalms and Hymns, comprised in the selection authorized and recommended by the General Assembly of the Presbyterian church, and that if there be no objection made by the congregation to their adoption they be introduced the first Sabbath of December next." There seems to have been no objection offered, for this collection came into use and continued to be the hymn book for use in public worship until 1859. This collection was a revision under the direction of a General Assembly Committee, of a previously existing collection of Psalms and Hymns by Dr. Isaac Watts, and it took the place of the early edition in the worship in our congregation. The earlier collection gave more prominence to the Psalms than to the hymns. Its hymns were arranged in three books, those "collected from the Scripture," one hundred and fifty hymns, those "composed on divine subjects," one hundred and seventy, and those

" prepared for the Lord's Supper," forty-five, a total of three hundred and sixty-five hymns.

How long this collection was in use in the congregation prior to 1834 is not known; but there is every reason for supposing that it was the first hymn book used by the congregation. The collection adopted in 1834 shows the tendency to an increasing use of hymns. There are fewer Psalms and more hymns. It was a thorough revision of the earlier book, especially in the section devoted to the hymns. Old hymns were omitted, new ones inserted, and the arrangement was more convenient, as the hymns were consecutively numbered. There were five hundred and thirty-one hymns, most, but not all of them, from the famous Dr. Watts. Doddridge, Montgomery, Mrs. Steele, Newton, Beddome, Heber, Cowper, Toplady, Fawcett, and noticeably Wesley are among the hymn-writers, whose productions the congregation began to sing in 1834.

This collection continued in use until 1859. About this date, possibly in October of that year, the "Church Psalmist" was adopted. This was a collection which had been published for several years as a private enterprise, and which was purchased by the new school General Assembly in 1857 and commended to the churches. The Psalms and hymns are still bound separately; there is a more systematic arrangement of the hymns; the hymns number eight hundred and fifty-eight and are drawn from a wider range of authors.

In November, 1874, Mrs. Eliza E. Haldeman, of precious memory, presented the church with over five hundred copies of the then new "Presbyterian Hymnal," which still continues to be the book used in public worship. This book is a radical departure from those in previous use in several respects. The Psalms and hymns are no longer kept apart, but are so mingled and undesignated that they cannot be distinguished from each other except by those familiar with the Psalms. The tendency to lessen the number of Psalms and increase the hymns has gained perceptibly since the earlier collections. In one thousand and six songs, probably not one in twenty could properly be called a version of a Psalm. The greatest change and the best is in the combination of tunes and words in the same book. This collection, while not ideal, was a great improvement over any other used by the congregation. This was the first time that the church had owned her hymn-books, and it was necessary that some provision be made in the pews for receiving them. Mr. William O. Hickok generously placed, at his own expense, racks in the pews for this purpose.

The records of the Session show that on March 10th, 1853, " Parish Hymns " was adopted for use in the lecture and prayermeeting. This subsequently gave place to the " Social Hymn and Tune Book ;" which, in turn, was succeeded by " Hymns and Songs of Praise " edited by Drs. Hitchcock, Eddy and Schaff. This is the book now in use. A new edition of this book by Drs. Hitchcock, Eddy and Mudge, is in use in the public services at Calvary Chapel.

Before 1856 " Union Hymns," a collection of five hundred hymns published by the American Sunday-School Union was in use in the Sunday-school. There is no record of its adoption. In 1856 it gave place to "Sunday-School

Hymns," compiled for the American Sunday-School Union by Mr. James W. Weir. There were three hundred and seventy-three hymns in this collection, many of them having been written by Mr. Weir. In later years there has been a great variety of Sunday-school music books in use. Every collection that had any merit, and some which had none, being adopted as it appeared. The present collection is " Winnowed Songs for Sunday-Schools," by Ira D. Sankey.

The Intermediate department has used two compilations of hymns selected by some of the musical people in the church and printed exclusively for use in this department. The last collection was made several years ago, and the expense of its publication was generously borne by Mrs. Eliza E. Haldeman.

This sketch, brief as it is, together with Mr. Graydon's, makes evident that the mother Presbyterian church of Harrisburg has had a history written in song and music, a history which reveals the high musical culture of its people and their sense of the important part music bears in the worship of God.

THE PRESBYTERIAN CHURCHES OF HARRISBURG.

The Centennial committee appreciating the fact that their church is only one of the Presbyterian churches in the city, and believing that the centenary of the mother would not be complete without a large recognition of her mother and her children, arranged for this evening to be devoted to the past history and the present condition of the several Presbyterian churches which sustain these relations to her.

The Rev. William A. West, the Stated Clerk of the Presbytery of Carlisle, now in charge of the Robert Kennedy Memorial Presbyterian Church at Welsh Run, and for many years the pastor of the Westminster Presbyterian Church of this city, was invited to preside on this occasion. Mr. West is greatly revered by this congregation, and his long residence as one of the pastors in this city made this selection eminently fitting. The service began with an organ prelude, Guilmant's "Marche Religieuse." In place of Dudley Buck's "Hark, Hark, My Soul," which had been announced for this evening, the choir sang "Holy Spirit, Come, O Come," a setting by Martin of an old Latin hymn, written about the tenth century, and attributed to King Robert of France. Rev. Reuben H. Armstrong, pastor of the Elder Street Presbyterian Church, read Philippians 2: 1-11. The Rev. Benjamin F. Beck, City Missionary, led in prayer. The congregation joined in singing hymn No. 232, vs. 1, 2, 3, 4:

> Jesus! the very thought of Thee
> With sweetness fills my breast ;
> But sweeter far Thy face to see,
> And in Thy presence rest.
>
> Nor voice can sing, nor heart can frame,
> Nor can the memory find,
> A sweeter sound than Thy blest name,
> O Saviour of mankind.
>
> O hope of every contrite heart,
> O joy of all the meek !
> To those who fall how kind Thou art,
> How good to those who seek !
>
> But what to those who find ? Ah ! this
> Nor tongue nor pen can show ;
> The love of Jesus—what it is,
> None but His loved ones know.

The PRESIDENT OF THE EVENING. I think it a great pleasure and privilege to be here this evening, and especially to have the honor of presiding at a meeting in which shall be given brief sketches of the dealings of God to and by the churches of this city. The history of one of these churches runs back a century, and of the others to different periods. It has been very properly arranged upon the programme that before hearing these sketches of the churches of the city, we should hear from the mother church, Old Paxtang, a name loved and revered not only in this immediate section, but throughout the Presbytery of Carlisle. It has been appointed that brief papers, not exceeding fifteen minutes in length, excepting that of the church in which we meet, to which thirty minutes have very properly been allowed, shall be heard. We will hear first from Paxtang, organized about 1726, through the Pastor, the Rev. Albert B. Williamson.

Address by Rev. Albert B. Williamson.

Owing to the fact that the sesqui-centennial celebration of old Paxtang Church is of such recent date, and that her history was then well-nigh exhausted in the comprehensive article by the ready pen of our able State Librarian, Dr. Egle, (these facts all being printed in the daily newspapers, and preserved in a beautifully bound volume that, most of you, without doubt, have in your possession,) it will be almost impossible for me to say anything to you that will be new concerning the first part of the subject that was given me for this evening.

Paxtang Church is situated three miles east of Harrisburg, taking the court house for a starting point. It was organized by Scotch-Irish Presbyterians, who unable longer to endure the oppression of the old world, sought new homes for themselves in this " land of the free," where they could " worship God according to the dictates of their own conscience," no one but Indians daring to molest and they could not make afraid. They came in their poverty, but they brought along with them their Bibles, catechisms, trusty rifles, and last, but by no means least, their brains. As a result they have established for themselves and their descendants a name for intelligence, resolute patriotism and stalwart christianity, that has distinguished Paxtang parishioners through the greater portion of two centuries.

Very soon after making homes for themselves in this new world, they built a log church in which to worship God, situated a few yards south of the present church building. Some few foundation stones of this structure could be seen in recent years. Exactly when this log church was built, how long it stood, and when it was torn down to make way for a more substantial one of stone, no one seems to know. Close by this log structure were the graves of the early pioneers.

Unfortunately all these graves with one exception were unmarked, and that one, we are told, was a rudely chiseled stone bearing the simple inscription, " Died 1716."

In 1740 the present house of worship was built, and this building " is the oldest house of Presbyterian worship in the entire State of Pennsylvania. There it stands to-day, firmer than the day it was built. The stones used in this building are rough surface limestones of all sizes and shapes, picked up from the surrounding fields, and put together with very little skill, and yet no firmer, better walls can be found, and why? Because the builders were the masters of a lost art, they knew how to make good mortar. The strength of the walls lies in the mortar which is as hard as the stones themselves. The storms of over a century and a half have had so little effect upon it that the marks of the mason's trowel are as clear as when they laid it."

The only thing about our past that I may be able to say this evening that will be new to at least a portion of you, will be about the old Paxtang charter, which by the way, is the oldest corporation charter in Dauphin county.

PAXTANG CHURCH.
ERECTED 1740.

This charter was granted by the Legislature to Paxtang Presbyterian Church, April 1st, 1784. This charter calls for thirteen trustees, one of whom is the pastor elect, " who is entitled to vote equally with any member of the Board of trustees." The trustees, whose names are in this charter, were "persons of prominence, reputation and property; farmers in the neighborhood." Their position is shown by their names and valuation found upon the assessment roll of 1785 and 1786.

Name.	Rate.	Tax.
Jacob Awl, ...	£800	£4– s0–d0
John Covert, ...		
Samuel Cochran, ...	230	1– 6– 8
Joshua Elder, ...	875	4– 12– 0
John Forster, ...	850	4– 0– 6
John Gilchrist, ...	500	2– 18– 9
John Harris (founder of Hbg.),	2.445	15– 0– 2
William Kerr, ...	525	3– 0– 0
Thomas McArther, ...	225	1– 2– 6
Alexander McClure, . . .		
John Wiggins, ...	250	1– 15– 0
John Wilson, ...	470	2– 10– 0
Rev. John Elder, ...	480	2– 0– 0

Rev. Mr. Elder was pastor and trustee of Paxtang Church fifty-six years. None of the descendants of these trustees now reside in the neighborhood of Paxtang church.

There are many distinguished men lying in old Paxtang grave yard without any mark to designate their resting place. Among those of known reputation who have headstones to mark their resting place, are Wm. Maclay, who was the first United States Senator from Pennsylvania; Wm. Wallace, Gen. Michael Simpson, and also the man, who not only gave his name to this city and laid out its streets, but was largely the means of having Harrisburg made the capital of this great Commonwealth, and donated for a capitol site a portion of the ground now known as capitol park, on which the capitol buildings are now situated. To me the only surprising thing in connection with this man is, that this city has never yet honored her founder by erecting on some suitable site a monument to his memory.

Throughout all these years the people of God have come up to this sacred spot to worship the God of their fathers. Swarm after swarm have gone off from the mother-hive and have found for themselves new hives which have grown larger and greater than the mother church. She has kept on in the even tenor of her way out under the old gray oaks for more than a century and a half.

The first offspring of Paxtang Church is Market Square, which has now not only reached the mature age of one hundred years, but is much larger and stronger than her mother. It is not, however, with trepidation and fear that the mother comes this evening before her giant child, but to rejoice in the strength of her offspring, to bring her greetings of love, and to cordially unite with her in the celebration of her one hundredth anniversary.

The life of a quiet country church may seem to be very unimportant. No wonderful deeds such as challenge the world are recorded in its annals; yet it may lie near the hearts and hopes of very many of God's children. As a birthplace of souls it is more hallowed than that of Marathon or Bunker Hill. The transformation of character effected in its midst is more important than the changes of empires; the fellowship of faith sweeter and more enduring than the ties of nature. Its worship and its employment give more joy and satisfaction than the deliberations of councils or the transactions of courts.

The church has within recent years renewed her strength, and now bids fair to hold her position for many years to come. In the winter of 1887 and 1888 the interior of the church was reconstructed and thoroughly modernized, and a sexton was employed to take charge of the church and grounds. In the summer of 1888 three new elders were added to the Session. They are now the only ruling elders the church has. The membership of the church, which was thirty-two in the year 1887, has been increased to sixty-seven. The women of the church are actively engaged in missionary work, both home and foreign. The young people's missionary band is nobly doing its part, and many hearts have been gladdened this winter by the gifts of clothing made by it. The Y. P. S. C. E. has an active membership of twenty-three and is a great help to both pastor and church. In 1892 lights were put in the church, since which time the cottage prayermeeting and the men's prayermeeting have united, and now worship every Wednesday evening in the church. The Sabbath-school is in a flourishing condition. This winter it held its first Christmas entertainment in the church.

The PRESIDENT OF THE EVENING. While it is pleasing to hear these tidings from the mother church, it will be also pleasing to hear from the sturdy daughter which has been doing such valued work during the last century in Harrisburg. It was a child whose birth was not hailed with joy and gladness by the mother, nor by its sturdy, strong-headed, stout-hearted pastor, Mr. Elder, of Paxtang Church. Notwithstanding that, she has grown and prospered and has been doing a good work for God and humanity. This evening my thoughts are turned back just fifty-one years ago to the winter of 1843, when, as a boy, I visited Harrisburg for about ten days or two weeks as the guest of Dr. Charles N. Hickok, now of Everett. During this time Dr. DeWitt was holding protracted services in the old church, which stood on Second street and Cherry avenue. Impressions were then made upon my mind which were deepened shortly after by hearing Dr. Oliver O. McClean, of Lewistown, and led me in April of the same year to take my stand on the Lord's side. So that I have always felt a peculiar interest in Market Square Church from that period to the present. We shall hear of the present condition of this church from the pastor, Dr. Stewart.

Address by Rev. George B. Stewart.

It is a matter of profound regret to myself and to all that Mr. McCarrell, who could so ably have spoken for this church at this time, is unable to discharge this duty. The state of his health is such as to positively forbid his undertaking it. It was not until a late hour that this became evident, and that it fell to my lot to take his place.

To-morrow evening the history of this church will be given by one than whom there is no other more qualified to narrate the story with accuracy, fullness and interest. To-night it devolves upon me to set forth the present

condition of the church. I shall endeavor to confine myself
strictly to the present condition, and shall only call to my
aid so much of the past as may be necessary to a clearer
presentation of the present.

It is a source of gratification that after a hundred years
of activity the church is to-day in a condition of growing
prosperity and strength. There are yet no signs of old age.
Her force is in no wise abated. The workers from time
to time change. The methods of work are successively
modified. The condition and needs of the field vary.
Nevertheless the church is as well qualified and equipped
to do her mission in this generation as at any preceding
time in her history. In celebrating this centennial of her
birth, we are not called upon to entertain fears of her speedy
dissolution. She is not decrepit, nor has her old age any
manifestations of failing strength. I ask you to consider
her present condition in respect of

I. *Membership.*

The present membership of the church is 768. Of this
number Mrs. Sarah Doll is the oldest, having united with
the church on profession of her faith in 1827. After her the
next in age is Mrs. Julia A. Briggs, who united with the
church on profession of her faith in 1834. In 1843 there
was a great revival, at which time the largest number who
ever united with the church on one occasion were received
into membership. Of this number the following remain
members still with us: Mrs. Susan Fleming, Mrs.
Elizabeth Kerr, Mrs. Caroline R. Haldeman, Mrs. Malvina L. Ingram, Mrs. Isabella S. Kerr, Mr. Alexander
Roberts, Mrs. Mary E. Vaughn, Mrs. Ann E. Zimmer-

man. There are thus ten members who have been communicants in this church for more than fifty years, or more than half of the period which we, on this occasion, celebrate. Two hundred and fifty persons united with the church in the twenty years that followed 1843, and yet only thirteen remain with us. They are Mrs. Ellen W. Stees, 1850; Mrs. Jeanette Fleming, 1853; Mr. Samuel D. Ingram and Miss Anna C. Weir, 1855; Mrs. Elizabeth B. Orth and Mrs. Elizabeth Reily, 1857; Mrs. Margaret F. Sumner, 1859; Miss Rachel T. Briggs, Mrs. Louisa C. Fahnestock, Miss Louisa C. Fahnestock, Mrs. Hanna M. Harvey, Miss Mary Vandling and Miss Elizabeth Vandling, 1862. Of those who were enrolled during the next twenty-one years, between 1864 and 1884 inclusive, there remain two hundred and twenty-nine, while of those received during the last nine years, there remain five hundred and sixteen.

II. *Organizations.*

The oldest organization in connection with the church is the woman's weekly prayermeeting, held on Friday afternoon of each week. The meeting can be traced back as far as 1812, and during all of this long history it has borne an important part in the work of the church. So signal has been the influence and the activity of the women of the church that it was at first thought the centennial services would not be complete without giving special prominence to this fact by having a meeting devoted exclusively to the consideration of the work the women have done. But that not being deemed desirable it seems best for me to lay emphasis upon the activity of the women of the past, and to bear particular testimony to the great value of their service in the present. There is a large amount of unwritten history in connection with this church which if it were recorded would be blazoned with the names of many godly and eminently useful women who have prayed and wrought to the glory of God and to the salvation of souls. You will pardon me for narrating an incident which has peculiar interest to me and probably to others. It is not likely to get into any history except as I might tell it. In 1884, it pleased this congregation to call me to its pastorate. After receiving that call, I held it under advisement for a considerable, I guess the congregation thought it an inconsiderable, time. After many days of prayerful deliberation, the day arrived on which my answer must be sent, and I had reached no conclusion. I was in great stress of mind as to where my duty lay between your call and the wishes of the beloved people I had served for six years. The letter must go on a train which left the city a few minutes after four o'clock. Three o'clock had arrived and my decision had not yet been made. In earnest prayer I sought, as I had previously sought, Divine guidance. I thought that I had received it and it became clear that it was my duty to accept your call. That was on Friday afternoon between three and four o'clock. I wrote the letter hastily, posted it and wired my decision to an elder of the church. He received my telegram, and a few moments later he met one of the women of the church and mentioned to her that he had received a telegram from me announcing my decision. She said, " I know what it is. I have just come from the woman's prayermeeting, where we have been praying that he might come, and we seemed to have the assurance that he will come." I cannot but feel the prayers offered in Harrisburg and at Auburn during that one common hour were instrumental in bringing the one common answer.

The woman's Friday afternoon prayermeeting is a lineal descendant of the early meetings of the women in the church, though much of the work which was originally done in connection with its weekly meetings is now carried forward by numerous other organizations. This meeting is now in about the same condition in which it has been for several years. The attendance remains stationary with a few new ones becoming regular attendants who take the place of those called away by death or removal. Probably fifteen or twenty comprise the number of those who attend this weekly meeting. A collection is taken at each meeting which is given for such objects of benevolence as the ladies may decide. These offerings annually amount to about $150, and are appropriated to missionary and other uses.

Another woman's organization is the Dorcas Society, which during the winter months meets each week to cut out garments and to do sewing for the destitute of the congregation. During this present winter this society, on account of the present distress, has been unusually active.

The ladies are also carrying on with great and encouraging results a sewing-school for girls, which has been in existence since February 1, 1879. No girl is allowed to become a member of the sewing-school unless she is also a member of the Sunday-school. These girls are taught the useful art of sewing from the most elementary up to dress-

making, fancy embroidery and fancy knitting. Mrs. Isabella
S. Kerr has been superintendent from the beginning, and,
notwithstanding her enfeebled health, is still the guiding
and inspiring mind. Thus far for this winter there are
enrolled about one hundred and sixty scholars.

The Women's Missionary Society was organized October
2, 1871, and meets monthly on the first Friday of each
month. This society does a most valuable work in the interest of Foreign Missions, though its collections gathered at
each meeting are divided equally between the Home and
Foreign work. The meetings are well attended, full of
interest and valuable as an agency for maintaining and
increasing the interest in missions. Our women are also
united with those of the several Presbyterian churches of
the city in the Women's Union Home Missionary Society,
organized in 1881. The ladies also co-operate with the ladies
of other churches in the McAll Auxiliary in the interest
of that mission work in France. There is a Ladies Aid
Society, which devotes particular attention to the care of the
church and its other material interests. It thus appears
that now as always in the history of the church the women
are foremost in every good work. By pureness, by knowledge, by zeal, they further the work of the Master here, and
their power has gone into all the world.

The Sunday-school was organized August 16, 1816. The
school is divided into Senior, Intermediate, Primary and
Chinese departments. The present superintendent, Mr. S.
J. M. McCarrell, has occupied this honorable office since
the death of Mr. Weir, in 1878, discharging the duties of the

same with eminent ability and success. The secretaries' reports for the past year show that we have enrolled in the church school twenty-five officers, ninety-eight teachers, one thousand and ninety-six scholars, a total of one thousand two hundred and nineteen. Many of these scholars are not otherwise connected with the church. The children of our own members are almost without exception communicant or baptized members of the church, are members of the Sunday-school, and are faithful in attendance upon the services of the sanctuary.

Among our young people we have a Young People's Society of Christian Endeavor and a Junior Society of Christian Endeavor. The former was organized Nov. 5th, 1886, and the latter Feb. 3d, 1890. Both are valuable and active organizations. The Young People's Society has a membership of about one hundred and forty. It holds a weekly prayermeeting every Sunday evening before church service, a bi-weekly missionary meeting and an occasional social, and other entertainments. The zeal, enthusiasm and energy of the young people is being wisely directed through this organization along all the lines of church work, and though it is so recent an agent, yet it is one of the most valuable.

The Junior Society is composed of boys and girls, and meets each Monday afternoon. It is under the management of five ladies, who are most enthusiastic in their work and have stimulated a real enthusiasm among the one hundred members. Just now the pastor is giving a course of lessons on the life of Christic. There is held a monthly missionary meeting, at which a collection for missions is taken. This amounts to about $40 a year.

In addition to these several organizations among the young, there are numerous mission bands—twelve, or more —organized for home and foreign mission work and other good purposes. These ordinarily meet monthly, and are accomplishing good results.

As one of the results of the revival in the winter of 1875-6 came the cottage prayermeeting, organized Dec. 12th, 1875. This meeting is held every Monday evening from house to house. While the immediate purpose for which it was organized has ceased to exist, and many of its most active supporters have withdrawn from it to enter upon larger and more important church work, nevertheless it seems to have a place to fill, and is accomplishing good, though not great' results.

For several years the music of the church has been led by a volunteer choir, which gives its services without compensation, with great heartiness, regularity and universal acceptance.

For several years the Pastor has conducted during eight months of the year a weekly Bible class for the careful and systematic study of the Scripture. This class is attended by a small number of ladies and gentlemen who are devoted to the work. It may properly be regarded as one of the organizations of the church.

It thus appears that the church is well organized for the prosecution of a large variety of work and for the preservation of its many interests.

III. Calvary Chapel.

In 1888, as a result of Sunday-school work carried on for many years in the neighborhood of Lochiel by the members of this church, there was erected a beautiful stone chapel, corner of South Cameron and Sycamore streets, and there was organized within it Calvary Chapel Sunday-school. This work has steadily grown from year to year. The school has outgrown its quarters, and a comfortable and attractive room has been fitted up in the basement during this past year for the use of a primary department, composed of the younger scholars. Since June 1st, 1891, the work has been in the more immediate charge of the Rev. David M. Skilling, who with conscientious fidelity, untiring devotion and great efficiency has carried forward the interests of this portion of the congregation. It is now a well-organized congregation in everything but the name. There are two preaching services, a Sunday-school and a Christian Endeavor meeting every Lord's day. During the week a Junior Christian Endeavor Society, a Ladies' Sewing Society, a Ladies Missionary Society, a Young Men's Association, a number of mission bands and Sunday-school class organizations hold their respective meetings. It is most gratifying to note also that there have been many conversions as the result of this work. The contributions of the Chapel congregation and the Sunday-school, together with the help of one or two friends of the work, defray the whole expense of the same, besides making generous contribution to missionary and benevolent causes. During the past year a free reading and social room has been established in the basement, and is

CALVARY PRESBYTERIAN CHAPEL,
CAMERON AND SYCAMORE STREETS.
ERECTED 1887-88.

open every night in the week for all who may come. Reading matter and games are provided in abundance. There is a gratifying attendance on the part of the men, old and young, from that portion of the city. We are much encouraged by the results of the experiment. Our affection for this work and interest in its prosperity is most sincere and unflagging.

IV. Official Boards.

The Session is the oldest of the Boards, its life being coterminous with that of the church. It was constituted February 16th, 1794, by the election of three elders. It now has five elders, all of whom have been elected, as were their predecessors, for life. Of these five, three, Elders McCarrell, McCauley and Miller, were ordained to this office April 15th, 1877, and two, Elders Harvey and Spicer, were ordained March 20th, 1887. As pastor of the church, being thrown into constant and most intimate relations with these brethren, I desire to bear testimony to their unvarying loyalty, fidelity and zeal in all the interests of the congregation in which God and the people have made them overseers. It is an unwritten law of the Session that no action is taken unless it is unanimous action. The venerated Alexander Sloan, who served as a member of the Session from 1834 to 1890, was in the habit of saying that he never had been present at any meeting of the Session which was marred by unpleasant disagreement between the members of that body. The same can be said up to the present time. I never have met a body of men who have been more careful to respect the judgment and protect the feelings of their associates, while, at the same time, being most free and independent in their thought and utterance. All of the numerous activities and grave responsibilities of this congregation have been committed to their charge, and they perform their duties with commendable fidelity and distinguished ability.

The youngest official Board of the church is the Board of Deacons, which was first constituted by the ordination of seven deacons on the 20th of March, 1887. The Board is elected according to the rotary system, and as the term of each class has expired the members of that class have been successively re-elected, so that the Board has the same members now as at the beginning, with a single exception. In 1889 the serious illness of Mr. John K. Tomlinson, one of the original members, forbade his re-election, and Mr. David Fleming, Jr., was chosen in his stead, and still is a member of the Board. This Board has charge of the poor of the church. They are the almoners of the charity of the congregation. They are most discreet and faithful in the discharge of their duties, and have come to be an indispensable part of our organization.

The first Board of Trustees, under the civil charter of the church, was elected in 1819. Prior to this there were trustees, though the congregation had no corporate existence. By the charter the temporal affairs of the church and its property are in the care of this board, composed of seven gentlemen from the congregation. The fact that we have such a large and valuable plant in the heart of the city, complete in all its appointments and in the best repair, that we have a beautiful and eligibly located manse for the use of the minister, that all of the financial obligations of the congregation are met fully and promptly, is abundant evidence of the ability and devotion of these servants of the church. Mention ought to be made of the fact that the Trustees, with the consent and under the direction of the congregation, during the past year purchased one of the most desirable building sites in the city, No. 127 State street, and erected thereon a most substantial, commodious, convenient and attractive residence for the minister. While the expense incurred by this has not been entirely met, yet it is safe to say that had not the city and country been suddenly and unexpectedly overtaken by financial distress after the building operations had been begun, the whole amount would have been provided for before this time. It is equally safe to say that the balance yet to be raised can, in the near future, be easily secured.

V. *Services and Meetings.*

As a matter of record on this occasion it is probably worth while to mention the various services that are held in connection with our church work. The Lord's Supper is administered four times each year, on the first Lord's day in each calendar quarter. For many years there has not been a Sacramental occasion at which there have not been some additions to our membership. The communicants of the church are uniformally regular in their attendance upon this ordinace.

The sacrament of Baptism is administered statedly on the days following each Communion service, and on Children's Day in June, and at such other times as may suit the convenience of the parents. Parents are, with rare exception, faithful in presenting their children for this ordinance.

There are two preaching services, at 10.30 a. m. and
7.30 p. m., respectively. Sunday-school at 1.30 o'clock,
and Christian Endeavor meeting at 6.45 each Lord's
day. Junior Christian Endeavor and Cottage prayermeeting on each Monday, with a monthly Session meeting on
the second Monday of each month. On Wednesday evening the lecture and prayermeeting, and following it the
teachers' meeting for the study of the Sunday-school lesson,
are regularly held. Friday evening is devoted to the pastor's Bible class. In addition to these services there are a
multitude of meetings of different organizations and for
various purposes held every week. It is entirely safe to say
that during ten months of the year the meetings held in
connection with the church will average in all about twenty-
five a week.

For several years the congregation has been in the habit
of observing with appropriate services, Children's Day, the
second Sunday in June, appointed by the General Assembly. This day is now generally observed throughout the
Christian world. We were one of the first congregations to
inaugurate the custom.

During the Civil War there was held on one occasion a
morning prayermeeting at six o'clock on the Fourth of July
to consider the nation's interests and to pray for its welfare
This prayermeeting has been held uninterruptedly ever
since and is well attended being participated in by our
citizens irrespective of church connection.

It has been the custom from time immemorial for this
church to assemble on the annual Thanksgiving Day
appointed by the President of the United States and the

Governor of the Commonwealth for services appropriate to the occasion.

Other services are held as occasion may arise, the church being responsive to all proper calls to worship and service.

VI. *Spiritual Condition.*

It is probable that the spiritual condition of the congregation will never be satisfactory. It is to be hoped that we will never reach such a point in our growth in grace as to be content with our attainments. May we ever have a hungering and thirsting after righteousness. There is much in the spiritual condition of the church to call for humiliation, and confession and prayer. Many hearts in Zion are burdened with the desire for a higher life for their beloved church. May the number of these who thus long for the most excellent things of God largely increase, and may their fervent prayers receive from our Heavenly Father speedy and gracious answer in the quickening of His own people, and the conversion of those who know Him not.

Nevertheless, we must not forget that active, earnest service for the Master, and true zeal in advancing His kingdom are evidences of spiritual life. I cannot but believe that the large and varied activities of this congregation, its zeal for a pure gospel in the mouth of its ministers, for the honor of God's name in this community and the spread of the glorious kingdom throughout the world, its efforts for the relief of the poor and for the maintenance of all the varied agencies of the church, are the product of true spiritual power. The large contributions which it makes, aggregating, now and for a number of years past, $20,000 per annum for the support of the gospel here and elsewhere, for benevolent and charitable undertakings of various kinds, is an evidence of the presence with us of the indwelling Spirit of God. That the fruit of the Spirit may be more and more largely manifested among us, that we may be rich in every good work, that we may grow in grace and the knowledge of Jesus Christ, is the fervent prayer of our hearts.

In closing, permit me to say a word to the other churches—our mother church and our children. To you my brother, the Pastor of Paxtang Church, the grandmother of us all, who, notwithstanding her venerable age, is renewing her youth and coming into the possession of an increasing inheritance, hearty greeting. We entertain for you true filial affection. Paxtang will always be dear to Market Square. Much of the blood of that venerable church still contributes to the life and power of this congregation. Never will we forget our debt and obligation to you, nor cease to cherish your interest as our own.

To you, my brother, the representative of the Pine Street Church, the eldest of those that have gone from us, on behalf of this church I extend the most cordial welcome to the enjoyments of this occasion. From the very first of your existence as a separate organization you have shared with us, share and share alike, the responsibility and honor of our denomination in the city. We rejoice in your magnificent usefulness and your increasing honor. We are more closely identified in interest, and purpose, and labors than ever before. I know that I voice the feelings of my people when I say, it is our earnest desire that this union in affection and activity may increase with our years.

We cannot forget that an elder and others from this congregation were instrumental in starting the movement out of which has grown the Elder Street Presbyterian Church. Your conservative and substantial work among the colored people of this city is gratifying to all the friends of your race and church. We welcome you to-night.

The large fields, the increasing prosperity, the acquisition of new and beautiful houses of worship which characterize the Covenant and Westminster Presbyterian Churches fill our hearts with gratitude. We welcome you.

The Olivet Presbyterian Church, the youngest of us all, is nobly resisting and successfully overcoming the perils of infancy, and undoubtedly has for itself an important and growing field in the eastern part of the city. Our heartiest greetings to the infant of months.

Dear brethren, we are not unmindful that a considerable portion of the life blood of this church has gone to advance your interests and we rejoice in it. We rejoice in your growth. Together with you we magnify the importance of your fields, and we bid you God speed in all your blessed work.

This is a happy family. We are united in heart, in interest, in purpose. We have no rivalries and no conflicts. The interest of one is the interest of all. Our Master has committed to us the work of our denomination in this city. It is a work of commanding importance. As one man we undertake the task. In speaking for myself and for these people, whose minister I am, my last and my most important word is this, our fervent desire and prayer is that this occasion may emphasize our unity and strengthen its bonds.

The PRESIDENT OF THE EVENING. In 1858 an earnest and devoted band of christian men and women went out from this church and organized the Pine Street Church. At the time it was a great trial to the pastor and to the co-pastor, Dr. DeWitt and Dr. Robinson. It was a great trial to the good people of this church. What the Lord was then doing they knew not. But as we look back over the past history, it seems to me that we can know as we behold the great and good work which has been done by that church. As I call to mind to-night the relation that these two churches sustained to myself and to each other in the work undertaken from year to year, I can bear delighted testimony that to my knowledge they have stood shoulder to shoulder and labored heart to heart and hand to hand in the aggressive work for a kindred faith in this city. We shall hear from Pine Street through Prof. Jacob F. Seiler, who from the time of its organization has been its honored Sunday-school Superintendent, and from a date shortly after its organization has been a ruling elder in that church.

ADDRESS BY JACOB F. SEILER, Ph. D.

On the 22nd of May of the year 1858, a committee of the Carlisle Presbytery met in Harrisburg to organize a new church. At this date there were in existence in the borough two societies holding to the Presbyterian faith and polity, viz: the English Presbyterian, and a congregation of colored people now known as the Elder Street Church. Sometime in the preceding March the first-mentioned congregation had lost their church edifice by a destructive

PINE STREET PRESBYTERIAN CHURCH.
ERECTED 1859-60.

fire. At this juncture a portion of the congregation, believing that the interests of Presbyterianism and religion in general would be promoted, requested the Carlisle Presbytery to grant them a distinct and separate organization; forty-two persons bearing certificates of good and regular standing from the English Presbyterian Church, and eight others bearing similar certificates from other churches, were organized into a Presbyterian Church, according to the directions of the General Assembly. They then elected as ruling elders: Messrs Francis Weyth, H. Murray Graydon and James McCormick, Jr. On February 1, 1859, the church was incorporated by act of the Legislature under the name of the Presbyterian Church of Harrisburg. The original trustees named in the charter were: Messrs James McCormick, A. B. Warford, Charles C. Rawn, E. M. Pollock, A. Boyd Hamilton, Joseph Casey and J. Donald Cameron.

Of the fifty who presented certificates on May 22d, the following persons are still in active membership: Mrs. Francis P. Rawn, Mrs. Sarah C. Wyeth, Mrs. Elizabeth E. Sharp, Mrs. Sarah E. Forster, Mrs. Isabella H. Hamilton, Mr. J. W. Simonton, Mrs. Sarah K. Simonton, Mr. H. M. Graydon, Mr. James McCormick and myself.

On June 6th a Sabbath-school was organized with three officers, eleven teachers and forty-two scholars. Of the fourteen teachers and officers present at the formation of the Sunday-school the survivors are: Mrs. Wyeth, Mrs. Rawn, Judge Simonton, James McCormick and the writer. An extract from the first narrative of the State of religion in the church is the statement, that " of the seven persons admitted to church membership, six are from the Sunday-school."

On May 12th, 1859, the corner-stone of the church edifice was laid with appropriate ceremonies. Addresses were delivered by Rev. Robert Watts (now of Belfast), and Rev. S. T. Lowrie, of Alexandria, Va. Mr. H. M. Graydon read a statement of the steps which led to the formation of the church. Rev. A. D. Mitchell, of Paxtang, and Rev. George Morris, of Silver Spring, assisted in the devotional exercises. The stone was laid to its place by the Rev. A. G. Simonton. The church site was the same as that of the present with somewhat less extension on Third street. On the previous January the lecture-room was sufficiently furnished for temporary occupation. In August of the same year work was resumed, and that portion of the church building was completed and occupied on November 19th.

On the 22d of July, 1860, a little over two years after the organization, the congregation dedicated the church edifice to the worship of God. It was a day of joy, and an occasion of public interest. Several churches in the city closed their houses of worship so that their members could participate in the services. The Rev. P. D. Gurley, D. D., of Washington city, and Rev. N. C. Burt, D. D., of Baltimore, preached on the occasion. Meanwhile from the date of organization to January 5, 1860, a period of eighteen months, the congregation had occupied four different places for various meetings: the lecture-room of the German Reformed Church, the lecture-room of the Baptist Church—Pine and Second, the hall of the Senate, and the hall of the House of Representatives. With the completion of the church building fairly in view, it was time to call a permanent pastor. Heretofore the congregation had been served uninterruptedly by temporary supplies. The spiritual oversight of the church had meanwhile devolved largely upon the elders; of the fifty-three admitted to membership, eighteen were added on confession. This responsibility, along with the labor of procuring and providing for supplies and the conduct of week day meetings, though a labor of love, was none the less a labor. Therefore, both they and the congregation heartily welcomed our first Pastor, the Rev. W. C. Cattell, who had been unanimously called March 3, 1860, and installed September the 22d. The two great events in the church's history for the year 1860—the calling of a pastor and the dedication of the building—were the occasion of much thanksgiving and congratulation, and it was a providential appointment that the congregation had so strengthened itself to meet the excitements and strains of the Civil War. Our town was turned into an armed camp. As many as ten thousand soldiers wearing the blue were posted in the then famous Camp Curtin, and threatened to swallow up every other interest. The tramp of men and the beat of drums ceased neither week day nor Sunday. Third street then as now was the great highway. The excitement was intense. On Sabbath morning, June 28, 1863, Dr. Cattell preached to a congregation of twelve persons. The evening services were omitted. More than once during the progress of this bloody war the female teachers and older scholars went from the Sabbath-school to assist in the various hospitals or to prepare for wants that could not wait for next day. Neither were our men idle or indifferent to the voice of patriotism. For at the call of country, according to the statistics prepared by the superintendent for the twenty-fifth anniversary of the Pine Street Church, forty-nine (49) members of the Sunday-school had served in the army and navy during the Civil War. The closing words of the report for the Sabbath-school covering the year 1864 are the following: " Eight deaths are recorded, among them those of Corporal John C. Lane and William Smith, of the Fifty-fifth Regiment of Pennsylvania Volunteers, and of the same company. Smith died in hospital and Lane's death was hastened by grief over the loss of his comrade." Old people will recall the anxieties and hopes, with all the varying sensations, which characterized those trying times to State and Church. But notwithstanding these distracting scenes, the Session in its narrative of the state of religion presented April 13, 1863, say: "Our Sabbath and weekly services have been well attended, and our Sabbath-school has been largely increased. The sum of our contributions to benevolent objects, we are happy to say, is fifty per cent. larger than last year, and three times as great as the year before. We have welcomed into our number sixteen persons." " On July 19, 1863," the record further says, " Jacob F. Seiler was ordained to the eldership." The Board of Elders remained unchanged until May 22d, 1887, when the number was increased to six, by the ordination of Francis Jordan and Daniel W. Cox. After a period of three years and two months, Dr. Cattell tendered his resignation, much to the regret of the congregation, and preached his farewell sermon November 29, 1863. He had accepted the presidency of Lafayette College. On November 15, 1864,

Rev. Samuel S. Mitchell, a licentiate of the Presbytery of New Brunswick, was ordained and installed Pastor of the Pine Street Church, and so continued for four years and three months, when he resigned to accept a call to the New York Avenue Church, of Washington city. The third pastor was Addison K. Strong. He was installed on the 14th of June, 1870. Dr. Strong continued in the pastoral office for three years and eight months, when, having accepted a call from Kalamazoo, Michigan, he was released by the Presbytery February 12, 1874. Once more the church was without a pastor.

The membership of the church kept steadily growing under the care and oversight of our rather numerous pastors. Upon the resignation of Dr. Strong the net membership was three hundred and twenty-four. But the Sabbath-school had at the same time increased to a total of eight hundred and twenty-one. From 1872 to 1875 the great question was to provide accommodation for its increasing members. Prior to 1870 the Seventh Street— now Covenant—had been organized by volunteers from Pine Street. Later, about the year 1872, many of our most useful and best trained co-laborers took part in founding the Westminster Sabbath-school. Notwithstanding this spirit of colonization, the rooms were so crowded that from 1872 to 1875 the urgent question was, how to provide for our growing numbers. An effort which had originated with the Primary department met with liberal response; yet these contributions would have secured but a fraction of the bare ground. This was the prospect as the Sabbath-schools were holding their fifteenth anniversary, when the problem was solved by the generosity of a single family. The superintendent then made the gratifying announcement that Messrs. J. Donald Cameron, Henry McCormick and James McCormick would purchase ground adjoining the property, and Mrs. Eliza McCormick and Mrs. Mary Cameron would erect the buildings thereupon. The erection and equipment of this stately and substantial building cost $41,600. How far this thoughtful liberality was justified may be learned from the then existing and subsequent facts. Year by year the church had gathered from the Sabbath-school. Out of the eight hundred and seventy-five additions to the membership of the church during these thirty years, seven hundred of the accessions had been from the Sabbath-school. Total membership of Sabbath-schools 1,927.

On December 3, 1874, Rev. John R. Paxton was called to the pastorate. He was installed Sabbath evening February 28, 1875. The Rev. Dr. D. C. Marquis, of Baltimore, preaching the sermon ; Rev. T. H. Robinson, of the Market Square Church, giving the charge to the Pastor, and Dr. Cattell the charge to the people.

On the 7th of April, 1875, the new Sabbath-school building was dedicated. Addresses were made by Rev. S. A. Mutchmore, D. D., and Dr. Cattell, and the Pastor, Mr. Paxton.

The church edifice was remodeled this year and alterations made, which completely changed the interior and added largely to the comfort of the congregation.

On the 18th of June, 1878, Mr. Paxton announced his intention of asking Presbytery to dissolve the pastoral rela-

BETHANY CHAPEL.
CORNER CAMERON AND CUMBERLAND STREETS.
ERECTED 1892-93.

tions. He had received and accepted a call to the New York Avenue Church, of Washington, D. C., following his predecessor in the Pine Street Church to the same pulpit in the capital of the country. On June 20th the request was acted upon by the Presbytery, and for the fourth time in twenty years the congregation was without a pastor.

BETHANY.

As early as 1875, the initial year of Mr. Paxton's pastorate, an experimental Sunday-school was located on Herr street, above Eleventh. Their first sessions were held in an unused church building owned by a society of United Brethren. This was located beyond the canal in a community notorious for disorder and immorality, and had some features of a foreign missionary enterprise. Success began to attend the effort, and in the year 1881 a substantial brick building was erected at the corner of Eleventh and Herr streets. The society was incorporated under the name of Bethany Presbyterian Sabbath-School, and the title to the property was vested in the trustees of the Pine Street Presbyterian Church. Mr. Samuel C. Donovan was the principal promoter of this last and very successful enterprise. Since December, 1884, Mr. Henry McCormick, jr., has been the acceptable superintendent. Prosperity attended the enthusiastic devotion and constancy of its officers and teachers to such a degree that it was necessary to erect a larger building. A new and beautiful edifice was built on the corner of Cameron (formerly Eleventh) and Cumberland streets. The last official report places the number of officers, teachers and scholars at 475. As yet there is no church organization.

The present Pastor, Rev. George S. Chambers, was called September 11, 1879, accepted the call in October, and installed November 11th of the same year.

During Dr. Chamber's pastorate there has been added to the church upon confession 427 persons; by certificate. 185; a total of 612 accessions. The present membership, on the 1st of January, 1894, was 724.

Since May 22, 1858, to this date, 867 persons have been admitted to church membership upon confession; and 631 by certificate; a total of 1,498. The amount of money contributed during these thirty-five years by the Pine Street Church is as follows:

To Home Missions, ...	$53,012 41
" Foreign Missions, ...	43,772 21
" Education,	14,437 01
" Publication, ...	3,344 50
" Church Erection, ...	12,450 56
" Ministerial Relief,	13,712 10
" Freedmen, ...	6,074 52
" Sustenation, ...	11,077 89
" General Assembly Fund, ...	1,015 00
" Congregational Purposes, ...	227,096 27
" Memorial Fund in 1871, ...	12,380 00
" Aid to Colleges, ...	36,881 46
" Miscellaneous Charities, ...	161,615 02
Total, ...	$596,868 95

Thus in accordance with the request of your committee, I have endeavored to set forth the past work of the Pine Street Church. Of the present work something ought to be briefly said. In the city of New York and elsewhere certain ecclesiastical societies have been called " Institutional Churches," a designation which characterizes a religious society which conducts not only purely spiritual exercises, but which also operates other agencies, such as educational, or physical, or which administers to merely pleasurable emotions by furnishing food to the hungry and amusement to the restless temptable crowd. It may be that Pine Street will get there in time. But at present she employs such agencies for her improvement, and that of the community at large, as Missionary Societies, Mission Bands for Home and Foreign work, Sewing Schools for the betterment of our neighbors' children, Mothers' Meeting for comfort and encouragement of over-worked mothers, Choral Societies, and a Boys' Choir to lend their trained voices on occasions ordinary and extraordinary, and of course a well organized and enthusiastic Christian Endeavor Society, a Beneficial Society for the promotion of thrift and honorable support against the day of adversity, besides her Home and Branch Sabbath-Schools in which Pine Street feels a proper pride. These agencies leave little talent unemployed. The Sewing Schools of Pine Street and Bethany have on their rolls 300 scholars, and the " mothers " of the two societies number 200, an aggregate of 500 to be instructed, cared for and comforted. All this imposes a great responsibility upon any church committed to such enterprises. But good organization and capable management, developed by gradual experience, has secured happy results under the blessing of God.

In complying with the committee's request to " represent

the Pine Street Church in an address in which the work of
that church, past and present, should be set forth," it seemed
necessary to enter into such details of statement as to furnish a historical narrative, based upon reliable records of
figures and facts. The sketch may savor of vanity, but it is
written in no such spirit. I am aware that spiritual results,
which are the most valuable, cannot be expressed by figures.
Bible study, power in prayer, a faithful ministry, modest
service, and true consecration cannot be placed in tabulated
columns. If the Pine Street Church has not manifested
these graces, she has learned little of her Master and failed
to catch the spirit of the mother church, which has set her
a noble example of liberal giving, pure devotion, and manifold works of love and zeal which have adorned the history
of the Market Square Church throughout the hundred years
of her sturdy and fruitful existence.

NOTE.—The writer of this article is entitled for many of the facts
to a discourse prepared and delivered by the Rev. George S. Chambers, D. D., on May 20, 1883, on the occasion of the twenty-fifth anniversary of the Pine Street Presbyterian Church.

Mr. West announced hymn No. 93, vs. 1, 3, and the congregation, having risen, joined heartily in the singing.

> Saviour, blessed Saviour,
>   Listen whilst we sing,
> Hearts and voices raising
>   Praises to our King.
> All we have to offer,
>   All we hope to be,
> Body, soul, and spirit,
>   All we yield to thee.

Great and ever greater
Are thy mercies here,
True and everlasting
Are the glories there,
Where no pain, or sorrow,
Toil, or care, is known,
Where the angel-legions
Circle round thy throne.

The PRESIDENT OF THE EVENING. Notwithstanding the loss sustained in the burning of its church edifice and the outgoing of the Pine Street Church in 1858, the Market Square Church addressed itself to missionary work in the city and was principally instrumental in the organization of the Elder Street Church. Though it has never been large in number, that church has always exercised great power and influence among the people of that race in our city. Mr. Cassius M. Brown, an elder of that church, will now address us.

ADDRESS BY Mr. CASSIUS M. BROWN.

We are glad to unite with you, and to bring gratefully to you, our garland of praise at this Centennial celebration, as we recollect what you have been and are to us as a race and church in the city of Harrisburg, as you review your seed-times and harvests, your summers and winters, your warfare and victory. In His name have you gone forth into this community to do, to dare, to die, if need be, for His work and worth. In His name you come rejoicing with all of your offspring, bidding them welcome, asking them to bring some signs of the coming of His kingdom. Our presence here is a sign, suggestive, helpful; founded upon principle instead of policy, far reaching in its bearings and consequences, awaiting greater reproduction to the glory of God, our Father and Friend, and to the better Christian development of many of his sons and daughters in many communities within the territory of our Presbytery, Synod and General Assembly. And if our presence is a sign of the coming of His kingdom, surely the origin, growth and present outlook of the Elder Street Presbyterian Church and Sabbath-school are equally and even more significant to this end. A church founded upon the Bible as the only rule of faith and practice must produce the very best type of Christianity in many of its members. It is not surprising, therefore, that as early as 1828 God put it into the heart of a Christian hero, in the person of Mr. Alexander Sloan, of precious memory, a member of your church, to begin teaching a class of boys in the old Methodist church, which then stood upon the corner of Third and Mulberry streets. Three years later, in 1831, this class was removed to the Presbyterian church, on Second street, and there the work was continued until 1836. For nearly twenty years longer there was no organized effort to teach the colored people of this community.

The unsettled condition of the Church brought about by the crisis of 1837–38 may have diverted the attention of many of God's children from more important work. The Methodist Church having removed to the corner of South street and Tanners avenue there had been some effort put forth to organize a Sabbath-school, but it resulted in failure. This fact came to the ears of some of the former teachers,

ELDER STREET CHURCH.
CORNER CAPITOL AND FORSTER SRTEETS.
ERECTED 1881.

and, the Holy Spirit leading them forward with some others, upon the 17th of April, 1855, they organized The Union Sabbath-School Association of Harrisburg. At the end of two years' labor the basement of the church was too small for the work, and a room, belonging to the German Reformed Church, corner of Third and Chestnut streets, was secured. In the autumn of the same year, 1857, the colored public school building, upon West avenue, was occupied by the school; and in 1858 they removed to the old armory, on West Walnut street, at the northeast corner of the Haldeman property. Up until 1871 the school retained the name of Union, since which time it has been known as the Sabbath-school of the Second, or of the Elder Street Presbyterian Church.

From a little pamphlet written by one of the elders of the church, Mr. George H. Imes, who departed this life about two years ago, we are indebted for the following compilation and words of commendation of the men and women to whom, above all others, we are indebted for religious training, as founded upon the word and works of Christ. At the head of this list of teachers who gave their time and talents to this work stand Mr. and Mrs. Alexander Sloan, Messrs. John C. Capp, George Capp, Alexander Graydon, Sr., John A. Weir, Mordecai McKinney, R. Jackson Fleming, Alfred Armstrong and Mrs. Alfred Armstrong, Mrs. Dr. W. W. Rutherford, Mrs. R. Jackson Fleming, Mrs. Harriet L. Westbrook, Mrs. Sanders, Mrs. Bucher, Mrs. Rachael Fenn, Mrs Lydia Ingram, Mrs. Devout and Rev. A. G. Simonton and sisters, Miss Agnes Crain, Miss Matilda Elder, Miss Boyd, Miss Bucher and Miss Graybill. Others may have labored in this part of the Lord's vineyard whose names we have not mentioned. They were all, whether mentioned or not, a noble army of martyrs, doing their duty as unto Christ and not unto man. For, in speaking of the conditions under which this work began and continued, Mr. George II. Imes says: "It is to be remembered that this work began in the midst of the terrific conflict over slavery. The courage that led and the fortitude that sustained these noble men and women command our highest admiration and praise. The hate toward them was quite as bitter as against those whom God saw fit to make of a different color. These lovers of Christ and of men taught amid this madness lessons of religion and true liberty. God's messengers were they in the gloom of the slave and the peril of the free, shedding holy rays from the inextinguishable light of the world." During the period from 1828 to 1876 the total enrollment of pupils was 3,250, the amount of money contributed $2,300. A large number have become teachers, and the most accurate record we could obtain shows nearly 1,500 who are active members in some church. Since 1876 the work has been kept up in the Sabbath-school, and many have been added to the kingdom of God through the precious truths of the Bible by which they know in whom and what they have believed. At present there are twelve officers and twelve teachers in the Sabbath-school, with an average attendance of about one hundred.

In 1858 the work in the Sabbath-school had produced a Presbyterian church. In the "Annals of Harrisburg" we have the following record: "About the 10th of September, 1857, Mr. Joseph C. Bustill, at the instance of Hon. Mor-

decai McKinney, of Harrisburg, called the attention of
Rev. Charles W. Gardner, of Philadelphia, to the necessity
of forming an additional Presbyterian church in Harrisburg. Induced by this representation Rev. Mr. Gardner,
visited Harrisburg on the 20th of September and conferred
with Rev. Dr. W. R. DeWitt and Rev. Thomas H. Robinson, and the Presbyterians of the first church upon the
subject, who experienced a lively interest in the matter,
and promised to extend liberal aid to the enterprise, provided a suitable place for worship could be procured."
The great financial troubles which at this period prevailed
throughout the country, however, caused a suspension of the
project until the spring of 1858, at which time several
members of the proposed congregation rented the large
and commodious room in the second story of the brick
building at the southwest corner of Walnut street and
River alley which was fitted up as a place of worship for
the congregation. Therein divine services were held every
Sabbath under the direction of the Reverend Doctors
DeWitt and Robinson.

The congregation thus formed invited the Rev. Charles
W. Gardner, who had returned to Philadelphia, to undertake charge of the work. This gentleman accepted the
invitation and arrived in Harrisburg April the 9th, and
preached his first sermon on Sabbath, April 11th, 1858. On
the 14th of October of the same year, the congregation sent
a petition to the Presbytery of Harrisburg asking to be
regularly organized, which was granted. On the 27th ·of
the same month a committee of the Presbytery met at the
church in Walnut street to perform that duty. The Rev.

William R. DeWitt, D. D., presided   An appropriate sermon was preached by the Rev. Conway P. Wing, D. D.,
from the following text, "And I say also unto thee, That
thou art Peter, and upon this rock I will build my church;
and the gates of hell shall not prevail against it " (Matt. 16:
18).   The Rev. James Calder, since deceased, of the Fourth
Street Bethel Church, was present and offered an impressive
prayer.

At 7 o'clock p. m., the following named persons were duly
organized into a church, viz: Jeremiah Kelly, Hannah
Kelly, Hiram Baker, Nancy Christy, Matilda Greenly,
Zillah Galloway, Sarah Hawkins, Curry Taylor, Sr., Elizabeth Taylor, William White, Sarah Kelly and Hannah
Humphreys, all of whom were received upon profession of
faith, except Nancy Christy, who presented a certificate from
the Presbyterian church, of Mercersburg, Pa.   Jeremiah
Kelly and Hiram Baker were respectively ordained as ruling elders.   The Second Presbyterian Church of Harrisburg
was chosen as a name for the new organizatton.   After the
organization of the church, addresses were made by Rev.
William R. DeWitt, D. D., Rev. Conway P. Wing, D. D.,
and Rev. John W. Davis.   The church made immediate
application to the Presbytery to be supplied with ministerial
services for the ensuing six months, whereupon the Rev.
Charles W. Gardner was selected to supply them.

The history of the Presbytery of Carlisle has the
following record of pastors and stated supplies down to
the present:

Rev. Chas. W. Gardner, S. S., 1858–1863.

Hiram Baker,* S. S., 1863–1869.

Rev. J. H. Cole, S. S., 1870–1872.

Rev. Hiram Baker, Pastor, 1872–1875.

Rev. Isaac W. Davenport, Pastor, 1875–1877.

Rev. George M. Bonner, Pastor, 1877–1883.

Rev. Lawrence Miller, Pastor, 1884–1885.

Rev. Reuben H. Armstrong, Pastor, 1886–

The Elder Street Presbyterian congregation has had two church buildings. The first was a frame structure. Not quite as large as the present building, located on the same lot on the southwest corner of Elder, now Capitol, and Forster streets. It was erected in 1866. The second, a substantial stone building with a seating capacity of about three hundred which was built in 1881, a year after the first building was burned. During the interim that intervened between the burning of the first and the building of the second structure, the congregation, through the Christian fraternity of the Pine Street Presbyterian Church, worshiped in their lecture room. We record this with most grateful remembrance of the same, and of other substantial and liberal aid extended to our congregation by the above church and many of its most active members.

Feeling that we have probably taken more than our share of your precious time we close with a statement, slightly modified, made by our present pastor upon another occasion. During thirty-six years the Elder Street Presbyterian Church has been preaching the blessed gospel of the Son of

---

*He was one of the first Elders of this church. He subsequently studied for the Ministry of the Gospel, and in 1863 was licensed by the Presbytery of Harrisburg to preach.—EDITOR.

God to a most needy people, a people that the Presbyterian church can and must reach, both North and South, East and West, if she believes her doctrines to be Biblical, as she does, and is ready to defend. She is a church, therefore, adapted to all people, the rich and the poor, the learned and the illiterate. The Elder Street Church has done a work in this community which can never be fully described nor appreciated in this life. Over two hundred have united with the church, while thousands have been taught in the Sabbath-school, helped, cheered and led to Christ by the ministry of her pastors and stated supplies, that are not members of our communion or denomination, but of a greater communion, fellowship with God, with Christ and with the Holy Spirit. We come to you, therefore, with grateful hearts. We come from the field of battle, not upon our shields, but with them in our hands, the Presbyterian shields, which have served us in many conflicts, not less because they are of the blue stocking material, but more because they are Biblical, and are used in His name, to His glory. If we are thankful to God for the past, with its fruitage ; if we rejoice at our present vantage ground, if we are hopeful for the future and will follow where He leads, " keeping close to Jesus all the way," no mind can conceive, no pen can picture what shall be your glory, who gave us being. We rejoice with you, whom our Father has highly honored in this community, and bid you God speed.

At this date, February 14th, 1894, the following are the officers and membership of Elder Street Church and Sabbath-school :

Rev. Reuben H. Armstrong, Pastor ; Thomas J. Miller,

William J. Adore, Cassius M. Brown, Turner Cooper Sr.,, and Walter W. Williams, Elders; James W. H. Howard, John Zedricks, Henry Coslow, W. W. Williams, Turner Cooper, Jr., Singleton G. Brown, Trustees.

Communicant members, sixty-five, Sabbath-school membership enrolled, one hundred and twenty-five.

The PRESIDENT OF THE EVENING. In 1866, under the leadership of Dr. Curwen, then superintendent of the Lunatic Hospital and a member of the Pine Street Church, the church which was known until lately as the Seventh Street Church was organized. For long years Dr. Curwen was the sole elder and almost the sole supporter of the church. On account of the location, it never prospered to any large extent, but since a more eligible site has been secured and the church has been removed, new prosperity seems to find entrance to those engaged in that work. So that we trust there is before it a prosperous and successful future. God in his providence recently took away the beloved pastor of that church, and this evening the representative of it in the person of Mr. Samuel H. Garland, an elder, will give us a short account of its history.

ADDRESS BY MR. SAMUEL H. GARLAND.

In the year of our Lord 1865, Dr. John Curwen conceived the idea of organizing a Presbyterian church in the extreme western suburbs of Harrisburg. Accordingly ground was secured and a building erected on the site of what is now known as the corner of Seventh and Peffer streets.

The church building was completed and ready for occupancy on July 21, 1866. The vicinity of the church property was but thinly settled and the congregation consisted chiefly of inmates and attendants of the insane hospital of which Dr. Curwen was then superintendent.

This church was then known as the Seventh Street Presbyterian Church, of Harrisburg.

Prior to this at a meeting of the Presbytery of Carlisle, held in the Big Spring Church, of Newville, April 11, 1866, a committee* was appointed to organize a church in Harrisburg, provided the way to accomplish this end be clear. The committee met for this purpose Saturday, September 8, 1866, and an organization was effected, the following persons presenting letters: Dr. John Curwen and wife, Annie Stewart, Mary Stewart, Mary McCullom and Eliza M· Todd from the church of Harrisburg; Dr. Graydon B. Hotchkin and wife from the church of Middletown, Delaware county, and Mrs. Margaret Cassady from the Presbyterian church of Letter-Kenny, Ireland. These certificates having been found in order, the committee passed the following resolution:

"*Resolved,* That the above persons, nine in all, be and are constituted into a church, to be known as the Seventh Street Presbyterian Church, of Harrisburg; to be connected with and under the government of the Presbytery of Carlisle, Synod of Baltimore and General Assembly of the Presbyterian Church of the United States of America."

A congregational meeting was immediately called for the

---

*The Committee consisted of Rev. James Harper, D. D., Rev. J. C. Bliss, Rev. Samuel S. Mitchell, Rev. A. D. Mitchell, Elders H. Murray Graydon and James Elder. Mr. Bliss and Mr. Elder failed to serve.—EDITOR.

COVENANT PRESBYTERIAN CHURCH.
CORNER FIFTH AND PEFFER STREETS.
ERECTED 1894.

purpose of electing a ruling elder; Dr. Curwen was unanimously chosen for that office. Of the original members, but one name, that of Dr. Curwen, remains on the church roll. He is still a ruling elder and takes an active interest in the church work at the present time, although having his residence at Warren. Soon after the organization of the church a Sabbath-school was organized; a corps of teachers coming from the older churches in the city, assisted greatly in making the Sabbath-school a success, and were a power in upbuilding the church congregation.

The church was served by different ministers,* until the spring of 1868, when the Rev. Charles A. Wyeth began to act as stated supply, serving in that capacity for two years, when a meeting of the congregation was called March 5th, 1870, at which he was unanimously elected regular pastor.

Accepting this flattering vote of the church for a continuance of his labors, he was duly installed on the 26th of June, 1870, serving for thirteen years in this capacity. The Presbytery dissolved the pastoral relation at his request, June 12th, 1883. Mr. Wyeth removed to Warren, and died there August 2d, 1889. His name and memory are held in the highest esteem by those of our church who knew him as its pastor.

A memorial window has been placed in our new edifice in his memory.

Owing to the removal of Dr. Curwen to Warren, and to the withdrawal of many of the workers in our church who

---

* These were Rev. Ambrose C. Smith, now of Fairfield, Iowa ; Rev. Stephen W. Pomeroy, now of Mill Hall, Pa.., and Rev. William A. McAtee, now of Danville, Pa.—EDITOR.

were members of the older churches, upon the departure of Dr. Wyeth, the tide of prosperous Presbyterianism seemed sadly on the ebb in West Harrisburg at this time.

Fortunately the church had remaining a few unshattered hopes in the person of Mr. J. M. Stewart, Mr. David Dunlap and Mr. William Wolfe. These three, whose interest in restoring the church work to its former prosperity was unflagging, held a conference with Mr. Gilbert M. McCauley, an elder in the Market Square Church, and a man of untiring energy, which gave new life and inspiration to the work of re-organization.

The services of Mr. John H. Groff, a member of Market Square Church, were secured as supply for the pulpit. Teachers for the Sabbath-school offered their services once more, and they were gratefully accepted. These devoted persons served in this way until the fall of 1887, when the church was enabled to supply teachers of its own, and in this manner the work was greatly revived.

Mr. John H. Groff served the church until the spring of 1886, at which time he took charge of the Steelton and Middletown churches. His earnest Christian character coupled with a loving, sympathetic nature, left him many fast friends in the church and Sabbath-school.

During the summer of 1886 the church was very acceptably supplied by the Rev. Matthew Rutherford, a student in Allegheny Theological Seminary, and now Pastor of the church at Avalon, Pa.

In the month of July, 1887, Rev. I. Potter Hayes began his ministry, and with convincing eloquence and untiring effort he aroused the congregation to a sense of their personal obligations.

The church was re-carpeted, painted and papered, a new organ purchased and the Sabbath-school made self-supporting. But it soon became evident, on account of the encroachment of the Pennsylvania railroad yards, with the noise and confusion incident thereto, that the progress of the church work must be greatly retarded. With his usual energy Mr. Hayes set about securing another location. Here again Dr. Curwen showed that amid his manifold duties as Superintendent of the Warren Hospital, he still held the interest of this church at heart, and came nobly to its assistance. A fine plot of ground, corner of Fifth and Peffer streets, the present location of the church was secured, and the church removed to its new location August, 1888, and its named changed from that of Seventh Street Presbyterian Church to Covenant Presbyterian Church.

Here the work of the church was greatly enlarged, in the midst of a growing community. The pastor and people were kept busy re-organizing the Sabbath-school and other work to meet their pressing needs. The work of God's spirit began to manifest itself and the long and arduous work of pastor and people began to bear fruit. A few months before Mr. Hayes removed to Wrightsville a gracious revival took place and many were brought to Christ. More than two score of people were at this time added to the church. Mr. Hayes served the church until March 15th, 1891, when he took charge of the church at Wrightsville. Mr. Hayes's work was of the highest order. Having found the church in a poor location with a meager working force, he had the satisfaction of seeing his efforts crowned with success; the church having been removed to one of the most desirable locations in the city, its membership united and largely increased—the working force was almost doubled—two ruling elders having been added, thus increasing the number of elders to five; the board of trustees having been re-organized and increased to five. Thus he left the church in excellent condition for future work.

But the church had many trials before it, and not the least of its many was the selection of a pastor. Finally at a congregational meeting held May 1st, 1891, Rev. Charles A. Evans was given a call. Mr. Evans took charge of the work and served as a supply until October 1st, 1892, when he removed to Rochester, New York.

The church was again thrown upon its own resources, a flock without an under-shepherd. However, at a meeting held January 13, 1893, the Rev. Robert Cochran was elected Pastor. Mr. Cochran was well known to most of the members of our church and was well received. He took up the work in a vigorous way, entering into it with his whole heart and being sustained by his people. The church began to revive, and with the advent of each communion service, the church received additional names to its roll. The Sabbath-school, with a Primary department, was brought to a high position of influence and usefulness. The result of the work done there bringing many to Christ and into the membership of the church. The Christian Endeavor Society was re-organized and is at present doing faithful and efficient work among the young people of the church and community. Mr. Cochran's work was of the evangelistic order, his earnest efforts being to point his hearers to Christ. In this work he was signally successful. He gave himself to the Lord and the Lord used him for the upbuilding of his cause.

It soon became evident to the Church Session that more room was necessary for Sabbath-school and church work. After due consideration it was decided to appoint a building committee, empowering them to do what to them seemed best in the way of improvements. The result of their deliberations and labors is our new and beautiful church edifice, including a model Sabbath-school room.

Mr. Cochran was untiring in his efforts to secure for us this new home. That the work of progress was hampered in our old building was not the only reason that we were inspired to erect a new and larger building. By the law of competition, mixed with a little pardonable Presbyterian pride, we were compelled, in view of the growth of the community and churches of other denominations in our vicinity, to keep pace with our neighbors and make our surroundings as comfortable and pleasant as theirs. Therefore our pastor and people determined to make a strong and united effort to secure better facilities whereby to carry forward our work. The work of building was begun July, 1893, and was pushed forward rapidly. All our people were looking forward eagerly for its completion. Already plans had been laid by our pastor for the extension of the work. The fond dreams of our people seemed about to be realized, when suddenly, like a thunderbolt out of a clear sky, a great cloud rested on our church and people. That dread disease, typhoid fever, laid its grasp on our beloved pastor and leader, when apparently in robust health. In his pastoral work this malignant disease had no terrors for him. He did not hesitate to enter the afflicted homes to minister to those who were its sufferers.

Having consecrated himself to the Master's work, he had placed his life in the Master's keeping, and when called, he was ready with the answer, " Speak, Lord, thy servant heareth." The Master in his infinite wisdom removed him from his labors October 15, 1893. Our people bowing their heads in sorrowful submission, said, " Thy will be done, not ours, O Lord." For a time it seemed that we could not withstand the shock occasioned by this severe blow, but we turned to his word and met with the passage, " Whom the Lord loveth he chasteneth." Taking up the work again we were greatly encouraged by our Moderator, Rev. D. M. Skilling, who was appointed by Presbytery immediately after the death of our Pastor.

Mr. Cochran, by his earnest Christian example, furnished a fine object lesson to his people and the community of what a thoroughly consecrated man can do. Having by precept and example, endeavored to lead his people near to Christ, when he was so suddenly called away, he left them a united praying people, ready to do the Master's work whenever called upon to do it. The large and beautiful memorial window erected to his memory in our new church was placed there by his brother ministers of the Presbytery.

Our past has been an eventful one, and one full of affliction, but we think we can see a break in the clouds. Our church is practically finished and furnished at a cost of $8,500.00. This is not all provided for, and owing to the stringency of the times, the money is coming in slowly. But we have faith that ways and means will be provided in the not far future to cover our indebtedness. With the debt properly secured we expect to dedicate our church in the early spring.

At a meeting held January 3d, 1894, the Rev. Curtis O. Bosserman, a student in the Senior class of Princeton Theological Seminary and a licentiate of this Presbytery, was given a unanimous call. Mr. Bosserman comes to us highly recommended by his Professors, and our people are ready and anxious to labor with him in the upbuilding of the Master's kingdom.

With a new and modern church building, a united and working congregation, a live Sabbath-school, having a good circulating library, a consecrated Christian Endeavor Society, a well organized and thoroughly equipped Ladies' Aid Society, a strong choir, and a talented and consecrated minister, we anticipate, and pray for, a bright future for Covenant Church.

The PRESIDENT OF THE EVENING. On the first Sabbath of February, 1873, under the auspices of the Market Square and Pine Street Churches, with Doctors Robinson and Strong at their head, mission work was undertaken in Harrisburg. Services were held in the evening in a room at the market-house on Broad street and in the morning in the Chapel at Lochiel. In the following June an organization was effected in the upper part of the city. That is just twenty-one years ago, and the church is of age, and, therefore, can speak for itself in the person of its present pastor, Rev. George S. Duncan.

ADDRESS BY REV. GEORGE S. DUNCAN.

. The Westminster Church to the Market Square Church " which is in God the Father and in the Lord Jesus Christ: Grace be unto you, and peace from God our Father and the Lord Jesus Christ." We remember " without ceasing your work of faith, and labor of love, and patience of hope in our Lord Jesus Christ, in the sight of God and our Father." As you enter the second century of your history, " may the Lord bless thee and keep thee; may the Lord make his face shine upon thee; may the Lord lift up his countenance upon thee, and give thee peace." Amen.

It seems fitting on this Centennial occasion that a brief history of the Westminster Church should be given. Its organization was due to the joint efforts of the Pine Street and Market Square Churches. In the year 1866 there is said to have been but one church above North street in this city. It was felt by many that some form of Christian work should be done in the northwest portion of the town. The population was steadily growing year by year and there were no churches in the community.

The Young Men's Christian Association, in January, 1867, organized a Sunday-school on the second floor of the stone market hall on Broad street. The officers and teachers were mostly young men, members of the Association. The Sunday-school was undenominational. There were about twenty-five present at the first session. The first superintendent was Mr. J. Samuel Detweiler, now a

WESTMINSTER PRESBYTERIAN CHURCH.

CORNER GREEN AND REILY STREETS.

ERECTED 1893-94.

Charles W. Bolton,
Architect

minister of the Lutheran Church. The school steadily grew in numbers and others, both young men and women, joined the number of workers. The quarters then occupied were found to be wholly too small and the public school house on the corner of Second and Broad streets was rented. The Sunday-school now had about one hundred and fifty scholars. Mr. John A. Borland was the second superintendent. This place also was soon found to be insufficient to seat the members of this growing school. Another flitting took place to the public school building at 126 Broad street. Here the Sunday-school numbered about three hundred scholars. The third superintendent was Mr. Walter F. Fahnestock, Sr., a member of Market Square Church. He was succeeded by Mr. Martin Stutzman.

Both churches felt that a Presbyterian church was needed in this portion of Harrisburg, and at once took measures to provide for preaching services. My beloved predecessor in the Westminster pastorate, the Rev. William A. West, was called to the work, and began his labors on the evening of February 2d, 1873. At this first preaching service there were about seven adults and a dozen of mission school boys. The preaching service was held every Sunday evening in the rooms of the market hall. At a meeting of the Presbytery of Carlisle held in Newville on June 10th, 1873, a paper signed by forty-seven persons residing in West Harrisburg was presented, asking the appointment of a committee to visit the field and organize a church if the way be clear. The request was granted, and Rev. Addison K. Strong, D. D., Rev. Thomas H. Robinson, D. D., Rev. Charles A. Wyeth, with Ruling Elders James McCormick,

John A. Weir and John Curwen were appointed a committee. The committee met on Thursday evening, June 19th, 1873, in the rooms over the old Market Hall, and after appropriate religious services proceeded to organize a church in the usual manner. Thirty-one persons were enrolled on certificate from other churches, and four were received on profession of their faith. Four elders were elected, namely, John L. Crist, Robert Trotter, William Jones and John E. Patterson. These were ordained on September 25th.

At a congregational meeting held on September 11th the name Westminster Presbyterian Church was adopted. The first communion service was held on September 28th. The need of a church edifice was keenly felt if the congregation was to prosper. A plot of ground on the northeast corner of Reily and Green streets was donated by Miss Rebecca L. Reily, a member of Market Square Church. Here a two-story brick chapel, thirty-three by seventy-three feet, was erected in the summer of 1874. After worshiping for one year and nine months in the old market hall rooms, the congregation moved into their new building, which was formally opened on the evening of October 27, 1874. Here the congregation and Sunday-school steadily grew in numbers.

Rev. William A. West resigned his charge at Westminster at the spring meeting of Presbytery in 1890. Immediately thereafter the present pastor, Rev. George S. Duncan, was called to and accepted the pastorate. His installation took place on the evening of July 1, 1890. It soon became evident that if the work was to prosper a large and attractive church building was necessary. At the annual congregational meeting in February, 1892, it was unanimously decided to take steps for the erection of a new church building. The designs submitted by Charles W. Bolton, of Philadelphia, were accepted and work on the new edifice was begun in August, 1892. The corner-stone was laid on November 26, 1892, when all the Presbyterian ministers took part in the services. The work has gone on ever since and in a few weeks the church will be completed. The dedication services will be held in May. The edifice is of undressed brown stone from the Walton quarries at Hummelstown and built in the Gothic style of architecture. The main audience room will seat 1,200 people, including the gallery, which is entered by two large stairways. Back of the pulpit is the choir and organ chamber, which is enclosed with a handsome arcade. The floor slopes toward the pulpit and the seats are arranged in arcs of circles. The audience room will be finished in oak. To the right of the preacher standing in the pulpit is the Sunday-school building, all of which can be thrown into full view of the pulpit by opening roller blinds. The first floor has a main Sunday-school room, infant room, two class rooms and a library. There is also a gallery with four class room, all of which can be thrown into the main room when occasion requires. The basement under the Sunday-school room will be fitted up with a kitchen, dining room and a reading room, to be open every evening. When the new building is completed a new era will dawn for the congregation, for the work, heretofore for lack of room, has been very much crippled. The growth of the city in the northwest end of Harrisburg will also be a most important factor in the success of the church.

Every department of the church is in a most flourishing condition. The ruling elders are John E. Patterson, William Jones, David R. Elder, J. Wallace Elder and John E. Daniel. The trustees are Harry Miller, J. Nelson Clark, W. S. Black, M. G. Baker, George E. Hackett, A. B. Tack, Wm. A. Moorehead.

The PRESIDENT OF THE EVENING. The Olivet Church in East Harrisburg is the youngest of the family of Presbyterian churches, and it is an important field that they occupy. We trust it has a future of great usefulness and of great prosperity. The pastor, Mr. William P. Patterson, will give a sketch of that church.

ADDRESS BY REV. WILLIAM P. PATTERSON.

Mr. CHAIRMAN, BRETHREN AND FRIENDS OF THE MARKET SQUARE CHURCH: I esteem it a privilege to represent, as I do to-night, the little church upon Allison's Hill; and I wish to say in the very beginning of my remarks that, in the offering of the very hearty congratulations of this most joyous Centennial season, the pastor, officers and members of the Olivet congregation desire to have no small share.

We join with the entire Presbyterian community in rendering sincere thanks to an all-good and gracious God, that this anniversary occasion is permitted to transpire; and we would praise Him, with heart and voice, for His favor during these two jubilees of years, and for the rare success, in His cause, He has enabled His people to achieve. We are deeply impressed with the fact that here a church of Jesus

Christ, a congregation in our beloved communion, has been drawn together to engage in the pure worship of Almighty God for the space of a century. We think of the hundreds of Sabbaths in that century, of the heavenly atmosphere encompassing the people of God as, obedient to the divine command, they have assembled to reverence Him, and to seek His guidance and blessing in the varied walks of the daily life.

We rejoice greatly in the amount of truth, profitable for doctrine, for reproof, and for instruction in righteousness, which has been proclaimed in the thousands of sermons and other religious discourses delivered here. Hallowed spot, verily where the voice of instruction, of admonition, of comfort, and of peace has been so long heard !

And with what an atmosphere of prayer are we surrounded to-night! Can it be that the prayers of God's people spend their force in the moment of their utterance at the throne of grace? It can not be. We believe, and truly, that their influence avails not only in securing present benefits, but also those for the days to come—their influence extends far into the future. Hence, the place whereon we stand is holy ground, consecrated by the agonizing, earnest, trustful petitions of our spiritual ancestors.

We think of the many times in which the command of love has been here obeyed—times when the followers of the Redeemer have delighted to draw near the sacramental feast, and to receive in faith the bread and the cup, emblematic of a Saviour's broken body and shed blood. They are not with us now in the body, it is true, but have passed joyfully and triumphantly into the better land, where they are enjoying the marriage supper of the lamb—nevertheless, as often as we ourselves are privileged to partake of the sweet memorials of love, we do indeed realize the communion of the saints, we feel as if drawn into special fellowship with those who have gone before.

How enrapturing the thought, that the time is rapidly approaching when the entire sacramental host, the redeemed of God, who have met here and elsewhere to worship God even with the imperfections of our human nature, shall be gathered in the temple not made with hands, there to unite in the thrilling anthem of that service in which they rest not, day nor night, praising God!

Olivet Church, as is well known, is the youngest in the Presbyterian family of churches in Harrisburg. Availing myself of the historical material at hand, I may be allowed to note briefly the origin of the infant congregation, and something of the work already accomplished within its bounds.

Referring, then, first of all, to the Year Book of the Market Square Church for the year 1888, I find it stated, that of two important movements of which this venerable church was already interested, one was the fostering of a Presbyterian enterprise on Allison's Hill, and that the Pine Street Church shared largely in such interest and care. On Tuesday, 22d November, 1887, the Presbyterians residing on Allison's Hill organized a Presbyterian association and inaugurated a prayermeeting. The secretary of that association, writing in the December issue of *The Church and Home*, just one month following the starting of the prayermeeting, says with deep significance, " we feel that the first month's experience of this meeting reveals that it is needed and enjoyed by the people in this portion of the city. Such is our distance from our churches it is with difficulty that any of us can attend the Wednesday evening meetings, and some of us are utterly unable to do so. This meeting gives us a weekly prayermeeting which we all felt we needed. May we be blest in this effort to do for ourselves, and the portion of the city in which we live. We desire the prayers of the members for our prosperity." If any justification for such a movement were required, we surely have it in this utterance, and it might well have secured for the new movement the perpetual sympathetic interest of those whose prayers are here so eagerly craved.

Not quite a year later we find that the association and prayermeeting, so auspiciously begun, no longer capable of being accommodated in the homes on the hill, has developed into a flourishing Sabbath-school, and obliged to take refuge in a church building on Derry and Kittatinny streets, providentially offering itself at the time. That is to say, on the 14th of October, 1888, in the church building referred to, a Sabbath-school was duly organized under the name of the Olivet Presbyterian Sabbath-school. The school was organized with eighty-two scholars, fourteen teachers and six officers. At the organization there were present Revs. George B. Stewart, D. D., Geo. S. Chambers, D. D., and W. H. Logan, Presbyterial missionary, all of whom spoke encouragingly to the school, and wished the organizers of the new movement God's blessing.

From this point onward, in addition to the invariable prayer service of each Tuesday evening, the occasional preaching of the Word was enjoyed. The entire work was a union movement of the Market Square and Pine Street Churches, and under the direction and control of a joint committee from the two Sessions. So pronounced was the growth of this new enterprise in the few months following, that on Sabbath, May 19th, 1889, Mr. Robert Cochran, of the Western Theological Seminary, at Allegheny, on invitation, took charge of the work, the Sabbath-school, which had been organized with only eighty-two members, having increased about ninety-three per cent.

It may be mentioned here, parenthetically, as an interesting item in this history, that Governor James A. Beaver had become very deeply concerned in the success of the young enterprise, and was now conducting an adult Bible class of thirty-five persons, who had banded themselves together for the purpose of benevolent operations among the poor, and also to assist in bringing adults and children into the Sabbath-school. The Bible-class work which Governor Beaver thus began is now very energetically continued by Mr. A. C. Stamm.

In July of this year we find the Sabbath-school numbering two hundred and fifty-one scholars, of whom between seventy-five and one hundred are in the Primary department; and so crowded are the quarters, that it is determined to erect a building at the rear of the church and connect with it for the better accommodation of the Bible and Primary classes. With the cordial assistance of interested friends that object was attained. In August of the same year a petition for an independent church organization was circulated and was signed by one hundred and thirty-nine

OLIVET PRESBYTERIAN CHURCH.
DERRY AND KITTATINNY STREETS.

persons, forty-five of whom signified their intention of·
becoming communicant members, should the church be
organized. Governor Beaver was one of the signers and
became a member and also a ruling elder in the new organization. That petition was presented to the Presbytery of
of Carlisle, at its meeting in Duncannon on the 8th of
October, 1889, was carefully considered and allowed, a committee of Presbytery being appointed to constitute the
desired church, if the way should appear clear. The committee raised for this purpose consisted of Revs. George S.
Chambers, D. D., George B. Stewart, D. D., Ebenezer
Erskine, D. D., and Messrs. Francis Jordan and S. J. M.
McCarrell. On Tuesday, 15th October, 1889, at 7.30 p. m.,
after proper publication of the matter, this committee
accomplished the object for which it had been named. In
the organization of Olivet Presbyterian Church the Rev. Dr
Chambers preached the sermon, the Rev. Dr. Erskine con-
ducted the ordination of the elders then elected, and the
Rev. Dr. Stewart made a brief address to the new church.
Governor James A. Beaver, William S. Shaffer, Jacob K.
Walker and Charles C. Steel were chosen and set apart to
the office of ruling elder. Since then Governor Beaver and
Charles C. Steel have retired from the Session and church,
removing from the city, and Abram L. Groff and Alexander
Adams have succeeded them.

In June of 1890 Mr. Robert Cochran was formally called
to the pastorate of the church and labored in the parish
until, at his own request, he was released in August of 1892.
The record of the church-life and work for this entire
period, making due allowance for the difficulties and com-

parative lack of resources incident to most new enterprises, is encouraging in a marked degree. Down to the retirement of Mr. Cochran from the pastoral oversight of the church, fifty-seven were admitted to membership on profession of their faith in Christ, and sixty-one by letters of dismissal from sister churches. The sum of $339.00 was contributed for benevolent purposes, and $4,306.00 for congregational uses, and $140.00 for miscellaneous objects.

In October of 1892 the present minister was called and, having accepted the call and entered at once upon the duties of the pastorate, was installed on Tuesday evening, 10th of January, 1893, the Rev. Dr. Chambers preaching the sermon, the Rev. Dr. Stewart charging the pastor and the Rev. David M. Skilling charging the people. Of the history of Olivet Church since the beginning of this second pastorate let others speak. I only desire, in closing my remarks, to express the conviction that, from the standpoint of organization at least, there can be but one judgment as to the promise for the future. Never before have there been brighter prospects of usefulness and of encouraging results in the justly-to-be-desired establishment of our common Presbyterianism on Allison's Hill. The field of operations is both large and interesting. We need, it is true, both friends and money, but given these plus the willing hearts and means already consecrated on the field, the issue can never be doubtful.

Grateful for what this venerable and beloved church has been divinely empowered to accomplish in the promotion of Christ's kingdom, and in the extension of Presbyterianism in this city during the century just closed, and fully appreciating the bright, hopeful outlook into the century just opening, we lift our hearts to our common Lord and Father, praying that he may be with you alway, and may bless you exceeding abundantly above all that your hearts can ask or think.

At the conclusion of Mr. Patterson's address Rev. Mr. West led in prayer, and then announced hymn No. 639, verses 1, 3.

Chorus—Shout the glad tidings, exultingly sing :
      Jerusalem triumphs, Messiah is King.

1. Zion, the marvelous story be telling,
    The Son of the Highest, how lowly his birth ;
The brightest archangel in glory excelling,
    He stoops to redeem thee, He reigns upon earth.

Chorus—Shout the glad, etc.

Chorus—Shout the glad, etc.

3. Mortals, your homage be gratefully bringing,
    And sweet let the gladsome hosanna arise ;
Ye angels, the full hallelujah be singing :
    One chorus resound through the earth and the skies.

Chorus—Shout the glad, etc.

After the Benediction by Mr. West, and Mr. Crozier's organ postlude, Guilmant's chorus in D Minor, the audience dispersed. Though in the nature of the case the exercises were unusually long, they were yet of unusual interest, and the attention of the large audience was unrelaxed throughout the whole service.

THURSDAY EVENING,

February the 15th, 1894, at 7.30 o'clock.

HISTORICAL EVENING.

This was the indispensable evening of the week. The other services, delightful as they were and appropriate, were yet not essential. In this evening centered the significance of the whole celebration. This fact raised the expectations of the large audience to the highest point. They came anticipating a rare treat and they were not disappointed. The occasion justified the high hopes of all concerned. The Minister of the church was requested by the Centennial Committee to preside at this meeting. The service was introduced by Mackenzie's "Benedictus," a quiet and tender prelude, which harmonized with the memories evoked by the occasion. The Minister led the congregation in repeating the Apostle's Creed, the foundation faith of the Church. The Rev. I. Potter Hayes, pastor of the Presbyterian Church Wrightsville, Pa., and formerly pastor of the Covenant Presbyterian Church of this city, led the congregation in prayer. Rev. Dr. George S. Chambers announced hymn No. 435, verses 1, 2, 3, 5.

> Our God, our help in ages past,
> Our hope for years to come,
> Our shelter from the stormy blast,
> And our eternal home !

Before the hills in order stood,
    Or earth received her frame,
From everlasting thou art God,
    To endless years the same.

A thousand ages in thy sight
    Are like an evening gone,
Short as the watch that ends the night
    Before the rising dawn.

Our God, our help in ages past,
    Our hope for years to come !
Be thou our guard while troubles last,
    And our eternal home.

Rev. John L. McKeehan, M. D., pastor of the Steelton Presbyterian Church, read the Scripture lesson, Psalm 89 : 1–11. At the conclusion of the Scripture lesson the choir sang the "Hallelujah Chorus" from Handel's "Messiah." As the first notes of this inspiring chorus came from the well trained voices the large audience rose as by a common impulse, and remained standing until the last notes of the holy praise died away.

The PRESIDENT OF THE EVENING. This evening is the jewel of this week. All that has gone before and that which is to come after is the setting, resplendent and full of delight, but still the setting. It is this night that gives significance to, and justification of, all others. We are celebrating the centenary of our church, and we are met to-night to hear the story of an hundred years of endeavor, of struggle, of trial and of achievement; and we are to hear it from one than whom there is none better to tell us the story, nor more competent to give us the correct interpretation thereof. And aside from this, there is a peculiarly tender and

significant reason why he should be invited to narrate this
history. He himself was an actor in much of it, bearing
his part nobly and well for thirty years, and for the last
ten years he has been a spectator, interested and closely
associated with the events as they have transpired. He is
bound to many in this audience by ties most tender. Your
thoughts to-night will follow his words as he tells you the
story of your ancestors and of yourselves. Before I give
place to him, I feel that in all sincerity I ought to say what
I am delighted to take the occasion to say, that since I have
been his successor in the pastoral office of this church he
has proved himself to be my wisest counsellor and my
firmest friend. The delight of serving you has been intensi-
fied by the delight of following him. I have learned the
reason of your love for him, and I desire to be enrolled in
that great company whose hearts are entwined around his
and whose lives are made richer, purer, better by having
learned to love him. I could have been treated in no more
cordial, helpful, fraternal manner than I have been by Dr.
Robinson. I bear this testimony that the century which is
to follow, may know, if it cares to know, that I love him
with all my heart, as you did, and still do. Dr. Robinson
will now speak to us upon the history of the church for
an hundred years, entitling his theme " A Century Plant."

"A CENTURY PLANT."

By Rev. Thomas H. Robinson, D. D.

Now go write it before them on a tablet, and inscribe it in a book. that it may be for the time to come forever and ever.—Isaiah, xxx. 8.

Walter Scott has very touchingly told us of Old Mortality, a religious itinerant of his times. He was first discovered in the burial ground of the Parish of Gaudercleugh. It was his custom to pass from one graveyard to another, and with the patient chisel of the engraver clear away the moss from the grey tombstones, and restore the names and the lines that Time's finger had well nigh effaced. It mattered little to him whether it was the headstone of some early martyr to the faith, or only love's memorial to some little child. It was his joy to do the quiet and unbidden work of bringing again to the notice of men the history and the heroism of some of God's nobility of whom the world was not worthy, nor less to honor the unknown ones who were laid to rest with unseen tears.

Our work to-day bears something of the same character. Like Old Mortality, we step softly and reverently among the graves of the past. Chisel in hand we pass from memory to memory. We clear away the gathered moss. We refurnish the ancient stones and read again the names of the departed, dropping here and there a tear as precious memories are awakened, and reminding ourselves anew of a fellowship that is only interrupted for a little time. The past is ours. We are its heirs. Its good comes down to us in an apostolic succession of benedictions. The links that bind us to past days and years are golden links. It is one of the choicest gifts of grace, that we may at the same time live three lives in one. Past memories and present experiences and future hopes do blend to make human life noble and attractive. Our holy faith commemorates the past, gladdens the present and brightens the future.

We stand to-day at the close of an hundred years. We stand also at the beginning of another hundred years. This Church is to-day one of the Century Plants in the earthly garden of our Lord. It has taken a century to grow to what it now is and a century to do the work that it has done. A mighty forest tree is what the revolving years, it may be the added centuries have made it. Day and night, sunshine and rain, seasons coming and seasons going, gentle winds and stormy blasts, the soil, the atmosphere, a thousand things have been conspiring in a happy partnership to lift that mighty trunk towards the sky. So with ourselves. No man creates himself. No man begins his own work. The roots of our being run back into the past generations. Our work began before we were born. Other hands laid the foundations on which we are building. So with a Church. Many workers toil in its uplifting. The men of to-day are carrying on and carrying out what others begun. There is a succession and dependence in all the labors of men. The generations reap the fields their forefathers sowed. The knowledge, the wisdom, the power, the numbers, the religious faith, which any Church of to-day possesses are largely a transmission from the past. It has been handed down, each generation retaining what it received from its predecessor and adding to the general stock for the benefit of coming ages. We are debtors to the past. The social, the political, the moral and the religious riches we are enjoying have been slowly accumulating. Other men prepared the way for our era of light and liberty. Other men who left no name behind them, helped to build our large estates of science, of art, of freedom and religion. It is because before us there were preachers of righteousness, and lovers of truth, men who were fearless against wrong and enamored of goodness, it is because we had fathers in the olden time who had patience and courage to work on for the better times that were to come to their children, that we now find the world getting ready for the Christ age.

We may well recall with gratefulness the history that leads us up to the present. We cannot, indeed rehearse all they were, nor all they did, who bequeathed to us our heritage. It will be all that we dare to hope, if we give a little life and vividness to our ancestral records.

One hundred years carry us back to seventeen hundred and ninety-four, the date of organized Presbyterianism, as a Church, on this spot. How changed the scene from that upon which we look to-day! The broad river with its beautiful islands, the wooded ranges of the Kittatinny rising like a protecting rampart, the glorious sunset and the overarching sky were here, but all else, how different. Large forest trees were standing upon the greater part of the ground now occupied by the city. The hills back of us were covered by the forests. Rugged country roads led to and from the little hamlet that gathered around the ferry across the river. The town began its growth from the region about the junction of Paxton and Front streets and from thence extended up the river and up the hill, with a width of but two or three streets. The little village of from one hundred to one hundred and twenty houses had been incorporated into a borough in 1785, nine years before, and had been named Harrisburg after its founder. Its dwellings were scattered somewhat irregularly below the place on which this Church stands. Very few houses were to be found above Market street or beyond Third. Leaving the corner of Market square from the door of this Church, one might pass down Second street then ungraded, and with quite a steep descent from Chestnut street to Paxton creek, thence out Paxton street to Front and up Front to Market street and to the point of starting, and he will have marched around the greater part of the town. In a small room of a log house which stood near the corner of Front and Vine streets, the first courts for the new County of Dauphin were held; and a short distance from this primitive court house stood the Pillory, a noted instrument of public justice in those days. The large stone house on Front street and Washington, the residence of the late General Simon Cameron, had been erected by John Harris the founder of the town in 1766, nearly thirty years earlier. It is one hundred and twenty-eight years old and bids fair to see the close of the twentieth century. There was in the town a population of a few hundreds. Families that were prominent in the organization of this Church had been resident here for some years. It was a mixed population consisting mainly of the

Scotch-Irish and German people, with a few families of direct English descent.

Of the Scotch-Irish families the following names may be mentioned as among the earliest residents: Moses Gilmor, Adam Boyd, Samuel Weir, James Murray, John Hamilton, James Mitchell, John Kean, Thomas Forster, William Graydon, James Clunie, Henry Fulton, Robert Sloan, Archibald McAlister, the Montgomerys, the Berryhills and others.

Presbyterianism on this spot antedates by many years the organization of the Church. Its households were connected with the long prior and more venerable Church of Paxtang, which for more than half a century was under the pastoral care of the celebrated John Elder. Joined with Paxtang under the same pastorate for forty-eight years was the Church of Derry. North of Derry and Paxtang along the Kittatinny Mountains lay the large congregation of Hanover, now for many years extinct. From these three once flourishing congregations came the founders of the Presbyterian church in Harrisburg. They were mainly from Paxtang as this region was within the boundaries of that congregation. They were a people of strong and clear and intelligent convictions, adherents of the Westminster Confession, and the Presbyterian polity of church government. A long line of pious ancestry in the mother land, had prepared them for the trials and triumphs of their new pioneer homes across the sea. They were the best materials out of which to build a free State and a free Church. They were a frugal, industrious, energetic people. Hardy, rugged and resolute. They have left their name and their mark wherever they have gone. They were men of peculiar and marked character. In their ways of thinking, their habits of life, the training of their families, and their religious customs and modes of worship, they were clearly distinct from the ordinary Englishman and the German. They were strict in their ways, rigid in the observance of the Sabbath, and were the very quality of human nature out of which to make good and useful citizens and great men. They were the firm friends of education, moral, patriotic, liberty-loving, tyrant-hating, God-fearing. They were plain and simple in manners. They founded pious homes, orderly communities and excellent schools, and never failed to plant the Church of Jesus Christ wherever they settled. They trusted God. They held by his holy truth. They thoroughly believed in religion. They worked and lived for a better and brighter future for their descendants, and doubted not that when they passed away the truth would live on and the Kingdom of God would grow, and Christ would win the final and complete victory. They had their faults. They were not the best and saintliest men that ever lived, but we may heartily thank God for their sturdiness and their devotion to what was good and sound and true.

A brief reference to the Church and its pastor, out of which this church sprung, seems to be necessary in forming a just estimate of the elements that entered into the early structure of the Presbyterian Church of Harrisburg.

The parish of Rev. John Elder was a large one. It extended along the banks of the Susquehanna from the Gap in the mountains at Dauphin, to the banks of the Swatara at Middletown, a distance of fully twenty miles. On the hill back of the village of Dauphin there stood in the early part of this century a small church building in which Mr. Elder was accustomed occasionally to preach. In width the parish extended back from the river to the mountain and to the borders of the Hanover congregation, a distance of from eight to twelve miles.

Mr. Elder's pastorate commenced about thirty years after the first establishment of Presbyterianism in this country, and continued through the bitter religious controversies of the early history, through ravages of border warfare with the savage Indians and through the seven years of the Revolutionary conflict, and until four years after the establishment of our present free and constitutional government in 1789; in brief, from 1738 to 1792, when Mr. Elder died in the eighty-sixth year of his age, and the sixtieth of his ministry, fifty-four of which were spent at Paxtang.

An account of Mr. Elder, given by Mr. Joseph Wallace, the grandfather of Judge McPherson, thus describes him. He was a large, fine-looking man, above six feet in height, well formed and proportioned, dignified in his manners, a fine specimen of an educated gentleman. He was beloved and respected by the people of his congregation and exercised a great influence for good among them. He retained, after his settlement in this country, the dress and manners of the early Scotch and Irish ministers abroad. On Sabbath morning he went from his dwelling, which was near the church, to the study, a small log building containing one room, which was used for the meetings of the Church Session, and there remained until the congregation had assembled and the time to commence service was at hand. He then came from the study, dressed in a gown, with a wig carefully powdered very white and surmounted by a small cocked hat. Thus attired he walked in a stately and solemn manner to the church door, speaking to no one, nor even looking at any until he had entered the pulpit and opened the service. He was a man of great activity in all the relations of life, resolute, fearless, positive in his opinions, stern and unyielding in what he believed to be right, and ready to maintain his convictions at any sacrifice. He was a good, sound preacher of the most approved orthodoxy. He was a man of great courage and of indomitable force of will, one of the men born to rule. His influence extended far beyond the boundaries of his own congregations. Very few men acted a more conspicuous and influential part in the history of Central Pennsylvania for fifty years than did Parson Elder. His public reputation as a citizen and a strong leader of men is attested by his commission as a colonel of militia during the stormy times of the Indian wars. It was under such a leader of men that the fathers of this church were trained. Nor should it be omitted from this sketch that some of the early as well as later members of the church were from the "Old Hanover" congregation, where they had been under the instructions of the sound and wise and devoted James Snodgrass, pastor of that church, from 1788 to 1846, a period of fifty-eight years.

After the borough was constituted and named, and made the seat of county government, the population increased more rapidly. Owing to the distance and the difficulties of travel, the Presbyterians of the town found it inconvenient to attend the religious services at Paxtang where they held their church membership. Many of them were tradesmen and mechanics and must find their way thither on foot and in all sorts of weather. The people were strongly attached to Mr. Elder, and were unwilling for a long time to sever their connection with him. But after the close of the Revolutionary war, in the fall of 1782, and the return of the people to habits of peaceful life, movements began towards an organization in the town. Mr. Elder was drawing near eighty years of age and becoming too infirm to meet the wants of so large a parish. Many ineffectual attempts were made to obtain Mr. Elder's consent to have occasional preaching by other ministers in Harrisburg. The attachments of more than half a century joined to the tenacity of old age made it impossible for him to consent to measures that looked towards the separation of the people of Harrisburg from his flock. He desired them to abide as they were until after his death. Some of the best of his people were in the town. He was jealous of all intrusions of neighboring ministers into his parish. The pastor at Silvers' Spring for many years was the Rev. John Hoge. He seems to have preached in Harrisburg without any invitation from Mr. Elder. It was regarded as a discourtesy and an offense. Mr. Elder made complaint to the Presbytery for redress, saying that a "certain hog had been rooting in his grounds," giving the pronunciation to his name that was common at the time.

It is a matter of tradition that the first sermon preached in Harrisburg, was given by the Rev. Joseph Montgomery, a Presbyterian minister who had been appointed the Register and Recorder of the county, by Gov. Mifflin. It is said to have been preached on a pleasant Sabbath afternoon in June, on the lot at the corner of Second street and Cherry alley, upon which the original Presbyterian church of the town was subsequently erected. The people of the place assembled in the open air and were sheltered from the sun by the shade of some forest trees that were standing and the apple trees of an orchard planted on the spot. It is however wholly improbable that Mr. Montgomery's sermon was the first one preached in a community whose origin dated back beyond that time for nearly half a century. Mr. Elder had probably often preached in the little community using the dwellings of his parishoners for the service. Neighboring ministers of the Presbytery, and occasional travelling ministers, had doubtless often preached, using private houses for the purpose of holding service out of doors.

In October, 1786, a petition was presented in the Presbytery of Carlisle from Harrisburg and the parts adjacent requesting that the people be erected into a congregation and be allowed to have a place of worship in the town, and to have supplies appointed to them. Owing to the absence of Mr. Elder no action was taken on these requests.

In April 1787, the Presbytery met at Carlisle The following account is taken from the record of that meeting:

"A representation and a petition of a number of the inhabitants of Harrisburg and others in the township of Paxton was laid before the Presbytery and read. The said representation sets forth that these people desire to be considered as a Presbyterian congregation and to have supplies appointed them by the Presbytery: and that in order to promote peace and harmony between them and the Paxton congregation, some proposals had been made to, and considered by, though not accepted by that Congregation, a copy of which was laid before Presbytery."

Mr. Elder gave a representation of the case as concerning those people and the Paxtang congregation. The Presbytery upon consideration of the case agreed to propose the following articles to the consideration and acceptance of these people which may have a tendency to preserve peace and union in that part of the church :

I. That Harrisburg shall be considered as the seat of a Presbyterian church, and a part of the charge of Rev. John Elder, in which he is to preach one-third of his time.

II. That Mr. Elder's salary promised by the Paxtang congregation shall be continued and paid by the congregation in common who adhere to these two places of worship.

III. That the congregation thus united may apply for and obtain supplies as assistant to the labors of Mr. Elder, to be paid by the congregation in common.

IV. That when the congregation may judge it proper, they shall have a right to choose and call a minister as a colleague to Mr. Elder to officiate in rotation with him.

Rev. Dr. Davidson, of Carlisle, President of Dickinson College, and Rev. Mr. Waugh, pastor of Silvers' Spring, were appointed a committee to attend at the church in Lower Paxton to moderate a meeting and assist in the matter.

At a meeting of the Presbytery held in June, 1787, Dr. Davidson and Mr. Waugh reported that the following articles had been agreed to by Mr. Elder and by the united congregation of Paxtang and Harrisburg :

I. That the congregation shall have two stated places of public worship, the one where Mr. Elder now officiates, the other in Harrisburg.

II. That the Rev. John Elder shall have and continue to receive during his life or incumbency, all the salary or stipends that he now enjoys, to be paid by his present subscribers as he and they may agree, and continue his labors in Derry as usual.

III. That for the present the congregation may apply to the Presbytery for supplies, which, when obtained, the expense shall be defrayed by those who do not now belong to Mr. Elder's congregation, and such as may think proper to join with them; and should such supplies be appointed when Mr. Elder is to be in Paxtang, then he and the person are to preach in rotation, the one in the country and the other in the town; but should Mr. Elder be in Derry, then the supplies shall officiate in the town.

IV. That the congregation, when able, or when they think proper, may invite and settle any regular Presbyterian minister they, or a majority of them, may choose and can obtain as co-Pastor with Mr. Elder, who shall officiate as to preaching in the manner specified in the third proposal."

Notwithstanding these arrangements, Mr. Elder continued to be the sole pastor of the two congregations of Derry and of Paxtang, including Harrisburg, until April 13, 1791, when the relation was dissolved. He died on July 17, 1792, at the venerable age of eighty-six years. His remains lie buried in the Paxtang graveyard. All honor to the memory of a sterling and stalwart man, who was conspicuous for more than a half century as one of the foremost men of his times.

After Mr. Elder's death the people of Harrisburg who held to the Presbyterian faith began at once to take measures for a distinct organization.

In an old volume belonging to the congregation, the following minute is found recorded in the handwriting of William Graydon, Esq.:

"July 30, 1793. At a meeting of the Harrisburg congregation, the following persons were chosen a committee to govern the affairs of the church, viz: Joseph Montgomery, Samuel Weir, Moses Gilmor, James Mitchell, and William Graydon." The first treasurer of the congregation, so far as can be learned from any existing records, was Mr. Henry Fulton, who, in 1790, gave place to Mr. John Kean, whose term of service continued for two years. How many years Mr. Fulton had served we have no means of ascertaining. From some loose papers containing a part of the treasurer's accounts we gather the names of a number of ministers who preached occasionally to the congregation prior to its organization into a church. It may be noted that nearly three years passed after the resignation of Mr. Elder before the church was organized. Of the men who supplied the pulpit at different times the following may be noted, viz: Robert Cathcart, pastor of the York Presbyterian Church for forty-four years; James Snodgrass, for fifty-seven years the pastor of the old Hanover church; Samuel Waugh, pastor of the Monaghan and East Pennsborough churches, now known as Dillsburg and Silvers' Spring, for twenty-five years; Joseph Hender-

NATHANIEL RANDOLPH SNOWDEN.
1793-1805

son, of Great Conewago, and Colin McFarquhar, of Donegal; David Denny, for nearly forty years pastor of Falling Springs Church, Chambersburg; Dr. Charles Nisbet, the distinguished President of Dickinson College; Dr. Robert Davidson, also President of Dickinson College, and for twenty-eight years pastor of the First Church of Carlisle; Dr. John Ewing, for thirty years pastor of the First Presbyterian Church of Philadelphia, and for twenty-three years at the head of the University of Pennsylvania; Dr. Samuel Miller, for thirty-six years a professor in the Princeton Theological Seminary; Dr. John McKnight, for twenty years a leading pastor in New York city, and other men less famous than the foregoing, but no less sound and good. The founders of this church enjoyed the privilege of occasional instruction from some of the most renowned men and ablest scholars in the Presbyterian church. The influences thus thrown about them had their bearing upon the character of the new organization.

In the latter part of the year 1792 the united congregations of Paxtang and Harrisburg secured the services of Mr. Nathaniel R. Snowden, a young man who was preparing for the ministry under the care of the Presbytery of Philadelphia, and during the winter of 1792–1793, he preached frequently to the congregations, giving his first sermon here on September 9, 1792. On April 10, 1793, he was taken under the care of the Presbytery of Carlisle, and a call from the three congregations to become their pastor was placed in his hands, and was accepted by him. Each of the congregations agreed to pay fifty pounds as their part of the salary. On the 2d day of October, 1793, Mr. Snowden was ordained and installed as pastor.

The Harrisburg congregation, however, was not yet a church. It had been kept in its minority for many years. But its hour had now come. In January, 1794, at a meeting of the Congregational Committee, it was agreed to call a meeting of the congregation for the purpose of electing five ruling elders to govern the affairs of the church that should then be constituted. This meeting was held on Tuesday, February 11th, 1794, and the five following persons were elected to the office of ruling elder: Samuel Weir, Moses Gilmor, Adam Boyd, Robert Harris and James Mitchell. The last two named declined to accept the office. On Sunday, February 16, 1794, after divine worship the remaining three, Messrs. Weir, Gilmor and Boyd, were ordained and installed, and this church became a regularly constituted and fully organized Presbyterian church. The three venerable men mentioned may be regarded as the fathers of the church Session, and the church had a name and a place among the sisterhood of Presbyterian churches in the earth. It was an independent organization with its pastor and its board of officers. It was an infant in age, but it was no weakling. It was made up of strong and intelligent men and women to whom the service of God was no new thing. They were trained and disciplined workmen. They had borne the cross for years. One of their elders, Moses Gilmor, had held the same office in the mother church of Paxtang, and all of them were men of large experience. The three elders were men of from forty-five to fifty years of age. They were no novices, nor raw recruits, but soldiers of many years service.

The young pastor gave the church but one-third of his time, preaching in Harrisburg but twice a month, and often but once. This was unsatisfactory to the people, and the burden of so large a charge was too great for their minister. In October, 1795, at his request, the relation between Mr. Snowden and the church of Derry was dissolved by the Presbytery. Derry was eleven miles distant, and along the whole distance, and for miles beyond, the families under his pastoral care were scattered. The toil involved in visitation as well as the time required, was a heavy burden. The two churches of Paxtang and Harrisburg were left under his care. Six months later the connection between Mr. Snowden and the Paxtang church was also severed by the consent of both parties. Derry and Paxtang then resumed their old alliance of more than half a century, and the Harrisburg church assumed the entire support of Mr. Snowden, and he gave to it all his time and energies. He continued to serve the church until 1805, when, at his own request he was released from the charge, after a service of about twelve years and a pastorate of eleven.

Mr. Snowden was a member of one of the oldest and most respectable families of Pennsylvania. Some of his descendants at the present day occupy high positions in civil and political life. Mr. Snowden was not a man of marked ability as a preacher or a scholar, but during his ministry here was very acceptable. A descendant of Old Paxtang thus testifies in regard to him: "Those of Paxtang congregation, whose memory runs back sixty years, will remember as an occasional visitant, this very worthy gentleman. In his sixties he looked hale and vigorous. He had grey eyes and a full face, and was about one hundred and sixty pounds in weight. His voice was strong and sonorous and he delivered his words with a measured deliberation."

During the years of the first pastorate of the church, it had no house of worship. Through the long delay of the Presbyterians of the town to organize a church distinct from Paxtang, other denominations that were later on the ground and feebler in numbers and in wealth, were first in the organization of churches, and in the erection of a church edifice.

As early as 1787, there was built by the citizens of the borough irrespective of denominational connections a small one-story log house on the northeast corner of Third and Walnut streets for the purpose both of worship and as a school building. It was used by the Lutheran and Reformed people for some months. The same year they jointly secured ground on the corner of Third and Chestnut streets, on the site of the present Reformed church. Here they built a log church fronting on Third street, the first church building erected in Harrisburg. It was one of the notable events of the time. All who were favorable to religion were invited to help in the enterprise, and to their credit be it said, all classes vied with each other in liberality and in labor. The two congregations, Lutheran and Reformed, for eight years worshiped together in happiest harmony, sharing equally in the support and government of the one church. It was a plain two-story building, with its side to the street, two windows in each story, and a door in the center of the side. The preaching was divided between the English and the German tongues.

Meanwhile the Presbyterians were without any fixed abode. For a time they held service in the loft of the old jail that was erected soon after the borough was formed. On the 17th of November, 1798, an application was made by the congregation for permission to fit up the upper room of the court house as a place of worship. The request was granted, and the room was occupied by the church for some time. The accommodations were very unpretentious. There were no family pews, nor cushioned seats, nor carpeted aisles, no stained glass nor memorial windows, no organ loft nor grand organ. Everything was simple and plain. The evening services were held at " early candle light," and the house was lighted by tallow candles of home-made manufacture. No bell summoned the worshipers to the house of God. Hard benches greeted their coming, but the God of the Covenant met them and blessed them.

In the accounts of John Kean, treasurer of that early period, we find some items of disbursements that speak clearly and pathetically of those early days:

Paid Robert Harris for one cord of wood, ten shillings.

Paid James McNamara for six benches for Church use, fifteen shillings.

Robert Sloan is paid nine shillings, four and a half pence for making two boxes to take collections in.

Paid Rev. Mr. Robinson for Presbytery, seven shillings and six pence. Other articles such as green baize candles, sconces, &c., are mentioned.

Gustavus Graham, the first sexton receives a yearly salary

of three pounds. John Sargint a sexton of later days gets sixteen dollars a year. Michael Rupp, furnishes twenty and a half pounds of stove pipe for the use of the congregation. Major William Glass is paid fifteen shillings for two new benches. The principal expense seems to have been for fuel and candles, and for the bread and wine used at the Sacrament of the Supper. The usual cost of a Sabbath's supply for the pulpit, was one pound in the currency of the times. One of the largest items is thus stated: "Paid Mr. Snowden for Missionaries to Indians, three pounds, seven shillings and six pence." The communion service was of pewter, and a frequent item of cost is for "scouring the pewter." The expenses of the congregation were met by Sabbath collections, supplemented, when necessary by subscriptions. These collections, prior to 1804 seldom rose above one pound or five dollars and were often not half that amount. On Sacramental Sabbaths the day for their largest congregations, the collections were twice or thrice the usual amount. To secure the amounts needed for the Pastor's salary and other expenses, collectors were appointed to visit all the families of the congregation. The lists of these collectors for the seven years prior to 1800 are on record. In the year 1795, Thomas Forster, George Whitehill, William Graydon and Alexander Berryhill are appointed, the latter two to solicit subscriptions through Paxtang on account of the poverty of the people in the town.

Baptismal ceremonies generally took place at the private residences of the people, at which sacred rite the friends of the family assembled and made the occasion one to be remembered.

The contrast between those early days and our own is very great. Their rude, small room in the loft of a log-jail, their bare benches, small windows and uncarpeted floors, their humble pulpit desk, their flickering tallow candles and pewter candle sticks, and our large, costly and elegant churches with carpeted aisles, cushioned and comfortable pews, our decorated and memorial windows, our high sounding organs, our gas and electric lights : their poverty, their collections and collectors, their narrow fields for church work, their little grasp of the great fields of missions and benevolence, and our rich and active and liberal Church of to-day, that feels that it must clasp the whole wide world in its arms and to its heart of love : their scanty literature, their narrow outlook, their meagre arts and sciences and inventions, their social world, their catechisings of the old and young in all their households, and our abounding literature in books and magazines and daily and weekly press, our multiplied agencies of benevolence for the round earth, our art and inventions : their plain home spun dress, simple manners, rugged, but friendly speech, and our manners, speech and dress molded by society and culture—these and a hundred other things serve to show what changes the Providence of God, and the progress of the times have made. We cannot decry the past. We have built upon its foundations. We cannot exult over to-day. God mold's the ages for himself. Our fathers had their noble work and we have ours. They met their mission. They believed in God. They studied his law.

They prayed and worked for the coming and broader times of Christ's kingdom. Wider, deeper, stronger than they knew were the foundations at which they set their hands. It remains to us in these richer times to carry on their work.

The next important step in the history of the congregation was that of providing for themselves a house of worship. The means taken would not be sanctioned in our day, but we must bear in mind that the course pursued was, at that day, neither legally forbidden nor morally condemned. It was in accordance with the customs of the times. Our fathers were poor. They determined to raise the needed funds for church building by a lottery. We are not aware that there was any opposition to the plan. At the close of the last century the finances of the entire country were in a desperate and dilapidated condition. Everybody was in debt. Money was in great demand. Credit everywhere was at the lowest ebb. To raise money lotteries sprung up as mushrooms in every direction. A lottery wheel might have been found in every city and in every town and village that were large enough to need some public improvement. If a bridge was to be built across some little stream, a school-house to be erected, a jail to be provided for criminals, a street to be repaired, a court house to be enlarged, or a church to be reared, a lottery bill was passed by the Legislature, commissioners were appointed, a wheel was procured, tickets were sold, and a day for the drawing was set. The mania was wide spread. Massachusetts sold lottery tickets to raise the money needed to pay the salaries of her public officials. The city of New York raised money by lottery to enlarge the City Hall. The court house of Elizabeth City was rebuilt, the library of Harvard University was increased and the Government of the United States erected some of its public buildings by lotteries. There was a mania for lotteries. They were a vast epidemic. Everybody seemed to be in haste to get rich in the foolish and criminal way of emptying the pockets of their fellow-men. The hope of winning prizes became a disease. It was amid this general use and approval of lotteries and this rage for them that the founders of this church lived. They were swept into the current.

During the winter of 1797–1798 an application was made to the Legislature for permission to raise $5,000 by lottery for the purpose of buying a lot, and building thereon a house of worship for the English Presbyterian Congregation of Harrisburg. In March, 1798, a law was passed appointing Robert Harris, George Whitehill, Adam Boyd, William Graydon, Christian Kunkel, George Brenizer, Archibald McAllister and Samuel Elder commissioners for that purpose. The law provided that before a ticket should be sold the scheme should be laid before the Governor of the Commonwealth and be approved by him, that the commissioners should take an oath diligently and faithfully to perform their duties, and that at least three of them should attend at the drawings of each day until they were completed. When we consider the strictness of the law, and the great respectability of the commissioners, who were charged with its execution, there can be no doubt that the law was rigidly observed, however much we may reprobate lotteries in this more enlightened age. The scheme was carried out and the lottery was closed on July 7, 1803. The time spent upon it, over four years, would indicate that the measure was not very heartily endorsed. It was not as successful an affair as was anticipated. Everything, however, was done in the broad light of day. Many of the best people of the community were interested and bought tickets. The pastor of the Church was among those who drew prizes. Some of the prizes were thrown into the treasury of the Church. They were generally small and no one amassed wealth by the lottery. It is clear that our forefathers did not imagine that they were encouraging immorality by their action.

On the seventh day of June, 1804, the commissioners having raised about five thousand dollars by the lottery, purchased the lot on the corner of Second street and Cherry alley, and soon after contracted with Messrs. William Glass, Peter Brua and Samuel Pool for the erection of a church edifice. It was ready for use in 1806, but was not formally dedicated until 1809. For the first twelve years in the history of the congregation it had no church building. The house now erected was a plain substantial brick structure, forty feet by sixty and stood with its side to the street, and about forty-five feet back from the pavement. It was two stories in height, and had two front entrances. It bore a striking resemblance in form and size to many of the fine barns that may be seen in the region about us. The space in front was a green sward fenced in from the street, and shaded by four stately lombardy poplars, a tree that was then greatly admired. The interior was comfortably arranged with large pews, built of yellow pine, but cushioned seats had not yet come into fashion among our hardy ancestors. The builders neglected to put chimneys in the new house. The fire was to be in the pulpit. The congregation had ample light and ventilation, but in the winter no heat. When the cold could be endured no longer, and the expedient of foot-stoves and hot bricks failed, the old-fashioned ten-plate stoves were put in and the pipes were run out of the windows. Evening services were not often held, the second service being placed in the afternoon. Some years after the erection of the church building, the congregation became too large to be comfortably accommodated, and in 1824 a gallery was built. The church was the finest and most capacious one in the town. The pulpit was built on the east side of the house and stood upon a small but convenient platform. It was elevated several feet above the seats of the people and had a closet underneath and a circular dais in front. It was entered by doors that were kept carefully closed during divine service. From this pulpit many of the great lights of our denomination preached sound doctrine to large and intelligent audiences. There was neither an Episcopal nor a Methodist Church in the town during the earliest years of the century. The adherents of those forms of church order generally attended the Presbyterian Church until they were strong enough to organize churches of their own faith. The names of some of the founders of these churches may be found in the lists of early pew-holders of this Church.* The use of the building was often granted to these denominations and the pulpit was occupied by their preachers. The venerable

---

* For a list of these pew-holders see Appendix, Note II.—EDITOR.

Bishop White, of Philadelphia, accompanied by the youth- ful Bedell, in later years the Bishop of Ohio, preached in it. Rev. Dr. Bascom, one of the most celebrated orators of the Methodist Church and of his times, gave a sermon that occupied more than two hours in its delivery and was a magnificent specimen of pulpit oratory.

The pastoral relation between the Church and Mr. Snow- den was dissolved, June 25th, 1805. An interregnum of four years occurred. The congregation was busy watching the slow uplifting of their first Church home. There was no cessation of public worship. Rev. Dr. Snodgrass was often called to preach at Sacramental occasions. Rev. Dr. Joshua Williams, for twenty-eight years the able and instructive pastor of the Big Spring Church at Newville; Rev. Dr. David McConaughy the pastor for thirty-two years of the Churches of Upper Creek and Great Conewago in Adams county ; Rev. Dr. John Moody who for fifty years filled the pastorate of the Middle Spring Church near Shippensburg ; and the Rev. John Linn who for forty-three years was pastor of the Centre Church, on Sherman's Creek, Perry county, frequently preached from the pulpit of the Church. Mr. Linn was a preacher of great power and impressiveness. He was the pastor of my own ancestry. George Robinson my great grandfather being among the first ruling elders of the Church.

An ancient book kept by the treasurer of the congregation gives quite a full financial history of the Church, its regular Sabbath collections, the names of the men who filled its pulpit, the amounts paid them for their service, the cost even of keeping the horse on which they traveled from

ENGLISH PRESBYTERIAN CONGREGATION.
SECOND STREET AND CHERRY ALLEY.
ERECTED 1804-6.

their homes, the weekly expenses and the sexton's salary. The old record is full of interesting reading for one of the present day.

It is a matter however of deep regret that while we have a record of this nature, the names and salaries of the sextons, the cost of candles and candle sticks and benches. there was no record preserved, and probably none kept, through the first quarter of a century in the history of this Church of the noble men and women, who were members of it, who sat at its communion table, who attended its weekly meetings for prayer and made it a leading religious power in the growing community. There is no record of the marriages, baptisms and deaths, none of the original members of the Church, no list of those who were added to the Church during the first twenty-five years.

To the original bench of elders, Messrs. Weir, Gilmor and Boyd, two others were added, John Stoner and William Graydon, but the date of their election and installation is not known. It was probably between 1809 and 1812. Of religious history, of revivals, of family and social life, of Christian work, but the barest account can be gleaned. We know the Church lived on and waxed stronger and stronger. We know their sons and daughters came into the Church communion. We find them there when the record opens. To us now, it is like a stream running underground and fed by numerous hidden springs, until it breaks out a strong, clear, cool river.

Names we have gathered here and there from lists of pew-holders, from collectors' records, from the treasurers' accounts, and other sources, that belonged to this ancestral house of ours, and they shall not be lost. Such a list of about three hundred names of men and of godly women, their fellow-workers in the gospel, is now in the possession of the Church. They belong to the first quarter century of its history.*

During the interregnum that followed the departure of Rev. N. R. Snowden, a call from the Church was extended to Rev. William Kerr, who was a frequent preacher in Harrisburg during the years 1806 and 1807. For reasons unknown he declined to accept and became the Pastor of Donegal. Five of his children in later years became members of the Church: Dr. James W. Kerr, for many years a Ruling Elder in the York Presbyterian Church; William M. Kerr, late president of the Harrisburg National Bank; J. Wallace Kerr, Mrs. Herman Alricks and Mrs. Dr. Edward L. Orth. The last named only survives and is a resident of Pittsburgh. Mr. Kerr died in the early years of his ministry.

The second Pastor of the Church was the Rev. James Buchanan. He preached his first sermon to the people on May 17, 1807, and during the rest of that year continued to fill the pulpit as a stated supply. He was a young man, not yet ordained to the ministry, but his services proved to be so acceptable to the congregation that he was called to be pastor. On September 29, 1808, he was ordained, and on February 13, 1809, after preaching to the congregation for nearly two years, he was installed. He remained in the pastorate until September 20, 1815, when he was released from the charge on account of ill health. His term of ser-

---

* For this list see Appendix, Note III.—EDITOR.

vice was over eight years, though as pastor he was with the
Church between six and seven years only. At his installation Parson Snodgrass, of Old Hanover, presided and gave
the charge to the young pastor, and Rev. James R. Sharon,
Pastor of Paxtang Church, preached the sermon. Mr.
Buchanan was called on a salary of one hundred and fifty
pounds for three-fourths of his time. The remaining fourth
was given to a small congregation at Middle Paxton, or
Dauphin. Fifty pounds more were given for this additional
service. The whole two hundred pounds was in the old
Pennsylvania currency and amounted to about five hundred dollars. After leaving this Church and recovering his
health, Mr. Buchanan was, for twenty-one years, the greatly
beloved Pastor of the Church in Greencastle. He died at
Logansport, Ind., in 1843, after a ministry of over thirty-six
years. Dr. DeWitt and others who knew him in later years
gave descriptions of him from which we draw the following
portrait:

He was a man of tall form, commanding presence and
great gravity of manner. No one could mistake either his
character or his profession. He was neat and scrupulous in
dress and courteous in his bearing. His grave and dignified
manner rebuked all levity and lightness, while his real
goodness, purity and sympathy with men attracted their
esteem and reverence. He was universally regarded as a
good man and a man of great force of character. His sermons were short, compact and precise, remarkably so for
that day, when sermons were often very lengthy and diffuse.
Few men, it has been said, could say so much as he in so
few words. He was not regarded as an eloquent preacher,

but he was a clear, able and instructive one, and his sincer- ity and deep earnestness made him very impressive. His discourses were prepared with great care, committed to mem- ory and then delivered memoriter. He had a very low esti- mate of his own abilities. Owing, doubtless, to a deranged condition of his physical system, he was nervous and subject to fits of depression, and at times fell into states of melan- choly. While at Greencastle he became so nervous and timid that he refused, for a time, to perform marriages even between members of his own congregation. The late be- loved elder of this Church, John A. Weir, narrated the fol- lowing incident in his pastorate: Having given out a hymn one Sabbath morning, the singers of the choir, for some unknown reason, neglected to sing. Mr. Buchanan closed the service abruptly, giving, on the following day, as the reason: "If the singers could not sing, the preacher could not preach." Mr. Buchanan was always remembered by this congregation as a man and a preacher who was worthy of highest confidence and affection. And, during his brief pastorate, the Church increased in numbers, intelligence and spiritual power.

This brief account of the pastorate of Mr. Buchanan would be incomplete were it to omit one event that has resulted in very great blessings upon the Church in all its subsequent history. They may not have been publicly recognized, but the greatest forces in nature and in grace alike work silently and unseen. Some time during that pastorate, probably about the year 1812, the Woman's Prayermeeting of this Church was started. Who were its originators and early members is not known. No record was kept of its weekly meetings. It was without doubt the first prayermeeting of the kind in Harrisburg and, so far as known, in Central Pennsylvania. Those early times were not favorable to the Christian activity of the female members of the Church. There was no men's prayermeeting in existence, and when in subsequent years the men of the church were drawn into the service of public prayer, woman's voice was never to be heard at the altars of public prayer. This meeting of the Christian women has been faithfully continued for some eighty years. It has been a quiet but mighty power in the spiritual history of the Church. The numbers attending it have never been large, but they have been the gifted and consecrated women of the Church. In times of spiritual depression and in times alike of revival this invaluable gathering of devoted women has met every week at the mercy seat, and carried thither in their hearts of love and longing the interests of this Church. Many years ago, it is not known how far back, the meeting joined alms with their prayers, and at times as large a sum as one hundred and fifty dollars have been given by it in a year to Christ's cause. Every true heart will say of this meeting "Esto Perpetua."

———

For four years after the departure of Mr. Buchanan, or until November 12, 1819, the Church was without a pastor and its pulpit was dependent upon irregular supplies. It did not sit down with folded hands. The history of one of the noblest organizations within this Church dates its origin in that interregnum of four years.

In the year 1804 a Sunday-school was started in the city
of New York by Divie Bethune, a member of a renowned
family of that name. It has the credit of being the first
Sabbath-school in America. But the honor must go farther
back. In 1793 a Sunday-school was started in the same city
of New York, by Katy Ferguson, a colored woman. Indeed
as early as 1786 we hear of one established by Bishop
Asbury, of the Methodist Church, in Hanover county, Virginia. Little is known of it save that it was started.

In the spring days of 1816, several earnest women in this
little Church, without a pastor, on the banks of the Susquehanna, determined to imitate the good example set elsewhere and start a Sunday-school. They do not seem to
have met much encouragement from their husbands and
brothers. It was wholly an undertaking of the women.
The first meeting for organization was held August 16,
1816, at the residence of Mrs. John Wright, then the post-
office, No. 13 South Market Square. It was a two-story log
house, weather boarded, and painted a dingy brown. The
report of the meeting says that "a respectable number of
ladies were present." There were no men in the company.
Mrs. Richard T. Leech, the wife of a subsequent elder of the
Church, presided, and Miss Rachel Graydon acted as Secretary. A constitution was adopted. The society was to be
known as "a society for the encouragement and promotion
of Learning, Morality and Religion by means of Sabbath-
schools, at Harrisburg." The society was to be composed
of persons of all the existing religious denominations then
in the town. It was to be unsectarian, but it was soon found
that none but Presbyterians were interested and active in

it. Officers were chosen as follows: *President*—Mrs. Captain Alexander Graydon; *Vice-President*—Mrs. Richard M. Crain; *Secretary*—Miss Rachel Graydon; *Treasurer*—Mrs. Henry Hall; *Managers*—Mrs. George Fisher, Miss Abigail Wyeth, Miss Eliza English, Mrs. R. T. Leech and Miss Catharine Hubley.

By special arrangement two of them were to alternate each Sabbath in performing the duties of Superintendent. The school was opened on September 22, 1816. An equinoctial storm of great violence was then prevailing, the day was inclement and dreary. The school met in the old academy building on Market street between Third and Fourth streets. There were present eighteen teachers and seventy scholars. There was no fire provided though the day was a cold one, and there were no seats for the teachers. They taught their classes standing and continued to do so during the first year. The names of the first teachers are given and they indicate that they, as well as the managers of the school, were all Presbyterians. They are all young ladies. Misses Juliana Fisher, Sally Hill, Sally Hanna [Jacobs], Rebecca Jones [Irvin-Allison], Louisa Kean [Powers], Juliana Stoner, Mary Hanna [Tod], Mary Miller, Elizabeth Hubley, Mary Wyeth [McKinley], Caroline Henry, Catharine Brunson, Rachel Graydon, Maria Murray, Jane Mitchell [Dr. Thomas Whiteside], Ruth Allen [John Whiteside], Eliza Ziegler [Hebt], and Mary Graydon [Hubbard]. Nearly all of them were in later years more widely known in the Church and community under their married names. They are the leaders in the large procession of

Sunday-school teachers of the Presbyterian churches of this city for seventy-eight years. All honor to their memory.

The names of the seventy scholars of that first day's session have also been preserved.* It was a mixed school, and made up of children. Thirty-three were white and thirty-seven were black. An examination of the names indicates that very few of them were from the regular families of the congregation. The enterprise was of a missionary character among the neglected and poor. Of the eighteen young women of this Church who took the original classes in this school, many in after years and down to my own pastorate were famous for their good works and high intelligence. It is to the honor of all concerned in the school that

---

Males, White.—Samuel Barnes, Joseph Russell, Peter Miller, John Young, Leonard Kline, George Geiger, James Gillespie, Charles McMullin, Henry Michael, John Maloney.

Females, White.—Catharine Young [Seig], Maria Newman, Susanna Vance, Catharine Stahl, Susan Weaver, Catharine Stence, Elizabeth Over, Mary Hill, Margaret Howard, Susan Lawyer, Mary Ann Michael, Peggy Ely, Julia Ann Weaver, Ellen McMullin, Ann Myers, Ann Brestle, Ann Johnson, Mary Over, Maria Clark, Nancy Rechkard, Peggy Whiting, Julia Ann McMullin, Polly Fager.

Males, Black.—Charles Butler, Samuel Dutcher, Sam. Green, Eli Norwoss, David Owens, Samuel Johnston, John Fayette, Henry Fayette, George Fayette, Henry Johnston, John McClintick, Wm. McClintick, Charles Butler, Sr., Lerin Johnston, Geo. Carr, John Davis, Wm. Crawford.

Females, Black.—Rebecca Anderson, Maria Capp, Catharine Irwin, Nancy Smith, Eliza Dutchess, Mrs. Polk, Fannie Fayette, Charlotte Owens, Judith Richard, Jane Chamberlain, Mary Ann Chamberlain Hester Dickinson, Mary Ann Dickerson, Maria Thompson, Daphna Baker, Matilda Dickinson, Mary Smith, Leah Blak, Sallie Randall, Mary Poole.—EDITOR.

no miserable prejudice against classes or against color hampered the flow of their Christian charity.

At the opening of the school a formal address was made by Dr. Samuel Agnew, of blessed memory, afterwards a Ruling Elder in the Church. And before the first year ends we find several men are named as General Superintendents, or patrons of the school, Rev. George Lochman, of the Lutheran Church, Rev. F. Rauhauser, of the Reformed Church, Rev. James Buchanan, Dr. Agnew and William Graydon, of the Presbyterian Church. The school started bravely and soon won favor and grew rapidly. The first semi-annual meeting of the society was held in a house that stood on the spot where this Church now stands. It will be impossible to follow in detail the very interesting history of the school. New managers and new teachers came in to bear a hand in the work. The school grew rapidly. In 1818, the second year of its life, there were one hundred and seventy scholars enrolled. In this year also male teachers were added to the corps, and gentlemen were also permitted to become subscribers to its support. The women, however, held the reins of management and finely did their work. The receipts of the society in 1818 for the support of the school amounted to seventy dollars. This was a noble sum for those days. There is no intimation that during those early years there were any collections taken up in the classes. The report of the library during the first three years gives us some hints about the character of the teaching and expenses of the school. There were seventy-one books in the library.

Mention is made of the following things as already owned or contributed by several donors whose names are given :

Nine dozen shorter catechisms, seven dozen testaments, one dozen and a half of spellers, three dozen and a half of primers, four psalm and hymn books and thirty-four tracts.

In 1819 the Lutheran and Reformed Churches, organized Sunday-schools of their own, and drew away many scholars. The original school now became distinctively a Presbyterian one. It had been under Presbyterian management and teaching from the outset, though in name, a union school. The change to three denominational schools took place with great harmony. The children of the Churches now came more freely into the Church schools. The original school was reduced in numbers by the exodus, but the number in the three schools was much greater than in the one.

On the first Sunday of January, 1820, the Presbyterian school opened with one hundred and thirty-eight scholars, of whom twenty-nine were black.* A few years later the

---

* The following are the names of the scholars :

Females, White.—Rose Wright, Sarah Dougherty, Rebecca Wills, Jane Wills, Margaret Berryhill, Catharine Clark, Sarah Curzon, Ann Keely, Elizabeth Nabb, Fanny Wagoner, Mary Ann Wright. Ellen McMullin, Mariann Capp, Emeline Armstrong, Margaret Campbell, Elizabeth Downings, Ann Mucheron, Polly Thompson. Catharine Heickel. Mrs. W., Polly Swartz, Hannah Smith, Kitty Gilespy, Lo Reeves, M. Megraw, Theodosia Graydon, E. Good, Betsey Sloan, Mary Ann Martin, Eliza Green, Sarah Floyd, Rebecca Dubbs, Mary Ann McKinney. Mary Allison, Anne Adams, Eliza Waggoner, Mary Frazer, Maria Irwin, Matilda Kunkel.

Males, White.—Solomon Waggoner. David Waggoner, William

black children were withdrawn to schools of their own. We recognize now in the list of the scholars the names of the children of the Church, among them two who in later years became ministers in the Church, Rev. Charles A. Wyeth and Rev. Benjamin J. Wallace, D. D., the brother of the late Mrs. Dr. DeWitt.

The school had heretofore been held in the old Academy and the court house. It was now removed to the Church on Second street and Cherry alley and occupied the audience room. After 1824, the unfinished gallery was put in order

---

Macchesney, C. Augustus Wyeth, Joseph Russell, George Kunkel, John Young, Joel Hinckley, Hugh Berryhill, Isaac Hyars, Michael Balsley, Samuel Lindy, Christian Lindy, Theodore Franks, Robert Harris, William Harris, William F. Bryan, Edward D. Bryan, Benjamin Wallace, Henry Stimmel, Albert Stimmel, Robert Elder, Henry Lyon, Lewis Wyeth, Richard Bryan, John B. Martin, Joshua E. Forster, Andrew Stewart, James Gillespie, George Johnson, Samuel Spahn, Franklin Cole, James Sloan, William Good, Peter Sowl, William Sowl, William Kelly, Lewis Kelly, John Sloan, Henry Cole, Robert McElwee, John Wagner, Thomas Lytle, John Lytle, Joseph Sowl: Jacob Sowl, Charles Perley, Eustus Perley, Wm. Reem, Irwin M. Wallace, Edward L. Orth, Richard C. Nabb, Augustus Gallaher, John Johnson, William Floody, George Balsley, Philip Linday, Joseph Wilson, William Dotterick, William Waggoner, Charles Floody, John Silsel, William Silsel, Joseph Grove, John Cannaday, John Thompson, Jeremiah Woler.

Females, Black.—Elizabeth Malson, Maria Malson, Mary Stewart Nelly Bradford, Margaret Allen, Jemima Ricketts, Sarah Rodrick, Fanny Williams, Rebecca Taylor, Dinah ———, Susan Layson.

Males, Black.—George Carr, Ezekiel Carter, Jacob Malson, Wm. McClintock, Chas. Coll, Eli Noovell, John Fiatts, Edward Davis, Charles Butler, Ben. Roberts, John Gould, James Taylor, Henry Davis, William Laughlin, Harry Johnson, John Lewis, John Baptist, Thomas Watson.

and used for the school, and by the year 1827, an annex
was built to the Church especially for Sunday-school
purposes. The school soon increased to its old numbers
before the departure of the Lutheran and Reformed scholars
and the interest of the Church in the school deepened.
Annual examinations of the scholars were held, which
were attended by members of the Legislature. In 1821,
the old system of managers who served as superintendents
alternately was abandoned and the present system of a
permanent superintendent was adopted. The first to fill
the office was Mrs. Gov. Snyder with Miss Juliann Fisher as
assistant. Mrs. Snyder served very ably and acceptably until
her death in 1823, when Miss Juliann Fisher was chosen to
fill her place. In 1822, a branch school of from 60 to 70
scholars was formed at Coxestown. In 1825,* Miss Juliann
Fisher, greatly to the regret of the school and its friends,
resigned her position as superintendent and Miss Abigail
Wyeth was chosen as her successor. By 1827, the school
had increased to three hundred and fifty enrolled scholars.

* July 3, 1825.—The following teachers "were present teaching
pupils, as numbered opposite their names," viz:

Females.—Miss Graydon, 7; Miss M. Graydon, 6; Miss Wyeth, 9;
Miss Hearne, 8; Miss Armstrong, 7; Miss Sturgeon, 6; Miss Rose
Wright, 11; Miss D. McKinney, 9; Miss McGonigle, 6; Miss Miller,
9; Miss Stoner, 9; Mrs. W. R. DeWitt, 8; Miss Hays, 7; Miss Sloan,
5; Miss Agnew, 5; Miss M. McKinney, 7; Mrs. Ritchey, 10.

Males.—Mr. McKinney, 9; Mr. Lutz, 4; Mr. D. Harris, 3; Mr.
Joseph McKinney, 7; Mr. Montgomery, 7; Mr. Sturgeon, 8; Mr.
Scull, 6; Mr. M. W. McKinney, 8; Mr. John H. Agnew, 7; Mr. H.
Stewart, 1.

This is the only list of teachers that can be found between 1816
and 1825.—EDITOR.

During that year the school was reduced by the departure of fifty scholars to form the Sunday-school of the newly organized Methodist Church. The school of this Church was the mother school of all the early schools of the city.

On Sunday, May 25, 1828, the infant school of this Church was organized with twenty-four scholars, whose names are on record.* Samuel W. Hays, who in 1840 became a ruling elder of the Church became its first superintendent and filled the office with great acceptance and faithfulness for nearly twenty-seven years, when he was obliged by failing health to resign. Mr. Hays was a warm friend and lover of the young and made a model superintendent.

In 1829, Miss Wyeth resigned the superintendency of the main school and Miss Juliann Fisher was again chosen, and filled the office until 1832. A new order of things was now inaugurated. Mr. Henry Cross was chosen superintendent in 1833, and filled the office for two years. During its infancy and childhood and until at the age of sixteen years it had grown into stalwartness, and had sent out from its fold three or four schools to other churches, the school was managed by the christian women of the Church. They filled its superintendency. They did it nobly and well. They have been from the birth of the school to this day of its great prosperity, the mightiest spiritual force in the

---

* These are the names: Catharine Murray, Cornelia J. Wright, Margaret Bennet, Julia D. Graydon, Elizabeth Harris, Harriet Thompson, Eleanor Graydon, Catharine E. Cameron, Mary Parker, Catharine Duncan, Mary Wayne, Lydia Rees, H. Thompson (colored), Catharine Black, Isabella Buffington, Elizabeth Buffington, William Mitchell, William Ayres, John Wilson, George Whitehill, John Martin, Richard T. Leech, Charles Mahon, Alexander Mahon.—EDITOR.

religious education of the children and youth of this congregation.

Mr. Cross resigned in 1835. The following record appears on the journal of the school for that year. "Resolved that Mr. James W. Weir be appointed superintendent in the place of Mr. Cross, resigned." March 12, 1835, a prince among Sunday-school Superintendents and among religious leaders had now taken his place at the head of the school. He continued to fill the place with remarkable power and universal favor until his death on March 14th, 1878, a period of forty-three years and two days.* At his death the present superintendent, Mr. Samuel J. M. McCarrell was chosen to fill the vacant office, and has occupied it with honor to himself and blessing to the school and Church for nearly sixteen years.

It is due to the Church in this historical record that a few words should be added concerning the superintendency of Mr. Weir. It was a custom of his, a fixed law, to make a thorough preparation for the fulfillment of his duties. The school was on his heart through the busy week. At the opening of each session it was his wont to deliver a brief address in connection with the reading of the scriptures. These addresses were usually about fifteen minutes in length. They were always looked for with great interest, by the teachers and scholars alike, and were remarkable specimens of condensed thought, strikingly illustrated by happy anecdote and incident gathered from

---

* As Mr. Weir was acting Superintendent during the year 1834, on account of Mr. Cross's illness, he really served more than forty-four years.—EDITOR.

JAMES W. WEIR.
SUPERINTENDENT OF THE SUNDAY-SCHOOLS, 1834-1878.

his wide course of reading and his intercourse with men. Very seldom were they devoid of deep interest. They were never trivial or common place. At times they were pungent and powerful appeals to the heart and conscience of all who heard them. Had they been preserved by any short hand reporter, they would have ranked high in the literature of Sunday school addresses. He made special preparation for the service. His thoughts were not random ones, nor were his words extempore. They were chosen and select. The school Bible which he used for years, will be found still to bear on its margins the brief notes and heads of some of his addresses. And the Sunday-school diary that he kept for years will give a great many illustrations of his skill in meeting this duty of the superintendent. Sometimes he would give on consecutive Sabbaths a series of connected addresses on the beatitudes, or the ten commandments or other themes, illustrating them with telling incidents. Sometimes he would select some particular passage in the lesson of the day and give a graphic address upon it. His Sunday-school prayers were also as remarkable as his addresses. They were fitted to the place and the occasion, and the minds he was leading to the throne of grace. Though blackboards were not in general use in his earlier days, and his own use of it was not extensive, he had one. Generally he placed upon it only a single sentence, but it was the very heart of his address. The passage which he left on the board at his death and that has been preserved and framed is a good illustration both of his facile hand and of the good use to which he put the

blackboard.*   He used it to make a point, to fix a truth, to
deepen an impression, to make a lodgment in the memory,
and he succeeded most admirably.   His intercourse with the
school was most genial and sympathetic.   He was always
thoughtful of others and the master of himself.   His
journal of the school, seen only after his death, reveals how
thoroughly he gave his heart and thoughts and powers to
the spiritual and eternal welfare of the school.   Even in
his last hours it showed itself to be the master passion of
his heart to care for the Sunday-school of this Church.   It
was in his own mind at the moment of his departure from
earth, and the last utterances that fell from his lips were
concerning it.

Some further record should be made of the Infant Sunday-
school.   As nearly as can be ascertained, the resignation by
Mr. Samuel W. Hays of the superintendency, took place in
1854.   During the period intervening between 1854 and
1858, the superintendency was held by Mrs. Sarah E. Dixon
for a part of the time, and a brief season by Miss Simonton.
After the destruction of the church building, March 30,

---

* It was the custom of the Assistant Superintendent, Mr. McCarrell, to prepare the blackboard after each session of Sunday-school
for Mr. Weir's use on the following Sunday.   On the last Sunday Mr.
Weir was in the desk, Mr. McCarrell was absent from the city, and
hence the weekly text written by Mr. Weir for that day remained
upon the board.   Before the next Sunday he was in his grave.   The
text which was thus left undisturbed, as his last word to the school,
was, " Leaving us an example that ye should follow in his steps," was
singularly fitting as the lesson of his life.   The portion of the board
containing the text was framed and still hangs upon the wall in the
room of the upper department of the school.—EDITOR.

1858, Mr. John A. Weir took charge of the school and directed its affairs with great success. Mr. Weir was a friend and lover of children, never more at home than when he was surrounded by them, and busy in their instruction and entertainment. His love for them was returned in bountiful measure by the children who were charmed by the methods of his teaching. Failing health compelled him in 1869, to resign most of the work of the school to Mrs. Matilda Feeman, retaining for himself only a general superintendency. He continued to be a welcome visitant at the school until his death.

On December 5, 1875, the school was divided into classes. On May 7, 1876, Miss Julia W. DeWitt was appointed superintendent and took charge with Miss Anna C. Weir as assistant superintendent. Miss DeWitt held the position with great acceptableness until October 12, 1882, when her place was filled by Mrs. David Fleming. Mrs. Fleming and Miss Weir still retain their positions after years of devoted and successful service, for which the Church is most deeply grateful. On May 13, 1883, the school was divided on account of the large numbers attending it into the Intermediate and the Primary departments, Mrs. Fleming and Miss Weir retaining their positions as superintendents of the former, and Mrs. G. M. McCauley and Mrs. Helen F. Bruner being appointed superintendent and assistant superintendent of the latter. The year 1883 was a memorable one in the history of the whole school. The new building so finely adapted to all the wants of the Church, and so elegant in its architecture, was dedicated on January 28th of that year. In March, the Intermediate department was formed into a

Missionary Band, called the Macedonian Band, and its record of gifts to Home and Foreign Missions and to Freedmen for the past eleven years has been a splendid one. On November 4, 1883, a library was presented to the Intermediate department by Mr. and Mrs. David Fleming in memory of a beloved son, Charles Mowry Fleming. The building in all its departments is beautiful and made sacred by the memorials to beloved and honored ones who were once connected with the school. The large and choice memorial windows to the two brothers and beloved superintendents, James Wallace Weir and John Andrew Weir, will continue we trust to speak for many years of their worth, and of the unfailing love of the Church. The stained glass windows, the clock presented by Mrs. I. S. Kerr, the speaking portrait, and the grand words, "Leaving us an example that we should follow his steps," the last traced by the "vanished hand" of our dead leader. Nay, may it be said, the whole building is a memoral of Christian love and unity.

Through all the years of its history since its early organization, September 26, 1816, the school has been the object of the warm affection of the Church. Its roll of teachers is a grand one. The piety and talent of the Church have here found a place to pour out their wealth of devotion to Christ. It has not been an uncommon thing for teachers to spend from twenty-five to forty years in the work of the school. Children have come up from the infant school to stand at length in the church, stalwart men and consecrated women, doing Christ's work, and passing away with the ripeness and honors of age.

WILLIAM RADCLIFFE DEWITT.

1818–1867.

FROM PHOTOGRAPH TAKEN AT THE AGE OF 70 YEARS.

THE first quarter of a century in the life of the Church has nearly passed. The trials of the wilderness are over. The community has grown into a borough of twenty-five hundred inhabitants. There are four churches in the town : the Reformed, the Lutheran, the Presbyterian and a small Methodist Church which had just sprung into being. There were but two pastors, the Rev. George Lochman of the Lutheran Church and the Rev. John Rauhauser of the Reformed Church, popularly known as the German Presbyterian.

The burial ground of the Presbyterian Church was for the first half century in its history on ground now occupied by the Pennsylvania Railway Station. An old subscription list signed by eighty persons in the congregation of the date 1818, still exists, providing for the purchase of additional ground. About the middle of this century the bodies of the dead buried there were removed to the present cemetery.

In September 1818, William Radcliffe DeWitt, a licentiate of the Presbytery of New York, who had been preaching during the summer months, his first sermons to two small congregations in central New York, visited this church on invitation of some of its members and preached to the people for two consecutive Sabbaths and during the week. He met a very hearty reception, and on the fifth of October he was unanimously called to the pastorate. He accepted the call, came on and took up his residence here. The call was signed by the four elders of the Church, Moses Gilmor, Samuel Weir, William Graydon and John Stoner, Adam Boyd having died May 14, 1814, and by sixty-one members of the congregation. Mr. DeWitt was ordained by the Presbytery of Carlisle on the 26th of October, 1819 and on the 12th of November following he was installed. This was Dr. DeWitt's first and only charge. He continued in the pastorate until December 23, 1867, the day of his death, a period of over forty-nine years of actual service, and over forty-eight years as an installed pastor. For thirty-six years he was the sole pastor and for the remaining thirteen he had a colleague. Of the sixty-five persons who signed his call but one outlived the youthful pastor. Among them were men who in subsequent years filled high positions in civil life or were called to offices in the Church. The following may be named. Chief Justice Gibson of the Supreme Court of Pennsylvania, William Findlay and Francis R. Shunk, governors of the Commonwealth. Messrs. Sloan, Agnew, Neilson and McJimsey in later years Ruling Elders in the Church and other men who became prominent in their professions. The Board of Trustees composed of noble men, all preceeded Dr. DeWitt into the other world.

According to a roll made out by William Graydon, one of the elders, the Church membership at the opening of Dr. DeWitt's ministry was seventy. This number was small compared with the large size of the congregation. The young people were not generally communicants in the church. They were not expected to make an early profession of religion. There were few, if any young people's organizations of any kind. The day of societies had not yet dawned upon the Church. There was very little to attract youth in the institutions of religion and very little for them to do. The Church had not yet learned the art of Christian Work and the joy of service. Dr. DeWitt has left on record

the testimony that it was only after some persuasion that
the elders and other lay members were induced to hold
meetings for prayer which could be attended by all, indis-
criminately, who desired to come. When these elders and
laymen took hold of Christian work and prayer, under the
leadership of Dr. DeWitt, they soon developed into
remarkably gifted men. The godly, praying women were
however then as they have always been the ornament and
glory of the Church. The prayermeeting first established
was held originally in private homes, until no private
dwelling could hold the numbers who desired to attend.
The log school house which stood at the foot of Capitol Hill
on the corner of Third and Walnut streets was then obtained.
It soon became too strait for the gathering crowds. The
Spirit of God was among the people. The heart of
the young pastor was cheered by a revival at the opening
of his ministry and the church sprung forward into
new life and unwonted activities. It grew rapidly. The
power of God was in it. It became influential in the
community and through all the years of Dr. DeWitt's
ministry it was the home of intelligence. The men of the
professions very largely attended it. It continued to be the
leading English Speaking pulpit, as the pulpits of the
Lutheran and Reformed Churches were divided between
the English and German, in their Sunday services for
several years. The executive officers of the State Government, the Legislators and the Judges of the Courts generally
waited upon the services of the Presbyterian Church. Of
the sixteen Governors of the State from 1790 to 1870, the
following were Presbyterians, and were attendants upon the

Sabbath worship of this Church : Thomas McKean, Simon Snyder, William Findlay, George Wolf, David R. Porter, Francis R. Shunk, William T. Johnston, William Bigler, James Pollock, William F. Packer, Andrew G. Curtin and John W. Geary. The last was a member of the Church for some years before his death.

Of the events that occured in the history of this Church during Dr. DeWitt's pastorate I must speak briefly.

On January 4, 1819, a charter was obtained from the Supreme Court of Pennsylvania for the congregation under the name of The English Presbyterian Congregation. That is still its legal title. The application was signed by seventy-one members of the congregation and the grant is approved by William Findlay, the Governor of the Commonwealth. The charter is still in the possession of the trustees of the Church.

The following additions were made to the Ruling Eldership of the Church during the sole pastorate of Dr. DeWitt :

On February 20, 1820, Dr. Samuel Agnew, Robert Sloan and Joseph A. McJimsey were ordained and installed to the office; and on September 11th, 1825, John Neilson, Richard T. Leech and John C. Capp were also ordained and inducted into the same office. In 1834 James W Weir, Alexander Sloan and Alexander Graydon were added to the noble band of Ruling Elders and leaders of the Church. In 1840 Samuel W. Hays and Alfred Armstrong, in 1845 William Root and William McClean were also ordained and installed. During the co-pastorate, Mordecai McKinney, John A. Weir and Robert J. Fleming,

ENGLISH PRESBYTERIAN CHURCH.
SECOND STREET AND CHERRY ALLEY.
ERECTED 1841-42.

in the year 1855, were added to the roll. Twenty intelligent, earnest, God-fearing men served the Church as members of its session and as its spiritual leaders during Dr. DeWitt's ministry. Rarely has a Church been honored with such a body of consecrated and irreproachable men.

During these early years in the pastorate of Dr. DeWitt, the church edifice, though enlarged by a gallary and otherwise altered, became too contracted for the numbers who desired to worship in it. In the spring of 1841 the old church was torn down, and the erection of a new one was begun on the site of the old one and of some ground added by purchase. During its construction the court house was occupied both for the regular Sabbath service and for the Sunday-school. The contractor for the new building was Mr. Peter Bernheisel, and it was opened and dedicated to God on the 13th of January, 1842. It was constructed of brick covered by white cement, and was universally regarded as a structure of peculiar neatness and beauty. Its dimensions were eighty-four feet by sixty-three. In front it was very tastefully adorned by a portico, supported by pillars of the Corinthian order, an exact copy, it was said, of a celebrated temple front erected on the street of the Tripos at Athens in the year 335 B. C. to commemorate a musical victory. The church was a two-story building. The basement story was above ground and contained a lecture room, a Sabbath-school room, and a studio designed for the pastor. The latter was also adapted to the uses of the original infant school of the Church. The audience chamber above was a fine large room, and with its three gallaries would accommodate fully a thousand persons.

The gallaries were called into use only on grand occasions, save that for the choir. The pulpit, constructed of finely polished Italian marble, was regarded as the cynosure for for all eyes, and unrivaled for chasteness and beauty. The whole structure was one of great beauty and fitness. After sixteen years of service it was totally consumed by fire on the evening of March 30th, 1858, the fire originating in some adjacent buildings. During the ministry of Dr. DeWitt the Church was visited by repeated and signal out-pourings of Divine grace, by which many were brought into its communion. The most noted of these seasons were in the years 1819, 1824, 1827, 1830, 1834 and 1843. While Dr. DeWitt largely devoted his thoughts and labors to train up around him a body of sound, intelligent and earnest Christians, and to develop the piety of Christian homes, and so secure a permanent and growing state of religious life as the best means of insuring a stable and progressive Church, he was thankful to God for these extraordinary tokens of Divine favor. The most noted of these revivals was in 1843, and it is well remembered still by a few in the Church who then found the Christ of their hopes and of their lives. The congrega-tion was stirred to its foundations. The entire community was awakened. For the space of two or three months all except necessary labors were laid aside that men might give themselves to the matter of salvation for themselves and for their fellowmen. The places of business were often closed. Religion was the theme of talk upon the streets. Men in the Legislature, then in session, left the halls of legislation that in the meetings for prayer they might seek the face of a forgiving God. Two senators were among the converts, one of whom subsequently became a minister in the Episcopal Church. Several young men came into the Church who have since that time served here and elsewhere as ruling elders. One hundred and thirty made a public profession of their faith on the same day and the membership of the Church reached its highest numbers under Dr. DeWitt's pastorate. The incidents of that happy period were often rehearsed in subsequent years by those who had shared in them. They were the more cherished in memory because they had followed so closely upon another series of events that threatened to be disastrous to the well being of the Church, and of which a brief record must now be made, as they had their bearing upon its history.

In 1838 the Presbyterian Church of the entire country was divided into two great branches, known as the old and the new school. The division continued for thirty-two years, or until 1870, when a reunion took place, which we trust will become more thorough and happy and strong until the second coming of the Great Head of all believers.

Into the causes and the history of that unhappy division it is not necessary to enter. It would involve very lengthy statements, too lengthy for a discourse on an occasion of this kind. It would also involve the expression of personal opinions and judgments upon the matters that had for years agitated the Presbyterian Church and that led to the disruption. The immediate occasion for the separation of the Church into two bodies may be found in the action of the General Assembly of 1837 that met in the Central Church of Philadelphia on May 18th. By a vote of one hundred and thirty-two ayes to one hundred and five nays, the Western Reserve Synod, with all its churches, was declared not to be a part of the Presbyterian Church in the United States. Four days later the three Synods of Utica, Geneva and Genesee were also by a vote of one hundred and fifteen yeas to eighty-eight nays, "declared to be out of the ecclesiastical connection of the Presbyterian Church" and to be "not in form nor in fact an integral portion of said Church." By this action of the General Assembly of 1837, four Synods, containing about thirty Presbyteries, several hundred churches and nearly one fifth of the entire membership of the Presbyterian Church of the country were exscinded from the Church. They were declared to be no longer a part of the Church of their birth, their training, their sympathies and their solemn vows. It was a very summary procedure, to say the least, to cut off, without impeachment and without trial, so large a number of ministers and elders and Church members from the Church which they loved and honored.

The Assembly of the next year, 1838, also met in Philadelphia. Commissioners appeared from the exscinded Presbyteries and claimed a right to seats in the Assembly. Their claim was denied and seats were refused them. A new Assembly was then constituted of the friends and sympathizers of the exscinded Presbyteries, whose members then withdrew to the First Presbyterian Church, of Philadelphia. This body was the first of the so-called new School Assemblies. The two Assemblies continued in session for several days, each claiming to represent the Presbyterian Church of the United States. This Church was called upon to decide with which of these two bodies it would cast its lot. A full history of the action taken by the congregation has been preserved in the handwriting of Rev. Dr. DeWitt, the pastor of the Church.* Three propositions were brought before the people and fully considered, namely, (1) To recognize and acknowledge as the General Assembly of the Presbyterian Church that body of commissioners who met in the Seventh Presbyterian Church of Philadelphia, or the body subsequently known as the Old School General Assembly; (2) To recognize and acknowledge as the General Assembly of the Presbyterian Church that body of commissioners who met in the First Presbyterian Church of Philadelphia, or the body familiarly known subsequently as the New School General Assembly; or (3) to decline the jurisdiction of either body and also of all the subordinate Synods and Presbyteries, and to assume the position of an independent Presbyterian Church. On July 2, 1838, the Church withdrew from the control of all the higher ecclesiastical courts and became an independent Presbyterian Church.

This action was taken with three or four voices dissenting. This action of the Church was without doubt mainly due to two causes. First, the Church by a very large majority sympathized with the new school branch of the Presbyterian body in the country and especially regarded the acts of the General Assembly of 1837 in the excision of the four Synods, and the proceedings that grew out of them as unconstitutional and unjust and unkind; and second, the Church was unwilling to have the pastoral relation between it and Dr. DeWitt dissolved, as he declared it would be necessary for him to withdraw from the pastorate should the congregation decide to acknowledge the juris-diction of the Old School General Assembly.

The independent position assumed by the Church was maintained until November 5, 1840, when it was received into the Presbytery of Harrisburg, in connection with the New School General Assembly, and so remained until all divisions were lost in the happy re-union of eighteen hundred and seventy. It was a severe trial to this Church to be severed from the great body of the Presbyterian Churches in Central Pennsylvania. It had walked with them in happiest harmony for nearly half a century. Two other churches, the First Presbyterian Church of Carlisle and the Presbyterian Church of York had preceeded this Church in recognizing the New School General Assembly. The Presbytery of Harrisburg was a very small body, made up of widely scattered churches. It required no small amount of courage and fidelity to principle for these few scattered congregations in the midst of a large body of churches to take and maintain for over thirty years the stand they had assumed, and that put them out of fellow-ship with old friends. The little Presbytery of Harrisburg was like a small but very happy household and this Church felt for about one third of a century the power of its attrac-tiveness.

Within a few years after the remarkable revival of 1843, a spiritual re-action occurred. It is no uncommon thing in the history of our fickle human nature. The Church be-came cold in its religious life and lost its power upon the

world. There were but few conversions and the membership of the Church decreased by death, by removal to other
communions and by a few defections from the faith. The
heart of the pastor became discouraged. The burden of
years was coming upon him and he determined to withdraw
from most of the active duties of the pastorate and commit
the work to such a colleague as the congregation might call
to co-operate with him in the care of the Church. On
February 6, 1854, his request that a co-pastor be associated
with him was presented to a meeting of the congregation,
and after resolutions expressive of regret and of their continued confidence, his request was granted. In pursuance
of this arrangement Mr. Thomas H. Robinson, who had just
finished his studies at the Western Theological Seminary,
Allegheny, Pa., was invited to preach in the pulpit on the
last Sabbath in June and the first Sabbath in July of 1854.
He preached on those Sabbaths and the Wednesday evening
intervening, and on July 5th was called to be a colleague
with Dr. DeWitt in the pastorate of the Church. He accepted the call and entered upon the work on the first
Sabbath of October of the same year. He had been licensed
by the Presbytery of Ohio a few days before his visit. He
was ordained to the ministry and installed in the pastorate
on January 21st, 1855. It was his first pastorate as it had
also been that of his three predecessors, and it proved to be
his only pastorate as it also was that of Dr. DeWitt. The
terms of service in the Church of the third and fourth pastors amounted to nearly eighty years, thirteen of which
were in common. The relations between the pastors were
most fraternal and kindly in character.

During all his ministry, Dr. DeWitt had proved to be a fast friend and supporter of missions, home and foreign, and the Church fully sympathized with him. His elders were greatly interested in these fields of labor. Both Dr. DeWitt and one of his elders, James W. Weir, were made corporate members of the American Board of Commissioners for Foreign Missions. The interest in foreign missions was stimulated by the many years of service of one of the members of the Church as a missionary in the Sandwich Islands, Miss Mary Ann McKinney, sister of Honorable Mordecai McKinney, and wife of Rev. William Patterson Alexander. She spent twenty years of devoted service on the Islands. One of her sons, William DeWitt Alexander, late a commissioner of the Provisional Government of the Sandwich Islands to the United States, has for many years been prominent in public affairs in those Islands.

There were at my coming, in 1854, about one hundred and seventy members in the communion of the Church. Forty years have since passed and but twelve of that number now remain on the roll. A few others are still living and are in the fellowship of other churches, but the great majority have departed this life in the faith of Christ's holy name.

Of this fourth occupant of the pastorate the following facts may be stated: He was born at North East, Erie county, Pennsylvania, January 30, 1828. In 1850 he graduated from Oberlin College, Ohio, and in May, 1854, from the Western Theological Seminary. In coming here he came back to the early home of his ancestry. Thomas Robinson, his ancestor of the sixth generation back, was among the first settlers of Donegal in the early part of the last century. Philip Robinson, son of Thomas, and his great great grandfather, was among the founders of Old Hanover Church, and resided on a farm at the mouth of Manada Gap. A fort, known as Robinson's Fort, and a place of refuge and of defence during the Indian wars about the middle of the last century, is mentioned in the Pennsylvania Archives.* His eldest son, George Robinson, removed to the head of Sherman's creek, Perry county, about 1754, and was one of the founders of the Old Centre Church, and one of its first ruling elders. Upon his farm also stood a fort, mentioned in the Pennsylvania Archives as George Robinson's Fort, into which the the inhabitants of the valley fled upon incursions of the Indians. He was also a captain in service during the times of the Revolution. My grandfather, Thomas Robinson, the youngest son of George R., removed to Erie county in 1798, and was among the first settlers on the shores of Lake Erie. He, with a few others, founded the first Presbyterian Church in that region, and was one of the original bench of elders. I came here a child of the Covenant, through many generations, a lineal descendant of the first settlers of Scotch-Irish blood and Presbyterian faith. It is needless to say I found myself at home. My ancestry lay buried in several of the ancient church yards of this region.

As in the case of my predecessor, Dr. DeWitt, the first year of my ministry was blessed and brightened by a gracious revival of religion. Several, who at that time made a profession of their faith in Christ, are still active and devoted

---

* It stood on Philip Robinson's farm.

workers in the Church of Christ. The Young Men's Christian Association, of this city, which has so long been an agency of blessing, was instituted in the Lecture Room of this Church on December 12, 1854, largely, I may claim, through my own urgency. It is my impression that it was the eighth association organized in the United States. His Honor, John W. Simonton, was chosen its first president, and a large proportion of its earliest officers and members belonged to this congregation. The Association should celebrate its approaching semi-centennary.

After the destruction of the second church edifice by fire on the evening of March 30, 1858, the congregation met for Sabbath worship, for nearly two years, in Brant's Hall, on Market street. Several of the other churches of the city vied with each other in kind and pressing offers of their own church buildings for our religious services. The gracious and Christian letters received from them are still preserved. During that period the Sunday-school was held, until October 16, 1859, in the upper room of the court house. On that day it took possession of the new school-room on the corner of Market Square and Second streets. The entrance upon the new home for the school was made an occasion of great rejoicing. The week-day lecture service was held on Thursday, and, by the courtesy of the Reformed Church, was held in their lecture-room, on Chestnut street, until Monday, October 17th, when the lecture-room of this church was dedicated to God, and has been in use until this day.

On the 18th of March, 1860, this Church was occupied for the first time, and was solemnly dedicated to the purposes

THOMAS HASTINGS ROBINSON.
1854-1884.

FROM PHOTOGRAPH TAKEN AT THE AGE OF 64 YEARS.

of divine worship. At both the morning and evening services the church was crowded, and many could not find an
entrance. The sermons for the day were both preached by
the eloquent Dr. Rosewell D. Hitchcock, of Union Theological Seminary. They were sermons of remarkable power
and great beauty. In the afternoon the Communion of the
Lord's Supper was celebrated. For over one-third. of a
century this room has been the Sabbath home of this congregation. It has lost none of its first attractiveness, and
through all these years sacred and precious memories have
been gathering in it that continue to enrich it. Here the
festal joys of marriage have been witnessed. From this
room the bodies of our beloved dead have been carried, and
laid away until the morning of the resurrection. Here
wondrous scenes of revival have gladdened the hearts of
Christians. Here, too, during the long struggle to save the
life of the nation, the people met, sometimes under depress-
ing fears and great forebodings, sometimes in periods of
intense excitement and sometimes for seasons of devout
thanksgiving.

Ere the congregation entered upon its new religious home
another event occurred that left a deep impression upon the
church and molded its history. We became two bands.
Quite a number of the Church, by the circumstances of birth
and early training, by their associations with churches of
the region, and by their own hearty convictions, had, for
years, preferred that section of the Presbyterian Church
known as the Old School. It was determined to organize
a new Church in connection with the Presbytery of Carlisle
and the Old School General Assembly. Letters of dismis-

sion were granted to all who asked for them, and the present Pine Street Church was constituted. The withdrawal reduced the Church to about one hundred and fifty members, the smallest number for many years. Painful as was the breaking up of many cherished associations, the departing of beloved friends and the rending of family ties, time and the gentle influences of divine grace have been busy healing the pains of separation, and the growth of two large and strong congregations, the enlarged activities of Christians in both Churches, and the rapid and substantial growth of Christ's kingdom in the city have demonstrated that the loving heart and hand of God molded the events of that hour to his own glory. As we look back upon the events of that time, at the close of these thirty-five years of Christian labors and victories and progress, the griefs and fears of the time pass away, and, exulting with the Apostle, we cry: "Herein we do rejoice and will rejoice." With larger hearts and clearer vision we recognize to-day the unseen hand that then guided us, that guides us now, and evermore will guide us to his own blessed ends.

At my coming to the city in 1854 the population was about ten thousand. It is not far from forty-five thousand now. Its churches numbered about twelve. They have increased to over fifty. There was but a single Presbyterian Church with a membership of about one hundred and seventy. The Presbyterian Church was failing to keep pace with the growth of the city. Its Sunday-school numbered two hundred and forty. The contributions of the Church, both for its own support and for benevolent causes, were less than twenty-five hundred dollars. Of this amount one thousand dollars were paid to meet the salaries of the two pastors, that amount being divided between them. There was no parsonage, and the pastors paid their own house rent. They were in no danger of growing rich upon their salaries.

According to the report made to the General Assembly of 1893 in May last, the Presbyterian Churches of the city now number six, with two large and flourishing missions and a prosperous growing Church just beyond the city limits. The number of Church members has increased from one hundred and seventy to two thousand and fifty-one. The growth of the city has been four and one-half fold, of the Presbyterian Church membership over twelve fold. The number in the Sunday-school has increased from two hundred and forty to four thousand eight hundred and and eleven, or twenty fold. The contributions of the Churches have increased from twenty-five hundred dollars for all objects, to sixty-five thousand, six hundred and ninety-six dollars during the last church year, or over twenty-two fold. Of this amount thirty-one thousand, five hundred and sixty-four dollars were given directly to benevolent objects, and thirty-four thousand, one hundred and thirty-one dollars were given to congregational expenses. These figures show how under the fostering care and smile of God these Churches have waxed in numbers and strength.

This Church alone has grown from a Church membership of one hundred and seventy to seven hundred and seventy-six, and from a Sunday-school of two hundred and forty members to one of seventeen hundred and eighty-nine, and from a contribution for all causes, its own home work and the work of general benevolence, from twenty-five hundred dollars per year to over twenty thousand. During the last forty years, the years through which statistics have been in some good measure, though not fully, preserved, the contributions of this church to all objects have been over half a million of dollars. Of this amount over one hundred thousand dollars have been given to Home and Foreign Missions. Large as these sums may seem to be, let it not for a moment be thought that they reach at all the height of our obligation to God and our fellow-men, or the height of our ability to give. No one has been made poorer by these gifts. The world has been enriched, and every liberal heart has grown in spiritual wealth. The benevolent causes to which these sums of money have been given are too many to be enumerated. In addition to those that are especially required by the General Church, there have been such as the following: The American Bible Society, The American Tract Society, The Sunday School Union, The Benevolent Society of Harrisburg, the Home for the Friendless, the City Hospital and numerous other causes.

Another series of events that had a great influence upon this church cannot be omitted from this brief history. It affected its growth and influenced its piety. It occupied very largely for several years its thoughts and directed its actions. The Church feels to this day the molding power of those events.

The stupendous war of the Southern Rebellion, which for nearly five years evoked the highest energies of the nation, and that came to the door of every home, and laid its

demands on every man, found this Church and congregation prepared for sacrifices. For many years there had been
an enlarging contest and struggle in the State and in the
Church over the questions that lay at the heart of the great
conflict. The fact cannot now be overlooked. I found the
members of this Church agitated upon these questions when
I came here in 1854, seven years before the dreadful war
opened upon us. The entire New School Church with
which this congregation was connected had for many years
been greatly affected and was far more pronounced on the
question of freedom for all men than the other branch of
the Presbyterian Church. But a small proportion of the
Presbyterians of the South, after the great division in 1838,
cast in their lot with the New School Church, and these few,
after the meeting of the Assembly in 1857, four years before
the outbreak of the Rebellion in 1861, withdrew from the
New School Church on account of its attitude on slavery
and formed a separate ecclesiastical organization. This
Church was in hearty sympathy with the body to which it
belonged in its love of the country and in its opposition to
the system of human slavery. It did not, however, dream
—few did in that day—how grave and terrible a conflict was
before the nation. The loyalty of the people was put to the
severest test and its faith in God was sorely tried. Its love
to the country stood the test of self-denials such as the
people had never thought themselves capable of making.
There were many dark hours during that memorable struggle. In the darkest the people did not falter. Large and
generous contributions to be reckoned by thousands of
dollars were made to the Christian and Sanitary Commis-

sions for the relief of the sick and the wounded soldiery. The women of the Church were indefatigable in their labors and boundless in their sympathies. They made garments and haversacks, before the general government was ready to meet the demands; they opened the hospitalities of their homes to the coming and going soldiers; they visited, like angels of mercy, the hospitals that were formed in the city for the sick and the wounded from the fields of battle. The junior pastor was permitted by the Church to leave his pulpit and spend months in the service of the Christian Commission in Virginia and Tennessee. Our city was often like a camp. The sound of martial music, the beating of drums and the waving of flags, the steady tramp of armed men, singing their patriotic songs on our streets, the coming and going of regiments and of brigades, the long trains of huzzahing armies passing through the city and crossing the river, with their faces away from their homes and turned to the seat of war, soldiers at our homes, at our meetings of prayer and in our Churches at Sabbath worship, the sight of Presidents and Professors of College, of Doctors of Divinity, of men high in the professions in the ranks, or as captains and as chaplains, and the sad trains filled with the sick and the wounded for our hospitals, or passing through to hospitals elsewhere, the strange, new sight of prisoners of war on our streets, these were some of the things that occupied our thoughts for nearly five long sad years of weariness and hope. And then, too, came the terrible strain as we waited for news from the battle-fields and scanned the lists of the killed and wounded to see if mayhap the names of any of our own beloved ones were there, the strain as we waited and wondered when the end would come and what the end would be, our hushed and solemn places of prayer, where we plead with God for our country; our days of fasting and our days of thanksgiving, too; our bated breath as we spoke of some great disaster, a battle lost, a great general fallen, and our lifted hopes as the tide turned; they were strange, thrilling days of which the children of to-day can scarcely form a conception.

The pulpit of this Church felt under bonds to truth and to the country to do its part in those trying times. Patriotic sermons, "War Sermons," as they were then called, were preached from time to time. In days of depression that followed any disaster to our armies, when saddened and despondent hearts need to be keyed up to a larger, firmer trust in God, and a firmer hope for the final issue in righteousness, peace and a united country. And in days of hopefulness and exultation when the spirit of thanksgiving to God needed to be called out, this pulpit spoke with no uncertain tones and this Church responded with no uncertain and wavering fidelity to the nation's peril and need.

Added to our larger concern for the whole country this Church had its own precious personal investments in the war. About fifty men and youth belonging to the families of the congregation then, or but a little time before, served with the army of the Union. They filled positions from the private to the general. Some are to-day bearing their scars. Some fell on the field of battle. One of the Elders of the Church lost a noble son. Another had a son who was brevetted as captain for gallant services at the battle of Weldon Railroad, Virginia, and who in that engagement received a wound that gave him trouble until his early death in 1883. Others lie with the unknown heroes who fell on the field and were hurriedly buried with no stone to mark their resting-place. This Church had its share in the fears and the tears of that sad conflict. It felt to its inmost heart the savage shot that laid the great and calm leader of the nation low. And when the end came and the white wings of peace fluttered over the battle-fields of strife and blood, this Church joined in the universal gratefulness to God that war was over and rest had come. It had been very hard to carry on the work of God amid the unceasing excitements of those perilous years. It was hard to get back again to the quiet and calmness of our holy Gospel.

After the close of the war, the years passed quietly and rapidly along. In 1867 the venerated senior pastor, now ripe in years, was called to his reward. Negotiations had already begun to heal the division in the Presbyterian Church. The years of separation had been continually demonstrating the substantial unity of the two branches of the Church in doctrine and polity, and in all forms of christian work. They had been drawing towards each other. The common struggles and sufferings for the salvation of the country had warmed the hearts of the people towards each other. The spirit of union was in the air. Hopes were entertained that there might be a fusion of all the families of the Presbyterian genealogy. We became especially interested in the re-union movement, because one of the conferences which greatly promoted it was held in this church during the session of the New School General Assembly in 1868. In fact it was in this Church and at that time that the report on the basis of re-union, as presented by the joint committee of fifteen through its chairman Rev. William Adams, D. D., of New York, was adopted by a unanimous vote. It was the harbinger of the good time coming.

A number of the great leaders of the two Churches were here, and this room resounded to their eloquent and fraternal addresses. Twelve who have filled the chair of Moderator in the New School General Assembly or in the Re-united Assembly, were present, viz: Rev. Drs. William Adams, Samuel Hanson Cox, Thomas H. Skinner, Henry B. Smith, George L. Prentiss, Samuel W. Fisher, Laurens P. Hickok, George Duffield, Jonathan F. Stearns, Robert W. Patterson, Edward D. Morris and Henry A. Nelson. There were present also as Commissioners from the Old School General Assembly to confer on the subject of re-union, Rev. Drs. Charles C. Beatty, Richard H. Richardson, Villeroy D. Reed, and Chancellor Henry W. Green, Robert Carter and Henry Day. Addresses were made by all the representatives of the other assembly. Telegrams of greeting and brotherly love were exchanged between the two Assemblies, and a common hour of prayer for one of the days of the week was appointed. The occasion was one long to be remembered. In the consummation of the union two years later, 1870, this Church most heartily rejoiced. It was brought again into closest and most happy relations with Churches from which it had been separated for a third of a century, and to their hearts and their homes the members of this Church once more welcomed the representatives of Presbyterianism in Cumberland Valley.

Fourteen years of the fourth pastorate now followed each other in quick succession. The years passed quietly away. They were years of mingled sorrow and joy. Gladness and grief alternated with each other. The Church grew in strength. It multiplied its agencies of usefulness. It increased its charities. Sometimes it moved along gently in the ordinary channels of grace. The family, the Sunday-school, and the sanctuary, social prayers, pious lives, gospel preaching, works of charity among the poor were evidences of the living power of true religion. The silent dew falling unseen when men are asleep has its mission in hastening on the harvest as well as has the breaking cloud which fills the thirsty earth and chokes the stream and swells the river to a flood. There were times when God came in gracious power to His temple, when He crushed the clamors of worldliness and awakened large numbers in a simultaneous concern for their salvation. Glorious times they were. But as the Master looks down into his vineyard, He rejoices also in those quiet days when under the light and warmth of His smile the leaves are putting forth and the buds are swelling, when the flowers and fruits of grace are quietly coming to perfection.

Through those years we had our marriage joys. Children blessed our homes with their songs and laughter, sinners came into the kingdom of grace, and saints left us for the kingdom of glory. New faces greeted us, and the friendly faces of many years passed out of our sight. Lifelong warriors laid their armor by and younger soldiers stepped into the ranks and the winning cause swept on towards the final victory.

The history of these years would be incomplete were we to omit from the record certain events that had a very great and marked influence upon the character of this Church and of Presbyterianism in the city. In the winter of 1875–1876 there occurred in the city a revival of religion of unusual power and extent, by which many hundreds were led to come out from the world and make a public confession of Christ. In the fall of 1875 it was very deeply felt that there was a pressing need for a quickening of religious life in all the Churches and an awakening of the whole city to the subject of salvation. An association of the evangelical clergy of the city discussed and prayed over the matter at its meetings. Several of the leading and most active Christian laymen were called into the conferences and it was decided to hold a series of union meetings of all the Churches. The union of Churches and ministers was very general. There was almost a complete breaking down of all denominational lines and a fusion of sympathies and labors. A very happy state of fraternal feeling prevailed. The religious movement became general.

James W. Weir, the beloved Elder of this Church, at one of the conferences urged that the Rev. E. P. Hammond, a widely-known Evangelist, should be secured. The great confidence felt in Mr. Weir by all the Churches led to an engagement for Mr. Hammond to come. Before he reached the city the daily meetings had become very large and very impressive. The Churches were awakened. The Pastors spoke with new power. The irreligious world began to question what it all meant. When the Evangelist came he found the Churches all united, earnest, praying, and assembling in large numbers.

Selecting this Church as the most central and one of the largest in the city, most of the services were held in it. At times the crowd in attendance was so large that the opera house was used. The services were held daily. Usually a service of prayer was held in the morning, and though it occurred during business hours, it was very largely attended. These morning meetings were greatly loved by the Christian people who attended them.

In the afternoon, generally at the hour when the public schools closed for the day a service was held for children. Mr. Hammond has been called "the children's preacher." He throughly believes in the conversion of children, even of tender years, and makes it a prime matter in his evangelistic work, to instruct and interest the children and bring them to know and trust, and love Jesus Christ as their personal friend and saviour. He was very clear and simple and graphic in his addresses to them and wielded a great and good influence upon them.

The evening services of the revival were the times of greatest public interest. Night after night for weeks this house was filled to overflow. Often many stood during the entire service and many were compelled to go away as a place to stand could not be had. At times the lecture room was also opened and another meeting for prayer was carried on at the same time.

The people came from all parts of the city and from all classes, the professions and the laboring men, the rich and the poor. They came in from the surrounding country.

They came on the railways from five to sixty miles. The evangelist seldom preached less than an hour, and spoke with great earnestness. He was at times dramatic in manner. His sermons were full of the Gospel, presented, argued, illustrated, enforced in every way to carry light and conviction and persuasion to the minds and hearts and wills of his hearers. He was thoroughly orthodox. The common people heard him gladly. The working classes from our rolling mills and manufactories and shops of every kind, after the day's work, would hasten to the service. The poor, the uneducated, were always ready to hear him. Some of the rich and fashionable and refined were not at home in the meetings. Religion was getting too common for them, too low, too obtrusive, too exciting. They could not comprehend nor endure the sorrows and tears of the penitent, nor the joys and happiness of the reconciled who had found their Saviour. At the close of the sermon all who desired to remain for conversation and inquiry upon the way of salvation were invited to do so. Often the entire audience would abide in their places, and the evangelist, with a large body of workers, the ministers present and earnest Christian laymen would pass through the house from pew to pew and seek to have a few words of personal appeal with those who had not come out on the Lord's side. Friends sought their impenitent friends, Sunday-school teachers sought their pupils, workmen sought their fellow-workmen. The roughest men of the city would be there, and moved by the strange scene, or by the singing of some sweet hymn, or the sermon, would wait for some one to come and talk to them about Christ and salvation. The lecture-room of the church

was at times crowded with penitents seeking the peace of
reconciliation with God. Marvellous scenes were witnessed
that cannot here be rehearsed. There was no disorder and
confusion for any one who was in harmony with the wonderful things that were transpiring. Religion was the
supreme topic. The results were very marked. All the
Churches of the city felt the power of the revival. The
country round about the city, the village and towns from
fifty to one hundred miles away were moved by reports
of the meetings, and delegations came and saw and heard
and carried away the sacred fire. Similar works of divine
grace and power were wrought in the whole region. Many
hundreds were received into the Churches. During that
year this Church welcomed into its communion one
hundred and forty-four persons. One hundred and twenty-
five of them on confession of their faith. Upon one Sabbath ninety-two were received, thirty-three of whom
received baptism, the remainder having been baptized in
infancy.

That revival brought to this Church a marked change in
its spirit and in its relations to society and the world. It
had been somewhat shut up in itself. Its own families had
been the objects of its greatest and tenderest care. Its outside
work had been largely that of a missionary character. It
was generous and liberal, and had welcomed into its Sunday-
school and into the communion from the families of the
working people and the poor, but it had gained, with some
injustice, the reputation of being exclusive. The revival ·
changed all this. Multitudes of the working people from
our mills and shops and manufactories had found peace

with God within these walls. They had been helped to
Christ by the loving guidance of the officers and members
of this Church. They loved the place and they came in
large numbers and knocked for admission at our doors.
They felt at home here. They wanted the help and sympathy of Christians here in their new life. The doors of the
Church were widely opened. From a membership of two
hundred and forty before the revival, it reached one of three
hundred and seventy-two after it, and the Sunday-school
membership rose from four hundred and eight to seven
hundred and thirty-seven. The Church became what all
Churches should be, a Church of the people, and so it remains
to this day, and, we trust, will ever remain. As in all past
years it has been guided by the wisdom and intelligence and
piety of its best members, so it will continue to be in all
coming years, showing how the religion of the great Master
can unite all classes of society in a loving and holy brotherhood. The revival, by bringing many into close connection
with the Church and the Sunday-school, speedily drew forth
the working power of Christian love in the new agencies which
for the past few years have been such a glory to the Church:
"The Cottage Prayermeeting," "The Sewing-School" of the
Church, "The Societies of Christian Endeavor," and many
other organizations for special forms of Christian work. The
revival of 1875–1876 helped this Church to recognize the
fact that as all men are equal before God, so in His Church
there ought to be no respect of persons. In the Church the
qualities of goodness and saintliness alone are to be recognized as honorable and distinguished. There is nothing to
be more dreaded than the separation of classes in the house

of God, or the separation of different houses of God to different classes.

The rich, the intelligent, the professional classes, who go to worship where only those of their order go, are doing their best to lower real and true religion in the eyes of the poor, the ignorant, and the manual laboring people, and so provoke social revolutions and hatreds. The salt that will preserve society is sympathy and communion between all classes in the highest and most serious of all interests, the religious and everlasting. The Church must honor, not wealth or rank or social standing, but the soul and its spiritual fitness to serve God. Let master and workmen, the rich and the poor, come together in Christ before God, and they will learn that mutual respect and regard will do more for order and peace in the State than all legislation. This Church and the other Presbyterian Churches of the city, by drawing in all classes to Church fellowship, are doing a good work for the city of which it is likely they have taken no note.

We had sad losses in our noble band of leaders from the Session of the Church, the brothers, Fleming, the elder of whom, R. Jackson Fleming, had for years led the service of song, and been a most faithful and consecrated worker in a mission among the colored people of the city that was transformed into the Elder Street Presbyterian Church, and the younger Dr. James Fleming, also for years a member of the choir, a teacher in the Sunday-school and at all times a Christian whose gentleness and consistency of character won for him universal esteem. The brothers, John A. and James W. Weir, whose names have already been mentioned

and will always hold a loved and honorable place in the
records of the Church; the guileless, sterling and true-
hearted Mordecai McKinney, poor in this world's goods, but
rich in faith, modest as a little child, but brave in doing
right as any martyr in all the Christian ages.

Memory recalls a multitude of names that are intimately
associated with the history of the congregation. The venerable
Joseph Wallace, for many years a trustee and a treasurer of
the congregation, a man of sterling worth and purest life;
John H. Briggs, among the foremost lawyers at the Bar,
prominent in municipal affairs, for twenty-seven years a
trustee of the congregation and for twenty-nine years a
member of the Church, an able counsellor, a patriotic citizen
and a generous friend; Hon. David Fleming, lawyer and
Senator, a trustee for many years, a member of the Church
for over two score years, and a faithful and intelligent
teacher in the Sunday-school for nearly, if not quite, a half
century; Dr. Edward L. Orth, the gentle, sympathetic and
skillful physician in so many of our homes, who filled our
hearts with grief by his sudden death at the opening of the
war; the hale and strong yet tender Dr. W. W. Rutherford,
who for forty years practiced his profession and won and
held the foremost place in it; and, leaving unnamed many
others towards whom so many of our hearts turn, yet two
more who have passed from our midst since the close of the
fourth pastorate must be mentioned, his Honor, Judge John
J. Pearson, closing a long and honorable career at the age of
eighty-eight years, with a reputation for signal fidelity to his
high trusts, and a character beyond reproach, and Henry
Gilbert whose life from boyhood was closely associated with

this Church, who delighted to be its servant, and who possessed in a remarkable degree the qualities of mind and heart that inspire esteem and trust and love.

The additions made to the Ruling Eldership during the years of Dr. Robinson's sole pastorate were, in 1868: Dr. James Fleming, William S. Shaffer and Walter F. Fahnestock, Jr.; on April 15, 1877: James F. Purvis, Dr. Jacob A. Miller, Samuel J. M. McCarrell and Gilbert M. McCauley. Messrs. Purvis and Shaffer are serving other Churches in the same office, the former in Kansas, and the latter in the Olivet Church, of this city. Messrs. McCarrell, McCauley and Miller are still members of the Church Session, and to them were added, on March 20, 1887, Messrs. John C. Harvey and J. Henry Spicer. The complete roll of the Session during the hundred years of history now ended embraces thirty-five names, five Pastors and thirty Ruling Elders. Among those elders may be found many who cannot be surpassed in the ability and the faithfulness with which they served the Church.

During the closing years of the fourth pastorate, Market Square and Pine Street Churches grew in power and numbers in Christian zeal, in organized and intelligent work, and new Churches were added to the forces of Presbyterianism in the city. The two older Churches have made splendid enlargements to their church buildings for Sunday-school operations, and have organized mission enterprises in needy parts of the city. These two Churches stand among the most prominent Churches in the denomination for their successful work among the young. Benevolent schemes in the city for the sick, for the poor, for the aged

and for orphans have not appealed in vain to this Church
for money, for labor and for counsel in their management.
Noblest of all during these years, aside from that spiritual
grace which nourished Christian lives and added the saved
to the communion of believers, was the marvelous development of Christian activity and power among the women of
the Church. Their names are conspicuous in the earliest
records of the congregation. The history of their labors
and sacrifices from the last century to this hour, and especially for the last twenty-five years, needs volumes for its
record and many hours for a fitting eulogy. It is with
grief, mingled with most delightful memories, that only
this passing allusion can be made to the quiet, but heroic,
lives of the Christian women of this Church.

In 1884 another change took place in the pastorate of the
church. Its pastor received a call from the Western
Theological Seminary at Allegheny, from which he had
graduated thirty years before, to the Re-Union Professorship
of Sacred Rhetoric, Church Government and Pastoral
Theology. After a prayerful consideration of the matter
for several months, he came to the conclusion that it was
his duty to accept the call, and so announced to the Church.
At a meeting of the Presbytery of Carlisle, held on April
9, 1884, the pastoral relationship between him and this
Church was dissolved, and Dr. Robinson was appointed to
declare the pulpit vacant on the first Sabbath in June.
This Church was represented at that meeting of the
Presbytery by Messrs. S. J. M. McCarrell, Charles L.
Bailey, M. W. McAlarney and William S. Shaffer, who
presented a strong protest from the congregation against

the severance of the bonds between it and the pastor. He continued to supply the pulpit until the last Sabbath in June, the thirtieth anniversary of his first sermon to the congregation in 1854.

At a meeting of the congregation held October 6, 1884, the Rev. George Black Stewart of Auburn, N. Y., was unanimously elected to fill the vacant pastorate. Mr. Stewart is a graduate of Princeton College and pursued his theological studies at both McCormick and Auburn Theological Seminaries and for five years was pastor of the Calvary Presbyterian Church of Auburn, N. Y. The call was accepted by him and on January 2, 1885, he was installed by the Presbytery of Carlisle as the fifth in the line of pastors, during a hundred years in the history of this Church. Nine years have now passed since this relationship was established. They have been years of unexampled activity and growth, surpassing all former years. All departments of church work have been invigorated, and new agencies have been created. The spirit of consecrated love and work has fallen upon the Church. Though this Church has reached the maturity of an hundred years its "eye is not dim nor is its natural force abated." There are no wrinkles of age upon it nor any signals of weariness. Its courts are thronged upon the Sabbath with worshipers, and its schools are filled with the students of divine things. Its places of weekly prayer are the resort of Christ's disciples. There is no going backward, but onward rather to meet the greater light and the larger responsibilities of the twentieth century. There is no defection in its teachings. Its pulpit is true to the word of God and to the immemorial

GEORGE BLACK STEWART.
1885.

faith of Christ's Church. It utters no uncertain and doubtful
sound. Its tireless, broad-minded and consecrated occupant
may be trusted to lead into no path that is not illumined
by the light that falls from the Holy Scriptures and
marked by the footprints of good men, and of the great
Captain of our salvation. The Ruling Elders who are
associated with him in the spiritual guidance of the Church,
have been wisely selected and have approved themselves as
worthy successors of the noble men who preceded them.
During the present pastorate the Church has most wisely
renewed the office of the Deacon vacant in the Church
since the death of a good old man of the earlier days,
Ebenezer Ward in 1864. He died at an advanced age and
for many years had laid aside the duties of the office. May
the Deacons of this Church serve well and so "gain to themselves a good standing and great boldness in the faith
which is in Christ Jesus."

By reason of the enlarged labors of the pastorate of the
Church and the growth of its mission enterprise in the lower
part of the city the employment of an assistant to the pastor
became a necessity. During the summer months of 1889
Mr. David M. Skilling, a member of the Senior class of
Western Theological Seminary, entered upon these duties
and so securely won the regard of the Church that upon his
graduation in May, 1890, he was recalled to the work and
has remained until this day. He has been fully ordained
to the ministry. The mission has grown under his fostering
care in numbers and spiritual power. The congregation
and the Sunday-school are already the strong foundation
for an active and successful Church. Through the large

generosity of members of this Church the mission has been provided with a stone chapel of elegant architecture and all the needed furniture of a house of worship. Mr. Skilling has brought to his field the scholarship and training of many years of college and seminary study and the consecration of a heart and life wholly devoted to the service of Christ.

I have left unsaid many of the things I most greatly desired to say. There are names unspoken in the heart that I wished to utter with words of veneration and praise. What a record of noble and saintly lives might be gathered from this century of years. What toils and strong purposes and love have gone into the uplifting of this Church of God here. What a history of prayers, of teaching and preaching, of glad sacrifices for God and for man, of souls born into the life that is everlasting, of Christian graces growing into splendid maturity, of a Christian faith that amid the decays of nature and in the chamber of death was radiant with the certainties of that world that is immortal. We have seen them as they reached the brink of the "deep river," and from their faces have caught what seemed like a "reflection of the sunbeams upon the city that is pure gold."

One hundred years! They take us back to a time that Bushnell has called "the Age of Homespun." The fathers and mothers who laid the foundations here were simply worthy men and women. They were sensible, wise-headed, upright men and women of plain and godly virtues. They never thought of being famous or historic. But from the rare simplicity and the homely virtues of that age we draw

DAVID MILLER SKILLING.
PASTOR'S ASSISTANT, 1891.

our royal lineage. Our inheritance has come from their sturdiness in well-doing and their reverent love of the things that are true and good. The greatest thoughts that brewed in their minds were thoughts of religion and of God. Little deemed they that the hundred years through which their successors and heirs have lived would form the most remarkable century in human history.

The " Grand Old Man," of England, who is about to lay down the work of his wonderful life, has said, that if he had been given his choice in what period of the world to live, he would have chosen the Nineteenth Century. It has been the age of invention and of discovery, the age of political change, of advancing science and art, of human liberty and of religious progress. What we possess to-day of privilege and power, of blessing and of hope, is but an heirloom. We have entered into the labors of our fathers. This Century Plant did not spring up in a night. The past was at its planting and many years have waited on its growth. The best spirits of three generations have been our benefactors. By the patience and courage, by the self-denials and the prayers of the hundreds of men and women who here loved their fellow-men, and served their God, this Church now stands on its height of attainment. Let us honor those who made us what we are. Let us bow our heads in gratefulness to the fathers and mothers who left us, not hoarded saving of perishing gold, but the memory and the power of their Christian lives. Some of them like the divinely-gifted James W. Weir stand forth with a brilliance all their own and unrivalled, but love weaves its garland's for hundreds of others who lived for us and left us their precious inheritance. Into the sympathy and goodly fellowship of these men and women who walked with the Son of God let us hasten to enter and there abide. By the goodness of our lives and by the fulness of our devotion to truth and to Christ, let us see to it, that by the close of the twentieth century, freedom and religion are high advanced towards the millenium.

At the conclusion of Dr. Robinson's address, Dr. Stewart announced Luther's Battle Hymn of the Reformation.

Our God stands firm, a rock and tow'r,
  A shield when danger presses:
A ready help in ev'ry hour
  When doubt or pain distresses;
For our malignant foe
  Unswerving aims his blow:
His fearful arms the while,
  Dark pow'r and darker guile;
His hidden craft is matchless.

Our strength is weakness in the fight,
  Our courage soon defection;
But comes a Warrior clad in might,
  A Prince of God's election;
Who is this wondrous Chief
  That brings this glad relief?
The field of battle boasts,
  Christ Jesus, Lord of hosts.
Still conq'ring and to conquer.

Then, Lord! arise: lift up thine arm,
  With mighty succor stay us;
Oh, turn aside the deadly harm
  When Satan would betray us,

That rescued by thy hand,
  In triumph we may stand,
And round thy footstool crowd
  In joy to sing aloud
High praise to our Redeemer.

As the audience joined heartily with the choir in singing the stately measures of *Ein, feste Burg*, it seemed a most fitting culmination of the praise to the great Head of the Church for his kind providence and infinite grace toward this people. Rev. David M. Skilling led the congregation in repeating the Lord's Prayer. The Benediction was pronounced by the Rev. Dr. Robinson, and the service concluded with the Chorus in E Flat composed by Guilmant.

FRIDAY EVENING.

February the 16th, 1894, at 7.30 o'clock.

SOCIAL RECEPTION.

Amiel in his Journal Intime makes some philosophical observations concerning social amenities. He looks upon social gatherings as occasions when "intellect and taste hold festival, and the associations of reality are exchanged for the associations of the imagination," and he adds : "Paradox or no, I believe that these fugitive attempts to reconstruct a dream whose only end is beauty, represent confused reminiscences of an age of gold haunting the human heart, or rather aspirations towards a harmony of things which everyday reality denies to us, and of which art alone gives us a glimpse." It must have been unconscious obedience to some such law as this which led the committee to plan the closing feature of Centennial Week. It was certainly a most happy thought which devised the social reception of Friday night. And it was a happy thought most admirably executed. The Reception Committee had a difficult task to perform. The problems confronting it were complex and full of unknown factors. Necessarily many of their arrangements were dependent upon the probable number of guests they would have to provide for, yet these arrangements had to be completed before this could possibly be known. It is no small praise when we say that their arrangements were perfect and admirably adapted to the circumstances, that they secured to those present a most enjoyable evening, and concluded the Centennial observances with a brilliant success. This committee with Mrs. Gilbert M. McGauley as chairman arranged the Sunday-school rooms in a tasteful and attractive manner, and provided ample refreshments for the twelve hundred to fifteen hundred guests. The Committee of Ushers with Mr. Peter K. Sprenkel as chairman ably assisted the Reception Committee in contributing to the comfort of the large company. This committee provided a cloak-room for the checking of hats and outer garments, which proved to be a great convenience. In addition to these two committees valuable help was rendered by the young people in distributing refreshments and in other ways. Among those who thus assisted were Misses Martha Worden McAlarney, Louisa A. Hickok, Anna Orth, Caroline Moffitt, Roberta Orth, Mary Hamilton, Nannie Orr, Caroline Bigler, Mary Fleming, Helen Boyd, Eva Vandling, Margaret Hamilton, Marion Weiss; Messrs. Ira Bishop, George Ridgway, Horace Segelbaum, John P. Kelker, George Martin, Charles Hickok; Masters Harris Stewart, John Hart McAlarney, George Stewart.

The night was clear and cold with bright stars above and the creaking snow beneath. The people early began to gather and evidently came prepared for a happy time, and they had it. The receiving party stood in the Intermediate Sunday-school room, and consisted of Dr. and Mrs. Stewart, Dr. and Mrs. Robinson, Mr. Skilling, and the Invitation Committee, consisting of Charles L. Bailey, David Fleming, Jr., Mrs. Julia A. Briggs, Mrs. David Fleming, Alexander Roberts, John H. Weiss, Dr. Jacob A. Miller, Mrs. Sarah Doll, Mrs. Jacob S. Haldeman, Miss Sibyl M. Weir, Samuel

D. Ingram, George W. Boyd, Lyman D. Gilbert. The hundreds of guests as they arrived were cordially received and made to feel at home. There was no lack of good fellowship. Because of the large number present the committees early began to serve the refreshments, and were kept busy throughout the whole evening.

About eight o'clock the impromptu musical programme began in the lecture-room. Messrs. Henry A. Kelker, Jr., J. F. Hutchinson, H. L. Vance, Charles F. Etter and Frank S. Morrow, members of the Harrisburg Banjo Club, played with spirit and precision two numbers. Mrs. Frank R. Schell and Mrs. David Fleming, Jr., gave as a piano duet, the overture to "Rienzi," by Wagner, in which their fine musical taste and skill were made evident. The voices of Messrs. George R. Fleming, Edward Z. Gross, William G. Underwood, and Lucius S. Bigelow, the Mendelssohn Quartette, blended perfectly in the ballads, so dear to the people's heart, "The Miller of Dee," "Ben Bolt," "Annie Laurie," "Blue Bells of Scotland." The surging throng which filled the social rooms made it difficult for hearing this excellent music.

At the same time, in the auditorium, a large company gathered to listen to the addresses given by some of the guests of the evening.

After Miss Reba Bunton and Mr. George R. Fleming had delighted the audience with the duet, "They Shall Hunger No More," in Gaul's cantata, "The Holy City," and Mr. Fleming had increased the delight by a solo, Coenen's "Come Unto Me," Mr. Stewart, the Minister of the Church, said: This is a flexible audience, and so is everything else to-night. There is nothing stiff or formal about this occasion. This is an evening of freedom and spontaneous good fellowship. It gives me very great pleasure to introduce the presiding officer of the evening, the Honorable John B. McPherson of Harrisburg, late of Lebanon.

The PRESIDENT. LADIES AND GENTLEMEN: Two or three of us were talking this afternoon as we were coming down the Bank and were wondering why it was that when Americans get together—and I suppose it is equally true of all English speaking-people—they always want two things; one is speech-making, and singularly enough the other is brevity in the speeches. The two do not always go together; but the effort this evening is to have them both; you will have several speeches, and I think you will have them short.

I will not refer to the reasons which make it most gratifying for me to be here on this occasion, but there is one suggestion which perhaps may touch others in the audience as well as myself. It is certainly most inspiriting to one who has anything to do with a small church, with a church that is struggling to live and is in the beginning of things, to come and see what is the result here of all these years of effort, and to reflect that after all somebody must go through the early stages of despondency, and that it may as well fall to your lot or to mine as to the lot of others. I am sure for such a person it will be easy this evening to get some inspiration and encouragement.

It is probably quite clear by this time of the week that the English Presbyterian Church of Harrisburg is celebrating its Centennial, but I hasten to add—and I believe

I am expressing your sentiments as well as my own—that it has never seemed to me as if our brethren of the Pine Street Church were really a separate Church. They shared our common worship for sixty-five years: there have been, and there are, so many ties between us, and those ties have been so intimate and so continuous during the last thirty-five years, that it never has seemed as if the churches were separate, but rather as if they were parts of the same congregation worshiping in different buildings. In that spirit I would like to present to you a gentleman whose name and face are not only familiar to you all, but are known and honored wherever the Presbyterian faith is honored throughout the land; I would like to call upon him as one who was formerly an associate pastor of the Presbyterian Church of Harrisburg—Dr. Cattell.

REMARKS BY DR. WILLIAM C. CATTELL.

I have taken a couple of days out of a very busy life, and have traveled many miles that I might be present at this Presbyterian reunion. For here in Harrisburg the happiest years of my life were spent. I have indeed happy memories of other places where I have lived, especially of Easton, where, among a refined and cultured people, I spent nearly thirty years, engaged in a work that awakened my highest enthusiasm, and that brought me into intimate relations with beloved colleagues in the Faculty and with the young and joyous life of college boys. Yet, I say frankly to you here, as I say everywhere, that my heart is in Harrisburg It was only four brief years that I lived here, but those were years in which I occupied a position which I believe to be the most blessed and delightful that can fall to the lot of man. I was the Pastor of a kind, loving, united people. So long as I live shall I cherish in my heart of hearts the memory of their love and loyalty which made my sacred work among them a supreme joy. I can say now, after the lapse of thirty years, what I said in my last words to them from the pulpit as I turned away from my happy home here to resume my college work at Easton: "I thank my God upon *every remembrance of you.*" That was the text, as some of you may recall, from which I preached my farewell sermon.

But the memories which have so endeared Harrisburg to me are not exclusively those connected with the people of my old pastoral charge. I had not lived here long without finding that in this "mother church," at whose invitation we are here to-night, were some of the most lovable people that ever lived.

Let me remind you that Harrisburg, in 1860, was only a large town, containing not much over fifteen thousand inhabitants. What were then open fields are now streets of closely-built houses. The palatial residences, everywhere to be seen now, were then unknown. The life here, a generation ago, was plainer and simpler than it can be in the great and busy city to which Harrisburg has now grown. People got to know each other easily. Neighbor was another name for friend, and the "neighborhood" was widely extended. It was, therefore, not long before the young Pastor of the Pine Street Church found that there were other good people here besides those of his own fold, although they, first and last and always, were the nearest to his heart. Naturally, he found these good people, first of all, and the most blessed of them all, in the old "mother church," and the friendships formed among them I have sacredly cherished all these years.

And so I rejoice to be here to-night. Many, indeed, of those I loved in this Church, and in my old pastoral charge have gone to the better land. Yet many remain. And it has been a great joy to me, as I passed through these crowded rooms, to take one and another by the hand—the two congregations so intermingled that those from one could hardly be distinguished from those of the other. Their kind greeting will be a precious memory to me for the rest of my life.

Yonder is my dear and honored brother, Dr. Robinson, who, as Pastor of this Church, so cordially welcomed me to Harrisburg nearly thirty-five years ago. We were both young men then. In his presence I should hardly dare to say about him all that is in my heart. But this I dare say While he has been called to a high position as a professor in one of our oldest theological seminaries, and the whole Presbyterian Church holds him in deserved honor, his old people here, and all of us who knew him, claim him to be in a special sense " *our* Doctor Robinson." Our respect for him and our personal love strengthen as the years go by.

And what shall I say of Dr. DeWitt, the venerable senior Pastor of this Church when I came to Harrisburg? I looked up to him with a reverence I have felt for few men. Of all those articles of historic interest collected in the adjoining room well worthy of days of careful study, nothing has so attracted me as the portrait of this venerable man. I stood long before it to-day, gazing upon those benign and well-remembered features, and recalling his rare and beautiful old age as he went in and out among the people whom he had so lovingly and so faithfully and so ably served for nearly half a century. Even in the declining years of his life he was a preacher of rare power. I recall a sermon I heard him preach shortly after I came to Harrisburg. A large tent was pitched upon the Capitol grounds in which meetings were held after the manner of the evangelistic services now so common. The patriarch took for his text, " Though your sins be as scarlet they shall be white as snow; though they be red like crimson they shall be as wool." Never shall I forget the deep impression made upon the great assembly as the silver-haired man, with a voice trembling with emotion, and in language of classic purity characteristic of all his sermons, pleaded with his hearers to accept God's mercy so fully and freely offered in the gospel. All around me were men in tears!

There comes to me a pleasant memory connecting Dr. DeWitt with our own services in the new church dedicated in 1860. Dr. Gurley, of Washington City, preached in the morning, and Dr. Burt, of Baltimore, in the evening, when this church was closed and both congregations met together and sent their prayers and sacred songs heavenward from the same altar. The next day I called upon Dr. DeWitt and invited him to preach on the following Sunday morning. He at once, and with his usual courtesy, accepted the invitation. But I saw he was under the impression that I had invited him as " a supply " in view of my absence from home that day, and I said to him: "No, Dr. DeWitt, I could not be away from my people when the very first sermon is preached to them in the regular ministration of the gospel after the exceptional exercises of the dedication. I shall be in the pulpit with you. But it is more fitting that this first sermon shall be preached by you than by the Pastor of the Church. You are the honored father of us all." And I shall never forget the pleased look with which the patriarch recognized that the invitation to him was intended, not to fill a vacancy occasioned by my absence, but to emphasize the high appreciation in which he was held by the community in which his whole ministerial life had been spent.

I should like to recall other pleasant memories I have of Dr. DeWitt and of the members of this Church whom I knew and loved in those far off days, especially among the elders; and I should not hesitate to name first of all that eminent man of God, Mr. James W. Weir. But there are other speakers to follow, and the reminiscences that crowd upon me would detain you too long.

But there comes to me a sad memory to which I must briefly refer—the civil war, which, during the last three years of my pastorate, transformed our hitherto quiet and peaceful town into one vast camp of soldiers. Their tents were pitched not only in the open fields around us, but in the public grounds and even in the streets. Preaching by their camp fires and ministering in the great hospitals soon established for the sick and wounded, all the pastors here found new and most sacred duties added to the work among

their own people. Our congregations upon the Sabbath day
were at times almost broken up with the excitement and
stir and confusion that everywhere prevailed. On that
Sunday—I remember it well—when the skirmish occurred
at Oyster's Point, but three or four miles from the city and
we could plainly hear the booming of the cannon, the congregation of the Pine Street Church numbered exactly
twelve! But in those dark days pastors and people in all
the churches seemed to be drawn nearer to each other as
all drew nearer to the throne to which their petitions were
sent for that help of which we all stood in such need. The
darkness around us deepened as the months slowly passed
away. In fact, in the second invasion of Pennsylvania by
the confederates under General **Lee,** Harrisburg became a
beleaguered city. Intrenchments for its defense were thrown
up on the opposite bank of the river—I myself worked upon
them with pick and shovel! All the State archives were
hurriedly removed for safety; women and children fled
from their homes. The sentinels were still keeping watch
and guard upon those outworks for the defense of the city
when I took leave of this dear place in the fall of 1863—
though in my farewell words from the pulpit to my beloved
people, I could even then point them to the **star of hope**
shining through the riven clouds of the war and betokening
the near hour when the fratricidal strife would be ended
and the restored Republic rise to a higher and nobler life.

But I will not detain you longer. Let me, as I take my
seat, thank you, Mr. President, for your kind words of
welcome this evening to the people of the Pine Street

Church as, with their first Pastor and the beloved man who now ministers to them in sacred things, they are gathered here with hearty congratulations, and best wishes and fervent prayers for the dear old mother Church. We highly appreciate such greeting from a man like yourself, whose Christian character and eminent endowments add luster to the high judicial office you hold. And upon all the congregation and their honored Pastor, whom I, too, like his own people, have learned to admire and love, I fervently invoke the continued and increasing favor of Almighty God.

The PRESIDENT: I need not remind you who was the first pastor of this Church. I do not intend to eulogize him after the address to which you had the pleasure of listening last night, but I may say that he must have been of remarkably good stock. Probably his harmonious balance of faculty was nowhere more admirably shown than in his selection of this congregation as one of his early fields of labor, and the congregation, I have no doubt, showed an equal balance of good judgment when they selected him as their first pastor.

We are exceedingly fortunate to-night in having two of his grandsons with us, who illustrate the excellence of the stock. Mr. Snowden's descendants have been distinguished in all the departments in which men can win distinction for themselves in civil, military and diplomatic life, and if there is any other position of trust or honor to which they have not yet attained, I am sure they are now upon the way to its attainment. I will call first upon General Snowden, grandson of the first Pastor of the Church.

REMARKS BY MAJOR GENERAL GEORGE R. SNOWDEN.

MR. PRESIDENT, LADIES AND GENTLEMEN: I am very glad to be here with you to-night on this interesting and historic occasion. A friend remarked to me not long since, that he thought I was a much better Presbyterian in theory than in practice. Without disputing his opinion, I confess to be among the best Presbyterians in theory. Because I believe that any man or woman raised in the Presbyterian Church, in her Sunday-schools, under the sound of the gospel as it has been preached from her pulpits in this country for the past 200 years, must realize that our civil institutions are based if not upon the confession of faith and the shorter chatechism at least upon her form of government. The theory of our federal union is based upon the form of government of the Presbyterian Church, as was once wisely said by Chief Justice Tilghman. The first principle of Presbyterian polity is republicanism. It is based upon the consent and intelligence alike of the governing and the governed. I do not think it too much to say that had not our Presbyterian forefathers come to this country and advanced to the Cumberland Valley, we would not now be living in a land of civil and religious liberty, wisely said by the Puritan poet, Milton, to be the most precious of all our earthly possessions. When the pioneers of this Church went forward to the wilderness they took with them the Bible and established the meeting house and the school.

There are no doubt sections of the country more noted in history than yours. Philadelphia has the State House and the Bell, and the achievements of New England have been celebrated by poet and historian. Our ancestors rushing on to clear the wilderness, to drive back the savage, to open the West to settlement, were too busy making history, to have time to write it. It is very gratifying now to see that in the last few years the deeds of Pennsylvanians are becoming better known. They were as distinguished, and our ancestors were as earnest and active in the Revolution as the patriots of Massachusetts, Virginia, or of any other part of our country. This section not so famous in history or known abroad as it ought to be, is one which can refer with the greatest pride to its course in the Revolution, to the part which it took in securing Independence and the Union. The spirit of patriotism was so strong that persons suspected of luke-warmness to the cause were subjected to trial and punishment as well in the church as the civil courts. It is no wonder considering the character of the early settlers of these valleys that here was recruited the most distinguished regiment which ever carried the flag, bearing it aloft in honor from Quebec to Yorktown, the First Continental. The men who went forth from Paxtang, Silvers' Spring, Carlisle and Chambersburg were ever at the front and yielded to none in devotion to the cause to which they pledged themselves and their fortunes.

From your valley proceeded South and West influences which led to the success of the Revolution and the formation of the Union. We have the authority of Washington that without the Presbyterians the cause would have failed. The swarms of Presbyterians, like bees, industrious but quick, if disturbed, to sting, which settled here and went on to the Southwest were the men who won the battle of King's

Mountain, and forced Cornwallis to Yorktown where he surrendered to the genius of Washington. The Declaration at Mecklenburg preceded that of Philadelphia. Our ancestors took a prominent and influential part in achieving the liberties of the American people and in forming the plan of government under which the country has so greatly grown and prospered.

It is the advantage of our free institutions that they develope the character of the individual citizen. I recollect very well when quite young commanding a company in the Army of the Potomac hearing the men in the ranks talk of their duty. Nearly all of them were from the humblest walks in life, yet they seriously considered the obligations resting upon them; they felt that they were fighting for the liberties of themselves and of their posterity, every man carrying a musket realizing that the success of the war was his individual concern. No armies of other countries could ever have that personal and patriotic sentiment. Those who march under the brilliant colors of England, Germany, or Russia cannot comprehend, for they have never felt, that sense of manhood and of citizenship which the American citizen entertained when he went forth as a volunteer. I speak of this, ladies and gentlemen, otherwise it might be out of place on this occasion, simply because I believe it to be largely owing to the teachings and the traditions of the Presbyterian Church. It was born in persecution; its flourished in spite of all assaults made upon it by weapons spiritual and militant, to reduce to servitude men who believed in this Bible. They drew from the teachings of the New Testament that all men are created free and equal; they believed that government is justly based upon the right of every man to a voice in it, and they learned from experience the necessity of every man's being ready when occasion requires with strong arm and resolute heart to defend his principles. The Scotch-Irish especially, coming into your valley, founded a community based upon liberty, upon the belief that man is capable and ought to govern himself.

There are not as many Presbyterians in the country as there should be; there ought to be more of them. I do not speak of the religious doctrines of the Church, others more capable have done so. But its polity I do not believe is equaled by any other religious organization in the world, and it is superior to all in unswerving and uncompromising devotion to civil and religious liberty. From its formation to the present its voice has ever been for the right of man to govern himself, to worship his Creator according to the dictates of his own conscience and to maintain that no one can come between him and his Master. It would, therefore, be better for the country if there were more Presbyterians, better for the welfare and permanence of our civil institutions. But there are enough of them, as we believe, to preserve our liberties to the remotest generation; at least enough to stand forth on every battlefield, in peace or war, to indicate these sacred principles. As long as the Presbyterian Church shall endure, to the end of time there will be a strong, perhaps a dominating element in the land which will have a controlling voice in higher politics, tending to the perfection and perpetuity of our free institutions.

At the conclusion of General Snowden's address, Miss Bunton sang with fine expression, "The Angel Came," by F. H. Cowen.

The PRESIDENT: I spoke of *two* grandsons, you will remember, and it gives me pleasure to say that the gentleman who will next address you has, like his cousin to whom you have just listened, a claim of his own upon your attention. He is not only the grandson of the first pastor of the church, but he is also one of the most distinguished members of the Pennsylvania bar—Mr. Ross Thompson, of Erie.

REMARKS BY COL. J. ROSS THOMPSON.

MR. PRESIDENT, LADIES AND GENTLEMEN: I am much indebted to·the pastor of this church, Dr. Stewart, and some warm friends for a kind invitation to be present and participate in the interesting ceremonies commemorating the Centennial anniversary of this church, of which my grandfather was the first pastor.

The one hundredth anniversary of the origin of this church naturally takes the mind's eye back over the records of the past and grasps in the stupendous results of these years and the wonderful strides taken in science and arts. Monarchies have risen and fallen. Republics, like meteors, have flashed across the pages of history. Wars of most stupendous character, involving momentous questions and fates of nations, have been waged. The pages of history are full of startling events, all in the life time of this church.

Steam, with its wonderful transporting powers, the electric wire encircling the earth, and on the wings of the lighting, carrying messages to the antipodes, the iron horse, the steam railroad, the steam boat, the sewing machine, the photograph and the thousands of inventions useful to mankind, have come into play in the life of this church.

In the centennial celebration of the adoption of the Federal Constitution, at Philadelphia, I saw an object lesson in the strides in transportation in the last one hundred years. First in the procession came the pack horses, with pack saddles, the first mode of transportation, then following the pack horses came the old Conestoga wagons, following this came the canal boat, following this a corps of civil engineers with their instruments, their levels and transits, following them the workingmen with the shovels and picks, next came the old fashioned locomotive, following this the modern engine of sixty tons, then the old fashioned railroad coaches, next the new and palatial cars, winding up with the grand Pulman palace car. Starting with the pack horse and winding up with the palace car, demonstrating the wonderful progress of transportation within the hundred years of this church. Our ancestors came here in the days of the pack horse and pack saddle. This was then the only mode of transportation.

In the same procession there was another object lesson, illustrating in a like manner the progress of civilization and the Christianized results of the work of the churches and within the life time of this church. I saw this procession headed by the savage Indians from the plains, decked in full war paint and the feathers of the untrained and uncivilized savage; following behind the men on horse back came a great array of little people dressed in gray, not with bows and arrows, but in their little arms carrying slates and pencils, and figuring and ciphering upon those slates.

Following them came the Indian girls in wagons working at the industries their Christian sisters worked upon; I saw them followed by the young Indians working at the trades, some at the saddler's and some at the tinsmith's trade. Starting in with the savage at the front and winding up with the Christianized man in the end. This in the age of this Church; from savagery to Christianity. I thought then of the grand school at Carlisle, where those Indians were educated, and of Carlisle as the home of my ancestors. The thought of those Indians at Carlisle recalled an incident in the life of my grandmother, the wife of Rev. Nathaniel R. Snowden, who resided there. The father of my grandmother was in Wyoming at the time of the massacre by the Indians. The Indian chief knew Dr. Gustine. My grandmother was a small child at the time. The chieftain had saved Dr. Gustine from the tomahawk and scalping knife of the Indians. As you recall, a portion of the massacre occurred in the day time. When night approached Brandt, the half-breed chieftain, took Dr. Gustine with his little daughter down to the Susquehanna, putting Dr. Gustine and his little girl into a canoe, told him to paddle for his life. He paddled down the Susquehanna to Harris Ferry, now Harrisburg, and went from thence to Carlisle with his daughter, who afterwards became the mother of my mother. I thought of that circumstance in relation to the Indian and the civilization marked in this century. I would say, Mr. President, that if the spirit of my grandfather should come down here to-day to see the strides made in this great

Church, to see this vast building with its beautiful arrangements, its organ, its beautiful windows, and would think of the little church he held over the jail, he would see in this one of the most wonderful strides made in the last hundred years.

I feel when I am talking here that I am talking, Mr. President, upon the ground that my ancestors occupied. I feel that when I am talking here I am recalling reminiscenses to people who are as much interested in them as I am myself. I can recall many curious things in my days. Some of you that are as old know that back in those days we did not have any hymn books. We had what we called the clerk, who sat in front of the pulpit. He had his tuning fork and would read off two lines and away we would go and then we would try again, then all would join in and sing. Some of you will recall this. There was a very peculiar characteristic of the preaching when I was quite a lad. I can recall with vividness, they always began with firstly, then secondly, lastly, allow me to conclude, and let me add. These things generally took about two hours and a half. Then, too, the prayers. They were very able prayers, but they were powerfully long. I recall when I was a lad visiting my grandfather's house that he always had prayers evening and morning. I could always tell when the old gentleman was about half through, for at this point he always prayed for the downfall of the Pope of Rome, the anti-Christ.

I want to say that in those days in my youth there were not the Christian liberality and spirit prevailing as to-day. We can recall how we Old School Presbyterians warred with

the New School, and how we warred with other denominations. But there is a Christian liberality all prevailing. It
seems sometimes to me as if while not agreeing on the non-
essentials, we all agree on the essentials.

My grandfather was very happy in his later days when
he could mount his old iron-gray horse, and with his old
saddle bags, travel to some brother pastor's church and
preach on Sunday. The old gentleman always spoke
kindly of Harrisburg. I have heard him say that when he
preached here it was scarcely a village. My mother was
born in this town. I feel as I am talking to-night that I
am talking to old friends of my family and myself. My
grandfather preached in various places throughout the
State, but he always had a kind corner in his heart for
Harrisburg and Harrisburg people He often spoke of his
church here and of the kindness of the people, and that
some of the happiest days of his life had been spent in the
city, or then village, for it was not even a borough, of Harrisburg. He belonged to the Old School of cast-iron Presbyterianism. He belonged to that class of men that Gen.
Snowden spoke about, who, with the axe on one shoulder
and the rifle on the other, went into the virgin forests, and
cleared them away and also drove out the savages. He
belonged to that stern class of Presbyterianism that in the
West sat with the Bible on top of the pulpit and the rifle
in the corner. These Presbyterians swarmed through here
into the Western States, diverging into those Western States
and conquering them. I am proud of the Presbyterian
Church, the Church of my grandparents, my parents, the
Church whose mark has been made in the history of our

common country. A Church that did more than any other
in winning the great West, the Church that has stood by
the country in all times of distress and trouble. A Church
that has produced more great divines, more great statesmen
than any other. A grand Church laboring in the cause of
religion and humanity and will continue its work until
time shall be no more.

The PRESIDENT: I quite agree with General Snowden, that
there ought to be more Presbyterians. Still, they are by no
means a feeble folk or few in number. This region contains
many of them, and in a neighboring town there is a strong
congregation of our brethren whose pastor is here to-night
to bring us their greetings and his own. I have great
pleasure in presenting to you Dr. Niles, of York.

REMARKS BY REV. HENRY E. NILES, D. D.

MR. PRESIDENT, LADIES AND GENTLEMEN: I am not here
to-night for the purpose of speech making, but had I come
for such object I think it would plainly be the part of
wisdom, at this late hour, not to trespass upon your time
and patience. Hindered from an earlier acceptance of the
kind invitation of your committee, to partake of the pleasures
of your various exercises on this anniversary week, I
was glad to come even at the eleventh hour. I wanted to
revisit scenes that have been familiar in the past, to reclasp
old bonds of friendship, to form others that shall be new,
and to drink in some of the intellectual and spiritual ozone
which I felt sure must be flowing about abundantly here.

I suppose I am called upon now, not so much for my own

sake, as because I may represent a Sister Church in a neighboring city, which, according to its charter, bears a similar distinctive name; which is, I believe, somewhat older than this; and also, for a portion of the last century, was associated ecclesiastically with this. I take pleasure, therefore, in presenting to the members of the "English Presbyterian congregation of Harrisburg," the fraternal salutations of the "English Presbyterian congregation of York." Your senior by several years and a little more venerable, perhaps, but a Church, I am sure, which, cherishes the most kindly interest in your welfare and rejoices that you have come to this period of maturity, with so many evidences of spiritual vigor and general prosperity.

If you want me to say more, it shall be in the line suggested by our dear brother, Dr. Cattell, for I too, am carried back to my first acquaintance with Harrisburg. It was in that time which tried men's souls, near the close of the war, when from an old dingy car that had seen hard service for the country, and was then filled with soldiers going towards the front, I first looked upon this goodly city. Of course, I had some general ideas of its character and importance, as the State Capital, but as from the window of that car standing a little while, on the other side of the Susquehanna, the view was presented, "beautiful for situation" seemed your loved city, which might well be the joy of the whole commonwealth. While I could not but notice the substantial buildings that lined the streets, symbolic of the character of the population, and those on the Capitol Hill, well suited for the legislators and other officials of the State, my attention was soon turned to a tall, symmetrical, beautiful spire which loomed up in the foreground, and which I learned was of the First Presbyterian Church.

Not long after, as I well remember, came my introduction to the pastors of the Church, the venerable, scholarly and accomplished Dr. DeWitt; and his junior colleague, concerning whom, here in his presence, I forbear to use such adjectives as my heart prompts me to employ, and such as I am sure your high appreciation of him would endorse.

The circumstances were peculiar. The events transpiring in our country were such as the world remembers with thrilling interest.

On Friday evening, April 14, 1865, the Presbytery, with which our churches were connected, convened in semi-annual meeting at York, and in connection with the usual business of that session, it was expected that I would be installed pastor of the York congregation. It was the evening of that memorable day when the stars and stripes, which had been, for four years, lowered at Fort Sumpter, were restored to their former position, Henry Ward Beecher being the orator of the occasion. This fact, together with the recent capture of Petersburg and Richmond, and the surrender of Lee and his army to General Grant, had filled the country with joy. Dr. Robinson preached the opening sermon of Presbytery, and on the next day it was expected that the regular business would be attended to, and on Sabbath, together with various popular meetings, would be the ceremony of installation. But on Saturday morning, how startling the intelligence that was flashed across the land, and filled every loyal heart with consternation! What a thrill of horror passed through our communities, on that 15th day of April, when successive telegrams announced, " President Lincoln assassinated !" " Secretary Seward simultaneously assaulted !" " Secretary Stanton and Chief Justice Chase imperilled !" " The President dead !"

When Presbytery convened that morning, no wonder that our expected delightful service was turned into a scene of anxiety and sorrow and shame ! And when the venerable Dr. DeWitt was called to lead us in prayer to the God of Providence, the Governor of the Universe, no wonder that we felt our help must be in Him alone. Next day, that church which otherwise had been decorated with symbols of joy and gladness, was hung with the black emblems of mourning. Although the appointed services were held, conflicting emotions were in our hearts. Under other circumstances, I might be tempted to say more in this connection. I have only alluded to that memorable time, as the beginning of my acquaintance with your pastors, in connection with the little " New School Presbytery of Harrisburg." " Little " she may have been " among the thousands of Judah," but by no means " least " in the loyalty of her devotion to Evangelical principles, in the readiness of her members for Christian service, and in the variety and liberality of her contributions for objects of Christian beneficence. Her ministers and elders met together as brethren, innocent of rivalries, rejoicing in each other's companionship, and confident in each other's fraternal affection.

But, when the reunion of our denomination in 1870 gave occasion for the readjustment of Presbyterial boundaries, the wedge of separation was driven between these churches, and some of us were brought into new ecclesiastical connections. From that time, though geographically neighbors, the churches of Harrisburg and York have had but little intercourse. And so, at length, I am here to-night, amid familiar scenes, yet somewhat as a stranger. Here, where I once felt so much at home, and in view of this pulpit where I often stood as a co-Presbyter, it almost seems that I need a fresh introduction !

Yet, I am not entirely ignorant of your history during these recent years. I have known something of your activity and power, and continued enlargement. I have marked "your work of Faith and labor of Love and patience of Hope in our Lord Jesus Christ, in the sight of God, even our Father, knowing brethren beloved, your election of God."

In conclusion, therefore, let me repeat to you, my dear Brother STEWART, and to your good people, the salutations of "The English Presbyterian Church of York," and assure you that, with thanksgiving to God for distinguished favors shown to you in the past, we will pray that, from the beginning of this new century on which you are entering, the Shechinah may be yet more constantly manifest among you, and the joy of the Lord be the delight of your souls!

The PRESIDENT: I do not know how we can better conclude the evening than by just one further word. It is probably out of the regular order from a chronological point of view, but sentimentally it seems appropriate to conclude this celebration with a few commendatory words from the Mother Church. I am glad to call upon one who bears a name so honored in this region as does Mr. W. Franklin Rutherford of the Paxtang Church.

Remarks by Mr. W. Franklin Rutherford.

Mr. President, Ladies and Gentlemen : Away back in those shadowy times, before the Quaker had crossed the Brandywine, or the famous cherrytree had been planted in the garden of Mr. Washington, a band of choice spirits from Ulster, composed of men, women and children had penetrated the wilds of Paxtang and appropriated to themselves the southern slopes of the beautiful hills, east of the spot upon which we now stand. And as a characteristic of the race wherever found, they brought with them the Church and the school-house, and with admirable taste, and a prescience not yet fully appreciated, located both in Paxtang Valley, and when history reached the place in 1732 as recorded in the minutes of Donegal Presbytery, she found there Old Paxtang Church.

The building thus found was of logs, and was replaced in 1740 by a stone meeting house, which like Concord, Lexington and Bunker's Hill, still remains, and there we hope, it will remain until the Church Militant shall have been supplanted by the Church triumphant. Every one knows that the history of Paxtang Church, down to the close of the Revolution, is in large measure, the history of this portion of Pennsylvania, but its history throughout has been so lately and so ably recited on several different occasions, that I shall not now inflict upon you a thrice told tale.

There is, however, one circumstance relating to the makeup of the congregation during the Revolutionary period, and for many years thereafter, which may be of interest to you as descendants, and which I think has never been brought out. And when I bring it out do not demand documentary evidence. I rely upon the deeper and more solid foundation of tradition, and follow the injunction which the Apostle Paul endeavored with all the force of his matchless eloquence to impress upon the Thessalonians, "Stand fast, and hold the traditions which ye have been taught." The minister of Paxtang and all his office-bearers were men of high military rank. Mr. Elder was a colonel, and his bench of ruling elders ranked from Captain to Brigadier, and were a body of men who never thought of shirking duty under cover of the old excuse implied in the question, "am I my brother's keeper?" Their meetings savored strongly of the camp: discipline was complete and the word of the reverend commanding officer was both law and gospel.

Trials before this body partook of the brevity and directness of a martial court, and the culprit was usually convicted. The laity was of like material, and ranked from Corporal to Major General, comprising magistrates and statesmen from constable to Senator of the United States, all patriotic to the backbone, and woe betide the unfortunate Tory or "Britisher," who dared to show his face within the portals of the old stone meeting house.

There is also a little episode in our history, which I think you will pardon me if I mention, as it has a very important bearing upon the present happy occasion, and, but for which you would have had no Centennial to celebrate After having passed successfully through the struggles of early youth and the bitterness consequent upon numerous civil and religious controversies, we had just settled down to the enjoyment of that peace and comfort which follows a consciousness of work well done, when suddenly trouble arose in the family, our eldest daughter, (a wayward child), began to scheme for a slice of our territory, upon which to establish a Church of her own. This proceeding was looked upon by the stern old rulers of Paxtang as treason and rank ingratitude,—and they must not be censured on this account, for, be it remembered, they lived in the tallow candle age, when the delusion prevailed that parents were wiser than their children, nor are we sure that the discipline then administered to our daughter, which restrained her impetuosity for at least a decade, was not a blessing in disguise, as it developed that fortitude and earnest endeavor to be worthy of the claim she then set up, which has characterised her career ever since, and has rendered her one of the brightest jewels in the crown of Old Paxtang's glory.

I wish to say further, that although the Mother Church, for a long time after the separation, sulked in her tent, and said some severe things about the daughter, she never permitted any one else to do so in her hearing, and was all the while secretly rejoicing in the prosperity and religious growth of the new enterprise. Long years ago all animosity ceased and from the beginning of Dr. DeWitt's ministry down to the present hour, her ministers have frequently filled the pulpit of the Mother Church, and have been almost as well known and as much beloved there as here.

And now in these commemorative exercises, which it is eminently fitting you should observe, I would say to our daughter, The Mother Church is here to rejoice with you· and to give voice to her pride in the noble record which

God has enabled you to make during the century just now folding itself away, and to bid you God-speed throughout all time to come.

At the conclusion of Mr. Rutherford's speech, the company in the auditorium returned to the social rooms, and resumed their participation in the social intercourse of the hour.

The evening wore on, and yet such was the delightfulness of the occasion that the company dispersed slowly, and it was not until after eleven o'clock that the last guests left the house, and Centennial Week came to a close. It was a fitting conclusion of a most delightful celebration. It could hardly be said to be anything less than a goodly fellowship of the saints. The whole celebration from Sunday morning to Friday night was one continuous, brilliant, gratifying success. Those who were most closely identified with it, and who lingered till the last in the sanctuary where it had been carried forward felt that as it began with the Doxology, it ought to close with the same.

> Praise God, from whom all blessings flow;
> Praise Him, all creatures here below;
> Praise Him above, ye heavenly host,
> Praise Father, Son and Holy Ghost.

CENTENNIAL GREETINGS.

GOD'S SURE COVENANT.*

By CHARLES NELSON HICKOK.

Lines suggested by an invitation to the centennial celebration of
the Market Square Presbyterian Church, Harrisburg, and by coinci-
dental recollections of the writer's membership and associations
therein, more than a half century ago.

'Tis said that sires were wont to tell
Their sons, in ancient Israel,
 The wonders God had wrought :—
How the oppressor's hosts were slain,
While, scathless, through the riven main,
 The chosen tribes were brought :—

How, by His own almighty arm—
Through tumult, danger and alarm :
 Their pilot, comfort, stay :
Their beacon through the baleful night :
Their shelter from the noonday blight—
 He led their devious way :—

How manna fell—by Heaven bestowed :—
From smitten rock how waters flowed,
 T' refresh the weary band :
Till safe, with neither scrip nor gold :
With sandals never waxing old,
 They reached the promised land.

---

*The centennial celebration called out several poems from members
and friends of the congregation. The Committee on Publication
being unable for lack of space to publish all of these contributions,
have selected the one written by the oldest person among the con-
tributors, himself for several years and until his removal from the city,
an honored member of the church.—EDITOR.

So, in these courts, God's people may
Recount His wondrous deeds to-day,
   Midst grateful, joyful tears ;
His myriad benefits recall,
His guiding, prospering hand through all
   The century of years.

A hundred times the tireless sun
His annual chariot-race hath run
   Back to his starting place ;
Yet every changing cycle past
Beheld, unchangeful as the last,
   God's covenant of grace !

Successive generations bear
Witness to His unfailing care,
   Whom our forefathers praised,
When to the wilderness they came
And, to the honor of His name,
   Their ebenezer raised.

The little flock, whom Jesus led—
By holy, faithful pastors fed—
   Has num'rous grown and strong ;
And it becomes their children well,
The numbers of His love to tell
   In a perpetual song ;

For precious is their heritage—
The holy birthright to engage
   In ministries divine :—
Theirs lineage of nobler blood—
The sons and daughters of our God—
   Than comes through royal line !

Bless'd flock ! Whom sweeter fruits regale
Than clusters, plucked from Eschol's vale,
   The sons of Judah fed !

Bless'd Shepherd ! By whose gentle hand,
Midst peaceful scenes of Christian land,
  Thy saints are comforted !

O Zion of Christ's plighted love,
Thy strong foundations who can move,
  Or, hopefully, assail ?
Though all the ranks of darkness swell,
Against thy Rock nor death, nor hell
  Hath power to prevail !

Dear House of Prayer ! How bless'd who wait
To meet The Lord within thy gate,
  Seeking to know His will ;
Learning, with Him, to bear the cross ;
Finding—midst conflict, grief. or loss—
  In Him, their refuge still !

Walking with God, no foes dismay !
With strength apportioned to their day,
  Nought can their hope destroy !
Oft sorrows cloud their " vale of tears,"
As oft The Comforter appears
  T' o'erflow their cup with joy !

And when —life's days of trial o'er—
Their feet draw near the darkling shore
  That borders death's cold sea,
Their faith discerns a heavenly form,
And hears the voice that still'd the storm,
  Of old, on Galilee.

Whether in Kalmia's* peaceful shade,
Or stranger-land their dust be laid,
  Or 'neath the ocean's wave.

* The name by which Harrisburg Cemetery was popularly known
forty years ago.—EDITOR.

Christ's covenant that dust secures :
His resurrection-pledge assures
   Their rescue from the grave !

Then let glad chants and hymns arise,
As fragrant incense, to the skies,
   With mighty organ's swell !
Join every voice in loud acclaim !
Shout to the heavens the matchless name
   Of our Immanuel !

Let youth and age, with one accord,
Proclaim the glories of our Lord,
   Th' Eternal God-head bless !
The fathers trusted well His love,
And children's children live to prove
   Jehovah's faithfulness !

BEDFORD, PENN'A, *February, 1894.*

RESOLUTIONS ADOPTED BY THE ELDER STREET CHURCH, HARRISBURG.

Resolutions adopted by the members of the Elder Street Presbyterian Church on the one hundredth anniversary of the Market Square Presbyterian Church :

" WHEREAS, God in his all-wise providence has blessed and preserved in our midst the Market Square Presbyterian Church for the period of a full century, and in that century God through the Holy Spirit and His Word has wrought miraculous temporal, moral and spiritual good to the community through the instrumentality of the church ; therefore, be it

" *Resolved,* That we, the members of the Elder Street Presbyterian Church, realizing that through the good men and women, who have been God's products and outgrowth of the Market Square Presbyterian Church, are grateful for our existence as a Church in this community and most heartily join with the Christian people of our city in extending congratulations to this Church which has labored so successfully in God's vineyard for the past hundred years, lifting up the fallen, building up and sustaining the weak, and advancing the principles of the Fatherhood of God and the brotherhood of man. We unite in prayer to God for continued prosperity and such an out-pouring of the Holy Spirit upon the congregation of the Market Square Church as they have never yet experienced; and we further pray that Presbyterianism as taught by the Market Square Church through the gospel of our blessed Lord and Saviour, may in this community do a greater work for humanity and Christ in the century to come than Presbyterianism has accomplished in the century just passed.

B. F. STEWART,

MRS. ELIZA ZEDRICKS,

JAMES H. W. HOWARD,

TURNER COOPER, JR.,

MISS ANNIE HIGGINS,

Committee."

LETTER FROM HON. A. LOUDEN SNOWDEN, GRANDSON OF REV. NATHANIEL R. SNOWDEN.

No. 1812 SPRUCE STREET, *February 13th, 1894.*

DEAR MR. STEWART:

I deeply regret that an unexpected call to New York on important business will deny me the pleasure of participating in the interesting ceremonies of your Church, of which my revered grandfather was the first pastor.

It was fully my intention to be with you, and to this end had accepted the polite invitation of my cousin, Mr. Henry McCormick, to be his guest. I can assure you that nothing but very important interests could prevent my being with you. I shall fully explain this in a letter to Mr. McCormick. I beg to assure you of my high appreciation of your considerate kindness in asking me to be with you, and of the sincere regret I have in not being able to meet your wishes. I am,

Respectfully yours,

A. LOUDEN SNOWDEN.

Rev. GEORGE B. STEWART.

LETTER FROM JUDGE JOSEPH ALLISON, A FORMER MEMBER.

No. 4207 WALNUT STREET, PHILADELPHIA,

February 13th, 1894.

LYMAN D. GILBERT, Esq.:

DEAR SIR: Yours of the 12th inst. has just been received at this 8:30 p. m.

Thanks for your invitation to be present during some portion of this week with the English Presbyterian congregation of Harrisburg during the Centennial Celebration of the founding of the Church.

It would give me no little pleasure to accept this invitation, if it was possible for me to be in Harrisburg during any portion of the week set apart for the services in commemoration of this interesting occasion; but I have been quite unwell for some time, and am now unable to make the journey to my native city, or to take part in the exercises in which I would be glad to share with the present congregation.

With respect, therefore, I must deny myself the pleasure of an acceptance.

Very truly yours,

JOSEPH ALLISON.

LETTER FROM MR. D. C. BUCHANAN, SON OF REV. JAMES BUCHANAN.

BARRACKS No. 21, SOLDIER'S HOME, NEAR DAYTON, O,

February 10, 1894.

REV. GEORGE B. STEWART:

DEAR SIR: My sister, Mattie B. Buchanan, of Logansport, sent me a letter written by you, inquiring if she knew of any likeness or picture of our dear father, the Rev. James Buchanan. I do not think there is one. Artists of any kind in the wilds of Indiana were very scarce in his day. The only likeness ever taken of him that I know anything about was from memory. An artist by the name of Geo. W. Winters settled in Logansport a short time before father's death. He said to me one day, "I hear you have no likeness of your father, a great pity. If you would desire one I can paint one from memory nearly as good, as if he were present. I thought your father one of the best representatives of the old divines we read about. I have often talked with Judges Stewart and Biddle here about it." "How much do you want for painting it?" "Forty dollars." "All right, with this understanding, if mother don't like the picture I am not to pay for it." "All right," he

said. After it was finished I took a great admirer of my
father to see it, by the name of Gen. Grover. He said,
" Winters, I have a much better likeness of Mr. Buchanan
over in my house than yours." " Whose is it?" " Gen.
William Henry Harrison, whom we elected President with
the help of coon-skins and hard cider. I have heard that
a great many times. I always thought Mr. Buchanan was
a finer looking man than Harrison." Mr. Grover said to
me, " Your mother won't take that picture. When you take
it out for her to see, I want you to take the Harrison picture
along and show her the Winter's picture first. I know she
will condemn it." As soon as she saw it she said, " My son,
that don't look like your father. It is more like an Italian
brigand. Tell Mr. Winters I don't want it." I then said,
" Hold on, mother; look at this one." Upon seeing it
she very quickly exclaimed : " I will take this one." Then
I explained matters to her. " Well, that is too bad. I am
not to have a likeness of your father after all," said she.
Gen. Grover was flattered a good deal when he heard
mother's report. I told him, " I can give you further proof
about your judgment. In the year 1836, when Gen.
Harrison made his political tour on horseback from the
Potomac through the Cumberland Valley to Harrisburg
(over the same route which Gen. Lee took in 1863, and met
his defeat at Gettysburg), some of my father's old Whig
friends requested him to ride at the head of the procession
with Harrison. Father, reflecting over the matter, told his
friends he did not think it would look very well for a minister of the gospel to be marching at the head of a political
procession, so declined going. The young ladies went along

the line of march to wave their flags and handkerchiefs to
salute the old hero of Tippecanoe. Three young ladies went
upstairs in Thomas G. McCullough's house as the procession came in sight. One cried out, ' Wait till Harrison
comes up, that first one is the Rev. James Buchanan, of
Greencastle.' So the old hero went by without their salute.
I got that from authority." That I thought was good.
Father graduated at Dickinson College, Carlisle, Pa. I
don't know the year. After he got what the Hoosiers called
his " sheep-skin " to preach, the Harrisburg church gave
him a call. When there he became acquainted with a
great belle and beauty, and the greatest dancer in all that
part of the country. People would say, " Can it be possible
that he would marry that flirt and coquette, Miss Hattie
Berryhill." Dr. Als. Berryhill, her brother, would say,
" Well Hatt, are you going to marry the preacher?"
" Don't you think I had better wait until he asks me?"
Miss Hattie was becoming seriously inclined now. " Hatt,
do you think you like him?" " Why not? He is certainly
the best looking and most intelligent gentleman in Harrisburg." " Oh, cracky, cracky, my young lady, you are froze
at last, goodbye, farewell." Many times have I heard her
say, "It was the most glorious day for me when I became
acquainted with your father, for he snatched me from the
brink of ruin and despair. Oh, what a wild, thoughtless,
giddy girl I was." If there ever was a true genuine Christian she was one. If my father would happen to be absent
over night she would lead in family worship, and she would
do it well, for her whole soul was in it.

I will tell you of one case of the good she did. Miss

Mary Shoemaker was at my mother's funeral. She came to me, the tears rolling down her cheeks, and said, "Oh, Mr. Buchanan, to that sainted mother of yours I owe all the glorious hopes I have. You know how I was raised almost an infidel. Thrice blessed may her memory be. Farewell, farewell, may her sweet prayers be answered on your behalf, for I may never see you again." This turned out to be the case. She is gone to her long home. It seems to me like a dream.

I have gotten too old to write much. I am seventy-two. About ten years older than my father at his death, and about ten years younger than my mother at her death.

Now if there is anything in this scrawl that you can use for the Centennial, it will pay for all my trouble. One thing is certain, it is all true as far as I know and believe.

My father's death was very sudden and unexpected. He went to church in his usual health. When about half through his sermon he told his congregation he was too unwell to finish it. He was taken with a congestive chill, gave out a hymn, went down the aisle, home, was taken to the church the next Sabbath a corpse,—one of the most sorrowful days I have ever seen, for I loved him with my whole soul and body. I was his favorite child out of nine. No one ever knew it until after his death, when mother told us. But I was about the last picked on. I was wild and full of vinegar. I am about worn out writing.

Yours respectfully,

D. C. BUCHANAN.

P. S.—I am the oldest son now living. Alexander, Wilson and I are the only boys living, and two girls, Martha in Logansport, and Maria, Mrs. Dr. Early, at Palmyra, Missouri. If I were as well off as I was ten or twelve years ago, I would come to your Centennial, but I am too poor to think of it.

LETTER FROM REV. JOSEPH R. VANCE, D. D., FORMERLY PASTOR FIRST PRESBYTERIAN CHURCH, CARLISLE, PA.

CHESTER, PA., *Feb. 6th, 1894.*

MY DEAR DR. STEWART:

Your kind invitation to the exercises of the 100th anniversary of the Market Square Church has just been received.

Thou hast been brought to the kingdom at a blessed time in the history of the grand old church.

In the days when Paxtang, Derry and Silvers' Spring were the chosen shrines, it was difficult for Harrisburg to gain recognition. For thirty years and up to the dawn of re-union, good Dr. DeWitt carried the flag of a small New School minority in Central Pennsylvania. One half of the faithful ministry of Dr. Robinson was spent in the little Presbytery of Harrisburg, but there is no " pent up Utica " for you and Market Square now. The good old Presbytery of Carlisle, the Synod of Pennsylvania, and the Woman's Boards are ready to second every motion you make.

When in A. D. 1894, we see the junior Dr. DeWitt and Dr. Robinson the exponents of the theological thought of Princeton and Allegheny, we conclude that it could not have been a very dangerous type of new schoolism after all, and seeing you in the van of Christian Endeavor columns, we say "He well represents the aggressive spirit characteristic of that Church. Like James Weir, he will never grow old." May the true consecration and determined aggressiveness of the past always charaterize the history of the church.   Very fraternally yours,

JOS. R. VANCE.

LETTER FROM MRS. MARY M. MCARTHUR, DAUGHTER OF THE LATE WILLIAM MCCLEAN A FORMER ELDER.

No. 636 N. MAIN STREET,

MEADVILLE, PA., *February 8th, 1894.*

MY DEAR MRS. DOLL: Please accept my thanks for your kind favor received. How much I wish I could be present and join in the very interesting services of the coming week. It was in that branch of the church (of sacred memory) with two elder brothers, I first made a public profession of my faith in Christ. Many pleasant and tender memories come crowding upon me as I recall the days of my youth in Harrisburg, of Christ's people, other friends and acquaintances, of the Sabbath-school, of my sainted parents, of respect shown my father, the confidence in him, and honor conferred in making him an Elder in the Church of God. I remember well several of the ladies and gentlemen whose names are on the committee.

I shall be with you in spirit as the programme is being carried out, praying that God's blessing may accompany each meeting, that his people there and elsewhere in Harrisburg may especially feel the influences of the Holy Spirit, and be greatly refreshed and strengthened, and many who are still out of Christ be brought to love and serve him. With love,   Your friend,

MARY M. MCARTHUR.

LETTER FROM REV. SAMUEL G. NICCOLLS, D. D., FORMERLY
PASTOR OF FALLING SPRING CHURCH, CHAMBERSBURG.

ST. LOUIS, *February 7th, 1894.*

MY DEAR BROTHER: I have received your invitation to
attend the One Hundredth Anniversary of the Market
Square Church. I greatly regret that it will not be possible
for me to be present. The invitation revives so many
pleasant memories of Harrisburg, and of my associations
with the old Presbytery of Carlisle, that I would like very
much to be with you on this memorable occasion. Your
old church has a grand history and has been a mighty
power for good in the Cumberland Valley. I know that it
has a life within it which prevents it from becoming old.
A living church always renews itself and laughs at Time.
With best wishes, I am

Fraternally yours,

SAMUEL G. NICCOLLS.

LETTER FROM REV. ROBERT F. McCLEAN, GRANDSON OF A
FORMER ELDER AND HIMSELF FOR MANY YEARS A MEM-
BER OF THE PRESBYTERY OF CARLISLE.

MUNCY, *February 7th, 1894.*

Rev. GEORGE B. STEWART, D. D., *Harrisburg, Pa.*

DEAR BROTHER : We are grateful for the invitation to the
Centennial of your church, though we will be unable to be
present. I well remember when a boy on a visit to Harrisburg, of seeing Dr. DeWitt, and the then black-haired Dr.
Robinson, together in the pulpit of the old church, and of
being in Mr. James McCormick's Sunday-school class of
boys. The grand work and the goodly fellowship of the

Market Square Church deserve commemoration. The fact of my grandfather being an elder, and Dr. Robinson and yourself such esteemed friends of my own give me deep personal interest in it.

Cordially yours,

ROBERT F. McCLEAN.

Many other letters of congratulation were received, but space is lacking for their publication. Among them were letters from

Colonel John J. McCook, New York City.

Rev. William H. Roberts, D. D., LL. D., Stated Clerk of General Assembly.

Rev. William S. Van Cleve, Gettysburg.

William M. Capp, M. D., son of a former Elder, Philadelphia.

Rev. S. S. Wylie, Middle Spring.

Mr. Abram B. Knapp, Elizabeth, N. J,

Mr. William J. Nevius, Jr., South Orange, N. J.

J. Bayard Henry, Esq., Philadelphia.

Mrs. Sibyl Fahnestock Hubbard, New York.

Mrs. Mary Fahnestock Reid, Allegheny.

Rev. Ezra A. Huntington, D. D., LL. D., Professor in Theological Seminary, Auburn.

Rev. W. T. L. Kieffer, Washington, Pa.

Miss Martha Buchanan, daughter of Rev. Jas. Buchanan, second pastor of the church, Logansport, Ind.

John Curwen, M. D., Superintendent of State Insane Hospital, Warren, Pa.

Ovid F. Johnson, Esq., and sisters, Philadelphia.

Rev. Martin L. Ganoe, pastor Ridge Avenue M. E. Church Harrisburg.

Geo. W. Mehaffie, General Secretary West Philadelphia Branch Y. M. C. A., Philadelphia.

Rev. Everard Kempshall, D. D., pastor First Presbyterian Church, Elizabeth, N. J.

Rev. J. Smith Gordon, Fannettsburg.

Geo. B. Ayres, Esq., Philadelphia.

Rev. Henry C. McCook, D. D., Pastor Tabernacle Presbyterian Church, Philadelphia.

Rev. William P. White, Financial Secretary for Lincoln University, Germantown, Pa.

Judge Henry H. Swan, of U. S. District Court, Detroit, Michigan.

Rev. Arthur S. Hoyt, D. D., Professor in Theological Seminary, Auburn, N. Y.

Rev. Timothy G. Darling, D. D., Professor in Theological Seminary, Auburn, N. Y.

Rev. John C. Barr, Dillsburg, Pa.

Mr. H. C. Doll, Denver, Col.

Gen. James A. Beaver, Bellefonte, Pa.

Rev. Edward D. Morris, D. D. LL. D., Professor in Lane Theological Seminary, Cincinnati.

Rev. J. R. Miller, D. D., Secretary of the Presbyterian Board of Publication, Philadelphia.

Hon. Samuel Gustine Thompson, Philadelphia.

President Patton, Princeton College, Princeton, N. J.

Rev. Willis J. Beecher, D. D., Professor in Theological Seminary, Auburn, N. Y.

OUR SECOND CENTURY.

It seemed fitting to the Committee on Publication that this volume should contain the first sermons of the new century, delivered in the church on Sunday, April 18th, 1894. It therefore requested them from Dr. Robinson and Dr. Stewart for such publication. By request of the minister, Rev. Dr. Robinson assisted him in the morning service and preached. He chose for his theme, "Characteristics of a True Pastor and a True Church." In the evening the minister preached upon the theme, "The Duty of Our Second Century." The usual order of service was observed on both occasions, and large audiences were present. Thus happily was the new century begun, with a deep sense of gratitude for the blessings received and an abiding consciousness of the ever-present duties of discipleship.

CHARACTERISTICS OF A TRUE PASTOR AND A TRUE CHURCH.

By Rev. Thomas H. Robinson, D. D.

Before I enter upon the subject of the morning I wish to say a word about the week that has just closed. It is a word of congratulation. The week has been a happy and most successful one. I rejoice in your unity and christian love. I rejoice in your brotherhood with all the Churches about you. I rejoice in the outlook for the coming years. I have been looking with gladness on the young faces that are to stand in your lot in the years to come. Perhaps some may feel that a great deal has been said about the Scotch-Irish and Presbyterianism ; too much it may be. Let us now submerge them. They are worth nothing save as they are Christian. Apart from Christ they are but worthless dust. The best and deepest thing in us is not ancestral blood, nor Presbyterian orthodoxy, but christian faith and life. In the vocabulary of Heaven, the words Scotch-Irish and Presbyterianism will not be found. There are no Scotch-Irish nor Presbyterians—as such in the glorious City of the Skies. Nationalities and denominations find no home there. Let us count it to be our chiefest glory now, as it will be then, to be simply the followers of Christ and the Children of God.

Philippians iv. 1-7.

Wherefore, my brethren, beloved and longed for, my joy and crown, so stand fast in the Lord, my beloved.

I exhort Euodia, and I exhort Syntyche to be of the same mind in the Lord. Yea, I beseech thee also, true yokefellow, help these women, for they labor with me in the Gospel, with Clement also and the rest of my fellow-workers, whose names are in the book of life. Rejoice in the Lord alway: again I will say, Rejoice. Let your forbearance be known unto all men. The Lord is at hand. In nothing be anxious: but in everything by prayer and supplication with thanksgiving let your requests be made known unto God. And the peace of God which passeth all understanding shall guard your hearts and your thoughts in Christ Jesus.

It was a very human and natural thing that as Paul drew near to the close of his letter to the Church at Philippi, he should indulge in some direct personal references. We do the same thing in our letters of to-day. We send messages to one and another of the absent friends. We recall by name the members of the household.

The main burden of the Apostle's thought in the Epistle is uttered and he is drawing to the end. The Good Bye is about to be written. The faces of the absent ones come before him, and it is very natural that before he lays down the pen he should add some closing admonitions, exhortations and messages. They are brief and pithy. The weight of thought and feeling that was upon him in the main body of the letter is cast off, and he comes out more the man than the great Apostle. We get at his heart and find how human he is.

These closing sentences may seem to be fragmentary and unconnected, and the Apostle may seem to be writing now just what occurs to him. He is not deeply thinking. Yet

I think we shall find his words are not quite fragmentary. They are not written at random. A definite line of thought underlies what he now says. The earlier part of the letter shapes the close of it.

It is so with ourselves. Letters of business, letters of friendship, letters of consolation and letters of family love, all have their own and their appropriate ending.

Paul was writing to one of the churches that he had founded and to which he clung with tenacious affection. He had been pouring out his soul on the subject of the true Christian life. He had revealed the deep sources from which it springs, the great channels in which it runs, and the conditions which surround it in this world, with its glorious attainments in the world to come.

But still he remembers we are here, not there. We are amid the petty details of human life on earth. Earthly things still have their strong hold upon us. These Christians at Philippi were human and weak. They were amid temptations. They were at the mercy of a great multitude of trivial and daily things that must be attended to. How could they keep the grand music of the Gospel, the sublime, uplifting anthems of the life eternal sounding in their souls amid the patter and stir and noise of a busy life amid earthly things!

Paul comes down to the case. In doing so he reveals to us some characteristics of a true pastor, and also some characteristics of a true church. Allow me to draw your minds along these two lines of thought.

I. The True Pastor.

The apostle brings out, unconsciously, one element in the

character of every true pastor. Unconsciously, I say, for he was not displaying and eulogizing himself.

He simply tells, in his own experience, how the members of a church should be esteemed by a true pastor. They should have the deepest, tenderest love, and the strongest and heartiest good wishes of the pastor. Listen to the words of Paul, this man whom many only think of as a great theologian and the massive thinker of the church, and so absorbed in the grandeur of his thoughts as to be above the ordinary affections of men. Paul's heart was as great as his intellect. Note how he addresses these Christians of Philippi:

"Therefore, my brethren, dearly beloved and longed for, my joy and my crown, so stand fast in the Lord, my dearly beloved." What an accumulation of strong epithets of affection are here. "Longed for." It was the yearning of a great, strong man. "My joy." The source of his joy was not in his apostleship, in his miraculous powers, in his grand acquirements, in his enlarging fame through all the churches. It was in those who had been converted to God under his ministry; in the beauty of their life and their loyalty to Jesus Christ. Our joy is in our homes and in our friends. The chief happiness of a true pastor is in the pure and Christlike lives of the people to whom he ministers.

"My Crown" adds the Apostle. He means that he prided himself in them. He gloried in them. It is not in these passages alone that St. Paul reveals his feelings for the people among whom he labored. It may be traced in all his letters. Elsewhere he writes. "My little children, for

whom I travail in birth till Christ be formed in your hearts."
And again—I ceased not to warn every one of you day and
night with tears—"we were gentle among you even as a
nurse cherisheth her children." "We were willing to have
imparted unto you not the Gospel of God only, but also our
own soul because you were very dear unto us." We think
of Paul usually, as the stern reprover, the dauntless hero,
the uncompromising champion of truth, the incomparable
theologian, but there were in his soul great fountains of
love and tenderness. Men who knew him loved him. They
fell on his neck and kissed him. In his gentleness lay
much of his power.

There are preachers who pride themselves on being "faithful", in preaching the whole truth, in telling the people
their sins. They are decided, they are heroic, they are
scathing in denunciations of evil, they bear their testimony
whether men will hear or forbear against popular evils.
But there is a hardness in their tones, and a harshness in
their manner, a self sufficiency and lack of sympathy that
make their ministry offensive.

The mainspring of the Gospel is the spirit of love. The
mission of the preacher is a delicate one. While he is to
preach the truth, and all the truth, he is ever to speak it in
love, never in haste, never in scorn, never in indifference. He
is to be filled with enthusiasm of humanity, a deep, true,
broad love of man as man. Like his great Master he is to
be a philanthropist—a lover of his kind. Narrowness, bigotry,
prejudice, sectarianism should never find a home in his
soul. Love should look through his candid, earnest,
solemn eye. It should gleam in every line of his counten-

ance. It should be heard in the intonations of his voice. His speech is always to be evangelical. He is the bringer of glad tidings. He proclaims the love of God to men. He speaks of boundless mercy. He tells of the love of the Incarnate God, of a love that was stronger than humiliation and pain. Stronger than shame and death—a love divine that bled for rebellious man. A love that knows no depth of sin that it cannot reach, no path of woe that it cannot travel, no foulness of the creature that it would not heal with tender touch. He tells of a love that opens a world of endless glory and happiness to the undeserving and guilty.

The man who preaches such a gospel, must have the spirit of love in every fibre of his being. Harshness, impatience, hoarse thunderings, are foreign to the true preacher. See what he has to do. He has to unveil to hard hearted men the tender fatherhood of God. He has to make them see the longing brotherhood of a Divine Saviour. He has to come to men in all their moods, their sins, their wants, as the representative of Him who tasted death for every man. He has to hear the heart's secrets of men in distress over their sins. He has to be present in human homes in the sacred hour of sorrow and speak in Christ's name. He has to be God's messenger of comfort to the desolate and broken-hearted, to stand by the bedside of dying saints and dying sinners, and tell each one of the Lamb of God who taketh away the sins of the world. He has to go where other men would be counted as intruders, into the deep and secret places of human woe, where mothers are clinging to their dead children—where grief is too deep for tears, and there bring the consolations of our divine faith.

How vain for any one to fill such an office whose heart is not delicate and sensitive under the refining power of real love. It is not sentimental weakness for which I plead. Paul was no sentimental weakling. He was a great, strong, brave, intellectual man—a very giant of a man. He knew what it was to argue with the wits and wise men of the world; what it was to stand before kings; what it was to be scourged and beaten with rods and to die daily. He was a man, a great, strong man everywhere. But the heart within him was a great, strong, broad heart, and it throbbed and beat as did the heart of the Master for men, for men everywhere. His words of endearment are not words of weakness but of strength. He looked upon men everywhere as given to him that he might win them for Christ, or keep them for Christ. His joys and his sorrows were connected with them. He was glad over them, or he grieved over them. He was never cold, never austere, never harsh. He was a true preacher.

II. The apostle also gives us some of the characteristics of a True Church.

If the pastor, like the Chief Pastor, the great and good Shepherd of the Flock, must have a loving nature, surely the disciples, the members of the church, must possess a lovable character. If he is among a people who are morally unlovable and unattractive, how can he be expected to pour out his affections upon them? The true church will be responsive. It will return love for love. It will display the winning graces and qualities of Christly character.

These qualities of character in the members of a true Church are brought out by the Apostle in three aspects:

1. What the members of a true Church are to each other.

2. What they are in themselves.

3. What they are towards God.

I. What the members of a genuine Church are to each other.

They are bound in spiritual unity. "I entreat Euodia and I entreat Syntyche to be of the same mind in the Lord." Two of the christian women of the Church at Philippi, women who, Paul says, had labored with him and with each other in the Lord, were unhappily at variance. We know nothing about the cause of the trouble. Paul gives no hints. He takes neither side in the alienation. One thing fills his mind. They must be reconciled. It may seem too little a thing to claim the attention and grieve the heart of the great Apostle. It may have been a thing of the commonest kind. It serves Paul as an illustration of how liable believing and loving lives are to be swayed and marred, and so to mar the beauty and weaken the power of a Church. The Church lives and speaks in all its members. It is one body. It must be sound and whole and harmonious in all its parts. There must be no schism in the body. Little grievances grow into great magnitude. In feeling, in friendship, in action, the genuine Church must be one. All hearts must beat in unison. There must be no discords in the music of the Church. All outward life, all intercourse with each other, our common labors, must all keep touch with the spring and source of our spiritual life. We must keep together in our Common Lord. In his glowing presence of tenderness and love all alienations must disappear. Unity—unity of affection, of sentiment, of aim, is the law for the genuine Church. In Him, in the glorified Christ, whose earthly struggles and sufferings were met for each, the members of the Church should be now and forever united.

The members of the genuine church are mutually helpful.

"I entreat thee, also, true yoke-fellow, help these women who labored with me in the Gospel, with Clement, also, and the rest of my fellow-workers."

Who this true yoke-fellow was no one knows. It does not matter. Who these other "fellow-workers" were, no one knows. It matters not. In a genuine church all are fellow-workers, all are true "yoke-fellows." The church is a loving workshop. All bear the yoke of service. One is the Master, even Christ. The law of mutual co-operation prevails. "Bear ye one another's burdens, and so fulfill the law of Christ."

For every one who has begun to follow Christ there is no other place but the Church of Christ. He belongs there as much as a soldier to an army; just as much as a child belongs in his father's house. He is out of his place if he is outside the church. He has no right to be outside.

And when he takes his place in the church he has no right to be an idler, to sit down and take his ease. "Lord what wilt Thou have me to do?" is the primal question of every genuine Christian; consecration to service, putting on the yoke, is a universal law. Then comes working in harmony. Yoke-fellows we are. It is a grand, good word. It tells of helpfulness. We pull together in rolling the car of salvation. We have entered into a holy alliance. God

in his almighty love, bids us love, and help, and serve and
bless each other. The old fable of the blind man and the
cripple is realized every day in the true church. The blind
man carries the cripple on his shoulders, and the cripple
becomes eyes to the blind man.

> "Heaven forming each on other to depend,
>   A master, or a servant, or a friend,
>   Bids each on other for assistance call,
>   Till one man's weakness grows the strength of all."

The members of the genuine church are mutually considerate. To these fellow-workers at Philippi Paul writes,
"Let your moderation be known unto all men. The word
meant forbearance—consideration—the state of mind that
does not overrate our own worth and our own plans, nor
insist on having our own will. Let every man look on the
things of others, Paul elsewhere says. The true church is
filled with magnanimous Christians—large-hearted, broad-
minded men and women. They are patient toward weakness, charitable towards the erring, gentle and forbearing
towards the sinful. The natural selfishness and impetuosity
of the human heart has been subdued by the unseen presence and influence of Christ. A great vision of faith keeps
the serene and loving Master near—a vision that calms the
human passion and brings the soul into a happy order. It
can now "believe all things, endure all things, hope all
things." Christ seen, felt, rejoiced in as personal friend
and Saviour, will make the members of the church forbearing, considerate, gentle to all men. A true, large-
hearted Christian is unselfish. He does not stand on his

strict rights. He is not punctilious over trifles. He imitates the large generousness of Jesus Christ.

II. The Apostle tells us what the members of a true Church are in themselves. He mentions two characteristics.

1. The first is that of Loyalty to Christ. "They stand fast in the Lord." We cannot stand fast against the forces of this world's evil, we cannot stand fast in our spiritual encounters with flesh and blood, with the principalities and powers of darkness, we cannot stand fast in charity and helpfulness toward all our christian brethren, we cannot stand fast in large-hearted love for all our fellow-men—in ourselves and by our own strength.

We must find our inspiration in Jesus Christ. Our firmness must come from being rooted in Him. We must have unshaken convictions about Him. We must have an everlastingly settled love towards Him—"rooted and grounded" "steadfast and immovable" in our faith and love towards Him. It gives our weakness heroic strength when we keep our hold on Christ. It kindles our cold hearts with the fires of a divine enthusiasm when we keep close in touch with Jesus Christ. It will sustain our courage, our fortitude, our constancy amid all perils and disappointments, amid every whirlwind of doubts and fears, if we keep up our fellowship with Christ. He is the vine, we are the branches. Apart from Him we can do nothing. United to Him we can join Paul in his word of triumph "I can do all things through Christ that strengtheneth me." Inspired with the life of Christ, living day by day in the light of Christ, happy in the love of Christ, glad to bear the easy yoke of Christ, we shall be able to stand. The fires of his love for mankind will burn in all our hearts. We shall look out on men with his generous pity and brotherly affection. The miseries and sins of the confederated millions of the human race will not appal us ; the troubles that assail the Church will not terrify us, for being one with Him, we are greater than we thought ourselves to be. His victory is ours.

2. One thing more, for I must leave a large part of my subject untouched.

A true Church will be full of religious joy.

This letter to the Philippians is like an anthem that has running through it from beginning to end a melody—a strain of music. Again and again you catch the notes of the sweet strain until as you listen, you wait for its recurrence and find that the whole anthem is built upon it. The undertone of this letter to the Philippians is Christian Gladness.

At the opening of the third chapter Paul had said: "Finally, my brethren rejoice in the Lord." Rejoice, be of good cheer, was the usual farewell salute of the early christians. It was the last, best word. It was the summing of the religious life. It best expressed the fulness of its meaning—Rejoice, it is the keynote of our faith. It is a strain, the undertone of our christian anthem. And so here, as Paul draws nearer to the end of his letter he resumes the melody : "Rejoice in the Lord always. Again I will say it. Rejoice."

Be happy in your religion, be happy in your great Saviour and Friend, is a divine command. Happiness is an essential element in genuine religion. Happiness is not only a privilege of the disciples of Christ, but a duty. It would seem as if it was as wrong for a Christian to be unhappy as to break any of the ten commandments. The command to rejoice is founded on the same authority as "Thou shalt not steal." It is repeated a hundred times more frequently.

Is joy possible? Is perpetual joy possible? Rejoice, rejoice in the Lord always; again I will say, rejoice! Old Testament believers were frequently exhorted to rejoice in the Lord Jehovah. New Testament believers are bidden to rejoice in the Lord—the Lord Jesus—God incarnate, God revealed. It is the necessary inference from their knowledge of Him, their belief in his being, character and work that they should rejoice in Him. If this Lord Jesus be what Christians believe Him to be, then there is a thousandfold more in Him to make them glad than there is in all the rest of the universe to make them sad. Christians ought to be always the happiest beings on the face of the earth. Despite their trials and troubles, despite their very sins, they ought to be. Joy is the logical outcome of true religion. The church should be the home of irresistible happiness.

But note it well, Christian joy is not joy in any form of mere earthly good, the things that make up the world's happiness; nor is it joy in our own sure hopes of heaven as forgiven and saved men—it is joy in a person—in the Lord Jesus.

This means two things. It means first, that we have learned to believe. We are the children of a fixed and positive faith. The greatest, the central object of our faith is Jesus Christ. We have a vivid sense of the reality of

Christ. We are in no region of mist and doubt, but one rather of certainty. It means that our minds work in reference to Christ, just as they do in reference to the things and persons about us, which are felt and known to be real persons and things. We do not doubt their reality; we see them; our hands touch them; we hear them, converse with them, deal with them in a real, substantial way. So stands Christ to us. He is real; He is living; He is our living brother. It matters not that to the dull eye of sense He is invisible. Faith sees him. Faith has full, free play in our souls as it turns to Him. It sees Him to be divine; it sees Him to be the Lamb of God that taketh away the sin of the world; it sees Him to be the invisible Ruler watching over and guiding all our affairs; it sees Him to be the great Advocate, who in heaven pleads for us in all trouble and danger; it sees Him to be the unfailing and almighty Friend, ready at all times to do us kindly service; it sees Him to be our ascended human Brother, who is preparing for the home coming of all the members of the family. It is the grand privilege of the Christian to have a faith about Christ; strong, clear and realizing, no wavering, changeful and frightened thing, but a thing of deepest convictions; a trust utter, unmovable, eternal, so that we may repeat the words of olden time, " We believe and are sure that Thou art the Christ, the Son of the living God."

This joy in Christ means another thing. We have learned to speak a second great word. That word is Love. Whom having not seen ye love. "Lord, Thou knowest all things, Thou knowest that I love Thee."

When Christ is realized to be what He is, love has no

difficulty. It leaps into being; it finds in Him all that it wants. In all earthly love there is need of caution, measurement and restraint. We cannot give ourselves up utterly to any human thing or human being. They have weaknesses. There are spots, flecks and shadows about the best and strongest of earth.

But there is no defect, no shadow, no stain about Jesus Christ. The perfection of humanity and the glory of divinity are His. We may love Him utterly and without reserve. He will meet it all, answer it all, satisfy it all.

Now comes joy. When through our deepest soul the conviction makes its way, of the reality of Christ, that He is divine, good, almighty; and that He is for me a friend, a saviour for me, and the soul surrenders to it all thoroughly; then love is born, and gladness flows through the whole being.

A firm faith and a hearty love—without any happiness? Impossible. The believing, loving soul must be a happy soul. The believing, loving church must be a happy church. The man who believes and loves Christ, as he ought, as he may, has in him the seed and the principle of a grand uplifting power of rejoicing. He cannot help himself. He must rejoice. He must be happy. It is a blessed necessity that compels every one who is in Christ by faith and love to be happy in Him.

Many in the world about us, many who stand high among the scholars and great men of the age give their sad answer to the question, Is this life worth living? They are pessimists. They see the heavy yoke that is on the sons of Adam. They note the weary and tragic sides of human history, the mystery, the bewildering evil, the want and woe. They are the malcontents, the disappointed, the suicides, for whom death is an escape from tedium or misery. They have lost their hold on faith and the unseen. They have failed to put God in the center of their lives and have exiled themselves from Christ. They have not tasted the good word of God, nor learned what it is to have life by believing in the Son of God, incarnate, crucified, risen, enthroned, and so they know nothing of that peace of God that swept away all the vexations of this mortal life.

Followers of the risen and glorified Christ, you ought to rejoice. If any in the world have a right to rejoice, it is you. You ought to be the happiest beings on the face of the earth. If you are sad and gloomy Christians, you should be filled with shame because of it. Believing in such a Saviour as you have, accepting Him as your eternal friend, accepted by Him, loved by Him, cared for by Him, it is a sin in you not to be happy all the day long. The world should see it beaming in your faces. The flags of joy should wave over every assembly of Christ's friends. He is worthy to be rejoiced in. "Rejoice in the Lord alway," again I will say, rejoice.

THE DUTY OF OUR SECOND CENTURY.

By George B. Stewart, *Minister*.

Psalms 16:6.

The lines are fallen unto me in pleasant places: Yea, I have a goodly heritage.

The events of the past week have brought to our attention in an emphatic and delightful way God's exceeding goodness to this congregation, the honor and the power which he has been pleased to bestow upon us. In view of the glorious past and the exalted present, every one of us is inspired to make the words of the Psalmist our own: "The lines are fallen unto me in pleasant places; Yea, I have a goodly heritage." We have been encouraged to retrospection—"looking backward" over the century of history in which many of us have borne some part, and in which this Church has had multiplied evidence of the divine presence and guidance. The last week has been one of unalloyed delight, of inspiration, of sincere thanksgiving.

The history of a hundred years has been no mean story. The struggles, the labors, the trials, the successes of the century have been rehearsed with mingled feelings of gratitude to our heavenly Father, and of legitimate admiration for our noble ancestors. Those who have gone before us bore a praiseworthy part in the establishment of the kingdom of Christ in this community. They were not faultless, but they were God's own; and they wrought well and nobly in his name. They have left to us a precious legacy in a good reputation. We are happier than ever in being identified with a Church whose name is honored in this community, and throughout the world. We have come into a goodly fellowship and we know better now than ever how priceless is our inheritance in this congregation.

Grateful as we are for the past, happy as we are for the memory of it, we nevertheless must turn from it. Centenary anniversaries are delightful occasions. It would not be surprising if we were disposed to say in the language of the old hymn:

> " My willing soul would stay
> In such a frame as this,
> And sit and sing herself away
> To everlasting bliss."

But that we cannot do. We cannot, we must not, tarry in these delightful fields of memory. It is our duty to raise our Ebenezer, to put up our monument to the glory of God and the praise of his servants, and then pass on. Duty beckons us to new labors, trials and achievements.

The Duty of Our Second Century.

I. Our duty stated broadly.

It is impossible within the limits of a single discourse to particularize all the duty that devolves upon us as disciples of Christ, as a congregation of his people. I can only hope at this time to draw your attention to certain duties which are emphasized by the occasion. Our feet are standing upon the threshhold of a new century. Our faces are turned toward the dawn of another hundred years. We have been looking over our possessions, examining our inheritance, rejoicing in the large accumulations of the past which are now ours, and we are sensible of the responsibility which wealth always brings.

Truly the lines are fallen unto us in pleasant places, and we have a goodly heritage. We must not be unmindful that the Psalmist used this expression with reference to Jehovah. "The Lord is the portion of mine inheritance, and my cup; thou maintainest my lot." Jehovah is his God, is to him the sum of all good. In the words of Paul, the great apostle, "All things are yours, and ye are Christ's, and Christ is God's." From our Jehovah comes all the blessing, all the treasure, all the honor. He always remains ours. Things may pass away, the portion of our lot may grow smaller and smaller, the generations may move on and disappear, but he remains the same yesterday, to-day and forever, our eternal possession. We rejoice in him, we magnify Him, we exalt Him above all other beings. We preach Christ, and Him crucified. In Him we glory. To all the world we proclaim that having Him we have all things; having Him we lack nothing. He truly is our inheritance and our portion. We rejoice that our noble sires, our sturdy forefathers accepted the Christ and the gospel when presented to them; that they took Him into their hearts and lives to be their Lord and Saviour; that they preserved the gospel in its purity and power; that they taught their children after them the blessed truth as it is in Jesus; and that each succeeding generation, believing in Him, told those who were to come after them the story of the cross, and inspired in them by their words and example a true loyalty to the Master and Saviour of men. Thus it has come to be that the Lord Jehovah is our inheritance; that Jesus is our Saviour; that the Holy Spirit is our Sanctifier and Guide. This is the sum of the blessing in which we rejoice. This is the priceless heritage to which we have fallen heir.

This is the heritage we are to transmit to our children. This knowledge of the living God, the everlasting Father, the Prince of Peace, we must give to others. We are custodians of the truth, not "to have and to hold," but to have and bestow. As we have freely received, we must freely give. We are debtors to the world by so much as we have the gospel of light and life and love.

II. Our duty stated more particularly.

The words of our text readily adapt themselves to the peculiar temper of our mind and heart at this time. Our lot has specially bright aspects which the century of history presents to us. In our great treasure-trove we note brilliant jewels in which we find peculiar delight. It is not difficult to mark them. To these I desire to call your particular attention, and to the duty growing out of them.

The duty of our second century, expressed in a single phrase, is loyalty to our traditions. This is the gist of what I am to say to-night. All that follows will be to illustrate and enforce this commanding duty.

Loyalty to our traditions does not mean narrowness, or bigotry, or conservativeness, or any ecclesiastical bourbonism. The whole spirit of progress, of aggressive, intelligent, large-minded, large-hearted sympathy with the present, of skillful adaptation of truth and activity to the needs of the hour are wrapped up in the observance of this one duty.

We have a goodly heritage and must keep it. The traditions of the Church are the character of the Church. New Churches are apt to be heterogeneous and unformed in their character but as the years lengthen out into decades, and scores, and centuries, they come to have their own particular way of doing their work, of viewing truth, of developing their life. They come to have an individuality which is recognized as their own. This means simply that they have each a mission to perform, and they go about it in their own way. The fact that some people like one Church better than another, feel more at home in it, or feel more in sympathy with its aims and spirit, is a recognition of this that each Church has its own individuality.

What we commonly call the traditions of a church are the marks by which it is known. It is not at all surprising that many of the traditions which I mention this evening as belonging to us to some extent belong also to other Churches. Everybody has a nose, and eyes, and ears; but there is just enough variety in these to make faces differ. Traditions are so combined and compounded in us as to give us an individuality which makes us, a Church, in no small degree, unlike the other churches whose fellowship we delight in, and whose magnificent progress we rejoice over. I call you, therefore, to note the traditions of this Church, as I understand them, and to press upon you loyalty to them, that is to say, to urge you to maintain the character of this Church. If it has gained anything during the past hundred years that is worth keeping, it is its character. The individual acts and events of the preceding generations have contributed toward its formation. The past activities have converged toward the present moment. A hundred years have written their lines upon our face, and men know us as we are. Our name stands for a distinct idea in this city, and of it we are justly proud, and for the maintenance of it we should bend our efforts.

I am constrained to say that I know no Church whose traditions are more to my liking; and, as I believe, more Scriptural. When, nine years ago or more, I was deliberating whether I should accept your unanimous call to become your Pastor, one of the considerations which led me to make a decision agreeably to your wishes was the character of this Church as I gathered it from the traditions current among you. I felt that I would be at home among a people whose past and whose present place the emphasis yours do upon certain phases of the Christian life. In this I have not been disappointed. As the Minister of this Church, "The lines have fallen unto me in pleasant places, and I have a goodly heritage." Each one of you is justified in making the same declaration in view of your membership here.

What are some of these traditions which indicate our past life and our present character?

1. Loyalty to your Minister, and those who have the rule over you.

The fact that you have had but five Pastors in a hundred years is evidence of this. If I read your history correctly there has been an unvarying loyalty to and an affectionate regard for, your Ministers. They have always felt that they could depend upon their congregation to sustain them in every good work. In time of crisis, when your Minister and your officers have been called upon to make momen- tous decisions as well as in the ordinary routine of church activity, they have not failed of your cordial and hearty support. To secure this co-operation in any undertaking it has only been necessary for them to make known to you that they deemed the undertaking expedient. Your trus- tees, your deacons, your elders have never appealed to you in vain for support in any good work. Happy are the official boards, happy is the Minister who are of a church with such a character as this. I cannot but believe that this will characterize your future attitude toward your Min- ister and officers. The second century ought to witness the same cordial, liberal and unvarying loyalty toward those who bear the rule among you. It is a tradition worth maintaining.

2. Large benevolence.

The reputation of this congregation in the city and Pres- bytery for liberality toward church causes and local char- ities, organized and unorganized, is truly enviable. For generations this has been your reputation. It has led many to infer that this is a rich Church, and to speak of it as such. The fact is, that this is not a rich Church, but a liberal one. And this is more to your credit. And it is more to the advantage of all good enterprises. You and your predeces- sors have counted it a great privilege to give generously for the advancement of every good work. This characteristic should continue. Every individual member of this Church should count it one of the highest privileges the Master bestows to give out of his abundance and out of his poverty for the support of good works. It is jokingly said by some, that we take a collection on every occasion. It is to our praise that we embrace every opportunity to give to the Lord's work. May we ever merit this praise.

There are vast undertakings, there are mighty interests, there are great causes to be maintained and advanced. We must bear our part, every one of us. Count this as a precious portion of your inheritance. Have you little, give little; have you much, give much. You who are young, upon whose mind the memory of this past week will linger for many years, will soon come into the responsibilities, the duties and the obligations of this Church. Begin now to cultivate the spirit of liberality. Count it your privilege to give out of your small possessions. This generation must not drop below the past in the liberality of our gifts. Every member of the congregation ought to be spurred by the magnificent generosity which has characterized the past years to an equally magnificent generosity in the days and years to come.

3. Activity in good works.

In reading the early history of the Church, and in listening to the history as it was so admirably presented by Doctor Robinson, I have been impressed with the disposition the members of this Church have always had to advance every good undertaking. In all moral reforms in the community, in every missionary enterprise, in all efforts to relieve the distress of the poor, to enlighten the ignorant, to lift up the degraded, to spread the knowledge of the gospel

in our own region, in our own country, and in all the
world, this congregation has been foremost. Illustrative of
this, it may be mentioned that the church organized the
first Sunday-school for all this region ; it was the prime
mover in the organization of the Y. M. C. A.; it was in the
forefront of the Washingtonian temperance work ; its women
organized what is probably the oldest woman's prayer-meeting in our Presbyterian Church ; when other Churches were
still indifferent to missionary enterprise, this Church was
awake ; it was the first to organize its women for home and
foreign work ; it had the first Christian Endeavor Society in
this city. In every forward movement of the Church, it
has been found in the front rank.

The record of a hundred years is the record of WORK,
readiness to further the interest of the community and
the world, and of achievement brought about by self-sacrificing and heroic endeavor.

I call upon you this evening as you enter upon the new
century, to resolve that this shall be the character of this
congregation in the future. Be quick to further every good
enterprise, to take firm hold upon moral reforms, to advance
the interests of the city, to exalt the name of the Lord in
the mission fields of the country, and of the world. Having
put your hands to the plow, look not back. Press steadily
onward in all the activities of the Church. There is much
latent and unused talent here. The working forces of the
Church might be easily and largely augmented if each individual member would set about his own particular task.
The condition of success, of growth, of life, is work. The
history which delights us is what it is because our fathers

"had a mind to work." May we, their children, have the
same mind. You have come into a large inheritance of activity. The Church is admirably equipped for all kinds of
endeavor. Everyone can find something to his liking.
Some kind of work for which he is especially and particularly adapted. Let him make his own selection. Let him
ask what kind of work he is to do in order to maintain
he tradition of this Church as a Church of intense enthusiasm and conse- crated activity.

4. Readiness to meet emergencies.

Those who have listened to the record of our history have
been impressed with the courage, intelligence, and wisdom
with which the various emergencies of the past have been
met. It is not necessary to rehearse any one of them. That
has already been ably done. I simply call your attention
to the fact that the crises in the life of this Church have
been ably and successfully passed. Through all its trials
and perils it has come with increased strength and renewed
vigor. Calmness, dignity, heroism, wisdom, are written on
the pages of our history in bold characters. I pray you
that in coming days there may be no lack of these great
virtues in our congregation. May we ever be ready to rise
to every occasion, and meet every exigency, embrace every
opportunity to do our duty with firmness, with zeal, with
heroism.

5. Attachment to our faith and order.

We are a Presbyterian Church, we never have been
anything else either in fact or in spirit. A hundred years
of loyal adherence to the doctrine of our Church has won
for us the right of claiming, what is not now disputed, that

we are in heart and life true Presbyterians. We love our polity; we believe it to be both Scriptural and wise. Its repose of authority in the whole church, and its jealous protection of the autonomy of each particular congregation we believe secures for us the best advantages of law and liberty. The doctrine of our Church we most cordially accept. Its system of faith as set forth in the Westminster standards we believe to be Scriptural. That it might be made more truly Scriptural in its emphasis, its proportion of truth, its language, this pulpit favored cordially the effort made three years ago to revise our Confession of Faith. May this pulpit and these pews ever favor the improvement of the Confession in these respects.

This doctrine has always been taught and accepted here. May we always retain our character in this respect. May we always be loyal in our adherence to a Scriptural polity and a Scriptural creed. May we never turn from the Bible as the only infallible rule of faith and life. May we never lose the spirit of Presbyterianism which exalts the Lord as the head of the Church, and regards the fellowship of the saints as the true type of Christian unity.

6. Christian fraternity.

The annals of this Church are marked by a large spirit of brotherly love, and of delightful Christian fellowship with the other Churches of this city. When there was but one other denomination we dwelt with it in delightful accord and mutual regard, and now that there are fifty or more other Churches, we desire to maintain the same spirit of brotherly love. I am pleased to state, as an indication of this fact, that when your committee was deliberating with reference to the matter of extending invitations to this centennial, it decided with unanimity and great heartiness to extend in the name of the congregation an invitation to every minister in the city, both Hebrew and Christian, Catholic and Protestant. I rejoice in the reputation which you so universally have of being a large-minded, broad and liberal Church. May no spirit of narrowness or bigotry ever take possession of this pulpit or these pews. May we ever be quick to recognize the image of our God in any man. May we delight to cultivate the broadest sympathies, the largest charity, the warmest fraternity for our fellow citizens in the community of men, and for our fellow disciples in the kingdom of God.

7. Love of liberty.

If our ancestors have given us one treasure more precious than the rest it is this. At the siege of Derry and elsewhere before and since, and among the hills of the Palatinate, they counted not their lives dear for their love of liberty. Anarchy either in the church or in the State has found no place in their creed or their practice. They loved order, they delighted in law, but they abhored despotism. They stood firmly on their feet in the maintenance of their manhood. They were willing to sacrifice everything save their independence. This they maintained against all comers in order that they might lay it at the feet of the one Sovereign of men, the risen and ascended Lord. Throughout the history of this congregation there is the same record of noble, respectful, loyal recognition of authority properly constituted and legally exercised, and along with it the most emphatic and unswerving resistance of every attempt at despotic rule.

When in 1837, for example, the spirit of despotism and intolerance of difference of opinion took possession of the church, and expressed itself in the exscinding acts of the General Assembly of that year, by which certain Synods, Presbyteries and congregations were cut off from the church, notwithstanding their protests of loyalty to both the creed and polity of the church, this congregation, pastor and people, were willing to take their stand with the exscinded churches in the maintenance of their rights. They claimed the liberty of interpretation, a claim subsequently acknowledged by all in the Reunion of 1870, and they would not surrender so sacred a right.

The traditions of these early struggles still remain with us, and the spirit of our fathers is the spirit of their sons. We delight in law, we recognize the authority of our tribunals, and we render true and loyal obedience; but we will not surrender our liberty at the command of any tribunal. May we never enter into slavery, and there is no slavery more debasing, more poisoned with death to the intellect, the heart and the life than slavery to opinion. We claim the right as true Presbyterians, and may we always claim it, to think for ourselves; to open the word of God, and to get from it its precious truths; to bow to the will of no man and no church in the matters in which God has revealed to us our path of duty. We continue to love the liberty for which our fathers fought, the liberty which they have secured for us in the wisely framed constitutions of State and Church. For there is nothing that the constitution of this country so jealously guards as the individual liberties of the people. There is nothing that the constitution of our Presbyterian church so plainly and emphatically secures as the liberty of both her ministers and her people. The whole framework of our church government was designed to secure to every man the enjoyment of his liberties, and the preservation of his individual rights. May we ever regard it as our highest duty to use the whole machinery of our ecclesiastical organization to thwart every attempt of Session, Presbytery, Synod or General Assembly in the tyrannous exercise of power.

This spirit we have inherited. Into this and like possessions we have come, and we must preserve our inheritance. The only way to keep what we have is to add to it. We rejoice in our character. We take it as a compliment whenever one of these characteristics of our congregation is referred to. May we intensify the significance of the praise by increasing our possession of the virtue. We stand on the crest of a hundred years. The mountain peak of the century furnishes us the vantage ground from which to look upon the vast possibilities of our life. A broad horizon is opened to our view. The way by which we have come is marked clearly for us in the monuments of past achievements, of past activity, of past nobility. The way by which we are to go is to a very large extent hidden from our view. We cannot see what the coming century has for this church, and we would not if we could. We are walking with God, he is our portion and our inheritance. We trust the way to him, we delight in his guidance, and repose absolute confidence in his leadership. Yet we are assured if the past has brought anything to us that is worth keeping, it is our character as a church. That character it is our solemn duty to maintain. These virtues which our fathers have won for us we must seek to increase. We build upon the past; we perpetuate its blessings in maintaining this noblest of characters. It is now ours; and, by the grace of God, we will make it our children's.

.

APPENDIX.

A CENTURY OF PASTORS.

REV. NATHANIEL RANDOLPH SNOWDEN.

Pastor 1793–1805.

By Major General GEORGE R. SNOWDEN.

The Reverend Nathaniel Randolph Snowden, fourth son of Isaac and Mary Coxe Snowden, was born in Philadelphia on the 17th of January, 1770, and received his baptismal name in honor of his grand-uncle, Nathaniel Fitz Randolph, of the New Jersey and Massachusetts family of that name, who started the first subscription paper to found the College at Princeton, and gave the ground on which was built Nassau Hall. His father, besides being President of the Board of Trustees of the College of New Jersey at Princeton, and member of committee to draft form of government of the Presbyterian Church, was Quartermaster in the Army of the Revolution, Commissioner for the Issue of Continental Currency. Treasurer of the city and county of Philadelphia, etc., etc. He was born in that city in 1732, and died in 1809, and was buried in the grounds of Old Middletown Presbyterian church in Delaware county, while the son was Pastor. His grand-father, Isaac, first, was a ruling elder and member of the first Session of the Second Presbyterian Church of Philadelphia, established in 1743, with which the family has been since continuously connected. His great-grandfather was John Snowden, elder of the First Presbyterian Church of that city, the first elder ordained in Pennsylvania and believed to be the first ordained in this country.

Nathaniel Randolph Snowden, graduated at Princeton in 1787. His four brothers also took degrees at the same college, three of them with himself becoming honored and useful clergymen in the Church of their forefathers. In 1788 he began the study of theology under Rev. Dr. Charles Nesbit, President of Dickinson College : then a Presbyterian institution ; taking a full course in theology he was licensed to preach in 1792, by the Presbytery of Philadelphia. In the same year he married Sarah Gustine, of Carlisle, who was the daughter of Dr. Lemuel Gustine, and granddaughter of Dr. William

Hooker Smith, both surgeons in the Revolutionary army, taking part in Sullivan's Expedition. Dr. Gustine was witness to the Treaty of Forty Fort and escaping with his family down the Susquehanna in a boat, landed at Harris' Ferry, and the daughter, Sarah, was the last survivor of the massacre of Wyoming. Through Dr. Smith she was descended from the distinguished Puritans, Governor William Leete and the Rev. Thomas Hooker; the latter, to whom a statue has been recently erected by the State of Connecticut, was especially noted for his services in the formation of free institutions in that Colony.

The first charge of the young minister was at Paxtang and Derry, where in 1793 he succeeded the celebrated Revolutionary hero, the Rev. Colonel John Elder, and Harrisburg, where he was the first pastor of the English-speaking, now known as the Market Square, Presbyterian Church.* His residence at Harrisburg was, perhaps, the most pleasant of his life, for here his children, save one, were born, and he always referred to his pastorate of this congregation in terms which indicated the warmth of his affection for his people and the tenderness of his recollections of them. A fine scholar, he conducted for some years Dickinson College, and at the places where he was settled he was seldom content without a class to teach in mathematics and the classics. In 1806, at Lancaster, then the State capital, he conducted with much usefulness an academy for young ladies. In the list of pupils appear the names of all the leading families. During a long and useful life, rather fond, perhaps, of seeking new fields he was, besides Paxtang and Harrisburg, the honored pastor of congregations at Williamsport, Chester, Pittsburgh and Kittanning. In his pastorate he followed the old customs in explaining the Psalms at length, and in social visits questioning the children in the Shorter Catechism, and joining with the family in prayer, in which he was remarkably fervent. His favorite book was the Greek Testament, his daily companion until failing sight denied him the comfort and consolation of reading it. Not especially noted for oratory, his sermons were clear, forcible, written with much literary taste and delivered with an earnestness in full appreciation of his calling. A fragment of a diary which remains, shows hardships which befell the early ministers of the gospel, but it also shows his entire trust in the divine Master and constant and fervid appeals to the throne of mercy.

*On April 10, 1793, he was taken under the care of the Presbytery of Carlisle, and a call from the three congregations of Derry, Paxtang and Harrisburg, having been put into his hands and accepted by him, he was, on October 2, 1793, ordained and installed over these churches. Subsequently he relinquished the charge of Derry in October, 1795, and of Paxtang in Spring of 1796. Harrisburg remained his sole charge until June 25, 1805.—EDITOR.

Admiring with pardonable pride the patriotic and valuable services of his father in the Revolution. he was fond of saying that he had heard, when a child, the bell ring to announce the reading of the Declaration of Independence. It is a tradition in the family that, with a number of other Presbyterian clergymen, he volunteered to form a company in the war of 1812-15 with Great Britain, but their services were declined. Two sons, however, Isaac and Charles, both quite young, well represented him in the ranks of his country's defenders. Of more than middle height, he had a fine physique and blessed with uniformly good health, was capable of great endurance.

At Freeport, Armstrong county, at the residence of his son, Charles, in 1850, he died in peace, and his beloved and accomplished wife, the companion of many joys and sorrows, followed him to rest in 1854. They left six children: Isaac Wayne, a surgeon with General Jackson in the South, severely wounded at Fort Scott : Charles Gustine ; Lemuel Gustine ; Mary Parker, wife of James Thompson, afterward Chief Justice of the Supreme Court : Nathaniel Duffield, and James Ross. Of these all were born at Harrisburg, except the youngest, who was born at Chester, and all are now dead. Four sons were leading and successful physicians, while James Ross was a lawyer and noted in public life, holding many positions of trust and honor—Speaker House of Representatives of Pennsylvania. State Treasurer, Director of the Mint, etc., etc., and an author of reputation. Of his grandchildren may be mentioned Archibald Loudon Snowden, late Superintendent of the Mint, United States Minister to Greece and Spain, etc., etc.: James Ross Thompson, an eminent lawyer of Erie : Samuel Gustine Thompson, late Justice of the Supreme Court : Dr. Samuel Gustine Snowden, a distinguished physician, of Franklin, now deceased, and George Randolph Snowden, Major General commanding the National Guard of Pennsylvania."

REV. JAMES BUCHANAN.

Pastor 1809–1815.

The *Church and Home* of August, 1883, contains the following sketch :

"The second pastor of the church was the Rev. James Buchanan. During the vacancy which succeeded on the departure of Rev. N. R. Snowden, Mr. Buchanan, then a young man and a licentiate of the Presbytery of Newcastle. was sent for and preached his first sermon to the people May 17, 1807. During that year he continued to hold that pulpit as a stated supply. His services proved to be so acceptable to the people that on the 5th of February, 1808, at a meeting of the congregation, presided over by the Rev. James Snodgrass, of "Old Hanover," he was called to be the pastor of the church. On the 15th of April he was received as a licentiate by the Presbytery of Carlisle, and taken under its care. The call from the Harrisburg church was placed in his hands, and accepted by him. He was ordained to the full work of the ministry, September 29, 1808, and Rev. Messrs. James Snodgrass, James Sharon and Joseph Brady, were appointed a committee to install him. Mr. Sharon was then pastor of Paxtang and Derry churches, and Mr. Brady, of Shermansdale, Perry county. The installation took place February 13, 1809, Rev. Mr. Snodgrass presiding and giving the charge to the young pastor, and Rev. Mr. Sharon preaching the sermon. Mr. Brady was not present. Mr. Buchanan was called on a salary of one hundred and fifty pounds for three-fourths of his time. The remaining fourth was given to a small congregation at Middle Paxtang or Dauphin. The original church, a log one, long since gone, stood on the high ground back of the village of Dauphin, and about a mile from the river. The village cemetery now occupies the site. Fifty pounds more were added to his salary for this additional service. This money was in old Pennsylvania currency, the two hundred pounds amounting to about five hundred dollars.

"It is not known how long Mr. Buchanan continued to preach in the Middle Paxtang church. His relation to the Harrisburg church continued until September 20, 1815, when it was dissolved, it is believed, on account of his ill health. He served the church as supply and as settled pastor for over eight years.

"For the following three years Mr. Buchanan preached but seldom. In 1818 he accepted a call to the church at Greencastle, preaching a part of the time at Waynesboro. He continued his charge at Greencastle until 1839, a period of twenty-one years, and was greatly beloved. He removed thence to Logansport, Indiana, where he died on the 16th of September, 1843, after a ministry of over thirty-six years.

"Mr. Buchanan is described as a man of tall form, commanding presence, and great gravity of manner. No one could mistake his profession or his character. He was neat and scrupulous in dress and courteous in his bearing. His sermons were short, compact and precise, remarkably so for that day of long sermons and diffusiveness of style. Few men, it has been said, could say so much as he in so few words. Though he was not regarded as an eloquent preacher, he was a clear, and able and instructive one, and his thorough sincerity and deep earnestness made him an impressive one. He had, however, a very low estimate of his own abilities. Owing probably to a deranged condition of his own physical system, he was nervous and subject to periods of depression, falling into states of deep melancholy, and was a great sufferer from these causes. He became so nervous and timid that, while in Greencastle, he refused, for a time, to perform marriages even between members of his own congregation. It was probably this nervous and depressed condition of mind that accounts for the following incident, narrated of him by the late John A. Weir. Having given out a hymn, one Sunday morning, the singers for some unknown reason neglected to sing, though there were some fine singers in the congregation. Mr. B. closed the service abruptly, saying, on the following day: "If the singers could not sing, the preacher could not preach."

"He was universally esteemed as a good man and a man of great force of character. Wherever he ministered he inspired reverence and trust, and where well known, sincere affection. His people both feared and loved him, perhaps the one as much as the other. His grave and dignified manner rebuked all levity and lightness, while his real goodness and sympathy and purity of life commanded reverence and esteem."

Mr. Buchanan, and his beloved wife, lie side side by in the old burying ground of Logansport, Indiana. Two plain, white marble stones, each about four feet high and three inches thick mark their resting-place. The following are the simple inscriptions upon these headstones:

Rev. JAMES BUCHANAN
Died at Logansport
Sept. 16, 1843
in the 62nd year
of his age

HARRIET BUCHANAN
wife of
Rev. James Buchanan
Died March 12, 1869,
aged 82 years.

Some interesting references to his father are contained in Mr. D. C. Buchanan's letter on pages 310 to 314 of this volume.

WILLIAM RADCLIFFE DeWITT, D. D.

Pastor 1818–1867.

By Rev. THOMAS H. ROBINSON, D. D.

Among the most ancient families of Holland descent that settled in the State of New York, was that of Tjenick Claase DeWitt, the first of the DeWitt family of whom we have any record. He was married in the city of New York, April 26, 1656, to Barber Andriesen, as appears by the records of the Dutch Church of that city. He is described as " van Grootholdt in Zunderlandt," and his wife as " van Amsterdam." The names of the succeeding line are as follows: I. Andriesen, son of Tjenick Claase; II. Tjerie, son of Andriesen; III. Petrus, son of Tjerie; IV. John, son of Petrus; V. William R., son of John.

Dr. DeWitt's ancestry were of that noble race of men, who were Calvinists in religion, and republican in politics, for many generations.

The Dutch were almost universally of the Reformed Churches in religious faith, and sturdy lovers of freedom in the State. Memorable in the Old World for their devotion to liberty and religion, the family of the DeWitts partook of the spirit of its race, and was early distinguished for its patriotism and devotion to country. Four generations have each furnished defenders in times of national peril. From some ancient relics in the family, we learn that Petrus DeWitt was a captain in the old French war, and fought under Wolfe, at the siege and capture of Quebec. His son, John DeWitt, during the entire Revolutionary war, was the captain of a company of minute men appointed to guard the loyal citizens against the incessant and troublesome raids of Tories, who abounded in the section of country north of New York. After the close of the war, he was elected a member of the Convention of the State of New York, and voted for the adoption of the Constitution of the United States.

William Radcliffe DeWitt, the sixth son of John DeWitt, was born at Paudling's Manor, Duchess county, New York, on the 25th of February, 1792. He was named after his uncle, the Hon. William Radcliffe, of Rhinebeck, Duchess county. The family of the Radcliffes, to which the mother of Dr. DeWitt belonged, were distinguished in civil life: one of them, Jacob Radcliffe, serving for several years as a Judge of the Supreme Court of the State of New York;

another, Peter Radcliffe, an eminent lawyer of the New York bar, and a Judge of the Court of Common Pleas of Kings county: and a third, William Radcliffe, for many years United States Consul at Demarara.

At the early age of ten years, he was deprived, by her death, of the counsel and love of a mother. After spending several of his earlier years in school, and receiving a common English education, William R. was employed as a clerk, first in his father's store in the city of Albany, New York, afterwards with his brother Cornelius, in Fairfield, Herkimer county, and later still in the store of his father and brother at Newburg, New York. At about the age of fifteen he entered into the employ of Cairns & Lord, dry goods merchants, of the city of New York, and continued with them until the year 1811. Whilst residing with them, and in their store, his mind became much exercised on the subject of his own personal salvation; and on January 8, 1810, he made a public profession of religion, connecting himself with the Presbyterian Church in Cedar street, then under the pastoral care of Rev. John B. Romeyn, D. D. Shortly afterward his attention was turned to the subject of the sacred ministry, and his own duty in respect to it.

After careful consideration and prayer over the matter, Mr. DeWitt felt called of God to relinquish all worldly ends, and prepare for the responsible office; and in 1811, then in his nineteenth year, he left New York and went to reside with Rev. Alexander Proudfit, of Salem, Washington county, New York, and entering Washington Academy, began a course of classical studies under the tuition of Mr. Stevenson, the principal of the school.

While still a student at Washington Academy, the second war with Great Britain broke out, and leaving his studies, young DeWitt enlisted as a volunteer in the regiment of Colonel Rice, that was called out to resist the invasion of the British at Plattsburg, and was on lake Champlain at the time of McDonough's victory, September 11, 1814, when the whole British fleet became the trophies of American valor. After the close of the war, sometime in the year 1815, he entered Nassau Hall, Princeton, New Jersey, as a Sophomore, and remained there until his senior year, when because of an interruption in his studies of the college, he withdrew and entered the senior class of Union College, Schenectday, N. Y.

Leaving Union College before the close of the senior year, Mr. De Witt returned to New York, and entered the Theological Seminary of the Associate Reformed Church. While in this Seminary Mr De Witt connected himself with the Presbytery of New York and was licensed by that body on April 23, 1818. The summer months of

1818 were spent in preaching in the State of New York, but early in the fall of that year, having received from a friend an invitation to visit Harrisburg, he came hither and spent two weeks, preaching to the people several times. The result was that a unanimous call to become Pastor was given him on October 5, 1818. The call was accepted and soon after he came on and commenced his ministry. Uniting with the Presbytery of Carlisle, at the earliest opportunity he passed the usual examinations required for ordination, and on the 26th of October, 1819, he was ordained to the office of the sacred ministry in the First Presbyterian church of Carlisle, and on November 12th, 1819, he was installed as Pastor of this Church, having already served in the pulpit over one year.

The main events in the history of the Church during the pastorate of Dr. De Witt are rehearsed elsewhere and need not be alluded to in this personal sketch. Dr. De Witt was twice married. His first wife, whom he married on June 22, 1819, was Julia Anna Woodhull, daughter of Rev. Nathan Woodhull, Long Island. This happy relation was sadly broken, within three years, by the death of Mrs. De Witt, May 1, 1822. Memories of her long lingered in the congregation as a woman of great personal beauty and attractiveness, of refined and winning manners, accomplished mind and unaffected piety of heart and life. On March 15, 1825, he married Mary Elizabeth Wallace, daughter of William and Eleanor Maclay Wallace, of Harrisburg. This union, by the kind providence of God, was continued until severed by his own death, a period of nearly forty years.

Dr. De Witt received the degree of A. M. in course from Union College, and on July 13, 1838, he was honored by the University of Pennsylvania, at Philadelphia, with the the title of Doctor of Divinity.

He was called by the Church courts of his own denomination to serve as Moderator and to discharge high and responsible duties. He was a member of several of the General Assemblies of the Church.

With the originators and leading men in that earliest and greatest of American agencies for evangelizing the world, "The American Board of Commissioners for Foreign Missions," he maintained a life long friendship and hearty co-operation, having been chosen a corporate member of the society in 1838, and in 1842 receiving the honor of an appointment to preach before the Board the annual sermon.

In the closing years of his life, when the burdens of the pastorate became heavy and he sought the aid of a colleague, he accepted the office of State Librarian that was pressed upon him by the Governor of the Commonwealth, and discharged its duties with great faithfulness through two terms, a period of six years.

Dr. DeWitt was a facile and elegant writer, but was disinclined to publish his writings. The following list comprises all that are known of his private discourses: 1. A Discourse in behalf of the Colonization Society: 2. A Sermon on the Death of Adams and Jefferson: 3. On the Evils of Intemperance: 4. An Address on the Death of Gov. F. R. Shunk: 5. A Pastoral Letter to the Churches under the care of the Presbytery of Harrisburg: 6. A small volume entitled, " Her Price above Rubies:" 7. The Sermon before the American Board of Commissioners for Foreign Missions: 8. An Address at the Dedication of the Harrisburg Cemetery: 9. A Sermon on the Death of Rev. Dr. Moody: 10, 11, 12. Three synodical sermons, entitled, "Ministerial Responsibility," "Prayer for Zion" and "The Church that Christ Loved;" 13. A Sermon when Seventy Years of Age.

The ties that bound him to this Church, the Church of his early and his life-long love, the only one among all the Churches of America that he had ever called his own, and for whose sake he had refused repeated calls and solicitations to settle elsewhere, seemed only to grow stronger as the burden of years divorced him from active labors in its behalf.

Here he had buried their dead and his own. To them he had given the dew of his youth, the strength of his manhood, the care and counsel of his ripest years. It was natural and reasonable that, after so long a pastorate, he should desire to live and die among the people to whom he had, for nearly half a century, preached the unsearchable riches of Christ; and that the bond between him and them, of pastor and people, should be broken only on the edge of the grave. It was a wish often expressed. The wish was gratified: for while he yielded to his colleague the active duties and pastoral care of the Church, he retained, to the moment of his death, his relation to the Church as its senior pastor. His official labors were now nearly accomplished. So long as he was able to go out at all, even when the increasing infirmities of years weighed heavily upon him, he attended the house of God, at the Sabbath service and the social meetings of the Church, taking his accustomed seat in the pulpit. His last public address was in behalf of the female prayer meeting of the Church, which, during the whole of his long ministry, had been regularly maintained, and had proved a most faithful ally to his labors. He spoke with great tenderness of its past history, and urged upon all the female members of the Church an attendance at its weekly gatherings. His last official duty is believed to have been the examination of a young candidate for the ministry. Sitting up in his bed, he faithfully and kindly, drew from the young man an account of his religious experience, of his views of the ministry, his call to the work, and purpose in entering upon it : and, with the experience of half a century before him, uttered his words of counsel and encouragement, and pronounced his benediction upon the youthful worker.

The elements of personal character and of personal power over others, very seldom proceed from the pre-eminence of one distinguishing trait : but usually from the combination of many qualities, physical, mental and moral. There was no one element in the character of Dr. De Witt that would instantly and universally be pointed out, as the source of his influence, or the characteristic of his life. There was rather a balance of qualities and elements in him that preserved him from all idiosyncracies.

There was weight in his personal presence. There was that in his appearance and bearing, when in his prime, or in his vigor of full health. that inspired respect and indicated power. His person was of full size, and good proportions, in early and middle life, and was the expression of manly vigor and dignity. Those who remember him as he entered upon his ministry here, speak of his handsome and imposing presence, his noble carriage, his finely developed frame, and glowing, manly countenance. And, at the latest years of his life, when his step was enfeebled and slow, and the body began to bend, his patriarchal aspect, as the whitened locks gathered like a crown of glory on his head, the calmness and gravity of a face so slightly altered by age, secured for him an involuntary homage and deference.

He was a man warmly social and genial in his temperament. His home life was filled with true and tender affections ; and they who have often met him in society, know that there were few who could better enliven and entertain than Dr. De Witt. He was a ready and fluent talker, a man of quick impulses and generous feelings, of ready wit, apt at repartee ; and when he opened his fund of reminiscences of earlier times and men, all were ready to listen. In the meetings of the Presbytery and Pastoral Association of this city, his presence was ever welcomed as that of a friend of peace, a genial spirit, a pattern of gentleness and forbearance. And in his own congregation, though often deeply depressed and despondent over his labors, there was never a substantial sorrow to which he did not give his presence, or a grief that lacked his sympathy.

Dr. Dewitt was a man of *self-depreciative and modest nature.* With a keen and high sense of his calling as a minister of the Gospel, and an honest desire to preach the Gospel worthily and powerfully, he seldom left the pulpit without a sense of failure and personal unfitness, wholly unwarranted by the character of his preaching, either in the matter, or the manner of its delivery. There was no self-glory in his nature.

Dr. Dewitt was a man of *unquestioned power as a preacher.* His position at this center of influence, the capital of the State, gave him uncommon opportunities of reaching many men of intellectual standing and of great influence from all parts of the State. He was a man of fine scholarship. He possessed a voice of great sweetness, clearness of tone and power. As a reader of the Holy Scriptures very few excelled him. In his early ministry, his preaching is said to have been peculiarly bold and eloquent in manner : and by the added novelty, beauty and pungency of his thoughts, stirred to the depths the elements of society. His discourses were written with great clearness and purity of style. Many of his sermons, in their matter. form, and in their delivery, were models of pulpit eloquence. He was impressive, dignified and graceful. Other men have excelled him in versatility of talent ; but it has fallen to the lot of few men to mould educational. moral and religious influences in so wide a sphere and through so many years. The end at which he aimed was the turning of men to God and the training of religious life of his people : and his chief instrumentality was the studious and careful preparation and the impressive delivery of good sermons.

He was eminently a *Christian preacher.* Converted in his early youth : brought under the influence of men whose praise was in the American Churches for their zeal, and piety, and deep devotion to the cause of Christ : drawn by his own youthful ardor into the ministry, the preaching of the Gospel was a work of love. And to his vision all truth arranged itself around one center—the cross of the world's Redeemer. From that center he seldom strayed ; seeking to obey the maxim of an old divine, to have enough of Christ in every discourse to point the way of approach to Him to any inquiring soul. He was decidedly evangelical and scriptural. He cared little for human speculations, dealt sparingly in what may be called the philosophy of Christianity ; but taking the truths of the Divine Word as they are revealed ; the lost, ruined, helpless condition of man as a sinner ; the provision which God has made for his recovery in a vicarious atonement ; the contrasts of law and grace ; the character and completeness of that righteousness of Jesus Christ which is "imputed unto us and received by faith alone ;" the regenerating and sanctifying influences of the Holy Spirit : the divine nature and kingly authority of Jesus Christ ; the relation of his atoning blood to all promises of good, all growth in Christian life, and all hopes of heaven ; as well as to all threatenings of evil, and the condemnation of the guilty ; in the region of these and their related truths, that bring the great facts and principles of the Gospel before the mind, Dr. DeWitt was a preacher of great power. Clearness, precision, force, characterized his demonstrations; fullness, fervor and pathos marked his appeals. Perceiving the glory and feeling the preciousness of the truth himself, he exhausted his powers to secure a like impression on the mind and heart of his hearers.

A Presbyterian by birth, education and preference, firm and decided in his theological views, in all the habits of his thoughts, conservative and jealous of the new and untried, he was yet liberal and catholic in spirit. Never wavering in his preferences for, and adherence to the church to which he was attached, there was yet no spirit of exclusiveness in him, that claimed for his denomination all truth and goodness. During a ministry of nearly fifty years in this city, he enjoyed the confidence of all his ministerial brethren. He was ready to assist them in every good work, and seldom, in public prayer, omitted to call down the blessing of God upon them and their churches. Toward all who loved the Lord Jesus Christ in sincerity and truth, he preserved a true affection, and upon them all besought the grace, mercy and peace of God.

Dr. DeWitt came here in his youth, but with a mind admirably trained for the work that was before him. For thirty-six years he stood in the pulpit of this church sole pastor. He was the teacher and guide of the people. He quietly planted the seeds of divine truth ; he worked about the roots of character. He infused his own conceptions of saving doctrine into the minds of two generations. He was the regular visitant upon multiplying families. He baptized the children, guarded inquirers, and welcomed hundreds to the table of communion. He linked his life with hundreds of other lives in beneficent influence, and buried sadly from his sight the generation that welcomed his coming.

During the last years of his life he preached but seldom, having relinquished to his colleague the care of the church, but he continued still to illustrate the beauties of Christian character and the power of the Gospel he had so long proclaimed. His mental power remained unimpaired. His thought of the coming world became softened and subdued by the light that was breaking upon him from the heavenly world. He spoke of his departure with calmness, yet with tenderness of feeling. His earthly cares were dismissed and he waited the summons of departure. It came as he had long desired—suddenly, and without pain and helplessness. In a moment " the golden bowl was broken," and he was gone from earthly intercourse to renew in another world the severed bonds of love and fellowship, and to greet the redeemed and holy ones who from the communion of this church had preceded him to glory.

It would be unjust to the memory of one who impressed her life very deeply upon the lives of many in the church not to mention briefly Mrs. Mary E. DeWitt, who for so many years seconded the labors of her husband by her own.

Mary Elizabeth Wallace, wife of William R. DeWitt, D. D., was the daughter of William Wallace and Eleanor Maclay. She was born in Erie, Pennsylvania, May 7, 1807, whither her father had removed from Harrisburg after his marriage. She was the first born of the household. The family returned to Harrisburg in 1810. Mrs. DeWitt was closely connected with prominent families in the town. John Harris, the founder of the town was her great-grandfather. William Maclay, the first Senator from Pennsylvania in the United States Senate, was her grandfather. Her father established the Harrisburg Bank and was its first President. A large part of her early life was spent in the Maclay house, now the Harrisburg Academy property and the residence of Professor Jacob F. Seiler. Her father died when she was but nine years of age, in 1816. He then resided on the southeast corner of Second street and Cherry alley. After his death the family occupied the Maclay house until the death of Mrs. Wallace, in 1823. The marriage of Mary E. Maclay and Rev. W. R. DeWitt took place in 1825, while she was residing with her great-uncle, Robert Harris, in the ancient Harris house on Front street, in later days the residence of the Honorable Simon Cameron.

One of her brothers, Rev. Benjamin J. Wallace, rose to eminence in the Presbyterian Church as preacher and writer, and as editor for years of "The Presbyterian Review." He died at an early age.

Mrs. DeWitt married at the age of eighteen, but her mind was already matured and peculiarly bright and strong. She entered at once and very heartily into the work of the church and until her death, fifty-six years later she was an honored and wise leader. For forty-two years in the ministry of her husband she was permitted to stand by his side, in the home, in society and in the church, and everywhere helpful and beloved. She was a woman of rare powers of mind, of wide information and admirable judgment. Her home acknowledged her beneficent sway. Society was charmed by her conversational powers, her tact, her winning courtesy and intelligence In the church she was at the head of the religious and benevolent work undertaken by the women of the congregation. For about fifty years she was a faithful and uncommonly able teacher in the Sunday-school of the church. The female prayer-meeting of the church, established in her childhood, received her hearty co-operation and regular attendance for more than half a century. Those who were favored in hearing her voice in these meetings testify to her remarkable power in prayer. Few laymen in the church equalled her in power of expression, range of thought and fluency, joined to spiritual fervor and tenderness. She was surrounded through life by those who trusted, admired and loved her. She was calm in temperament, hopeful in spirit, broad in her charity and judicious in her utterances. Few have evinced so high, so tenacious and so courageous faith. Kind and liberal in her feelings and words toward all, she lived and died without enemies. Though suffering severely in her last days from physical pain, she retained all her faculties of mind unimpaired. Her trust in God, her composure of spirit and her love towards others never failed her. Death found her peaceful and serene and could not disturb her repose in God. A very precious memory survives her in the city and in the church where the greater part of her life was spent.

REV. THOMAS HASTINGS ROBINSON, D. D.

Pastor 1854–1884.

BY THE EDITOR.

Thomas Hastings Robinson, son of William Andrew Robinson and Nancy Cochrane was born January 30, 1828, in the township of North East, Erie county, Pennsylvania. His ancestors were Scotch-Irish, those on the father's side having come to this country about 1730 and settled in Lancaster (now Dauphin county, Pennsylvania), near the Susquehanna, and those on the mother's side coming in 1802 and settling in Ripley, Chautauqua county. N. Y. Both families were from the region of Belfast, Ireland, and were from time to time immemorial Presbyterians in religious faith. Mr. Robinson received his early education in the common school, and in an academy at Ripley. N. Y. Subsequently he entered Oberlin College, Oberlin, O.. 1846, and graduated from it in 1850. The vacations during his college course were spent in teaching, and for over a year after graduation he was engaged in teaching a classical and English Academy at Ashtabula, O., and a normal school at Farrington, O.

Having made a public confession of Christ during his college course, he determined to devote his life to the gospel ministry. In the winter of 1851–1852 he entered the Western Theological Seminary, Allegheny, and completed its three year's course in May, 1854. He united with the Presbytery of Ohio, since divided into the Presbyteries of Pittsburg and Allegheny, June 15th, 1854, and on the same day after an examination in his college and theological studies, was licensed to preach the gospel. His first sermon as a licentiate was delivered on June 20, 1854, in the First Presbyterian Church of Pittsburg, of which he was a member.

Upon the last Sabbath in June, the 27th, 1854, and the first Sabbath in July, 1854, and on the Wednesday evening intervening he preached by invitation in the English Presbyterian congregation of Harrisburg, and on July 5th he was unanimously called to be colleague pastor of the church with Rev. William R. DeWitt, D. D. The call was accepted, and he came to Harrisburg early in the following October and took up the duties of his office.

On October 17th he was received as a licentiate into the Presbytery of Harrisburg, and on January 21st, 1855, he was ordained and installed as co-pastor over this church. For the first ten years of the co-pastorate Dr. DeWitt continued to preach occasionally. In 1864 he resigned all the active duties of the pastorate, and now Mr. Robinson continued to serve as pastor until the relationship was dissolved by the Presbytery of Carlisle, to take effect on the first Sabbath of June, 1884. He continued to fill the pulpit until the last Sabbath in June, the thirtieth anniversary of his first sermon to the congregation, when he preached his farewell discourse.

In November, 1883, he was called by the directors of the Western Theological Seminary to the Re-Union Professorship of Sacred Rhetoric, Church Government and Pastoral Theology. After several months of consideration he accepted the call, but was unable to enter upon the duties of the Seminary until January, 1885. This position he still holds.

His residence at Harrisburg for thirty years called him to many duties outside those of his pastorate. He was for many years a trustee of the Harrisburg Academy and of Wilson Female College at Chambersburg, from 1875 to 1887, a trustee of Princeton College; from 1875 to 1884 a director of the Western Theological Seminary, and for some years past has been a trustee of Washington and Jefferson College and of Pennsylvania Female College.

He was the moderator of the Synod of Pennsylvania (N. S.) in 1861, and at the reunion of the churches in 1870 was made the stated clerk of the Synod of Harrisburg, and held the office until the consolidation of the four Synods in Pennsylvania into the single Synod of Pennsylvania, when he was chosen to the same office in that body, and continued in it until he entered upon the duties of his professorship, when he resigned, having held the office fourteen years.

During the war he was a member of the Christian Commission,

directing its work in Central Pennsylvania, and serving in its behalf for two or three months in Virginia and Tennessee.

In 1868 he was given the honorary title of Doctor of Divinity by Hamilton College, New York.

He was a member of the Assemblies (N. S.) of 1858 and 1866, and of the reunited Assemblies of 1873, 1882 and 1892. And was a delegate to the Alliance of the Reformed Churches holding the Presbyterian system that met in London in 1875 and in 1889.

On May 10th, 1856, he married Mary Wolf Buehler, daughter of Henry Buehler and Anna Margaretta Wolf. Their children are Henry Buehler, who died in infancy; Anna Margaretta, who died December 23, 1881, in her twenty-third year; William Andrew, Professor of the Greek Language in Lehigh University; Eliza McCormick, wife of George R. Fleming, Esq.; Edward Orth, Thomas Hastings, Jr., and Mary Buehler, the last three being still members of their father's household in Allegheny.

During his pastorate he became greatly endeared to his congregation, and enjoyed the confidence and esteem of the whole community. The action taken by the Church a short time prior to his resignation is illustrative of the strong hold he had upon the affection and confidence of this people throughout his long and useful ministry here. When it became known that he was considering a call from the Western Theological Seminary to a professorship in that institution, a meeting of the congregation was held on Wednesday evening, November 28th, 1883, to consider the matter.

Mr. Charles L. Bailey was elected chairman, and Mr. Alex. Roberts secretary. On motion of Mr. Samuel J. M McCarrell, a committee of five, consisting of Messrs. M. W. McAlarney, Henry Gilbert, Adam K. Fahnestock, James Fletcher and John C. Harvey, were appointed to prepare a letter expressive of the feelings of the congregation, which committee reported the following:

HARRISBURG, *November 28, 1883.*

TO REV. THOMAS H. ROBINSON, D. D.

VERY DEAR SIR: The congregation of the Market Square Presbyterian church, having heard with unfeigned regret of your call to a professorship in the Western Theological Seminary, hereby expresses its gratitude to you for your long, faithful, efficient and sympathetic pastoral service, as also its unanimous and earnest desire that you shall not accept the new position tendered you, nor ask a dissolution of the pastoral relation with us. While we are not insensible to the honor which your call to this professorship bears with it, we feel that we must protest against its acceptance for many reasons, among which are the following:

1. Your long and efficient pastorate, your unswerving fidelity and boldness as an ambassador of Christ, have given you a commanding influence in your city, your Presbytery, your State, which influence the cause of Presbyterianism demands, shall not be removed from its pulpit and active pastoral work.

2. Your church is united and prosperous under your pastorate and your labors here have been followed by a continual stream of blessed influence and result, and have been frequently and but recently crowned with marked tokens of Divine approval.

3. Your whole ministerial life has been spent with us; you have broken to us the bread of life for more than a quarter of a century: you have been at our homes in seasons of joy and sorrow; you have solemnized our marriages: you have wept with us at the graves of our loved ones: and we most earnestly ask that the tender ties thus binding us together shall not be severed.

4. No other man can fill your place among us as acceptably as yourself and we do not wish to take the hazard of divisions, bickerings and strife in seeking another to occupy your pulpit and assume your work in this church, so dear to you and ourselves. In the light of these and many other reasons which we might urge, we earnestly request that you remain with us.

And in testimony of our gratitude and unwavering affection for you as our pastor, we cause this letter to be subscribed by the chairman and secretary of this congregational meeting, and by the committee appointed to present a paper expressive of our views upon the subject for the consideration of which this meeting was called.

The letter was unanimously adopted, the meeting adjourned, and the congregation proceeded in a body to the house of their much loved pastor, where the letter was read to him. Dr. Robinson, in replying, said that this call had been a source of much grief to him; that his whole life had been spent in this city, and that here he had hoped to end his days: that he loved the people, and that the friendships formed here could never be broken this side of the grave. But he proceeded to say that, as yet, he had not determined which path duty required him to follow—to go or to stay, and that he had until the first of the year to decide, and in the meantime he could only hope and pray that the Lord would enable him to decide as his heart now prompted.

When, a few months later Dr. Robinson requested Presbytery to dissolve the pastoral relation, the congregation made a strenuous protest against granting the request. Though he has been absent from the Church and city for ten years, yet he is still cherished with the sincerest affection in the hearts of the people, and is always greeted upon any of his frequent visits with true cordiality.

His wise leadership, unsparing activity, spotless character, left their impress upon the Church and made it the strong, broad, generous, aggressive church it is to day.

He was always in sympathy with all movements that were evidently in the interest of progress, an avowed friend to the temperance reform, though not a political prohibitionist, and a courageous leader in every good cause. As "a conservative-radical," so he speaks of himself, he directed the life of the Church into channels of the largest usefulness and most permanent development.

A CENTURY OF ELDERS.

By Rev. THOMAS H. ROBINSON, D. D.

The history of "The English Presbyterian Congregation," of Harrisburg, which celebrated its centenary February 11-16th, 1894, would be incomplete without the following sketches of the Ruling Elders, now deceased, who were connected with it during the hundred years and helped so largely in giving it its character and power. For a portion of the facts contained in these sketches we are indebted to the able and accomplished Dr. William H. Egle, State Librarian, and author of a number of very valuable historical publications.

The first Board of Ruling Elders in the Church was composed of the following persons : Samuel Weir, Moses Gillmor, Adam Boyd.

They were elected to office on February 11, 1794, and on the following Sabbath, February 16th, they were ordained and installed, each of them holding office until his death.

SAMUEL WEIR.
Born September 29, 1744.
Died August 15, 1814.

Samuel Weir, the eldest son of James Weir, was born near Ballymony, County Antrim, Ireland. His ancestry was numbered among the heroic defenders of Derry during the famous seige of 1689-1690, by King James, when almost incredible hardships were endured in the cause of Protestantism and freedom of faith. Heir-looms of that memorable time are still held in the family and are greatly prized. Samuel Weir came to America in 1775, and located in the township of Derry, Lancaster county, now Dauphin county, Pennsylvania. The Revolutionary war had already opened at Lexington, and British ships of war were scouring the seas, searching for, seizing and impressing British subjects whenever found. The vessel on which Mr. Weir came was boarded and searched, but by a happy providence he escaped, and was saved from fighting against the country to which he was coming for larger liberties than he had found in the old world. A year had scarcely elapsed before he was in the army of the Revolution, defending his adopted country. In 1776 and 1777 he was a First Lieutenant in Col. John Rodgers' battalion (eighth) of Lancaster

County Associators, rendering important service. He served under General Washington, at the crossing of the Delaware, at Trenton, Princeton, Brandywine and Germantown. At the close of the war he removed to a farm he had purchased near Harrisburg, but shortly after, in 1787, he became a merchant in the town, and one of the most prominent business men of the borough. He assisted in the organization of the Presbyterian church in 1794, and was chosen one of its first Ruling Elders. In person he was of stout, heavy build, strong and muscular. In civil life he was a man of probity and honor. In the Church he was very active, greatly devoted to its interests and the recipient of its esteem and love. He was noted for his large and generous hospitality to the ministry of his day, making his house their home as guests. He was twice married. By his first wife he had a son named James, who died young, and by his second wife, Mary Wallace, he had three sons, Samuel, who removed to South Carolina, John Andrew and James Wallace, both of whom succeeded him in the Eldership. He died in the seventieth year of his age, and in the twentieth of his office, as Elder.

MOSES GILLMOR.

Born, September 6, 1749.

Died, June 10, 1825.

Moses Gillmor was born in the township of Burt, parish of Templemore, county of Donegal, six miles from the city of Londonderry, province of Ulster, Ireland. Until his seventeenth year he remained in Ireland, when he came with an uncle to America, and settled in Hanover township, Lancaster county, now Dauphin. Having returned to Ireland on business connected with his father's estate, the war of the Revolution broke out during his absence and delayed his return until after the declaration of peace in 1783. The next year, November 1784, according to Parson Elder's marriage record, he married Isabel Wallace, third daughter of Robert and Mary Wallace, of Hanover. When, in 1785, Harrisburg was made the county seat of the new county, Dauphin, Mr. Gillmor removed hither, purchased a lot on Market Square, and established himself in the business of a merchant, which he carried on successfully for a number of years. He was prominent in local politics and an influential member of society. He was one of the founders of the Presbyterian Church, and is said to have been an elder in the Mother Church of Paxtang. Mr. Gillmor died in Harrisburg in 1825, after serving the church for thirty-one years, having reached the age of seventy-six. His body, and that of his wife, who died three years later, were buried in

Paxtang Church grave-yard. The older members of the church gave descriptions of him to the writer, as he was before age had bent his form or impeded the elasticity of his step. He was a man of fine personal appearance, tall and well-proportioned, grave and dignified, and wore, as was customary with gentlemen of his standing in society, the cue, cocked hat, short breeches and silver-buckled shoes of that earlier generation. He was a man of stately bearing and courtly manners, and his tall, manly form clothed in the dress peculiar to "gentlemen of the old school," would command involuntary respect. He was a most worthy citizen and a man of sterling integrity, sincere, incorruptible and straight-forward in all his dealings. In Christian character he was decidedly old style, and would be regarded in this easier age as severe and cold and Puritanic: but in his reverent and high-toned piety there was a substantial solidity that might bless these modern times were it more frequent. He died revered by all.

ADAM BOYD.

Born,   , 1746.

Died, May 14, 1814.

Mr. Boyd was the son of John Boyd and Elizabeth Young, and was a native of Northampton county, Pennsylvania. He was of Scotch descent, his grandfather, John Boyd, having been born in or near Edinburgh in 1690. He was one of the earliest settlers in the so-called "Irish Settlement." By occupation, he was a carpenter. He was in the prime of early manhood when the war of the Revolution opened, and entered into the service with patriotic ardor. He was an early associator, and received a commission in the Pennsylvania Navy, and was in the conflict between that fleet and the British ships in May, 1776. He was subsequently transferred from the navy to the army, served through four campaigns and participated in the battles of Brandywine and Germantown and Princeton as an officer. At the close of his military career he held the place of chief of transportation. He removed to Harrisburg in 1783, and made it his permanent home. Mr. Boyd bore a high reputation among his fellow-citizens, and was often chosen by them to positions of public trust and honor, serving as the presiding officer of the first town council, as County Treasurer for many years, as County Commissioner, and a Director of the Poor. He was honored with office by the people as long as he would accept it. He was a man of fine abilities and literary taste, decided in his opinions, industrious in habits, and of strictest integrity. In person he was stoutly built, of blue eyes, sandy hair and fair complexion, genial in countenance and courteous in bearing. As an officer of the Church he was greatly esteemed and beloved, enjoying the confidence of all. His death occurred in the sixty-eighth year of his age and the twenty-first of his Eldership. He left at death one daughter, Mrs. Rosanna Boyd Hamilton, wife of Hugh Hamilton. A grandson, Mr. A. Boyd Hamilton, still survives in honored and useful age.

At some unknown period between the years 1808–1812 probably, the following persons were added to the church Session : John Stoner, William Graydon. No record remains to fix the date of their election and induction into office.

JOHN STONER.

Born, March 24, 1748.

Died March 24, 1825.

John Stoner was the son of Jacob Stoner and Juliana Baker, and was born in Lancaster county, Pennsylvania. His father was a native of the city of Berne, Switzerland. His mother was a native of Holland. Fleeing from persecutions abroad they came to this country and settled in Lancaster county in the early part of the last century. John was the youngest child of the family, and was educated in Philadelphia. Returning home, he remained there until the death of his father, which occurred a short time before the breaking out of the Revolutionary war, when he removed to a farm he had purchased on the Susquehanna, about three miles above Harrisburg. Shortly after the opening of the war he sold his farm and raised a company for service, of which he was elected and commissioned first lieutenant. Most of the expenses of equipping the company and of its term of service was borne out of his own purse. The company belonged to the second battalion of the Pennsylvania Rifle Regiment, commanded by Colonel Miles. Mr. Stoner's first commission was dated March 15, 1776. He was promoted captain December 4, 1776, and transferred to the Tenth Pennsylvania Regiment of the line. He resigned, on account of ill health, on November 22, 1777. He was a hearty and thorough patriot, ready for any sacrifices.

After leaving the army he took up his residence in Harrisburg, where he married the widow of Thomas Murray. Her maiden name was Mary Berryhill. The two families of Murray and Berryhill were prominent in the early history of the church. He was an active citizen in the new town, taking a prominent part in civil affairs. He was chosen an Elder at an advanced age, probably not less than sixty years, and held the office between fifteen and twenty years, dying at the age of seventy-seven.

Captain Stoner sustained the reputation of being an honest, sincere and hearty Christian : a man of very kind and affectionate disposition, and of much and earnest prayer. He served Christ in humility and faithfulness, died a peaceful and happy death, departing to the "Rest" of the children of God. Mr. Stoner was the third of the earliest Elders of the church who were officers in the Army of the Revolution.

WILLIAM GRAYDON.

Born, Sept. 4, 1759.

Died, Oct. 13, 1840.

William Graydon, the son of Alexander Graydon and Rachel Marks, was born near Bristol, Bucks county, Pennsylvania. He spent his early life in Philadelphia, where he acquired a classical education, and studied law under Edward Biddle, Esq. He came to Harrisburg upon the organization of the county of Dauphin, and entered upon the practice of his profession, being admitted at the May term, 1786. He was the first notary public of the county, was a justice of the peace and a member of the town council for several years, the president of the council and one of the burgesses of the borough. He was the author of " Forms of Conveyancing " in two volumes, and edited "An Abridgment of the Laws of the United States in 1802." Mr. Graydon was well educated and a man of cultivated literary tastes, and in the many trusts committed to him by his fellow citizens, he sustained a character of unblemished integrity. He was highly esteemed as a gentleman of the old school in his manners, courteous and refined, of high and honorable principles, and in the church and the walks of Christian life a man of true piety and deep devotion. He filled the office of ruling elder between twenty-five and thirty years. Mr. G. W. Harris in his " Reminiscences of the Bar," says : " He was a man of medium height, of very gentlemanly manners, neat, if not precise, in dress, of dark, lively eyes and of an intelligent countenance. His portrait, painted by Francis, is in existence, and is an excellent representation. He wore a cue tied with a ribbon and had his hair powdered." He was humane and benevolent, and an acknowledged leader in charitable enterprises. Of his children, one, Alexander Graydon, became an elder of this church some years prior to his father's death, and another, H. Murray Graydon, Esq., has been an elder in the Pine Street Presbyterian Church since its organization in 1858. A third, William Graydon, M. D., was for many years an elder in the Presbyterian Church of Dauphin, and now holds the same office in the Memorial Presbyterian Church, Philadelphia, and a daughter, Rachel Graydon, was the wife of Hon. Mordecai McKinney, for many years an elder in this church.

On Monday evening, February 7, 1820, the following persons were elected Ruling Elders of this church : Robert Sloan, Samuel Agnew, M. D., Joseph A. McJimsey.

And on the 9th of April succeeding they were ordained, and installed in office.

ROBERT SLOAN.

Born 1769.

Died Dec., 1833.

Robert Sloan was born in Hanover township, Dauphin county (formerly Lancaster), Penna. He was of Scotch-Irish descent, his ancestors coming to America prior to 1736. His father, Robert Sloan, Sr., was an Elder in the Old Hanover Presbyterian church, one of the land marks of the Scotch-Irish settlement in Pennsylvania. His grandfather had also been a Ruling Elder, and as his son Alexander succeeded him, there is the record of four generations in direct line of Ruling Elders in the Presbyterian Church. The early years of Mr. Sloan's life were spent on the farm with his father, but manifesting a genius for mechanical pursuits, he left home, and without any apprenticeship, entered upon his life work, that of a cabinet-maker. On the 30th of March, 1799, he married Sarah McCormick, of Hanover, and soon after removed to the city of New York, and joined the Presbyterian Church, under the pastorate of Rev. Dr. Milledollar. In the year 1812 he returned to Harrisburg, where he passed the remainder of his life. He was regarded as a very superior workman, a man of peculiar mechanical skill, and was most faithful and diligent in business. Mr. Sloan was eminently a good man, a Christian full of faith and prayer and good works, a man of singular modesty and uprightness. He possessed the confidence of the community where he resided to an unbounded degree, and they who knew him intimately, had for him a regard that deepened into affection. He was a most faithful office-bearer, always at his post in the sanctuary and the meetings for social prayer. In the matter of prayer he was peculiarly gifted, being evidently taught of God and blessed with an unction from the Holy Ghost.

He was a layman of wide and accurate theological knowledge. After the severe toils of the day he was wont, when not engaged in outdoor work for the Church, to spend his evenings in reading the standard Christian literature of the times, especially the sermons and other works of the old Puritan divines. The doctrines of the Presbyterian Church, as taught in her standards, he heartily embraced as the system of theology contained in the sacred Scriptures, and adhered to them through life with unwavering fidelity. It may be said to his honor, that no man possessed more completely than Robert Sloan the confidence of the Church as a man of God, noble and blameless in his uprightness. He was of a thoroughly Christian and Presbyterian stock, for beside those of his line already mentioned as Ruling Elders, a brother served as an Elder in old Hanover church, and another brother in the First Presbyterian church, of Williamsport, Pa. Mr. Sloan died at the age of sixty-four and in the thirteenth year of his Eldership.

SAMUEL AGNEW, M. D.
Born 1777.
Died Nov. 25, 1849.

Samuel Agnew was the son of James Agnew and Mary Ramsey, and was born near Millerstown, Adams county, Pennsylvania. His parents were Scotch-Irish Presbyterians, being members of the Associate Reformed church. His father and three brothers, uncles of Samuel Agnew, were all elders at the same time, and tradition says in the same congregation. The father was also a soldier in the Revolutionary army and was wounded in one of the battles in New Jersey. The family was noted for intellectual culture, strength of mind and decided piety.

Mr. Agnew was set apart by his mother for the ministry. Trained under the best of religious influences he became very early the subject of divine grace. In the later years of his life, he stated, in answer to the question, "When were you converted?" "I cannot tell. I cannot recall a period from my earliest childhood when I was not a child of God, with the experiences of a true Christian."

He received a classical education, graduating from Dickinson College in 1798. On leaving college, greatly to the disappointment of his mother, he chose the profession of medicine, studied with Dr. McClellan, of Greencastle, and graduated from the University of Pennsylvania in 1801. In college he was the classmate of two men who became distinguished in western Pennsylvania, Rev. Francis Herron, D. D., of Pittsburgh, and Rev. Matthew Brown, D. D., President of Jefferson College.

Dr. Agnew first settled in the practice of his profession in Gettysburg, remaining there for several years, and winning a large patronage and the confidence of the people. While there he married Jane Grier, daughter of Major David Grier, of the Revolution. but in

1804 he removed to Harrisburg, where he remained until 1835. While in Harrisburg he became distinguished in his profession by his " Treatise on the efficacy of kine pock inoculation as a preventive of the contagion of the small pox." He originated a plan for the general distribution of kine pock by the establishment of a lottery which proved to be successful. In the war of 1812, he was one of the first, perhaps the first officer, who offered his services, and that of a company comprising the very best men of Harrisburg, one hundred and twelve strong, to Governor Snyder. As there was no call for men the company disbanded in 1813. In March, 1835, Dr. Agnew left Harburg and after a sojourn of a year at Lewistown, Pa., removed to Missouri, and while there became an elder in a Presbyterian Church. Meeting some reverses of fortune he remained but a few months, returned east, first to Pittsburgh, and thence to Philadelphia, where he remained but a year. In 1839, he went to Butler, Pa., where for eight years he resided with his daughter, the wife of Rev. John R. Agnew. Here he continued the practice of his profession, and by his skill, joined to his labors for the spiritual interests of the people, won the highest favor. He became, while there, an elder in the First Presbyterian Church and the Superintendent of the Sunday-school of the Church. The Pastor of the Church in that place thus speaks of him. " His memory is precious in Butler. Thanksgiving Day was almost turned into a day of mourning for us, as the news of his death had only reached us the day before."

On the removal of his daughter to Greencastle, Pa., in the spring of 1847, Dr. Agnew accompanied the family and made his home there for two years. In 1849, while on his way to Temperanceville, a suburb of Pittsburgh, he was violently thrown from a packet boat into the canal and received injuries from which he did not recover, dying on Sabbath evening, November 25, 1849.

Dr. Agnew was a ruling elder in the Church at Harrisburg for fifteen years. Few laymen have been better fitted by natural talents, by education, by personal character, and by public position, than Dr. Agnew for a wide and permanent influence of the best and highest kind over their fellowmen. He was a man of notable qualities. In the eyes of the world he was one of the marked men of society. Both in social and professional life, as well as in the church he was promptly accorded the place of a leader. Possessed of a sound, clear and vigorous mind, well disciplined and polished by a thorough course of collegiate and professional studies, a man of great activity, of fine bearing and of a refined courtesy that made his presence always welcome, it was but natural that he should stand at the head of his profession and exert in every sphere where he moved a controlling influence. He was a frequent contributor to the medical journals of his day, and was often called to make literary, scientific and religious addresses. Both as writer and speaker he displayed marked ability. Generous and kind hearted, charitable in his judgment, affable in his manners, uniformly cheerful and hopeful, he gained universal respect and friendship. As husband, father, and friend; as neighbor, professional man, and citizen, he had the esteem and respect of all.

But it was in the Church and as a Christian man he stood highest. He lived a life of steady, uniform and consistent, godliness, making the service of God the great business of his life, seldom allowing any professional duties to interfere with his attendance on the public rites of religion or on his duties as an officer of the church. He was a man of public spirit, of broad charity and of a familiar acquaintance with the great religious enterprises of his day. The Sunday-school and tract societies, and temperance organizations of the time; and all benevolent operations within and without the Church received his active and earnest support. The cause of Foreign Missions was especially dear to his heart. He was elected a corporate member of the great missionary organization, the American Board of Commissioners for Foreign Missions and attended its annual meetings as long as age would permit. His religious life was peculiarly marked. The testimony is very strong to his unquestionable piety and devotion to the Saviour of men. In all his life shone forth the evidences of an abiding and unquenchable personal love of Jesus Christ as his Friend and Saviour. In the midst of great trials, involved through others in pecuniary difficulties, reduced to extreme poverty, compelled in old age to struggle for earthly maintenance, he still was strong in faith, giving glory to God. His fervor, his child-like confidence, his warm evangelical spirit, his holy importunity and his scripturalness in public prayers made his presence most welcome in the meetings of believers. And when at length eternity dawned upon him the serene and calm repose of his heart on God was not at all disturbed. His departure from earth was as calm and hopeful and beautiful as the clear setting of the sun when the day is done. Seldom has the memory of a man been more precious to his fellowmen than that of Dr. Samuel Agnew.

JOSEPH A. McJIMSEY.
Born December 16, 1780.
Died September 20, 1821.

Mr. McJimsey was born in Chester county, Pa. But few records or traditions of him can be found. He was of Scotch-Irish descent, was educated at an academy in Philadelphia, learned surveying, and for several years filled a clerical position in that city. He was a popular citizen and a man of public affairs and had an established reputation as upright and honest, a man of integrity and wisdom. He was elected clerk of the State Senate in Lancaster in 1809, and when the State Capital was removed to Harrisburg, he continued to serve in that body until his death. Within a year and a half after his election to the eldership in this church he departed this life in the forty-first year of his age. He is said to have been a man of excellent Christian character, a good, exemplary man. The late Mr. John A. Weir who knew him in his own youth spoke very highly of him.

At an election held in the church, August 17, 1825, the following persons were chosen Ruling Elders : John Neilson, Richard T. Leech, John C. Capp.

They were ordained and inducted into office September 11, 1825.

JOHN NEILSON,
Born June 16, 1780,
Died March 10, 1856.

John Neilson, son of Robert Neilson, of Scotch descent, was born in New Castle county, Delaware. His parents died in his early life, and in his youth he resided with relatives at Wilmington, Delaware. After his marriage, he settled in Middletown, Pa., and filled for some years the office of cashier of the Swatara bank. Upon the removal of the bank to Harrisburg in 1815, Mr. Neilson came with it, and held his office until the bank was closed. Subsequently he was appointed Cashier of the State Treasury and held the position for twenty-one years. He was a faithful officer, rendering most faithful service with complete fidelity to the State and great honor to himself. He was a man of gentlemanly manners, of pleasant, fair countenance and of quiet and an unobtrusive life. He continued to serve the church until the latter part of the year 1838. The closing years of his life were spent in Baltimore, where he died March 10, 1856, in the seventy-sixth year of his age.

RICHARD TREAT LEECH.
Born October 3, 1775.
Died August 26, 1850.

Mr. Leech was born at Cheltenham, Montgomery county, Pennsylvania. He was of English descent, his paternal ancestors having emigrated from Cheltenham, Gloucestershire, England, in 1682. Purchasing a tract of land in the Province of Pennsylvania from

William Penn, they settled upon it and gave it the name of their old English home. Four generations possessed the land, and the bodies of these ancestors of Mr. Leech lie buried in the old church yard at Abingdon, Pa. Richard Treat Leech was so named in honor of his step grandfather, Richard Treat, one of the early professors of Princeton College, New Jersey. His opportunities for education were only such as were furnished by the schools of his neighborhood, though he subsequently became known as a man of extensive general knowledge and a writer and speaker of more than ordinary power. In the year 1809–1810 he was elected to the Legislature of the State, then sitting at Lancaster. Here he married Miss Eva Henrietta Steinman, of Lancaster.

Returning to his home he remained there until called to Harrisburg by Gov. Simon Snyder, in 1813, to fill the office of Surveyor General of the State. He was re-appointed to the same office by Gov. Snyder in 1815. During the war of 1812–1814 Mr. Leech, with every clerk in his office except one, joined the army. The regiment to which they were attached lay at York, Pa., for some weeks, but was not called into action, further than a march to Baltimore. He was a member of Captain Richard M. Crain's company, of Colonel Kennedy's regiment. In this company served five of the subsequent Trustees of this church : Capt. R. M. Crain, First Sergeant Alex. M. Piper, Third Sargeant James R. Boyd and Privates R. T. Leech and Alex. Graydon, Jr. Messrs. Leech and Graydon were also subsequently Elders in the Church. In the ranks with these men served other members of the congregation : Francis R. Shunk, William S. Findlay, Dr. Luther Reily and others. After the expiration of his term of office as Surveyor General, in 1818, he went to Pittsburgh, and engaged in mercantile pursuits, but returned to the State capital in 1821. In 1825 he was chosen a Ruling Elder in this church and continued to serve it faithfully till 1837, when he again removed to Pittsburgh, where he died August 26, 1850, in the seventy-fifth year of his age, having filled the office for twelve years.

In personal appearance, Mr. Leech was tall and slender, fair in complexion, with bright blue eyes, benign in their expression. His manners were courteous and attractive. He was a man of fine abilities and of very firm and decided character. For the many years in which he occupied public position at the capital of the State, he bore an unstained reputation. In all his official relations he was greatly esteemed. He was an ardent lover of his country, and in a letter written by him when he was in the army he expresses his readiness to die in defence of his native land and her liberties. The course of public events was watched by him with the deep and jealous interest

of a thorough christian patriot, and every violation of true principle
in the conduct of civil and national affairs gave him pain as a blow
struck at the life of a dear friend.

In social life he was an example of urbane manners, of warm and
generous friendship and of generous hospitality. In the Church he
stood high as a counsellor, and a faithful member and officer. He is
said to have been uncommonly gifted both in the spirit of prayer and
in the fluency and elegance of his language. He loved the kingdom
of Christ, and gave to its welfare, his toils and prayers and cares. He
was generous in the support of its ministry and of its various benevolent agencies. Lowly in spirit, sympathizing and faithful, he left
behind him in the Church, after a service of twelve years as an
elder. the fragrant memory of a noble character and a good and useful
life.

JOHN CHARLES CAPP,

Born   1800,

Died March 3, 1876.

Mr. Capp was the son of John Capp and Catharine Chamberlain,
and was born in Philadelphia. He was of German descent. His
father was for many years a justice of the peace and was a man of
great integrity of character. The son was educated in Philadelphia
and brought up in mercantile pursuits, but came to Harrisburg while
yet a youth. He was a member of the Sunday-school of this church
in its earliest history and a teacher in it as early as 1817, when but a
boy of seventeen. He united with the church in 1820 and was looked
upon as a model young man of large promise. Such was his activity
and zeal in the religious life and so great was the confidence of the
church in his piety and good judgment that he was chosen an Elder
in the twenty-fifth year of his age. His subsequent history fully confirmed the act of the church as a wise one, Mr. Capp proved to be a
most worthy man and valuable church officer. He was ready for all
labors, active in duties, earnest in prayer, self-sacrificing and consistent in all his life, winning for himself the esteem of the church,
and especially gaining the confidence of the youth of the congregation over whom he exerted the most happy influence. Very few of
the Elders of the Church have been more beloved, more regretted in
their departure, or have left a more enviable memory than John C.
Capp. After a brief eldership of six years he removed to Philadelphia. From 1837 to his death in 1876, thirty-nine years, he served as
an Elder in the Central Presbyterian Church. In 1829 he married
Sarah Singer of Philadelphia. One of his sons, Rev. Edward Payson

Capp, went as a missionary to China, and died at Yokohama, Oct. 20, 1873. Two of his sons reside in San Francisco. A fourth, the youngest, Dr. William M. Capp, is a physician of prominence in Philadelphia.

On October 6, 1834, the following persons, James Wallace Weir, Alexander Graydon, Alexander Sloan, were chosen Ruling Elders, and on Sabbath morning October 19, 1834, they were ordained and installed.

ALEXANDER GRAYDON,
Born September 18, 1791,
Died December 12. 1868.

Alexander Graydon, eldest son of William Graydon, an Elder of this Church, and Rachel Marks was born in Harrisburg. He was educated at the Harrisburg Academy, entered the hardware trade, and for many years conducted a successful business. He was chosen an Elder in 1834, and served the Church faithfully until his removal to Indianapolis, in 1844. At Indianapolis he became an honored Elder in the Fourth Presbyterian church of that city, holding the office until his death in 1868.

Mr. Graydon bore an enviable character as an earnest Christian worker, a man fearless in the discharge of whatever he deemed to be a duty, even at the cost of reproaches and pecuniary sacrifice. He was early known, as was his brother Elder and life-long friend. James Weir, as a warm friend of the oppressed, at a time when the anti-slavery movement was u popular and obnoxious in the State, and a heresy in the Church. To be an Abolitionist and a friend of the down-trodden black man was a crime in the eyes of the great majority, and exposed a man to many social trials and insults, often interfering with his business and church relations, and sundering the ties of friendship. Mr. Graydon was unflinching and fearless in maintaining the equal rights of all men of every color and nation. He was honorable and fair in business, faithful to his vows as an office-bearer in the Church, studious of the highest interests of the cause of Christ, and was trusted by all as a true man, a servant of God, and a lover of human kind. The men of this generation can scarcely imagine the amount of opprobrium that was heaped in those earlier days upon the reformer of the political and social evils that had become entrenched and strong and invested with legal rights and moral respectability. In his new home and long residence at Indianapolis Mr. Graydon continued to be revered and honored by good men for his sterling Christian principles and his firm and conscien-

tious conviction of duty towards God and man. In the good providence of God his useful life was spared until after the close of the
war, when he had the joy of seeing that he was on the winning side
in the great conflict of righteousness with wrong.

JAMES WALLACE WEIR.
Born August 9, 1805.
Died March 14, 1878.

James Wallace Weir, the youngest son of Samuel Weir and Mary
Wallace was born at Harrisburg, Pennsylvania. The father was one
of the triumvirate that formed the first Board of Ruling Elders in
"the English Presbyterian Church" of Harrisburg, and was of the
sturdy Scotch-Irish people. Mary Wallace was of the same origin,
and grandsires on both sides, Weir and Wallace, fought side by side
in the gallant defense of Derry against King James, 1689-1690.
From such an ancestry Mr. Weir inherited a mind, strong in natural
faculties, keen in its search for truth, and a will strong and positive.
He and his older brothers were brought up on the Bible and on the
catechisms and the confession that were brought hither from the
mother county. The home of his childhood and youth was one where
serious religious earnestness was commingled with household love
and care. Mr. Weir showed while a mere youth the effects of home
training in his mental powers, in the rapid mastery of his studies and
in his taste for the most solid and substantial literature of the day.
Before the age of seventeen he was a fluent writer for the press, was
well read in the natural sciences, indulged in the calculation of
eclipses and made astronomical drawings of a high order. His love
of study and reading drew him toward the printing office. He became
journeyman printer in the office of John S. Wiestling and a contributor to the paper published by him. After his apprenticeship he
spent some time in the printing office of Messrs. Johnson, Philadelphia. While there his righteous soul was greatly stirred by an event
that he witnessed and that aroused great feeling—the mobbing of
some anti-slavery men and the burning of the hall where they had
met. The scene confirmed him in his hatred of human slavery.

On the 26th of November, 1833, having been chosen teller in the
Harrisburg Bank he accepted the position and held it until October
30, 1844, when he was chosen its cashier. When the institution
became a National bank in 1874 he was unanimously elected its
cashier and held the office until his death, having been an officer in
the bank for over forty-four years. As a bank officer and financier
he gained an enviable distinction for his uniform courtesy, for his

unimpeachable integrity and for ability of the highest order. Few bankers in the Commonwealth or the country have left a record equal to his in years of service, in successful administration of affairs in periods of financial disaster, and for such rigid honesty. Through nearly half a century he handled millions of money and by no single act of his ever stirred the faintest suspicion against the purity of his dealings.

But not alone as a banker was he distinguished. As a man among brother-men he won universal confidence. Men felt that they knew him he was so transparently unselfish, reliable and sympathetic.

He was gifted with rare social qualities, and a graceful wit, with a rare knowledge of men and books, and the events of his time, with refinement of manners, which gave a charm to his home and his presence, not often met in men of business. This kindly, social nature, moulded by divine grace made him foremost in the reformatory, benevolent and religious movements of his time. The poor and the lowly, the tempted, the fallen, the enslaved, found him ready with love and pity for their woes, and with a hand to help them out of their sins into manliness and Christliness.

His literary taste and ability were of a high order. He wrote for the secular and the religious press, was a contributor to the *Theological Review* of his own denomination, was a compiler and a graceful and facile writer of hymns, the writer of several religious tracts and Sunday-school papers of value, and the author of two volumes of prayers, that have passed through several editions. For over forty-three years he was a Ruling Elder in active and devoted service in this Church, and a superintendent of its Sunday-school for forty-three years. He was a life director of the American Board of Commissioners for Foreign Missions for nearly twenty years, and his wise and prudent counsel was sought there, and in the higher courts of his own Church and in numerous public conventions. His conversion to God was a remarkable one, and his subsequent Christian life was characterized from its beginning to his death by the elevating power of Christian principle and religious faith. He was above all things else a Christian. It moulded all his life. He felt the awe of God upon his soul, the loving awe of an earthly child to a Father infinitely holy and unmeasureably good. His Christian life was steady and even and strong as the stars in their courses. He was a close and loving student of God's word and his wonderful prayers at his home altar and in the church were models in their rich quotations of Bible language.

For more than thirty years he was a constant sufferer, often from very severe pains, but under them all was one of the brightest and

most cheerful of men, helping others by his buoyant spirit. He was
a man of uncommon beneficence, giving for years half his income, and
often much more to charitable and religious purposes. He was a
large believer in the things divine and eternal. He walked by them.
He lived among them. They were to him the sublimely real things.
He had a firm grasp on things that other men were groping after.
And so his life was a steady, triumphant victory.

This church was peculiarly dear to him. Upon it he bestowed his
affections, his solicitude, his labors, his gifts. To its welfare he consecrated all the years of his rich Christian life and powers. More
than any other man he moulded its character and inspired its work.

Mr. Weir was most happily married to one who for twenty-seven
years joined him in church labors and presided over his home with
engaging manners and a beautiful piety, Hannah A. (Fahnestock)
Mahany, a sister of Mrs. John A. Weir. Her death preceded his,
and with his departure the household became extinct.

ALEXANDER SLOAN.
Born October 9, 1802.
Died August 2, 1890.

Alexander Sloan was the son of Robert Sloan and Sarah McCormick, and was born at Harrisburg. His father was one of the early
Elders of the Church. The son was educated in the select and private
schools of Harrisburg, especially under Mr. James Maginness, who
was well known as an eminent mathematician. He learned the trade
of cabinet maker with his father, and after his death conducted the
business alone up to 1864, and from that date for several years with
Messrs Boyd. He was chosen an Elder of the Church in 1834, and for
a period of fifty-six years continued to serve in that capacity. Mr.
Sloan, though a quiet and modest man, was very well known in the
city where he had spent eighty-eight years, and wherever known
there was unvarying testimony to his virtues. He faithfully and
most acceptably for more than half a century, discharged the duties
of a Ruling Elder, giving a loving and efficient service. He loved the
" gates of Zion " and was seldom absent from the Sabbath or week-
day services. Mr. Sloan was characterized by his kindness of judgment and of speech concerning all his fellow-men. He was genial
and warm-hearted, ready to forgive and slow to wound by word or
deed. He lived and walked among men with a warm and brotherly
heart, esteemed by all, and leaving behind him the record of a consistent and unblemished life. No word of reproach assailed his long

and useful life. At peace with all men, at peace with God, and in comfortable hope of a blessed immorality he passed his declining years in quiet happiness. He was the last in the line of a band of remarkable man who were spiritual officers in the Church, entering into its service in the first half century of its existence. He served in the Session with twenty-two of the Elders of this Church and was beloved by them all, for his genial brotherly traits of character, his wise counsel and upright life. Mr. Sloan married, September 19, 1833, Mary Todd, daughter of James and Sarah Todd, of Hanover. Two of her brothers were worthy and acceptable ministers of the Gospel. Of his children but one remains, Sarah, the wife of H. Murray Graydon, Esq., of this city.

On November 5, 1840, the following persons were elected Ruling Elders in this church : Samuel Wallace Hays, Alfred Armstrong. They were ordained and installed on the first Sabbath of December, 1840.

SAMUEL WALLACE HAYS.

Born October 30, 1799.

Died May 18, 1855.

Mr. Hays, as with nearly all the Elders of this church, was of Scotch-Irish ancestry. Some of the family received honorable notice for bravery in the patriotic wars of the mother land. His grand-parents came hither in 1789. In the year 1819 Mr. Hays connected himself with the First Presbyterian Church of Carlisle. In 1821 he removed to Harrisburg, where he resided until 1825, when he went to Philadelphia and spent three years, returning to Harrisburg in 1828 and taking up a residence here. His permanent connection with this church dates from that time. He began business here and carried it on successfully through the rest of his active life. Mr. Hays from the date of his confession of Christ was an active and earnest disciple of his Master. When in Philadelphia, and still a young man, he taught a class of young men in a mission Sunday-school connected with Rev. Dr. Janeway's church. It was called " The Galilean Society." Before going to Philadelphia he and John C. Capp, a young man like himself, had charge of the first Sunday-school established among the colored people of this city. Upon his return to Harrisburg in 1828, he organized in October of that year, in connection with this church the first infant Sunday school of Harrisburg, and continued to superintend it with great acceptance for nearly twenty-seven years. A few months before his death, failing health obliged him to give up his charge. He died in the fifty-sixth year of his age and the fifteenth of his eldership. For thirty-six years his life was full of Christian labors. He was a quiet and modest man, during his last years a patient sufferer. He was a very warm friend and lover of the young, kind and happy in his intercourse and an amiable teacher.

ALFRED ARMSTRONG.
Born February 14, 1801.
Died October 21, 1884.

Alfred Armstrong, son of James Armstrong and Mary Stevenson, was born in Carlisle, Penna. He was a descendant of one of the oldest and most distinguished Scotch-Irish families of Cumberland Valley. His grandfather, Gen. John Armstrong, resided at Carlisle and was an able and brilliant leader of the colonial troops during the Indian wars of the last century, and the hero of the famous victory over the Indians at Kittanning in 1756. The county of Armstrong was so named in his honor.

Mr. Armstrong was educated at Dickinson College, graduating from it in 1823. That institution was then a Presbyterian college, under the presidency of the celebrated Rev. Dr. John M. Mason, and was at the height of its usefulness and power. During the last year of his college life Mr. Armstrong and many others of his classmates and fellow-students were subjects of an extensive revival of religion— and made their confession of Christ, uniting with the First Presbyterian church, of Carlisle. Quite a large number of these young men subsequently entered the ministry and attained high positions of honor and usefulness in the Presbyterian Church. Among them may be mentioned : Rev. Drs. Geo. W. Bethune, Erskine Mason, J. Holmes Agnew, George A. Lyon, Daniel McKinley, J. Chamberlain, John M. Dickey and others.

Mr. Armstrong's life was devoted almost entirely to the teaching of classical schools, for which he had a peculiar fitness, and met with large success. Several years were spent in the charge of an academy at Bellefonte. He came to Harrisburg in 1831 and assumed control of the Harrisburg academy, retaining it until 1846. Many young men were fitted for college and the professions under his tuition. A large number of the leading men of this city were among his pupils, and they regarded him with veneration and respect. His reputation as an educator was of high character, and his training was thorough.

He united with this church at his coming in 1831, and on the first Sunday of December, 1840, he was ordained and installed in it as Ruling Elder. He continued to serve the church until his removal from the city in 1846. Returning to Harrisburg in 1862, he again united with the church and was again chosen an Elder, and installed in office, 1868. He held the office, serving the church with great faithfulness, until 1871, when he removed to Washington city. There he resided until his death in October, 1884, in the eighty-fourth year of his age. While in Washington he held a position in the Post Office Department.

Mr. Armstrong was thrice married. In 1829 to Mary Rankin, of Bellefonte, daughter of John Rankin and Isabella Dundas. He married his second wife, Anna Carothers, daughter of Thomas Carothers, of Carlisle, in 1833. His third wife, whom he married in 1863, was Mary Hamill, daughter of William Hamill and Dorcas Galbraith.

One of his sons, Lieutenant James Armstrong, was killed at the battle of Fredericksburg.

Mr. Armstrong was a man of strong character and commanded the notice and respect of his fellowmen wherever he was known. He possessed natural powers of a high order. His mind was keen and active and through life he was a student of men and books, of the word and the ways of God in the history of the church and the world. His conversation and his public addresses revealed a wise, strong and thoughtful man. He was also a man of sincere and thorough consecration to truth, the good of men, and the triumph of God's kingdom in the earth. His sympathies were very broad. The rights of all men, the overthrow of all forms of social and political evil, the spread of temperance, the preservation of the Sabbath, religious education, in brief every good and Christian movement enlisted his sympathies and won his co-operation. He was a man of prayer, gifted and earnest, and a wise and reliable counsellor of the church, and was always ready for duty. That he was called twice to the eldership in this church and was chosen to sit in the higher courts of the church several times, indicates the large esteem in which he was held. He was noted for his dignified and courtly manners, and was beloved and venerated for his pure and steadfast Christian character, his unswerving attachment to Jesus Christ and his stainless life.

On Wednesday evening, December 10, 1844, the following persons were elected to the Eldership of this church : William McClean, William Root, and on January 5, 1845, they were set apart to their office.

WILLIAM McCLEAN.

Born August 4, 1778.

Died December 23, 1846.

William McClean, son of Moses McClean and Sarah Watkins was born in Franklin township, Adams county, Pennsylvania. His ancestors were from the north of Ireland, his grandfather coming to this country about the middle of the last century. All the men of his father's family, five brothers, were surveyors by profession. Two of them, his father and an uncle, were employed under the authority of Great Britain in running the famous Mason and Dixon line. One of his uncles was Deputy Surveyor of York county and a man of prominence, and the father of William McClean and himself assisted him in his duties.

Mr. McClean was reared in the church of Upper Marsh Creek. York county, which was then under the pastoral care of Rev. John Black, a man of high order of talent, moral courage and pulpit power. The father, Moses McClean was an elder in that church and was a man of high standing. At that very early day, in the close of the last century, a temperance society was organized, one of the first of the country, whose members were pledged to abstain themselves from strong drinks and not to furnish them at harvestings. house-raisings. and corn-hustings, the popular gatherings of that day. It was a noble pioneer band to the great host of later days.

In the midst of such moral and religious influences, Mr. McClean spent his youth, and as long as he lived spoke of his early pastor with rapture. In 1794 the family became connected with the Lower Marsh Creek Church, which for forty-nine years was under the pastoral care of Rev. William Paxton, D. D., an ancestor of Rev. William M. Paxton. D. D., now of Princeton Theological Seminary. Under his administration Mr. McClean. while a youth, made a public confession of Christ and became a communicant in the church.

Mr. McClean was twice married : first to Sarah McGinley in 1800, who died six years later, and second to Hanna McPherson in 1816. His children became persons of prominence—one, Judge Moses McClean, was for many years a resident of Gettysburg. Rev. Dr. O. O. McClean, now spending the closing years of his life, after a long and able ministry, in Lewistown. Pa., Dr. Alex S. McClean. of Springfield, Mass., and the subject of this sketch.

Mr. McClean removed to Gettysburg, Penna., in 1816, and about the year 1829 was chosen a Ruling Elder of the Presbyterian Church of that place. In 1839 he came to Harrisburg and served in the office of the Surveyor General of the State for several years. removing his family hither in 1841. So rapidly and completely did he win the confidence and love of the church, by the purity of his life, by his marked abilities and by his Christian courtesy and earnest devotion to the cause of religion that in little over three years after his union with the church as a member, he was chosen Elder by a nearly unanimous vote of the people, receiving one hundred and twenty votes out of one hundred and twenty-five.

He proved to be the man for the place. He was a Christian of spotless life, and of strong and ardent faith, amid many and severe trials. He met with reverses, afflictions and misfortunes, but abode unchanged in character. He was a man of large benevolence, giving out of his limited means regularly and liberally to objects of Christian charity. He was admirably fitted for a leader, being intelligent, active, fluent in speech and a prompt and wise counsellor. Above all these gifts he was a man of prayer and of friendship with God. His prayers were fervid and earnest, clothed in chaste language and from a heart warmed from on high and a mind familiar with the wants of the Church and the world. He was a good man, greatly beloved and respected, and his death within two years after his installation as an Elder filled the Church with mourning and was felt to be a great bereavement. His pastor, Rev. Dr. Wm. R. DeWitt, ever spoke of him in terms of uncommon praise and love. He had often expressed the desire, if the Lord willed, to die a sudden and painless death, and sought to be always in readiness for it. The wish was gratified. On December 26, 1846, he fell suddenly dead in the market place, when in the sixty-ninth year of his age.

WILLIAM ROOT.
Born January 10, 1798.
Died August 25, 1848.

William Root, son of Josiah Root, was born in Southington, Connecticut, and was the one of New England descent brought into the Eldership of this Church. He came to Harrisburg about the year 1834, and was engaged in the tin and iron trade until his death. He was a man of very large and muscular frame and of wonderful vigor of body, of great weight, powerful, yet active and quick in movement. His feats of strength were long remembered and rehearsed after his death. This peculiarity led in some degree to his sad and sudden exit from life. He fell when about to lift some timbers upon a bridge in process of erection across the Susquehanna, and death resulted from the injury sustained.

In the gracious and extensive revival that occurred in the year of his arrival in Harrisburg he was converted and made a public confession of Christ. Mr. Root, though not a man of much intellectual culture, was a very earnest and active Christian, and possessed the entire confidence of the Church. He was modest and retiring in disposition, and yet had in him the stuff of which heroes and martyrs are made, the spirit of almost unlimited personal sacrifice for the good of his fellow-men and the glory of the Redeemer whom he served. It was in fact the distinguishing trait in the character of William Root. Great in body he was large in heart also. He was ready to do or to die, prompt in every duty, cheerful at all times, never morose or disheartened, and his name was promptly given a place in the memory of his brethren and on the honor roll of the Church. His term of office was but a brief two and a half years. The two men, Messrs. McClean and Root, were ordained at the same time, were alike honored and beloved in the Church and were alike removed by sudden and startling death in about two years after their induction into office. Mr. Root died at the age of fifty, leaving his wife and an only daughter. The latter is residing in the West, having married George Bushnell, of Cromwell, Connecticut.

At the eighth election, on June 20, 1855, for Ruling Elders, the following persons were chosen: Mordecai McKinney, John Andrew Weir, Robert Jackson Fleming. On Sabbath evening, June 24th, they were ordained and installed.

MORDECAI McKINNEY.
Born ——, 1796.
Died December 17, 1867.

Mordecai McKinney, son of Mordecai McKinney and Mary Chambers, daughter of Colonel William Chambers, was born near Carlisle, Pennsylvania. His parents resided on a farm and were of that numerous body of Scotch-Irish who were the first settlers of Cumberland Valley. His early studies were pursued at Dickinson College, where he spent six years, graduating while quite a youth. He began the study of law in the office of Judge Duncan, of Carlisle, and after his removal to Harrisburg, completed his studies, in the office of Hon. Amos Ellmaker, Attorney General of the State, and was admitted to the bar in May, 1817. In 1821 he was appointed District Attorney of Union county, and October 12, 1827, Governor Shultze appointed him one of the associate judges of Dauphin county, Pa. He served five years. Subsequently Judge McKinney turned his attention to the compilation of law books and published "McKinney's Pennsylvania Tax Laws," and other works of value to the profession. Later still in life he published a volume of labor, research and worth, entitled, "Our Government," an explanatory statement of the system of government in this country in its various departments of the State and the Nation. He was a man of extended and accurate knowledge in his profession, an honest and conscientious counsellor, but so modest and retiring that he shrank from the public contests of the bar.

Mr. McKinney married Rachel Graydon, daughter of William

Graydon. Her death occurred at Harrisburg, April 12, 1856. Mr. Mckinney principally wrought his mission in the world by his Christian life and character. His life as a man and a citizen was completely transfused by his religion, sanctified and elevated by it. He was one of the most guileless of men, a man of sterling honesty and conscientiousness, and was remarkably free from selfishness and pride, spending all his years in comparative poverty, no more contented, trusting and happy man walked the streets of the city. He was a friend to all that was venerable and good, a defender of law, and a supporter of all that promised to promote the welfare of society.

Though he could give but little he was distinguished as a philanthropist, giving what is often far better than money, time and attention and his most hearty sympathy. A true-hearted man, he "counted nothing foreign to him that was human," giving in genuine unselfishness a faithful and earnest devotion to the outcasts and Pariahs of society. He knew no ambition beyond the simple doing of right, and though so lowly and unassuming in all things else, in this he was as brave a man as ever faced an enemy. No notions of policy or of expediency ever swerved him from his course. He was the friend of the slave, of the poor, of the despised, and his loyalty to their rights and wants merited universal admiration. And touching as was the tribute to his worth when on the day of his burial, the officers of the court and members of the bar at their head, the president judge passed beside his coffin, taking their last and silent look and giving their unspoken farewell to their old friend and associate who died as poor in worldly goods as he was morally great, it was by no means so noble and so impressive a testimony to his goodness and worth as when the long procession of parents and children from the colored population of this city passed, and with the touching eloquence of sobs and tears told all, that they had lost their best earthly friend.

It is, however, as a devout Christian that Mr. McKinney will chiefly and permanently live in the history of the Church. For half a century he was an active member of its communion, for fourteen years a member of its Board of Trustees, and for thirteen years a Ruling Elder. The Presbyterian Church was his by descent, by education, by love of its doctrines and order. It was a pride and a pleasure to him to sit, as he was permitted to do, in her various courts, the Presbytery, the Synod and the General Assembly.

Judge McKinney was a great student of the Bible. His brethren of the bar were wont to find open on the table where lay his commentaries on human law, the volume of Divine Law, and with its contents he was more familiar than with any work of human origin. He was a theologian of the Scriptures.

For many years most of his active christian labors were given freely, and as the chief reward the pleasure of doing good, to the colored people of the city. He sought no public notice. He was ever at his post. His life was a life with God. A life of kind thoughts, pious deeds, charity toward men and of trust toward God. It was closed by a calm and quiet death of entire trust in the Great Redeemer, for whose speedy second coming he had longingly waited. His death was the result of injuries from a street car, and when he was told by his pastor that in a few hours he would stand amid the scenes of eternity, he heard the announcement with all the composure and calmness of one who hears of the most common event of life. The half a century of prayers, labors, counsels and godly living that Judge McKinney gave to this Church are of inestimable worth.

JOHN ANDREW WEIR.

Born January 10, 1802.

Died October 10, 1881.

John A. Weir, second son of Samuel Weir, and Mary Wallace, was born at Harrisburg. His father was one of the first three Elders of the Church, and a man of high character. The mother, who survived her husband several years, was greatly esteemed by her sons, and by all as a woman of great worth. Mr. Weir received an education in the private schools of the borough and in the Harrisburg Academy. The best teaching he had, by his own testimony, came from his mother. He learned coach-making, but did not pursue the trade to any large extent in subsequent life, taking up the hardware business in preference and somewhat later connecting with it the drug business, associating with him his nephew, Daniel W. Gross.

During the administration of Gov. Ritner, 1835–1837, he served as a clerk in the office of the Secretary of the Commonwealth. In 1840 he was elected Prothonotary of Dauphin county, and held the position for six years. While serving in this position he became a Director of the Harrisburg bank, and later a teller in it, and so continued until 1880, when the infirmities of age obliged him to retire. He was also from 1850 to 1880 the Treasurer of the State Lunatic Hospital at Harrisburg. His peculiar fitness for such duties brought him many trusts as administrator and executor of estates and the guardian of minor children. In his many and difficult responsibilities he proved to be eminently worthy of all confidence.

He made a public confession of Christ in the year 1820 at the age of eighteen, and for sixty-one years, as a member of the church, maintained a Christian character that was worthy of all praise and imitation. He was summoned to many duties by the Church, serving it as a Trustee for sixteen years, as the Treasurer of the congregation for a number of years, as Superintendent of the infant school about fifteen years, and from 1855, until his death, a period of twenty-six years, as an honored and beloved Ruling Elder. For a long time, with his first wife, he was a member of the church choir. They were both excellent singers.

He was above most men a genuine lover of children, and a model in all his intercourse with them. He was beloved and held in memory by all who were under his training.

In the graver duties of a Ruling Elder, he was a wise and safe counsellor in the Session and in the higher courts of the Church. In private and public life his character was conspicuous for its beautiful consistency and uprightness. No man in the city had a more unsullied reputation for all manly Christian virtues than John Andrew Weir. He was a man of large and unfailing liberality. He kept himself informed of wants of the Church and of the world and was prompt to meet them to the fulness of his ability. He was a great and true friend of all moral reforms, steadfast and devoted to the temperance cause, closely connected with Bible societies from early manhood, one of the first and staunchest friends of the anti-slavery movement and of the negro in the North. He had also the courage of his convictions. He was one of the best and truest of friends, genial, cheerful and brotherly. Wherever he went he brought sunshine and peace. The house was brighter after he had been there, faces were sunnier, hearts were lighter. He came with a benediction and left with a blessing. He was one of the gentlest of men. Life has been happier, its burdens have been easier, its crosses lighter, and faith in God and faith in man have grown stronger for many a fellow mortal because of the true and Christian friendship of John Andrew Weir.

Mr. Weir was twice married, first to Catharine Wiestling, sister of the late George P. Wiestling, and second to Matilda M. Fahnestock, sister of the late Adam K. Fahnestock. Of the family of Mr. Weir but two survive, Misses Anna C. Weir and Sybil M. Weir, who reside in the family home, for many years the residence of Mr. Weir.

ROBERT JACKSON FLEMING.

Born November 16, 1803.

Died December 2, 1874.

Robert J. Fleming, the son of Samuel Fleming and Sarah Becket, was born in Hanover township, Washington county, Pennsylvania. He received an academic education, and while yet a young man, in

1829, became a teacher and lecturer on English grammar, and took a trip to the west, lecturing on his favorite topic. His parents had removed in 1813 to Hanover, Dauphin county, Pa., whence came a number of the earlier families of this church. Mr. Fleming was a lover and also a teacher of vocal music, and was the chorister of the church from 1834 to 1850. In 1834 he established the coach-making business on a large scale in Harrisburg, and continued it with success until June 15, 1865, when his entire establishment was destroyed by fire. He built at his shop the first eight-wheel passenger car which ran on the Pennsylvania railroad between Columbia and Philadelphia. Also the first on the Williamsport and Elmira railroad, taking it up the canal on a flat boat. In 1861 he was appointed notary public, and held the office until his death, doing the business of the Harrisburg National Bank in this capacity. He married June 5, 1845, Sarah Ann Poor, of McConnnelsville, O.

Mr. Fleming was deservedly honored by his fellowmen as an upright and enterprising citizen, and a man of intelligence and high moral character. He united with this church on confession of his faith, March 31, 1842, and was ordained and installed a Ruling Elder June 24, 1855.

Mr. Fleming was earnest and active in the work of the church, being greatly interested in the young. For many years also, with his wife and others, he devoted himself to Christian work among the colored population of the city. He was a hearty opponent of human slavery. Self-denying, generous, true-hearted, he wrought good and noble work for Christ and his cause. He died in the seventy-first year of his age.

At a meeting held for the purpose on February 19, 1868, the following persons were elected to the office of Ruling Elder: Alfred Armstrong, Dr. James Fleming, William S. Shaffer, Walter F. Fahnestock, jr.

The latter three were duly ordained and installed on Sabbath evening March 8, 1858. Mr. Armstrong being already ordained, was installed at the same time.

JAMES FLEMING, M. D., D. D. S.,

Born June 25, 1810,

Died January 30, 1875.

James Fleming, son of Samuel Fleming and Sarah Becket, was born in Washington county, Pennsylvania. In 1812 his parents removed to Hanover township, Dauphin county, Pennsylvania. He received a good education, being ambitious to excel in his studies.

Thrown upon his own resources at the early age of eighteen, he resolved to help himself by alternately acting as teacher and pupil. He pursued this course for seven years and became conversant with the higher mathematics, with one or more of the ancient languages and with French. He taught in various schools and academies spending some time in the States of Ohio and Kentucky. In 1838 he graduated with honor from the Jefferson Medical College, Philadelphia, and entered upon the practice of medicine in Harrisburg. For some years he practiced his profession, but finding the duties too severe for a slender constitution his attention was drawn to the science of dental surgery, then comparatively in its infancy. He went to Philadelphia and acquired a thorough knowledge of the science, and returning to Harrisburg he met with a deserved success in his new profession and prosecuted it through the rest of his life. He was one of the originators of the Pennsylvania Association of Dental Surgeons, aided in establishing the first Dental College in Philadelphia, it being the second of its kind incorporated in this country. He was a frequent contributor to both medical and dental journals and occasionally to the newspaper press. He was tendered a professorship in the Dental College at Philadelphia, but declined it He twice received the honorary degree of Doctor of Dental Surgery. He was also a director in the Harrisburg National Bank, and President of the Board of School Directors, showing himself to be a man of public spirit and ability.

He made a profession of his faith in Christ and united with the Presbyterian Church March 2, 1843. He at once entered upon Christian work and was for many years a teacher in the Sunday school. He was ordained an Elder in the Church March 8, 1868, and met his duties with fidelity until his death, eight years later. He was a man of pure and noble character, retiring in his ways, gentlemanly, obliging and courteous to all. He was a man of generous instincts and actions, a man of sincerest piety and of real worth. He married, in 1852, Jeannette Street, daughter of Col. Thaddeus Street and Martha Davenport Reynolds, a lineal descendent of Rev. John Davenport, the founder of New Haven. The widow and two children, Mrs. D. P. Bruner, of Philadelphia, and William R. Fleming, of New York survive him.

WALTER FRANKLIN FAHNESTOCK, Jr.
Born October 8, 1844.
Died May 19, 1879.

Mr. Fahnestock was the son of Walter F. Fahnestock and Louisa C. Heisley, and was born at Harrisburg. He united with this

Church on July 2, 1865, and was active in the work of the Church and of the Young Men's Christian Association. He gave large promise of usefulness and of success and was called into the Eldership and ordained March 8, 1868. After a brief service of four years he removed to Philadelphia, severing his connection with the church. He died while still comparatively young at his father's house in Harrisburg.

Mr. William Stowe Shaffer served the Church for twenty-one years with sincere devotion. Since the organization of the Olivet Church in 1889, he has been an active and earnest Elder in that organization.

On April, 15, 1877, the following persons were added to the goodly roll of the Eldership of the Church by ordination and installation. They were chosen to the office on April 4: James Franklin Purvis, Samuel John Milton McCarrell, Jacob Augustus Miller, Gilbert Martin McCauley. After serving the Church with ability and universal acceptableness until December 26, 1882, Mr. Purvis removed to Kansas, where he still resides. He has been a Ruling Elder in the Presbyterian Church of Holton, Kansas, since a short while after his removal there. The remaining three are still amid the active duties of the office. To them were added by ordination and installation on March 20, 1887, John Craig Harvey and John Henry Spicer. The complete roll of the ruling eldership contains thirty names. The foregoing record will show what noble and able men have served God and the Church in that office.

THE CHARTER OF THE CORPORATION.

To all whom these presents may come : know ye, that we, whose names are hereunto subscribed, citizens of the Commonwealth of Pennsylvania, having associated together for the purpose of worshiping Almighty God, agreeably to the gospel of our Saviour, Jesus Christ, and desirous of acquiring the powers and immunities of a body politic in law according to the form of an act of the General Assembly of the said Commonwealth, passed the sixth day of April, Anno Domini, one thousand seven hundred and ninety-one, do hereby declare that we have associated ourselves together for the purpose aforesaid, by the name, style and title, and under the articles and conditions following, that is to say :

ARTICLE I. The name, style and title shall be THE ENGLISH PRESBYTERIAN CONGREGATION OF HARRISBURG.

ARTICLE II. The subscribers and such others being citizens of the said Commonwealth as shall hereafter become members of the said congregation, and who maintain and adhere to the system of religious principles declared and exhibited by the General Assembly of the Presbyterian Church in the United States, shall become and be a corporation and body politic in law and fact to have countenance by the name, style and title of the English Presbyterian Congregation of Harrisburg.

ARTICLE III. The subscribers and their successors respectively shall have full power and authority to make, have and use one common seal with such device and inscription as they shall respectively deem proper, and the same to break, alter and renew at their pleasure, and by the name, style and title by them respectively provided and declared as aforesaid, shall be capable in law to sue and be sued, plead and be impleaded in any court or courts before any judge or justices in all manner of suits, complaints, pleas, causes, matters and demands whatsoever, and all and every matter or thing therein to do in as full and effectual a manner as any other person or persons, bodies politic and corporate within this Commonwealth may or can do, and shall be authorized and empowered, and they are hereby respectively authorized and empowered to make rules, by-laws and ordinances and to do everything needful for the good government and support of the affairs of the said corporation ; *Provided, always,* The said by-laws, rules and ordinances, or any of them, be not repugnant to the Constitution and laws of the United States, to the Constitution and laws of this Commonwealth, or to this instrument upon which the present association is founded.

ARTICLE IV. The subscribers and their successors respectively by the name, style and title declared as aforesaid shall be able and capable in law according to the terms and conditions of this instrument, to take, receive and hold all and all manner of lands, tenements, rents, annuities, franchises and hereditaments and any sum or sums of money and any manner or portion of goods and chattels given and bequeathed unto them to be employed and disposed of according to the objects, articles and conditions of this instrument or according to the articles and by-laws of this corporation or of the will and intentions of the donors: *Provided always, nevertheless,* That the clear yearly value or income of the messuages, houses, lands and tenements, rents, annuities or other hereditaments and real estate of this corporation, and the interest of money lent shall not exceed the sum of five hundred pounds.

ARTICLE V. A board of trustees consisting of seven members (four of whom shall be recognized by the Church Session as being in full communion with the church) shall be chosen by ballot in church on the first Monday of January next, of which previous notice shall be given two weeks from the pulpit; and until trustees shall be elected in virtue of this instrument, the temporal affairs of the congregation shall be managed as heretofore.

ARTICLE VI. The persons capable of voting at the election of trustees and at all other elections shall be pew holders and shall possess at least one half a pew in the church which has been in his or her occupancy one year, at least, previous to the election (except that the five large pews occupied as aforesaid shall be entitled to four votes, provided so many persons occupy them as are otherwise qualified to vote; *Provided, nevertheless,* That no one shall be permitted to vote at any election whose pew rent shall be six months in arrears and unpaid.

ARTICLE VII. The trustees shall meet on the first Monday after their election (four of whom shall be a quorum) and afterwards as often as business shall require. They shall choose from their own number a President, Secretary and Treasurer.

ARTICLE VIII. The power of the board of trustees shall extend to making by-laws for their own government and that of the temporal concerns of the church, such as providing regulations and keeping in repair a burial ground, providing and keeping in repair a house of worship, renting pews and collecting pew rents, receiving and paying all debts due to or by the congregation, employing, paying and dismissing a sexton, fixing and paying the salary of a clerk, but they shall be chosen by the Session. The trustees shall not have power to alien the real estate of the congregation or to expend more than three hundred dollars without the consent and approbation of a majority of the congregation.

ARTICLE IX. Meetings of the trustees may be called at any time by the president, or at the request of two members.

ARTICLE X. Congregational meetings may be called by the trustees or at the request of six pew holders, of which at least three days previous notice shall be given.

ARTICLE XI. The trustees shall lay before the congregation at each annual election a full account of all the transactions of the past year.

ARTICLE XII. The choice and salary of a pastor shall be determined by a majority of the congregation entitled to vote.

ARTICLE XIII. In case of a vacancy in the board of trustees the President shall call a meeting of the congregation (on one week's notice from the pulpit) to fill the vacancy.

ARTICLE XIV. The trustees at the first meeting after their election shall divide themselves into three classes, two of which shall consist of two members each and the third of three ; the first class shall continue for one year, the second for two, and the third for three years. An election by ballot shall be held annually on the first Monday of January in church to fill the vacancies respectively in rotation, of which previous notice shall be given two Sabbaths from the pulpit.

ADOPTED October 5th, 1818.

John Stoner,	Thomas Smith,	Ira Woodworth,
Joseph A. McJimsey,	Geo. Bryan,	Jno. Fisher,
Isaac Meguier,	Robt. Harris,	Rachel Awl,
William Murray,	Sarah Mooney,	James Emerson,
Robert Sloan,	Hester Hall,	P. C. Nabb,
Hugh Hamilton,	Richd. M. Crain,	William Graydon,
Henry McKenney,	J. Wallace,	Samuel Agnew,
Warum Holbrook,	Hillary B. Talbot,	James Sayers,
Moses Swan,	James S. Espy,	Elizabeth Elder,
A. S. Dearmond,	John Neilson,	A. M. Piper,
James Trimble,	Charles Hinckley,	Jno. Frazer,
J. W. Buffington,	Moses Gillmor,	James Roberts,
James Alricks,	Tho. Walker,	W. N. Irvine,
John McChesney,	Wm. Shannon,	John Woodward,
James R. Boyd,	Robert Dickey,	William Armstrong,
George Whitehill,	Mord. McKinney,	H. Antes,

Samuel Sees,	Joseph Smullen,	William Michael,
Gilbert Burnett,	Mary Hanna,	Sarah Barr,
Rebecca Orth,	Thomas Whiteside,	Eleanor M. Wallace,
Samuel Weir,	Frs. R. Shunk,	Joshua Elder,
Andrew Mitchel,	Rt. McElwee,	John B. Thompson,
William Allison,	Rose Wright,	Nancy Anthony.
Abiathar Hopkins,	J. Kearsley,	J. Montgomery.
James Peacock,	Mary B. Potts,	

I certify that I have perused and examined the within instrument and association, and am of opinion that the objects, articles and conditions therein set forth and contained are lawful.

AMOS ELLMAKER.

HARRISBURG, *November 16, 1818.*

We, the Justices of the Supreme Court of Pennsylvania, do certify, that having examined and perused the foregoing instrument of writing, we concur in opinion with the Attorney General that the objects, articles and conditions therein set forth and contained are lawful. Witness our hands the 14th day of December, Anno Domini, 1818.

WILLIAM TILGHMAN,
JOHN B. GIBSON,
THOMAS DUNCAN.

Fee $1, charged by Judge Gibson.

PENNSYLVANIA, *ss :*

In the Name and by the Authority of the Commonwealth of Pennsylvania.

WILLIAM FINDLAY, *Governor of the said Commonwealth.*

To Thomas Sergeant, Esquire, Secretary of the said Commonwealth. Sends greeting .

WHEREAS, It has been duly certified to me by Amos Ellmaker, Esquire, Attorney General of the said Commonwealth, and by William Tilghman, Esq., Chief Justice, and John B. Gibson and Thomas Duncan, Esquires, Associate Judges of the Supreme Courts of Pennsylvania, that they have respectively perused and examined the annexed act or instrument for the incorporation of, "The English Presbyterian Congregation of Harrisburg," and that they concur in opinion, that the objects, articles and conditions therein set forth and contained are lawful : now know you, that in pursuance of an act of the General Assembly, passed the sixth day of April, in the year of our Lord one thousand seven hundred and ninety-one, entitled, "An act to confer on certain associations of the citizens of this Commonwealth, the powers and immunities of corporation or bodies politic in law," I have transmitted the said act, or instrument of incorporation unto you, the said Thomas Sergeant, Secretary as aforesaid, hereby requiring you to enroll the same at the expense of the applicants, to the intent that, according to the objects, articles and conditions therein set forth and contained, the parties may become and be a corporation and body politic in law and in fact, to have continuance by the name, style and title, in the said instrument provided and declared.

Given under my hand and the great seal of the State, at Harrisburg, the fourth day of January, one thousand eight hundred and nineteen, and of the Commonwealth the forty-third.

By the Governor.

THOMAS SERGEANT,
Secretary.

SECRETARY'S OFFICE, *January 4th, 1819.*

Enrolled in charter book, No. 2, page 523, containing a record of acts, incorporating sundry religious, charitable and literary societies.

Witness my hand and the lesser seal of the State at Harrisburg, the day and year above written.

THOMAS SERGEANT,
Secretary.

Note IV. on page 243.

ACTION OF THE CONGREGATION IN 1838.*

The following proceedings took place at a congregational meeting of the Presbyterian Church of Harrisburg, July 2d, 1838. The meeting was held in consequence of a recommendation to that effect, made by the Session and Board of Trustees conjointly, and which had been read by the pastor of the church from the pulpit on Sunday, the first of July, 1838. The proceedings of the Session and the Board of Trustees embodying this recommendation, it was thought proper to introduce into the minutes of the congregational meeting of July 2d, 1838, and it is believed they are nowhere else preserved. This copy of these proceedings is taken from a copy carefully examined, compared and attested by Charles C. Rawn, one of the secretaries of the meeting.

The pastor of the English Presbyterian Church and congregation of Harrisburg, read from the pulpit on Sunday, the first day of July, 1838, the following statement:

Harrisburg, June 13th, 1838, the Session and Trustees of the English Presbyterian Church on invitation of the Session met in the lecture-room of the church for the purpose of mutual consultation in reference to the ecclesiastical relations of the church with which they are connected. President William R. DeWitt, Moderator of the Session; William Graydon, John Neilson, Alexander Graydon and Alexander Sloan, members of the Session; Robert Harris, William Allison, Gilbert Burnet, Mordecai McKinney and James R. Boyd, trustees. The meeting was opened with prayer. After some consultation Herman Alricks, Alexander Graydon and William R. DeWitt were appointed a commitee to take into consideration the subject of the ecclesiastical relations of the English Presbyterian Church of Harrisburg, Pa., whether any, and if any, what action in reference to the relations shall be recommended to the church and congregation. Adjourned.

June 30th, 1838. The Session and Trustees met in the lecture-room of the church. Present, William R. DeWitt, William Graydon, John Neilson, Alexander Sloan, Alexander Graydon and J. W. Weir, members of the Session; Robert Harris, William Allison, Herman Alricks, Gilbert Burnett, James R. Boyd, Mordecai McKinney and

---

* This is taken from a document in the hand-writing of Dr. DeWitt, which is preserved in the archives of the church.—EDITOR.

John A. Weir, Trustees. The meeting was opened with prayer. Rev. William R. DeWitt was appointed Moderator and J. W. Weir Secretary. The minutes of the last meeting were read.

The committee to whom was referred the subject of the ecclesiastical relations of the English Presbyterian Church, Harrisburg, Pa., and whether any, and if any, what action by the said Church should be recommended report: That in consequence of the Commissioners chosen to represent the Presbyteries of the General Assembly of the Presbyterian Church in the United States of America, appointed to meet in the Seventh Presbyterian church, Philadelphia, Thursday, May 17th, 1838, having separated and organized two bodies, each claiming to be the General Assembly of the Presbyterian Church in the United States of America, and claiming the right to exercise, as such, ecclesiastical jurisdiction over all the subordinate judicatories and churches in connection with the said General Assembly; it seems important and necessary that this Church should either decline the ecclesiastical jurisdiction of both bodies, and all the subordinate judicatories that adhere to them or declare to which body they adhere and submit to as the General Assembly. That although the ecclesiastical relations of the Church can effect only the members in full communion with the Church, and although it has been the practice of Churches of Pennsylvania to submit all questions involving their ecclesiastical relations to her members in full communion, yet as the pew-holders may feel interested in the question, and as it is desirable to continue and promote by every possible means the harmony which has so long distinguished this congregation, it be recommended that all the members of this Church recognized by the Session to be in full communion together with all the pew-holders assemble on Monday evening, July 2d, at half-past seven o'clock in the church, for the purpose of deciding on their future ecclesiastical relations.

In pursuance to the foregoing the said congregation assembled in the Presbyterian church in the borough of Harrisburg, Monday evening, July 2d, 1838, at 7:30 o'clock, and organized the meeting by calling Robert Harris to the chair and appointing James W. Weir and Charles C. Rawn Secretaries.

On motion it was agreed that the Rev. William R. DeWitt, Pastor of the congregation, open the meeting with prayer, which was done.

On motion it was agreed that the proceeding of the Church Session and Board of Trustees as above in part should be read. Whereupon the same was read with the further proceedings of the said Session and Board of Trustees following, to wit:

"That when thus assembled the Pastor of the Church be desired to invoke the divine blessing upon the deliberations and actions, and also to give a brief statement of the facts which render some action on the part of this Church necessary. That he then state that the Session and Trustees conjointly have had this subject under serious deliberations, and have concluded to propose the three following resolutions to be offered and acted upon by the meeting in the order in which they shall be read, and to recommend and urge an acquiescence in whichever of the resolutions shall be adopted by a majority of the meeting.

WHEREAS, The Commissioners chosen by the different Presbyteries to represent them in the General Assembly of the Presbyterian Church in the United States of America, appointed to meet in the Seventh Presbyterian church, of Philadelphia, on the seventeenth of May, 1838, separated and constituted two bodies each claiming to be the General Assembly of the Presbyterian Church in the United States of America, and also claiming jurisdiction over the subordinate judicatories and Churches connected with the said General Assembly; wherefore,

1. Resolved, That this church and congregation recognize and acknowledge as the General Assembly of the Presbyterian Church in the United States of America the body composed of commissioners from the Presbyteries which assembled in the Seventh Presbyterian Church and organized by electing Rev. William Plumer, of Virginia, Moderator, and Elias W. Crane, Temporary Clerk, and which continued their sessions in said church until their final adjournment, June, 1838.

2. Resolved, That this church and congregation recognize and acknowledge as the General Assembly of the Presbyterian Church in the United States of America the body composed of commissioners from Presbyteries which assembled in the Seventh Presbyterian Church of Philadelphia May 17th, 1838, and organized by electing Samuel Fisher, D. D., Moderator; Erskine Mason, D. D., Stated Clerk; E. Gilbert Permanent Clerk, and John W. Blatchford, Temporary Clerk, and after that adjourned to meet in the First Presbyterian Church, Philadelphia, where they continued their Sessions until their final adjournment, June, 1838.

3. Resolved, That the English Presbyterian Church in Harrisburg, Pa., decline the jurisdiction of either body, and also the jurisdiction of all subordinate judicatories, which are or may be organized, and which may claim in virtue of the former ecclesiastical relations of this church the right to exercise jurisdiction over it."

The Rev. W. R. DeWitt, pastor of the congregation then proceeded to make a detailed statement of the proceedings of the Genera

Assembly of the Presbyterian Church of 1837, referring at large to the alleged causes leading thereto, to the plan of union formed in 1801, and to such matters connected with the whole subject as were calculated to possess the meeting with a more perfect knowledge of the business and duties it had been assembled to attend. He also very feelingly referred to the long and affectionate relations of nineteen years and more that had subsisted between him and his congregation, during which time he had received only accumulating evidence of the kindest regard and esteem from them. He stated a continuation of the harmony and Christian fellowship, which had during all the time of his ministrations among them so peculiarly and unprecedently distinguished their intercourse as a church, congregation and people, was to him an object so desirable that he would sacrifice his personal feelings and wishes (without compromising principle) rather than interpose any obstacles thereto. And that should the congregation decide by a reasonable unanimity to acknowledge the jurisdiction of that body as the General Assembly which organized in Philadelphia on the 17th of May, 1838, by electing the Rev. William Plumer, Moderator he should most cheerfully acquiesce in such a decision and unanimity, though it would compel him to withdraw from their pastoral charge and oversight, and tear himself from friendships and places consecrated by ties strong and lasting as the affections of his nature, as he had ever regarded the acts of the Assembly of 1837 in the excision of the four Synods and the proceedings which had grown out of them as unconstitutional, unjust, unkind, and could perceive no reasons for changing his opinions. He also further stated that should they similarly decide to acknowledge the jurisdiction of that body as the General Assembly of the Presbyterian Church, which organized in Philadelphia on the 17th of May, 1838, by electing Samuel Fisher Moderator, or decline the jurisdiction of either or both of said bodies and all subordinate judicatories which adhered to them or either of them he would continue with great satisfaction to minister to them in the pastoral office. After Mr. DeWitt had closed his remarks, C. C. Rawn moved that the general rules for judicatories found in an appendix to a book containing the Confession of Faith of the Presbyterian Church in the United States of America be adopted so far as applicable for the regulation of the proceedings of this meeting.

William McClure moved to postpone said motion, which was agreed to, and the said rules were not adopted. John M. Foster then moved the adoption of the following preamble and resolutions :

WHEREAS, This meeting of the English Presbyterian congregation of Harrisburg and members of the church in communion with the same, sincerely regret that dissension prevails in the General Assembly of the Presbyterian church in the United States, to such an extent that that once united and respected judicatory of our church has separated itself into two distinct bodies, each claiming to be the rightful and legal General Assembly, and appealed to the laws of the land for a decision of their respective claims to that character ; and,

Whereas, During the pending of that appeal it would be as indecorous in this meeting, as it is foreign from their intention, to volunteer any expression of opinion on the merits of the legal controversy ; but in the meantime this meeting has the right, which it may exercise without disrespect to any tribunal, legal or ecclesiastical, to indicate their future course in matters connected with that controversy, over which neither tribunal has any absolute or binding control ; and,

Whereas, The congregation and church, composed of the members of this meeting, have now, for the long period of twenty years, had for their pastor one endeared to us all by many considerations, one whom we admire for his talents, confide in for his integrity, love for his virtues and revere for his piety, such a connection pleasant and happy as we know it to have been in times past, and which we see no just reason to apprehend will be less so for the future, we cannot and will not, on our part, voluntarily sever, as the condition on which we may be connected with or continue by any church judicatory whatever ; therefore,

Resolved, That we will not consent to any acknowledgment of the ecclesiastical jurisdiction of either party, now claiming to be the General Assembly of the Presbyterian church in the United States, nor to any connection of the church and congregation, with any Presbytery or church judicatory, which shall exact as the condition of such acknowledgment or connection, a dissolution of the subsisting relation between us and our pastor, the Rev. William R. DeWitt.

Charles C. Rawn moved to postpone the consideration of the preamble and resolution, offered by Mr. Foster, for the purpose of introducing the following preamble and resolution :

WHEREAS, It is absolutely necessary that the government of the church be under some definite form ; and,

Whereas, We hold it to be expedient and agreeable to the Scripture and the practice of the primitive Christians that the church be governed by congregational, Presbyterial, Synodical and General Assemblies ; therefore,

Resolved, That we will as a church anxiously avoid any action calculated to destroy or impair the regular legitimate succession of such ecclesiastical tribunals :

Resolved, That no official joint meeting of the Church Session and Board of Trustees as such for the church is recognized by or known to the Form of Government and Discipline of the Presbyterian Church :

Resolved, Therefore, that this congregational meeting possesses no other or greater authority by virtue of the particular recommendations causing it, than any other voluntary assemblage of the members of said congregation after request or notice for that purpose ;

Resolved, That it is now unnecessary and inexpedient, if not wholly unauthorized by the forms of the Presbyterian Church government and discipline for this congregation to assume the decision of the question proposed for its consideration and action :

Resolved, That the Session of this church is the regularly constituted tribunal to deliberate and decide upon ecclesiastical relations, and that we do most cheerfully confide in the body we have so constituted for a regular decision at proper and expedient time of those questions now presented and all others requiring its action.

And on this question he called for the yeas and nays.

The chairman asked the meeting whether it was their pleasure that the yeas and nays should be called on the question of postponement, which was decided in the negative. The question was then taken on the postponement, and it was lost without a division.

Joseph Wallace then moved to postpone the preamble and resolution of Mr. Forster for the purpose of considering the third resolution stated by the Session and Board of Trustees. On this motion the yeas and nays were called, but the call was subsequently withdrawn and the motion was lost.

Joel Hinckley then moved to postpone the preamble and resolution offered by Mr. Forster for the purpose of considering the second resolution stated by the Session and Trustees, and on this question the yeas and nays were called. The call was subsequently recalled and the motion to postpone was lost.

The question then recurring on the preamble and resolutions offered by William Fosser, they were carried, three or four votes dissenting.

(Signed)   ROBERT HARRIS.
Chairman.

Attest :
(Signed)   CHARLES C. RAWN,   *Sec's.*
              JAMES W. WEIR,

From this date, July 2d, 1838, to November 9th, 1840, two years, four months and seven days, the church and congregation continued independent. On the 9th of November, 1840, the church and congregation resolved to apply to be received under the watch and care of the Harrisburg Presbytery, Mr. Alexander Graydon, Ruling Elder, was appointed to make the application. It was made, and the church and congregation was received into the Presbytery.

FORMS IN USE DURING A PORTION OF DR. DE WITT'S PASTORATE.

NOTE.

The First Presbyterian Church of Harrisburg, Pennsylvania, as a consistent member of the Presbyterian Church in the United States of America, adopts the Westminster Confession of Faith, the Larger and Shorter Catechisms, as the statement of our faith, fellowship and discipline, Form of Government and Book of Discipline, and to this the Ministers and Ruling Elders of the Church subscribe at their ordination. But as this Church re-affirms what our fathers at the adoption of the Constitution of the Presbyterian Church did formally declare and what the General Assembly of the Presbyterian Church has since reiterated, namely: That we are willing to receive one another as Christ has received us, to the glory of God, and admit to fellowship in sacred ordinances all such as we have grounds to believe Christ will at last admit to the kingdom of heaven (see act preliminary to the adoption of the Westminster Confession of Faith —Minutes 1729, page 96): and, that we fully recognize the authority of the command, "Him that is weak in faith receive ye, but not to doubtful disputation;" in its application to the reception of private members of the Church (see Pastoral Letter of the General Assembly of 1822, in Minutes of that year, page 30), we deem it proper to require of private members, on their public admission to our communion an assent only to a brief summary of leading doctrines, while all are required to submit to the government of the Church administered according to the Book of Discipline, and are expected to become familiar with the Shorter Catechism, and as opportunity permits to study the Confession of Faith and Larger Catechism which we regard as the best uninspired summaries of Christian doctrine.

FORM OF PUBLIC ADMISSION TO THE COMMUNION.

By the proper authorities of this Church you have been examined as to your Christian knowledge and piety; and on the profession of your faith in Christ, and promise of obedience to his commands, you have been received by them into its membership. You now present yourselves in this public manner, to confess Jesus Christ before men, to testify your faith in him, and your consecration to his service. We hope you have well considered this important transaction. It will live long in your remembrance, and be followed with everlasting consequences. The vows you this day make will be recorded in heaven, and meet you again on your trial at the last great day. But these solemn considerations need not dishearten you. In the name of Christ you may venture thus publicly to commit yourself to God in a covenant never to be revoked, and to trust to his promised faithfulness, for strength to fulfill your engagements.

Attend now to the profession of your faith.

1. You believe in one God subsisting in three persons, Father, Son, and Holy Ghost, the same in substance, equal in power and glory.

2. You believe that the Scriptures of the Old and New Testaments were given by inspiration of God, and are the only infallible rule of faith and practice.

3. You believe that God created man upright in his own image, in knowledge, righteousness, and true holiness, but that left to the freedom of his own will, he fell from the estate in which he was created, by sinning against God, and by his fall brought all mankind into an estate of sin and misery.

4. You believe that the Son of God, the second person in the Godhead, assumed our nature, and in the room of sinners obeyed the law of God and offered up himself a sacrifice to satisfy divine justice, and that God is now just in justifying the ungodly who believe in Him.

5. You believe that all who are justified have been born of the Spirit, and, by Him persuaded and enabled to embrace Jesus Christ freely offered to us in the gospel, and that all such are kept by the power of God through faith unto salvation.

6. You believe there will be a resurrection of the just and unjust and a final judgment when the wicked shall go away into everlasting punishment, and the righteous into life eternal.

All this you do believe, do you?
Attend now to your covenant:

You now confess and deplore your sad apostasy from God, your want of original righteousness, the corruption of your whole nature, the unbelief which has led you so long to reject the Saviour, and the manifold transgressions of your lives, all which sins you condemn and forever renounce. In the presence of God, angels and men you do solemnly avouch Jehovah to be your God, the object of your supreme love, the Lord Jesus to be your Saviour from sin and death, and the Holy Spirit to be your sanctifier, comforter and guide.

To this God, Father, Son and Holy Spirit you do now give yourselves in a covenant never to be revoked, to be his willing servants, to obey his commandments, and to observe his ordinances, in the sanctuary, in the family, and in the closet. You bind yourselves by covenant to th's church, to seek our peace and edification, and to submit to the government and discipline of Christ as here administered. All this in reliance on divine aid, you do severally profess and engage.

(Baptism here administered to unbaptized adults.)

(The members of the church will here arise.)

In consequence of these professions and engagements, we, the officers and members of this church, do welcome you to our Communion, to a fellowship with us in the duties and labors, in the hopes and joys of the gospel, and on our part engage to watch over you in the Lord, to pray for you, and to seek your edification, as long as you continue among us.

(The members of the church will here resume their seats.)

And now, beloved in the Lord, let it be impressed on your minds that you have entered into solemn relations which you never can renounce. Should you have occasion to remove from us within the bounds or neighborhood of another church, we shall hold it to be our duty to give, as it will be your duty to seek, a recommendation from us, which will place you under the watch and care of that portion of the family of Christ. For hereafter you can never withdraw from within the pale of the church, or live in the neglect of sealing ordinances without a breach of covenant. Rejoice with exceeding joy in these indissoluble bonds which connect you with Christ and his people. Walk worthy of your vocation; be faithful unto death, and you shall receive a crown of life.

The Lord bless you and keep you.

The Lord make his face to shine upon you, and be gracious unto you.

The Lord lift up his countenance upon you and give you peace.

FORM OF INFANT BAPTISM.

Dearly beloved, you have now presented your children before God n his sanctuary, to devote them to his service, and to enter into covenant with him, in their behalf, that they may become interested in the covenant of grace, of which the water of baptism is the seal.

Remember, therefore, that your children are involved, with the rest of his race, in the consequences of the fall of our first parent, that they are by nature the children of wrath even as others, and that they need the application of the blood of Christ and an inward cleansing of the heart through the influence of the Spirit of God, blessings, of which bapism by water is only the sign, which it can never impart, but which you are to seek of God in their behalf in the faith of that blessed promise, "I will be your God, and the God of your children after you, in their generations."

You do now publicly renew your covenant engagement with God and his Church. Should your lives and the lives of your children be spared, you engage to teach them, or cause them to be taught, to read the Word of God, and to instruct them in the principles of our holy religion as therein revealed, to make them acquainted with that excellent form of doctrine contained in the Shorter Catechism adopted by our Church, to pray with and for your children, to set them an example of piety and godliness and conscientiously to endeavor, by all the means of God's appointment, to bring them up in the nurture and admonition of the Lord.

Relying upon the all-sufficiency of divine grace to make you faithful and to crown your efforts with success, these things you solemnly promise, in the presence of God and His Church, to perform.

PASTORS.

Nathaniel Randolph Snowden, October 2, 1793-June 25, 1805.
James Buchanan, February 13, 1809-September 20, 1815.
William Radcliffe DeWitt, D. D., November 12, 1819-December 23, 1867.
Thomas Hastings Robinson, D. D., January 20, 1855-July 6, 1884.
George Black Stewart, D. D., January 2, 1885-

ELDERS.

Samuel Weir, February 16, 1794-August 15, 1820.
Moses Gillmor, February 16, 1794-June 10, 1825.
Adam Boyd, February 16, 1794- May, 1814.
John Stoner, about 1814-March 24, 1825.
William Graydon, about 1814-October 30, 1840.
Samuel Agnew, M. D., April 9, 1820-March, 1835.
Robert Sloan, April 9, 1820-December, 1833.
Joseph A. McJimsey, April 9, 1820-September 20, 1821.
John Neilson, September 11, 1825-1838.
Richard T. Leech, September 11, 1825-1837.
John C. Capp, September 11, 1825-1831.
James W. Weir, October 19, 1834-March 14, 1878.
Alexander Sloan, October 19, 1834-August 2, 1890.
Alexander Graydon, October 19, 1834-1843.
Alfred Armstrong, December, 1840-1846.
Samuel W. Hays, December, 1840-May 18, 1855.
William McClean, January 5, 1845-1846.
William Root, January 5, 1845-1847.
John A. Weir, June 24, 1855-October 10, 1881.
Mordecai McKinney, June 24, 1855-December 17, 1867.
R. Jackson Fleming, June 24, 1855-December 2, 1874.
James Fleming, D. D. S., March 8, 1868-January, 1875.
William S. Shaffer, March 8, 1868-October 11, 1889.
Walter F. Fahnestock, Jr., March 8, 1868-March 13, 1872.

Alfred Armstrong, March 8, 1868–October 11, 1871.
James F. Purvis, April 15, 1877–December 26, 1882.
Samuel J. M. McCarrell, April 15, 1877–
Gilbert M. McCauley, April 15, 1877–
Jacob A. Miller, M. D., April 15, 1877–
John Henry Spicer, March 20, 1887–
John C. Harvey, March 20, 1887–

DEACONS.

John K. Tomlinson, March 20, 1887–March 24, 1889.
Charles W. Foster, March 20, 1887–
Peter K. Sprenkel, March 20, 1887–
Melancthon S. Shotwell, March 20, 1887–
Luther R. Kelker, March 20, 1887–
Jacob J. Franck, March 20, 1887–
Samuel C. Miller, March 20, 1887–
David Fleming, March 24, 1889–

TRUSTEES.

George Whitehill, 1819–1820.
James Trimble, 1819–1834.
William Murray, 1819–1822.
Andrew Mitchell, 1819–1822.
William Allison, 1819–1830 ; 1835–1846.
Robert Harris, 1819–1839 ; 1841–1842.
Richard M. Crain, 1819–1821.
Gilbert Burnet, 1821–1839.
John Brooks, 1822–1828.
John Berryhill, 1824–1826 ; 1840–1841.
John Neilson, 1824–1826.
Alexander M. Piper, 1826–1833.
James R. Boyd, 1827–1839.
Alexander Graydon, 1829–1834.
William M. Carson, 1831–1833.

John A. Weir, 1834–1842; 1847–1855.
Mordecai McKinney, 1834–1844 ; 1852–1855.
Samuel Capp, 1835–1835.
James Wright, 1837–1837.
Herman Alricks, 1838–1854.
Henry Walters, 1840–1851.
Samuel W. Hays, 1840–1840.
Joel Hinckley, 1842–1842.
William Root, 1843–1844.
Andrew Graydon, 1843–1850.
Francis Wyeth, 1843–1844.
Robert J. Ross, 1845–1855.
John H. Briggs, 1845–1872.
Augustus Burnett, 1846–1857.
Joseph Wallace, 1851–1857.
William M. Kerr, 1855–1864.
Alexander Hamilton, 1856–1857.
Edward L. Orth, 1856–1861.
Alexander Roberts, 1856–1868 ; 1869–1886.
Henry Gilbert, 1858–1888.
David Fleming, 1858–1890.
Charles L. Bailey, 1862–
Dr. George Bailey, 1865–1876.
William S. Shaffer, 1863–1868.
David McCormick, 1866–1873.
Robert H. Moffitt, 1878–
Augustine L. Chayne, 1878–
M. Wilson McAlarney, 1887–
Samuel W. Fleming, 1887–
Spencer C. Gilbert, 1889–
George R. Fleming, 1891–

CHURCH CHOIR.

George R. Fleming, *Director.*
David E. Crozier, *Organist.*

SOPRANO.

Mrs. David Fleming, Jr.,	Miss Lillian M. Kline,
Miss Addie Geiger,	Mrs. Gilbert M. McCauley,
Mrs. William M. Graydon,	Miss Sara J. Miller,
Miss Margaret P. Grayson,	Miss Margaret B. Mowry,
Mrs. Edward J. Hardy,	Miss Marie A. Segelbaum,
Miss Maud A. Hench,	Mrs. J. Henry Spicer,
Miss Mary Killough,	Miss Elizabeth F. L. Walker.

CONTRALTO.

Miss Reba Bunton,	Mrs. John C. Harvey,
Miss Sara B. Chayne,	Miss Annie R. Kelker,
Miss Elizbeth Given,	Miss Cora L. Snyder,
Miss Louisa Given,	Miss Mabel E. Vaughn.

TENOR.

Mr. David Fleming,   Mr. George R. Fleming,
Mr. Peter K. Sprenkel.

BASS.

Mr. J. Roberts Given,	Mr. George B. Roberts,
Mr. Henry A. Kelker, Jr.,	Mr. John B. Roberts,
Mr. Samuel C. Miller,	Mr. Geo. F. Sharp,
Mr. Clarence Platt,	Mr. Wm. G. Underwood,

ROLL OF COMMUNICANTS.

February 16th, 1894.

[The year indicates the date of their admission to the church, and "P." and "C." indicate respectively that they were admitted on Profession or by Certificate, and the figure after the last name in each year shows the number now remaining on the roll for that year.]

1827.—Mrs. Sarah Doll, P.—1.

1834—Mrs. Julia A. Briggs, P.—1.

1843.—Mrs. Susan Fleming, P.; Mrs. Caroline R. Haldeman, P.; Mrs. Malvina L. Ingram, P.; Mrs. Isabella S. Kerr, P.; Mrs. Elizabeth Kerr, P.; Alexander Roberts, P.; Mrs. Mary E. Vaughn, P.; Mrs. Ann E. Zimmerman, P.—8.

1850.—Mrs. Ellen W. Stees, P.—1.

1853.—Mrs. Jeannette Fleming, C.—1.

1855.—Samuel D. Ingram, P.; Miss Anna C. Weir, P.—2.

1857.—Mrs. Elizabeth B. Orth, P.; Mrs. Elizabeth Reily, P.—2.

1859.—Mrs. Margaret F. Sumner, P.—1.

1862.—Miss Rachel T. Briggs, P.; Mrs. Louisa C. Fahnestock, C.; Miss Louisa C. Fahnestock, C.; Mrs. Hanna M. Harvey, C.; Miss Mary Vandling, C.; Miss Elizabeth Vandling, C.—6.

1864.—Thomas. B. McCord, P.—1.

1865.—Mrs. Henrietta Z. Miller, P.; Mrs. Margaret G. Parsons, C.—2.

1866.—Mrs. Ellen R. Bent, P.; Miss Maria L. Boyd, P.; D. Truman Boyd, P.; Spencer C. Gilbert, P.; John C. Harvey, P.; George W. Parsons, P.; Miles Rock, P.; Mrs. Elizabeth M. Russell, P.; Mrs. Isabella T. Sheesley, P.; Miss Sibyl M. Weir, P.; Robert M. Zimmerman, P.—11.

1867.—Mrs. M. Elizabeth Cathcart, C.; William M. Fahnestock, P.; Miss Rebecca Kline, P.; Samuel J. M. McCarrell, C.; Mrs. Mary C. Goodman, P.—5.

1868.—Mrs. Anna M. Bigler, C.; Miss Clara Marshbank, C.—2.

1869.—Mrs. Laura D. Huston, P.; Miss Annie M. Marshbank, C Dr. Jacob A. Miller, C.; Mrs. Maria M. Miller, C.; Samuel C. Miller C.—5.

1870.—Mrs. Sarah P. Boyd, C.; Miss Margaret B. Mowry, P.—2.

1871.—Charles A. Fahnestock, P.; Mrs. Caroline Hickok, C.—2.

1872.—Miss Lucretia H. Frowert, C.; Miss Mary E. George, P.; Miss Julia T. Harris, C.; Miss Sallie L. Harris, P.: M. Wilson McAlarney, P.: Mrs. Ada McAlarney, C.; Mrs. Rebecca W. McCarrell, C.— 7.

1873.—Mrs. Mary M. Applebaugh, P.; Miss Henrietta Guissinger, C.; Mrs. Sarah J. McCord, P.: Dr. Henry L. Orth, C.—4.

1874.—Miss Sarah Beatty, C.: Miss Emma F. Beatty, C.; Miss Isabella DeHaven, P.; Samuel W. Fleming, P.; Mrs. Agnes M. Hardy, P.; Mrs. Louisa H. Hickok, C.; Gilbert M. McCauley, C.; Mrs. Sarah E. McCauley, P.: Mrs. Eliza Ogelsby, C.; Miss Caroline Pearson, P.: Dr. Cherrick Westbrook, Jr., P.—11.

1875.—Mrs. Mary Ferguson, P.: Mrs. Catharine Harris, F.; Mrs. Kate G. Orth, C.; Mrs. Mary E. Quickel, P.—4.

1876.—Charles L. Bailey, C.: Mrs. Emma H. Bailey, C.: James R. Banford, P.; Mrs. Rebecca Bowers, P.: Leroy J. Bowers, P.: Mrs. Virginia F. Brant, P.; Augustine L. Chayne, C.; Mrs. Catharine Chayne, C.: Miss Sara B. Chayne, C.; Miss Sarah C. Cowden, C.; Miss Marian E. Darr, P., Mrs. Mary E. DeHart, P.; Martin Deisroth, P.; Mrs. Kate Denney, P.: Mrs. Emma W. Dirosa, P.: Mrs. Helen Dwyer, P.: George M. Ehrisman, P.; Mrs. Mary J. K. Ewing, C.; Frank G. Fahnestock, P.: Mrs. Mary M. Fleming, C.; James Fletcher, P.; Mrs. Eliza A. Fortenbaugh, P.; Jacob J. Franck, P.; Joseph R. Henning, P.; Peter A. Hershey, P.: Mrs. Lydia E. Hershey, P.; Mrs. Clara V. Ingram, P.; Mrs. M. Ellen Jopp, P.; Luther R. Kelker, C.; Mrs. Agnes K. Kelker, C.; Miss Mary A. Kelker, P.; Miss Mary W. Kerr, P.; Harris Kerr, P.; Samuel M. Killough, P.: Miss Mary Killough, P.; Mrs. Maggie E. Kline, P.; Mrs. H. Jennie Ludlow, C.: Miss Sarah D. Milliken, P.: Dr. Robert H. Moffitt, P.: Mrs. Rebecca Moffitt, P.: Mrs. Rebecca Morrison, P.; Miss Annie M. McCord, P.; William McCormick, C.; Mrs. Catharine E. O'Brien, P.: Joseph R. Orwig, C.; Mrs. Jane W. Orwig, C.; Mrs. Mary Oves, P.; Charles W. Palmer, P.: Mrs. Rebecca J. Palmer, P.: Mrs. Mary H. Pearson, P.; John E. Peters, P.; Harvey Phelps, P.; Mrs. Mary F. Phelps, P.; Rev. Thomas D. Reese, C.; John W. Reily, P.; James Roberts, P.; George Roberts, P.; Alexander Roberts, Jr., P.; John F. Snow, P.; Mrs. Regina Steinmeier, P.: Miss Mary A. Steinmeier, P.: Mrs. Catharine M. Tann, P.: John H. Taylor, P.: Morris Taylor, P.; George W. Taylor, P.; Thomas A. Woods, C.; Mrs. Mary A. Woods, C.; George W. Young, P.; Mrs. Catharine Young, P.—69.

1877.—Mrs. Effie Ehrisman, P.; Joseph G. Ewing, P.; Mrs. Carrie M. Kerr, C.: Mrs. Catharine B. Mitchell, C.: Miss Mary Mitchell, C.; Miss Jennie F. Mitchell, C.; Mrs. Mary J. Quickel, C.: Henry F. Quickel, C.: Mrs. Carrie R. Shotwell, C.; Charles A. Spicer, C.; Mrs.

Nancy W. Spicer, C.; J. Henry Spicer, C.; James C. Stoner, C.—13.

1878.—William K. Fenn, P.; Mrs. Anna Grayson, P.; Mrs. America W. Sheafer, C.; Miss Caroline B. Sheafer, C.; Mrs. Mary E. Snow, P.; Sharon Stephens, C.; Mrs. Catharine A. Taylor, P.; Mrs. Mary L. Ward, P.; Mrs. Isabella S. Wilson, P.—9.

1879.—Horace A. Chayne, P.; Miss Emma M. Cummings, C.; Thomas Gosney, C.; Mrs. Mary A. Gosney, C.; Mrs. Margaret A. Woods, P.—5.

1880.—Henry W. Knight, C.; Mrs. Angelina B. Knight, C.; James Newby, C.; Mrs. Zella P. Newby, C.; Melancthon S. Shotwell, C.; Mrs. Jane Stewart, C.--6.

1881.—Miss Julia E. Fenn, P.; William H. Gregory, P.; Mrs. Catharine E. Gregory, C.; Mrs. Letitia P. Johnston, C.; Abram E. Kingport; C.; Mrs. Maggie E. Kingport, C.—6.

1882.—William E. Bailey, P.; Mrs. Sabra M. Bell, C.; Mrs. Anna S. Bergner, C.; Mrs. Hanna A. Burn, C.; Miss Lizzie J. Burn, C.; Mrs. Ellen Gibbins, P.; Mrs. Delilah Hess, P.; T. Frank Newby, C.; James N. Ohail, P.; Charles F. Spicer, P.; Mrs. Marian E. Willetts, P.—11.

1883.—Mrs. Susan Baer, P.; Mrs. Annie L. Baker, C.; Mrs. Susannah E. Bankeley, P.; George W. Boyd, P.; Mrs. Henrietta Boyd, P.; Miss Bessie Cathcart, P.; James W. Dougherty, P.; Miss Agnes Ferguson, C.; David Fleming, P.; George R. Fleming, P.; Spencer G. Frowert, P ; Miss Alice A. Glass, P.; Mrs. Elizabeth M. Groff, P.; Mrs. Ella T. Heck, C.; Mrs. Mary A. Herman, C.; Benjamin F. Kendig, C.; Mrs. Mary M. Kendig, C.; Miss Elizabeth K. Kingport, P.; Miss Florence M. Kingport, P.; Mrs. Carrie E. Leidich, P.; Mrs. Elizabeth B. Lyne, P ; David Martin, C.; Mrs. Elizabeth Martin, C.; Mrs. Florence Payne, P.; Miss Bertha M. Payne, P.; Miss Sarah Raymond, P.; Christian Reichart, P.; Miss Ida L. Rogers, P.; Augustus G. Shantz, P.; Mrs. Julia H. Snyder, C.; Miss Cora Lee Snyder, P.; Harry M. VanZandt, C.; Mrs. Lizzie W. VanZandt, C.; Mrs. Mary Lyle Weaver, P.; Mrs. Catharine B. Westbrook, C.; Charles H. Woods, P.; Mrs. Emma Woods, P.—37.

1884.—Miss Annie Culp, P.; Charles W. Foster, P.; Mrs. Mary W. Foster, P.; Nicholas I. Hench, C.; Mrs. Annie Hench, C.; Henry S. Jenkins, C.; Mrs. Sallie T. Jenkins, C.; Harvey J. Miller, P.; Mrs. Elizabeth McCord, P.; Thomas H. Redmond, P.; Mrs. Jane Redmond, P.; Frank J. Roth, C.; John K. Tomlinson, C.; Mrs. Lydia Tomlinson, C.; Geary M. Willetts, P.; Miss Elizabeth M. Willetts, P.; William H. Windsor, P.—17.

1885.—James B. Bailey, P.; Miss Anna C. Bell, P.; B. Frank Bishop, C.; Mrs. Barbara E. Bishop, C.; Miss M. Elizabeth Bishop, C.; Ira N.

Bishop, P.; Miss Stella Bishop, P.; John R. Bockus, C.; Mrs. Anna M.
Bockus, C.; Mrs. Kate Border, P.; Samuel V. Border, P.; Mrs. Esther
Bricker, C.; Mrs. Lucy S. Brown, P.; Wilson S. Cornman, P.; Mrs.
Harriet S. Cornman, P.; George W. Deisroth, P.; Miss Elizabeth
Dunn, P.; Miss Helen Ewing, P.; Mrs. Carrie Fahnestock, C.; Miss
Lulu Farmer, P.; Mrs. Lena Fuller, P.; Alexander Gibbins, P.;
Mrs. Katie Goehringer, P.; Henry W. Gough, P.; Mrs. Jennie L.
Gough, P.; Mrs. Catharine D. Hamilton, C.; Edward A. Hartwick, P.;
Miss Carrie Harvie, P.; Miss Maud A. Hench, P.; Miss Lillie A.
Hench, P.; Abram M. Hess, P.; George K. Hoy, P.; Mrs. Grace
Hoy; Mrs. Elsie J. Kelly, P.; Mak-Yu-Chung, P.; Mak-Ling-Ching,
P.; Miss Lizzie M. Martin, P.; Miss Clara V. Mehancy, P.; Henry G.
Metzger, P.; Robert C. Michael, P.; Miss Silvia Millard, P.; John S.
Miller, P.; Luther R. Moffitt, P.; George P. Montgomery, P.; Mrs.
Barbara Myers, P.; Miss Cornelia W. Newby, P.; Miss Margaret M.
Orwig, P.; Miss Clara B. Orwig, P.; Mrs. Mary Ott, P.; Mrs. Lillie E.
Palmer, P.; Miss Alva Pannebecker, P.; Jefferson Payne, P.; Jacob
K. Probst, P.; Miss Annie E. Raymond, P.; Joseph Redmond, P.;
George W. Reily, P.; Miss Caroline Reily, P.; Miss Alice J. Sanders,
P.; Mrs. Mary K. Sharp, P.; Mrs. Rosanna Shive, P.; Edward
Shuey, P.; Mrs. Annie E. Spicer, P.; William C. Spicer, P.; Peter,
K. Sprenkel, C.; Mrs. Lillie A. Sprenkel, C.; Mrs. Mary A. Stewart,
C.; Mrs. Eva C. Stewart, P.; Miss Alice V. Taylor, P.; Miss Annie
S. Vandling, P.; Mrs. Lucy M. Weaver, P.; Miss Sarah J. Win-
ters, P.—71.

1886.—Edward Deisroth, P.; Mrs. Emeline Dickey, P.; Mrs
Emma L. Garman, P.; Haldeman Bigler, P.; Adam Bricker, P.;
Mrs. Annie E. Hartwick, P.; Mrs. Frances S. Jackson, C.; David R.
Junkin, P.; Mrs. Sarah J. Marsh, C.; Miss Jennie A. Marsh, C.; Miss
Fannie R. Marsh, C.; Miss Mima K. Marsh, C.; Miss Annie M.
McKee, P.; James O'Brien, P.; J. Ralph Orwig, P.; Miss Rosa Place,
P.; Mrs. Carrie H. Schell, C.; Miss Catharine J. Sheesley, P.; Mrs.
Leah Shuey, P.; William R. Steinmeier, P.; Mrs. Mary Tress, P.;
William R. Weaver, P.; Miss Anna M. Williamson, P.; Isaac Woods,
P.; Miss Elizabeth A. Wooley, P.; Harry Zeiter, P.—28.

1887.—Amos M. Anderson, C.; George Edwin Arnold, P., Wil-
liam R. Bain, P.; Rush E. Banford, P.; Miss Mary Bates, P.; Edward
M. Bierbower, P.; Mrs. Emma L. Bowers, P.; George L. Bowersox,
P.; Harry H. Boyd, P.; George H. C. Brant, P.; Mrs. Edith K.
Buehrer, P.; Miss Rachel A. Burn, P.; Mrs. Clarissa Carpenter, P.;
Mrs. Mary Crutchley, P.; Mrs. Mary A. Dougherty, P.; Mrs. Mar-
garet J. Durkees, C.; Mrs. Mary E. Emerick, P.; George W. Etter,
P.; Miss Mary Ferguson, P.; Charles E. Frowert, P.; Miss Mary E

Garver, P.: Miss Julia W. Geety, C.: Mrs. Eliza R. Given, C.; Miss Elizabeth Given, C.: Miss Louisa Given, C.; John Roberts Given. C.: John H. Grayson, P.: Miss Margaret P. Grayson, P.; Mrs. Carrie L. Hale, P.: Miss Arabella Heister, P.; Mrs. Teressa E. Hogentogler. P.; William H. Hoke, P.: Robert W. Hoy, P.: William H. Huber. P.: Miss Annie R. Kelker, P.; Miss Ellen Kelker, P.: Mrs. Agnes A. Kirk. P.: John W. Lyne, P.; David H. Martin, P.; Mrs. Mary Michael, P.: John J. Moffitt, P.; Robert H. Moffitt, Jr., P.; Mrs. Rosanna Morgan, P.: Miss Mary E. McCormick, C.; Mrs. Hattie F. McNeal, C.: Miss Elizabeth McMullen, C.; Miss Fannie J. Null, P.: Miss Mary G. Orwig, P.; Mrs. Kate Peace, P.: Mrs. Lillie M. Peace, P.: William C. Pfouts, C.; Mrs. Amy S. Pfouts, C.; Miss Carrie L. Place, P.; Mrs. Annie L. Rauch, P.: William H. Reindel, P.: John W. Reitzel. P.; Mrs. Jennie Reitzel, P.: Mrs. Maggie S. Robinson, P.; Mrs. Mary E. Rodenhaber, P.; Mrs. Sylvia H. Roth, P.; S. Grant Sawyer, P.; Jacob S. Shaffer, P.: George M. Shuey, P.; John R. Silvius, C.: Mrs. Anna E. Silvius, C.: Mrs. Sallie A. Smith, P.; Edward James Stackpole, C.; Mrs. Alice M. Stephens, P.; Miss Millie Stine. P.: William G. Underwood, P.; Jeanetta D. Vandling, P.; Conrad O. Zimmerman, P.—73.

1888.—Charles J. Bechdolt, C.: Mrs. Bertha S. Darby. P ; Mrs. May Daugherty. C.: Miss Josephine Derr, P.; William Emerick, P.; F. Byron Ewing, C.: Miss Ella Gouldin, C.; Alfred M. Hawn, P.; Mrs. Alice Hawn, C.; Nicholas Pall Hench, P.: Annie Weakley Hench, P.; Mrs. Millie Hogentogler, C.: Mrs. Ivy J. Huber, P.; Miss Mary E. Huber, P.; J. Geiger Ingram, P.; Miss Lydia M. Kapp, C.: Warren Z. Meck, P.: Adam H. Millard, P.; Miss Sarah J. Miller, C.; Mrs. C. Lizzie Morris, C.: Richard W. Morrow, P.; Dr. John B. McAlister, C.; Mrs. Margaret McClure, C.; Mrs. Jennie McCormick, P.; Ashton D. Peace, P.; Miss Annie E. Pearson, P.; Mrs. Rachel Powell, C.; Mrs. Mary Probst, C.: Filmore Scantling, P.; Miss Marie Antionette Segelbaum, P.; Mrs. Estelle Spicer, C.; Mrs. Gertrude M. Wiestling, P.; Mrs. Margaret Wooley, P.—32.

1889.—Miss Bertha W. Burrow, P.; Miss Ella LeRue Hart, C.; Charles W. Hartwick, P.: Mrs. Laura C. Heckendorn, P.; Mrs. Mary D. Horst, P.; Lewis Jenkins, P.; Mrs. Sarah Lehr, P.; J. Hall Musser, C.; Mrs. Alice R. Musser, C.; W. Henry Musser, P.: John A. McCord, P.; Daniel E. McGinley, P.; Mrs. Jennie McGinley, P.; Miss Florence Orth, P.; Miss Helen Payne, P.; Andrew Redmond, C.; Martin Richards, C.; Mrs. Julia Richards, C.; Miss Catharine, Richards, P.: George F. Sharp, P.; Valentine H. Wiestling, P.; Walter H. Yingst, P.—22.

1890.—Mrs. Agnes Adams, C.; Edward Bailey, P.; Mrs. Elizabeth R. Bailey, P.; James Baker, P.; Mrs. Isabella Beck, P.; Miss Anna M. Bender, P.; Mrs. Mary A. Bender P.; Joseph A. Berryhill, P.; Mrs. Araminta Berryhill, P.; Albert H. Buchanan, P.; Miss Margaret A. Bumbaugh, P.; Fred. B. Carnes, P.; Mrs. Margaret Chellew, C.; Miss Josephine A. Coldren, C.; John T. Cope, P.; David E. Crozier, C.; Daniel E. Crutchley, P.; Miss Harriet A. Crutchly, P.; Edwin E. DeHart, P.; Mrs. Lulu E. DeHart, P.; Edwin Drennan, P.; William E. Ehrisman, P.; Mrs. Ida M. Ehrisman, C.; Mrs. Laura E. Essig, P.; Mrs. Virginia M. E. Fenn, P.; James M. Fessler, P.; Mrs. Norene K. Fetrow, P.; John Flickinger, P.; Miss Mary E. Fry, P.; Joseph T. A. Fuller, P.; Charles H. Garberich, P.; Mrs. Virginia Garberich, P.; Miss Bertha Gingher, P.; Miss Sadie E. Gingher, C.; Mrs. Pearl E. Graydon, P.; Nathaniel G. Grayson, P.; Edward L. Groff, P.; Mrs. Ada D. Groff, C.; Miss Fannie S. Gruber, P.; Miss Mary W. Hamilton, P.; Harry C. Hoffman, C.; Miss Pearl E. Hogentogler, P.; Miss Ivy J. Huber, P.; Miss Florence H. Hursh, P.; Mrs. Mabel C. Jones, C.; Miss Alice C. Kingport, P.; Miss Lilian M. Kline, P.; Miss Lyra M. Leeser, C.; James Hasbruck LeFever, C.; Mrs. Sarah E. Leidich, P.; Rody R. Lyter, P.; J. Roberts Magee, C.; Mrs. Sarah Magee, C.; Mrs. A. Carrie Meck, P.; Albert J. Metzger, P.; Mrs. Mary H. Meyers, P.; Mrs. Laura S. Middleton, P.; Mrs. Carrie O. McCord, P.; William D. McNeal, C.; Miss Jeannette I. Notestine, P.; Mrs. Agnes G. Nunemacher, P.; Miss Frances E. Pannebecker, P.; Harry Peters, P.; Dr. Hugh Pitcairn, C.; Mrs. Annie M. Pitcairn, C.; Roy C. Pitcairn, C.; Frank R. Pitcairn, C.; Mrs. M. Ellen Record, P.; J. Harry Reel, C.; Miss M. Margaret Reel, P.; Charles P. Reel, P.; Lincoln M. Reigle, P.; Edwin S. Reigle, P.; Mrs. Mary H. Rice, P.; Mrs. Mary F. Rust, P.; William H. Shaffer, C.; Mrs. Emma R. Shaffer, C.; William S. Shaffer, Jr., C.; Miss Edith B. Shaffer, C.; Helen N. Sharp, P.; Mrs. Sarah L. Sheesley, P.; Miss M. Alice Small, P.; Mrs. Louisa Smith, C.; James E. Sollers, P.; Miss Bessie W. Spicer, P.; Mrs. Kate Hummel Stackpole, C.; Mrs. Ella Stees, P.; Jesse K. Stephens, P.; B. Edward Taylor, P.; Mrs. Mary N. Thomas, P.; John R. Thompson, C.; Mrs. Mary J. Thompson, C.; Bertha A. Tippett, P.; Miss Minnie R. Trout, C.; William B. Wenrich, P. Mrs. Ida M. Wenrich, P.; George G. Young, P.; Mrs. Sarah Young, P.—98.

1891.—William H. Anderson, P.; Mrs. Mary Anderson, C. Mrs. Emma Bentz, P.; Miss Caroline H. Bigler, P.; Mrs. Catharine Black, C.; Miss Anna M. Bowman, P.; Charles P. Boyd, P.; Lewis H. Carpenter C.; Mrs. Maggie S. Carpenter, C.; Richard Chellew, P.; Mrs. Clara Cowan, C.; Frank Deihl, P.; Mrs. Mary Deihl, C.; Miss

Alice V. Drawbaugh, P.; Miss Bessie R. Ehrisman, P.; Mrs. Emma
H. Eisenberger, P.; Miss A. Laura Eisenberger, P.; John L. Essig,
P.; Mrs. Eliza R. Fleming, C.; Elcinda M. Geiger, P.; Mrs. Emma
W. Hepperle, P.; Harry G. Hogentogler, P.; Miss T. Edith Hogen-
togler, P.; Miss Janet M. Horst, P.; Mrs. Martha M. Junkin, C.;
Miss Clara Knipple, P.; Miss Anna Lantz, C.; Miss Lizzie A. Lindsey,
P.; Mrs. Melinda Leeds, P.; William W. Lynch, P.; Miss Mary E.
Lynch, C.; George C. Martin, P.; Howard F. Martin, C.; Mrs.
Lillian C. Martin, C.; Mrs. Nellie R. Millard, P.; Samuel W. Miller,
P.; Mrs. Emma Miller, P.; Miss Caroline R. Moffitt, P.; George R.
Moffitt, P.; Mrs. Ellen M. McCormick, P.; Mrs. Nancy McCoy, C.;
Edwin S. McCoy, P.; Miss Mary E. McGinley, P.; Miss Ida Note-
stine, C.; Miss Maud A. Peace, P.; Mrs. Annie E. Phillips, C.; Miss
May O. Phillips, C.; Miss Fannie E. Phillips, C.; Mrs. Anna M.
Reese, P.; Mrs. Lena Reichart, C.; Miss Minnie M. Rineer, C.; Miss
Susie O. Rose P.; Mrs. Ida M. Schmidt, P.; William H. Sharp, P.;
Harry F. Sheesley, P.; Miss Catharine Shuey, P.; Mrs. Frances E.
Simmers, P.; Miss Marcie A. Snodgrass, P.; H. Clement Sweatman,
C.; Mrs. Louella Sweatman, C.; M. Harvey Taylor, P.; Miss Maud
Tippett, C.; Mrs. Emma H. Underwood, P.; Miss Roberta Vaughn,
P.; Miss Mabel E. Vaughn, P.; Mrs. M. Virginia Weiss, C.; Miss
Mary J. Wooley, P.; Mrs. Annie P. Young. C.—68.

1892.—Miss Clara M. Anderson, P.; Mrs. Anna T. Beachler, C.;
Miss Mary C. Bidaman, P.; John Black, P.; Miss Mary J. Boyd, P.;
Mrs. Harriet N. Crozier, C.; Thomas J. Crutchley, P.; Mrs. Gertrude
S. Dunkin, C.; Mrs. Mary A. Hefflefinger, C.; Miss Harriet S. Gilbert,
P.; Miss Louisa A. Hickok, P.; Edward O. Hogentogler, P.; William
Hunter, C.; Miss Catharine Jacobs, P.; Mrs. Ella I. Johnson, P.;
Miss Eva R. Johnston, P.; Rudolph F. Kelker, jr., P.; James C.
Leidy, C.; Mrs. Annie W. Leidy, C.; Mrs. Sarah Leib, C.; Miss
Emma E. Leib.; C.; Miss Anna Magee, P.; Miss Mary E. Mehaffie,
P.; Miss Annie E. Miller, P.; Oliver B. Montgomery, P.; Miss Edith
Montgomery, P.; William H. Myers, P.; Miss Martha W. McAlarney,
P.; Mrs. Sarah A. McCann, P.; Miss Annie V. McCord, P.; Harris
B. McCormick, P.; Mrs. Lizzie McCroskey, P.; Mrs. Helen B.
Newby, C.; Miss Susie Nichols, P.; Frederick J. Pearson, P.; Miss Ida
M. Pearson, C.; Mrs. Annie M. Peters, C.; Miss Lizzie J. Redmond,
P.; Miss Edith K. Reel, P.; Miss Ada M. Richards, P.; Mrs. Sarah
Roberts, P.; Mrs. Eliza E. Roberts, P.; Miss Elizabeth L. Robinson,
P.; Miss Martha K. Ross, C.; A. Fisher Russell, C.; Henry K. Samp-
selle, C.; Mrs. Eliza Sampselle, C.; Mrs. Louisa Seasholtz, C.; Mrs.
Lizzie Shearer, C.; Miss Bertha Small, P.; Mrs. Agnes Smith, C.;
Miss Phœbe Emma Smith, P.; Stanley G. Smith, P.; Mrs. Emma S.

Taylor, P.; Miss Bertha M. Unger, P.; John W. Urban, P.: Mrs. Sarah Urban, P.; Miss Elizabeth F. L. Walker, P.; Warren H. Wasson, C.; Mrs. Alice B. Wasson, C.; Miss Mary Wheeler, P.; Wallace Willis, P.; Mrs. Hannah R. Wilt, C.; Miss Jennie Woods, C.; Miss Cora M. Young, P.—65.

1893.—Miss Elizabeth S. Baker, P.; Dr. Thomas S. Blair, C.; Miles Brown, P.; William J. Clark, C.; Edwin C. Conrad, P.; Miss Bessie L. Eckenroth, P.; Alonso H. Eby, P.; Mrs. Mary M. Franck, C.; Miss Margaret P. Hamilton, P.; Henry C. Heilman, C.; William Orville Hickok, P.; Ross A. Hickok, P.; Charles N. Hickok, P.; William O. Hickok, 1V., P.; Mrs. Carrie L. Ingle, C.; John P. Kelker, P.; Miss Edith Kelker, P.; Miss Josephine B. Knight, P.; John J. L. Kuhn, P.; Mrs. Mary G. Kuhn, P.; Miss Wilma Z. Leffingwell, C.; Mrs. Kate Lewis, P.; Miss Mary Z. Miller, P.; John H. McAlarney, P.; Elizabeth C. McCoy, P.; Miss Bertha M. Myers, P.; Mrs. Catharine J. O'Brien, P.; Miss Nancy C. Orr, P.; Miss Anna Shipley Dixon Orth, P.; Miss Roberta Elizabeth Orth, P.; Miss Frances Annie Payne, P.; Miss A. Elizabeth Pearson, P.; Norman B. Pitcairn, P.; Miss Mary Myrteth Ramsay. P.; Miss Elizabeth S. Reel, P.; Miss Mary E. Reily, P.; John B. Roberts, C.; Mrs. Mary Roberts, C.; William P. Schell, P.; Orville H. Schell, P.; Miss Louisa W. Sears, P.; Miss Bertha M. Shertzer, P.; Mrs. Elizabeth Shuler, P.; Miss Edna M. Sprenkel, P.; Miss Anna B. Stewart, P.; Miss Helen Stewart, P.; Miss Martha Carrie Weiss, C.; John Fox Weiss, C.; Mrs. Mary A. Wentz, P.; Robert W. Woods, P.; John E. Woolley, P.—51.

1894.—Samuel F. Compton, C.; Mrs. Ella G. Compton, C.; Mrs. Lottie Conrad, C.; Miss Emma M. Cummings, P.; Alexander S. Koser, C.; Mrs. Ella L. Koser, C.; George W. McCurdy, P.; Mrs. Emma J. Tress, P.; William C. Young, P.—9.

Total Communicants, February 16th, 1894, 768.

OFFICERS.

February 16, 1894.

PASTOR.

GEORGE B. STEWART, 127 State Street.

PASTOR'S ASSISTANT.

DAVID M. SKILLING, Y. M. C. A. Building.

ELDERS.

SAMUEL J. M. McCARRELL, 1877.   DR. JACOB A. MILLER, 1887.
GILBERT M. McCAULEY. 1877.   J. HENRY SPICER, 1887.
JOHN C. HARVEY, 1877.

CLERK OF SESSION—JACOB A. MILLER, M. D.

DEACONS.

Term Expires 1894.

PETER K. SPRENKEL.
CHAS. W. FOSTER, *Secretary.*   MELANCTHON S. SHOTWELL.

Term Expires 1895.

LUTHER R. KELKER, *Treasurer.*   DAVID FLEMING.

Term Expires 1896.

JACOB J. FRANCK, *Moderator.*   SAMUEL C. MILLER.

TRUSTEES.

Term Expires 1895.

AUGUSTINE L. CHAYNE.   SPENCER C. GILBERT.

Term Expires 1896.

M. WILSON McALARNEY,   SAMUEL W. FLEMING, *Secretary.*

Term Expires 1897.

CHAS. L. BAILEY, *President.*   ROBERT H. MOFFITT.
GEO. R. FLEMING.

TREASURER.

SAMUEL W. FLEMING, 32 North Third Street.

ORGANIST.

DAVID E. CROZIER.

SEXTON—CHARLES A. DAVIS, 1629 Logan Avenue.

MEMBERS RECEIVED.

Prior to 1819, . . 331	1845, ... 6	1871, ... 10
1819, ... 46	1846, ... 6	1872, ... 21
1820, ... 20	1847, ... 10	1873, ... 24
1821, ... 23	1848, ... 5	1874, ... 30
1822, ... 9	1849, ... 3	1875, ... 96
1823, ... 12	1850, ... 27	1876, ... 80
1824, ... 26	1851, ... 7	1877, . . . 35
1825, ... 4	1852, ... 10	1878, ... 26
1826, ... 8	1853, ... 3	1879, ... 22
1827, ... 34	1854, ... 5	1880, ... 19
1828, ... 11	1855, ... 60	1881, ... 15
1829, ... 12	1856, ... 12	1882. 25
1830, ... 61	1857, ... 20	1883, ... 69
1831, ... 7	1858, ... 22	1884, ... 32
1832, ... 27	1859, ... 18	1885, ... 97
1833, ... 5	1860, ... 17	1886, ... 40
1834, ... 50	1861, ... 9	1887, ... 97
1835, ... 8	1862, ... 15	1888, ... 49
1836, ... 11	1863, ... 4	1889, ... 31
1837, ... 2	1864, ... 7	1890, ... 113
1838, ... 7	1865, ... 18	1891, ... 76
1839, ... 10	1866, ... 39	1892, ... 70
1840, ... 7	1867, ... 21	1893, ... 54
1841, ... 10	1868, ... 12	1894, to Feb. 16th, 11
1842, ... 27	1869, ... 41	
1843, ... 134	1870, ... 11	Total, ... 2,462
1844, ... 10		

THE PRESBYTERIAN COLORS.

Perhaps there are very few who call themselves "Blue Presbyterians"—who really know why that color is given to them. "'Twas Presbyterian true blue," is found in Hudibras 1, 1. The allusion is to the blue apron which some of the Presbyterian preachers used to throw over their small, high pulpit—their "preaching tub," as it was called—before they began to address the people.

The term, "blue stocking," is quite misapplied to Presbyterians, as that has nothing to do with the church, but was applied to a social club formed in Venice in the year 1400—distinguished by the color of their stockings. This club appeared afterwards in Paris, and later in England, and finally disappeared entirely in 1840.

When Presbyterians say they are "*true blue*"—"dyed in the wool," they refer to a blue cloth and thread made at Coventry, noted for its permanent dye—and blue or azure is the symbol of divine eternity.

The old *Covenanters* wore *blue* as their badge in opposition to the scarlet of the royalty. They based their choice on Numbers xv. 38, "Speak unto the children of Israel, and bid them make fringes in the borders of their garments, and that they put upon the fringe of the borders a ribbon of blue."

In one of the Rump songs we read of a person going to hear a lecture, and the song says:

> Where I a tub did view,
> Hung with an apron blue ;
> 'Twas the preachers, I conjecture.

REV. JOHN ROAN'S SCHOOL.

The Rev. John Roan had a Theological school in the neighborhood of Derry, at the which were instructed the Rev. Samuel Eusebius McCorkle, Rev. Joseph Montgomery, a member of the Continental Congress, and Rev. William Graham, founder of Washington and Lee University, Virginia, than whom none are more celebrated in the annals of the Presbyterian Church in America. - EDITOR.

INDEX.

www.ingramcontent.com/pod-product-compliance
Lightning Source LLC
Chambersburg PA
CBHW031812270326
41932CB00008B/397